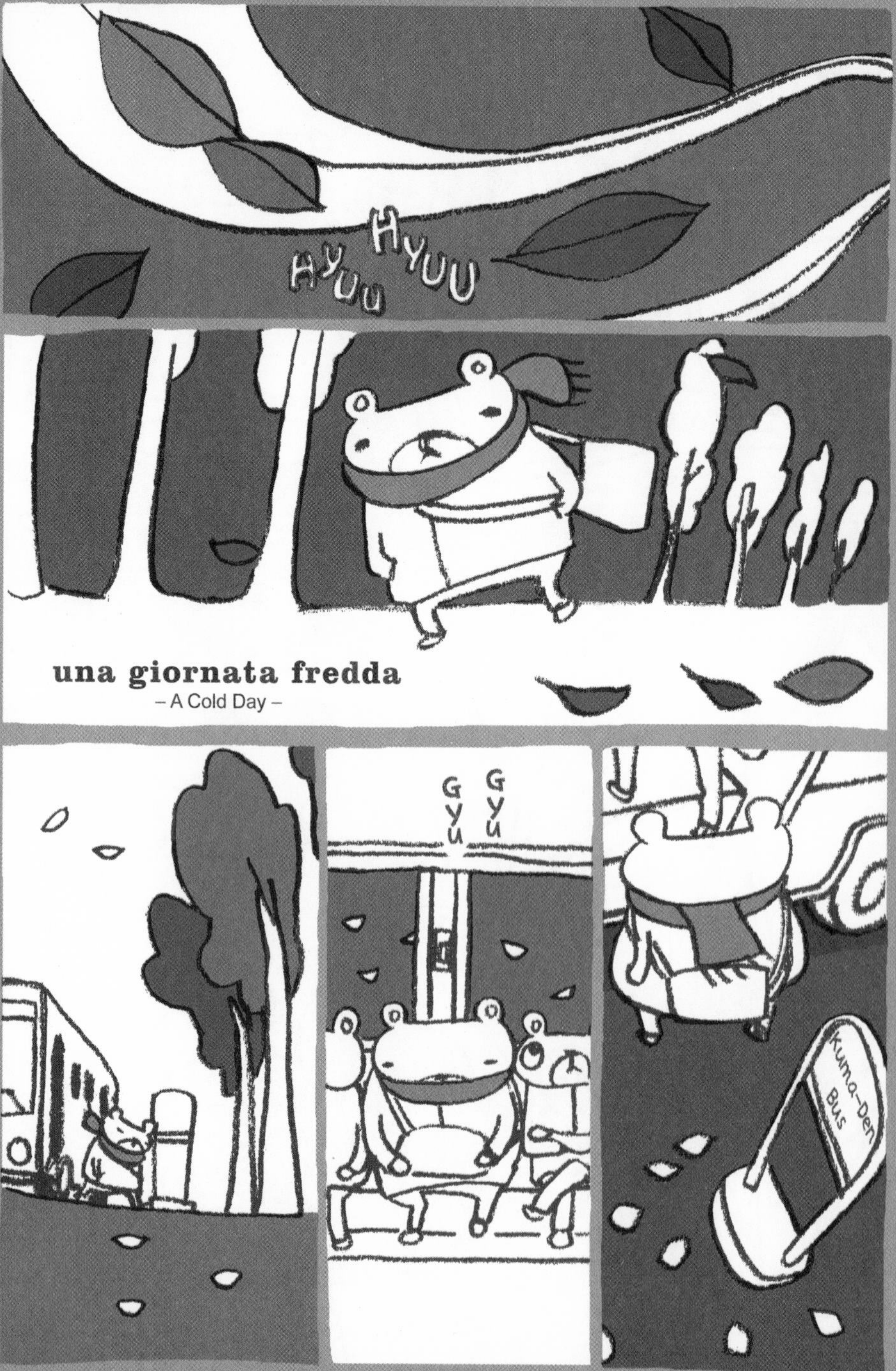
HYUU HYUU
una giornata fredda
– A Cold Day –
Kuma-Den Bus
Gyu Gyu

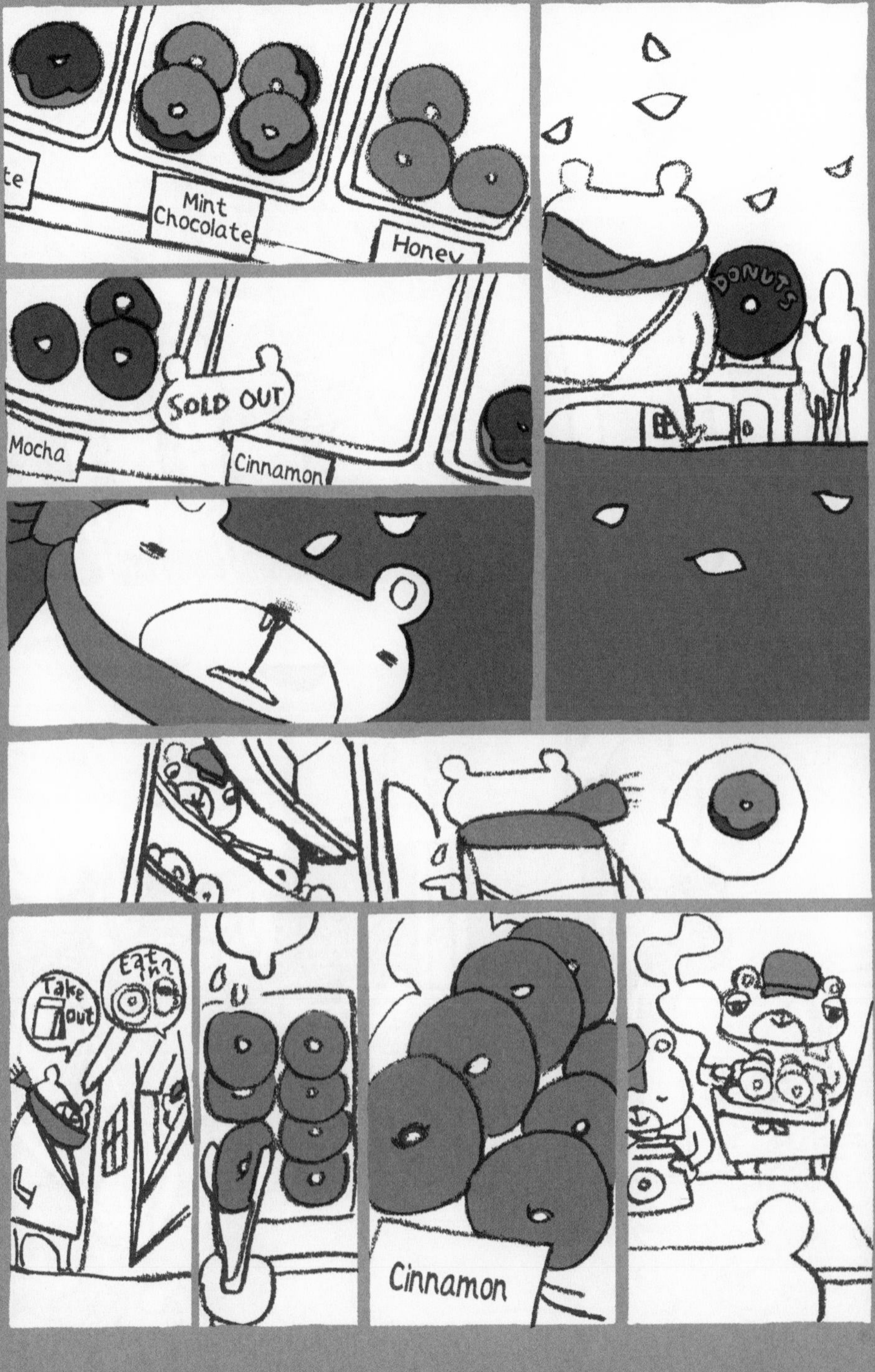

DONUTS
te
Mint Chocolate
Honey
SOLD OUT
Mocha
Cinnamon
Cinnamon
Take out
Eat in?

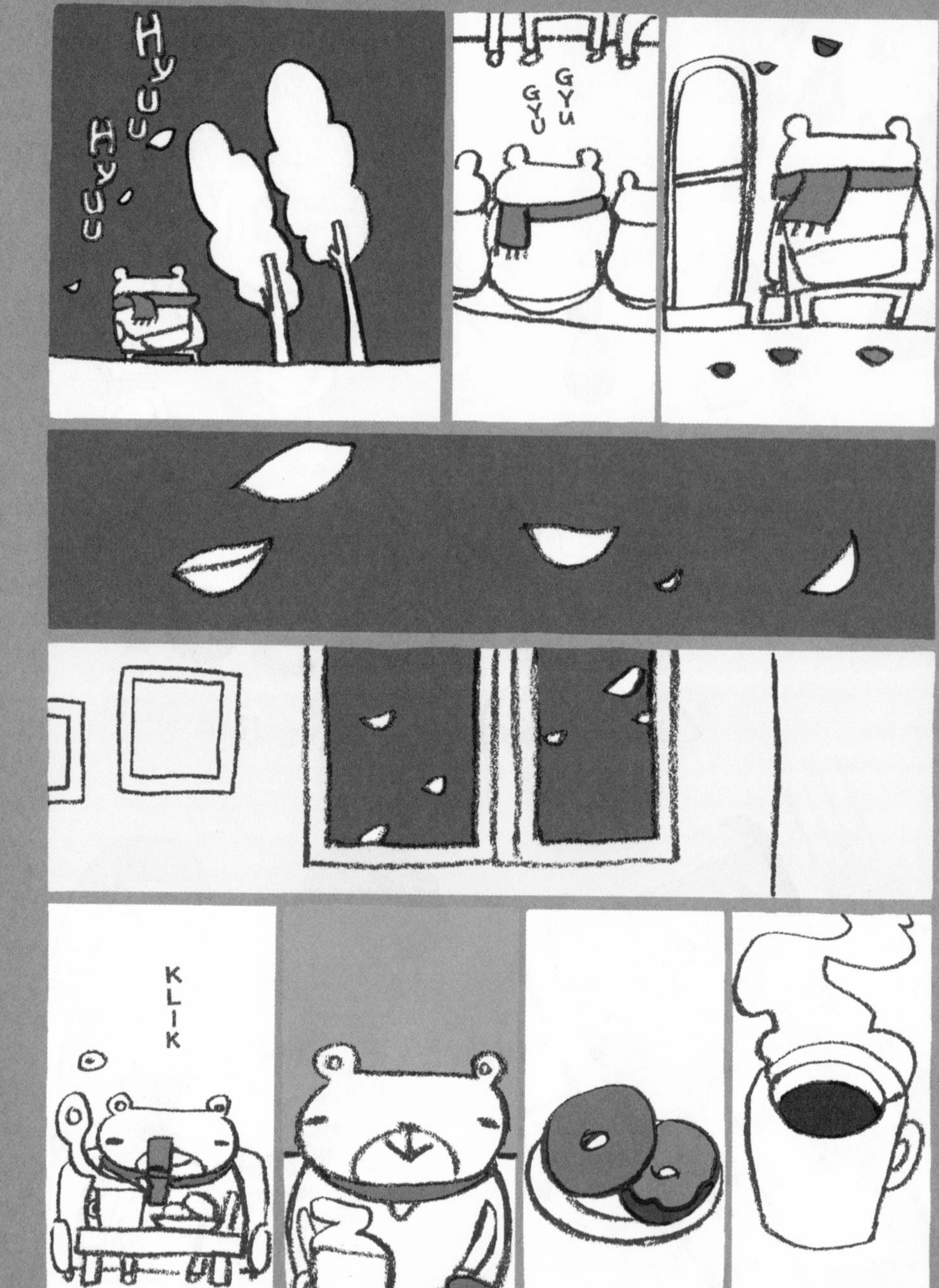
GYU
GYU
HYUUU
HYUUU
KLIK
fine.

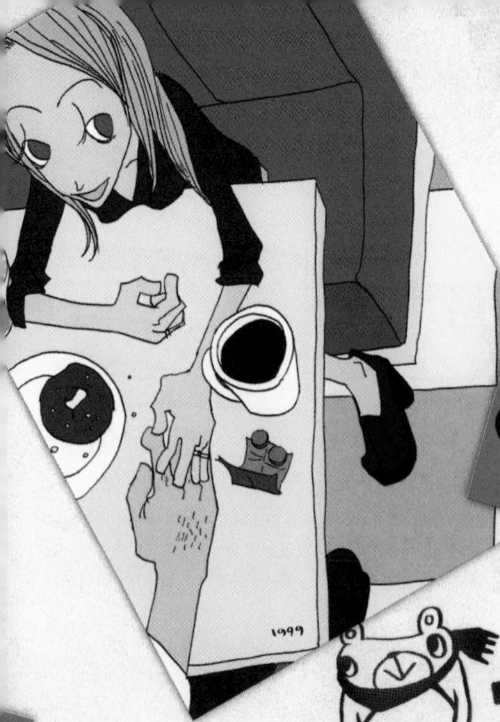
1999

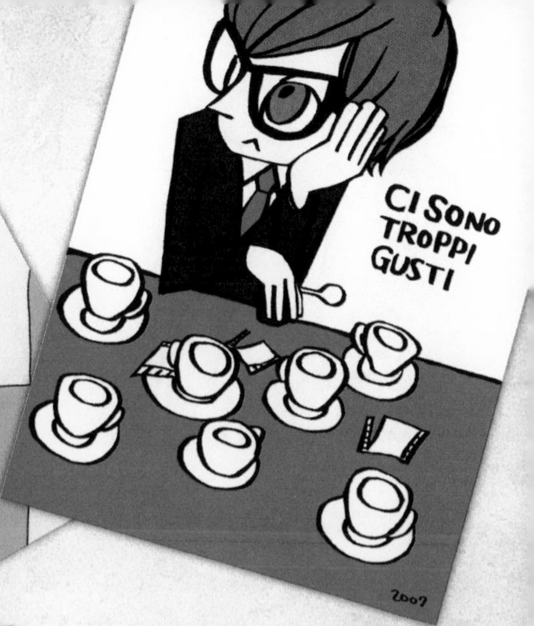
CI SONO
TROPPI
GUSTI
2007

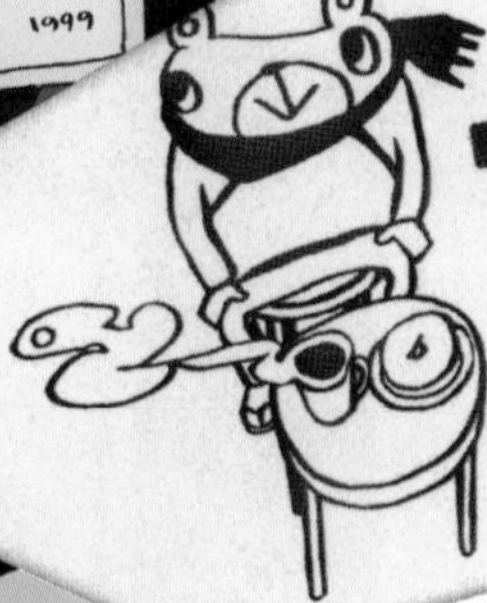

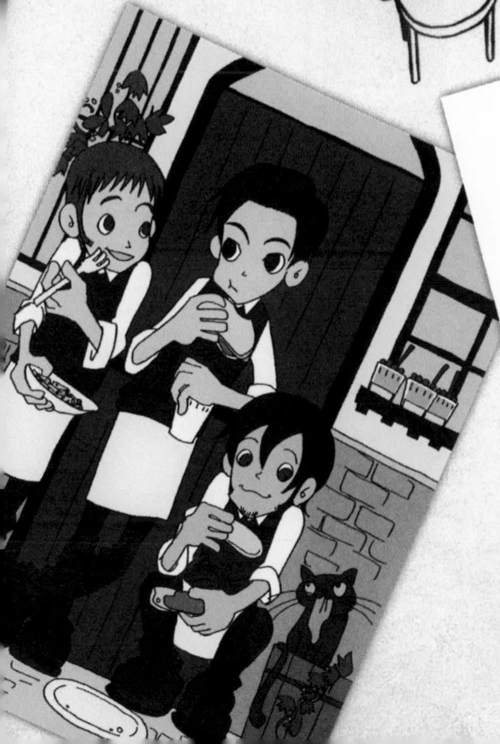

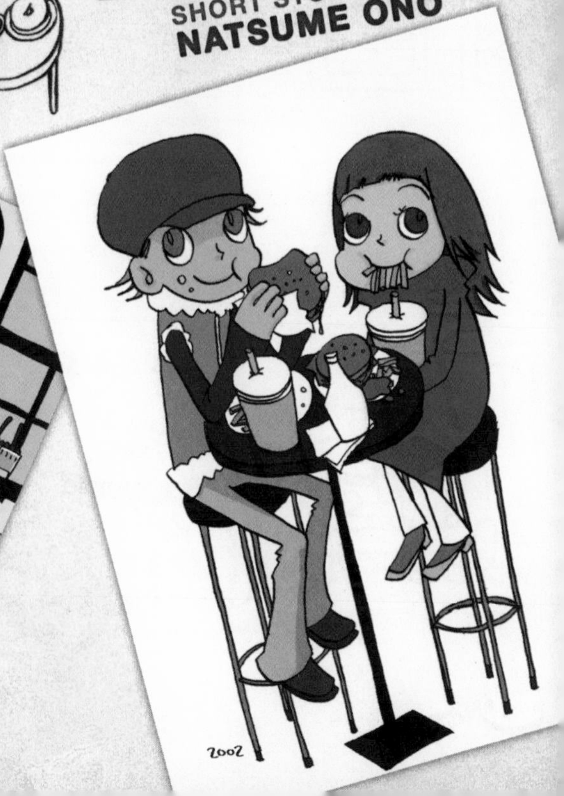
2002

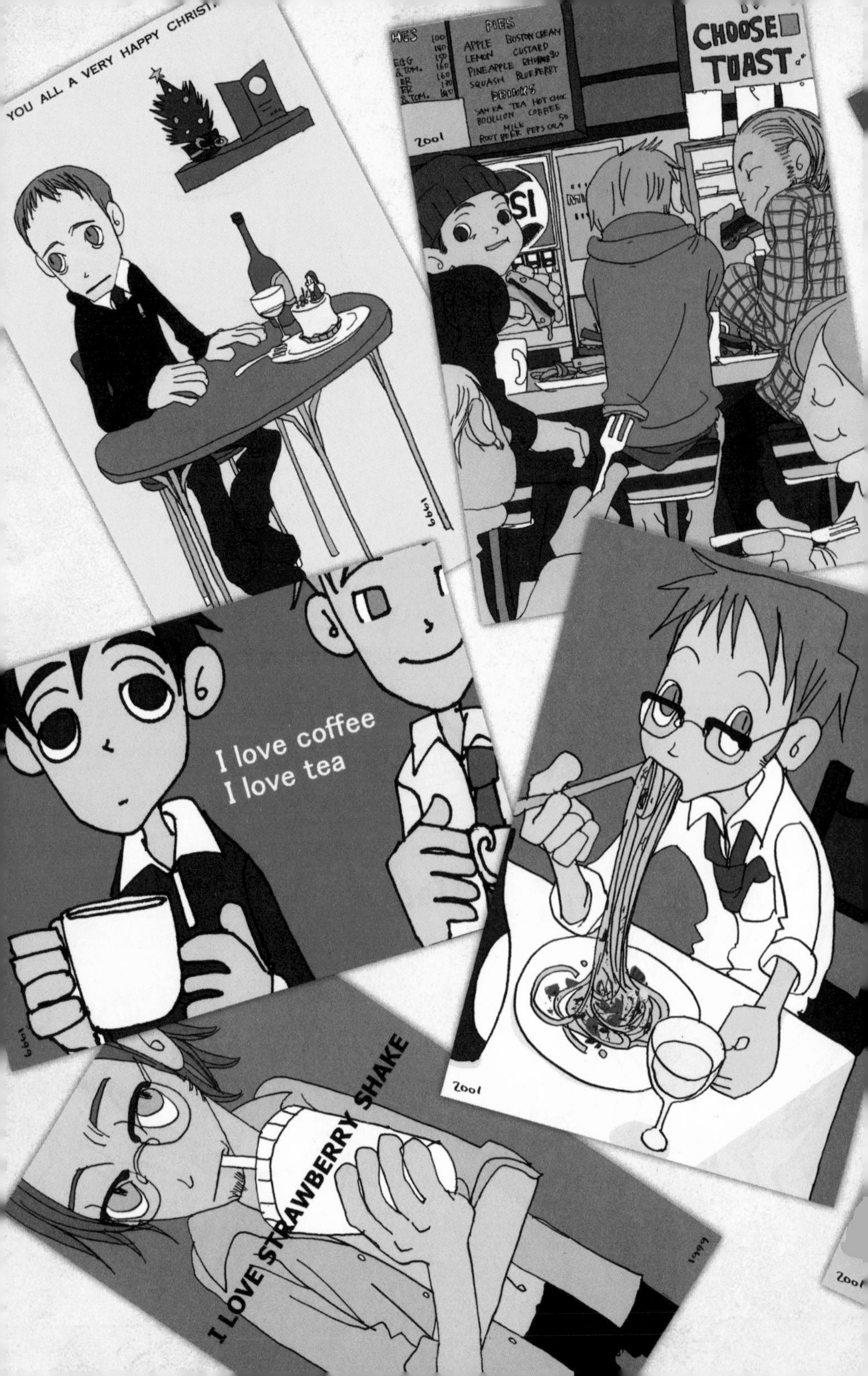
YOU ALL A VERY HAPPY CHRIST
1999
PIES
APPLE BOSTON CREAM
LEMON CUSTARD
PINEAPPLE
SQUASH BLUEBERRY
DRINKS
SANKA TEA HOT CHOC
BOULLION COFFEE
CHOOSE
TOAST
2001
I love coffee
I love tea
1999
2001
I LOVE STRAWBERRY SHAKE
1999
2001

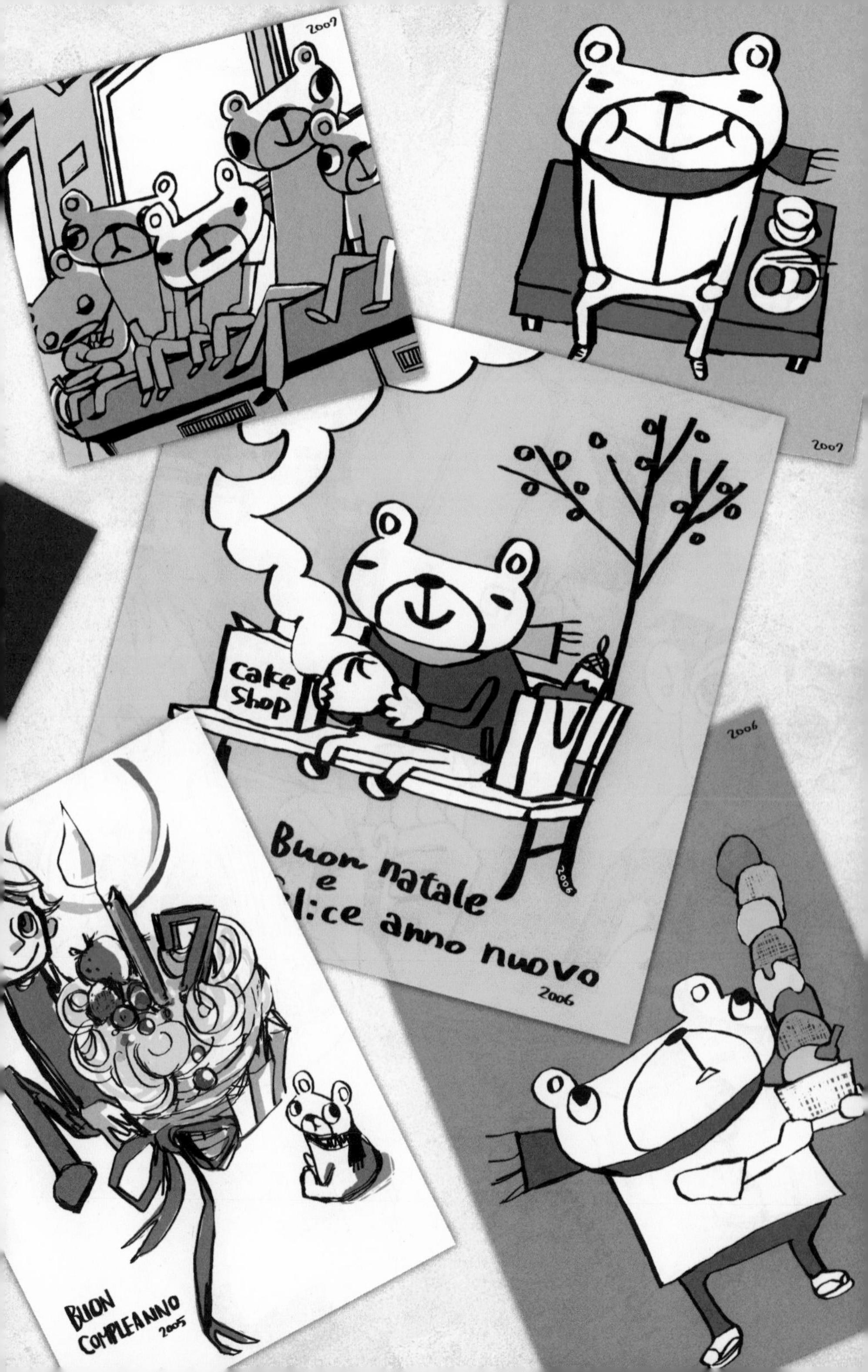
2007
2007
Cake Shop
Buon natale e felice anno nuovo
2006
2006
2006
BUON COMPLEANNO
2005

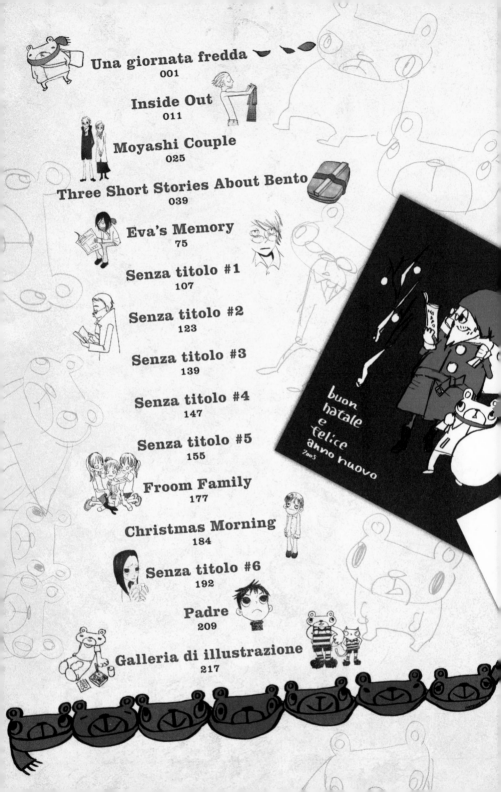

buon
natale
e
felice
anno nuovo
2005

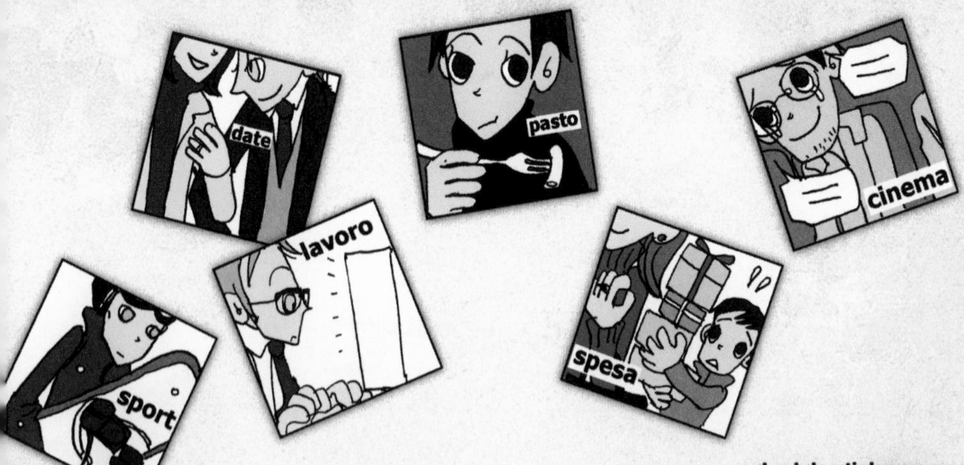
date
pasto
cinema
lavoro
spesa
sport

schedule stickers 1999

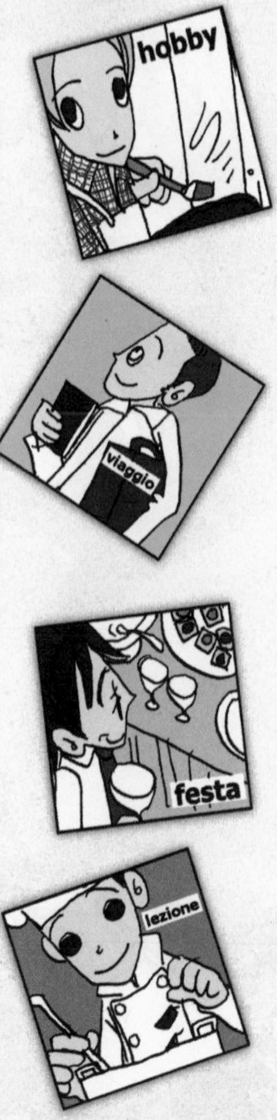
hobby
viaggio
festa
lezione

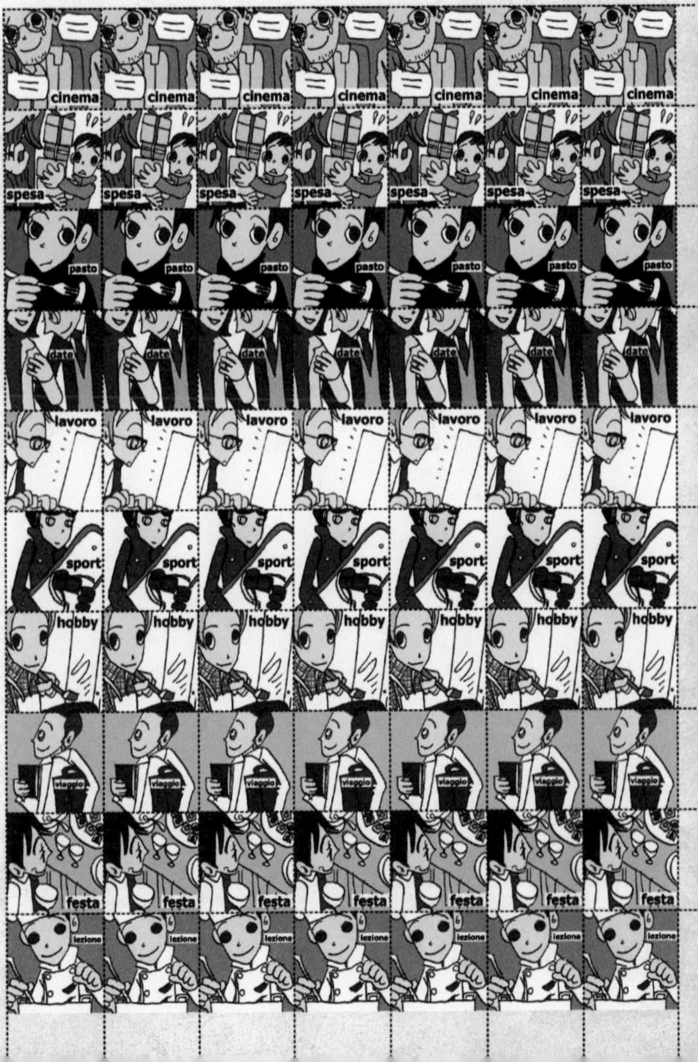
cinema
spesa
pasto
date
lavoro
sport
hobby
viaggio
festa
lezione

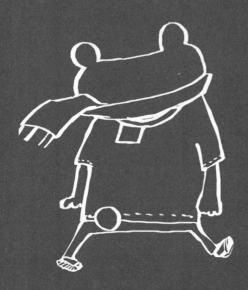

Natsume Ono
Tesoro

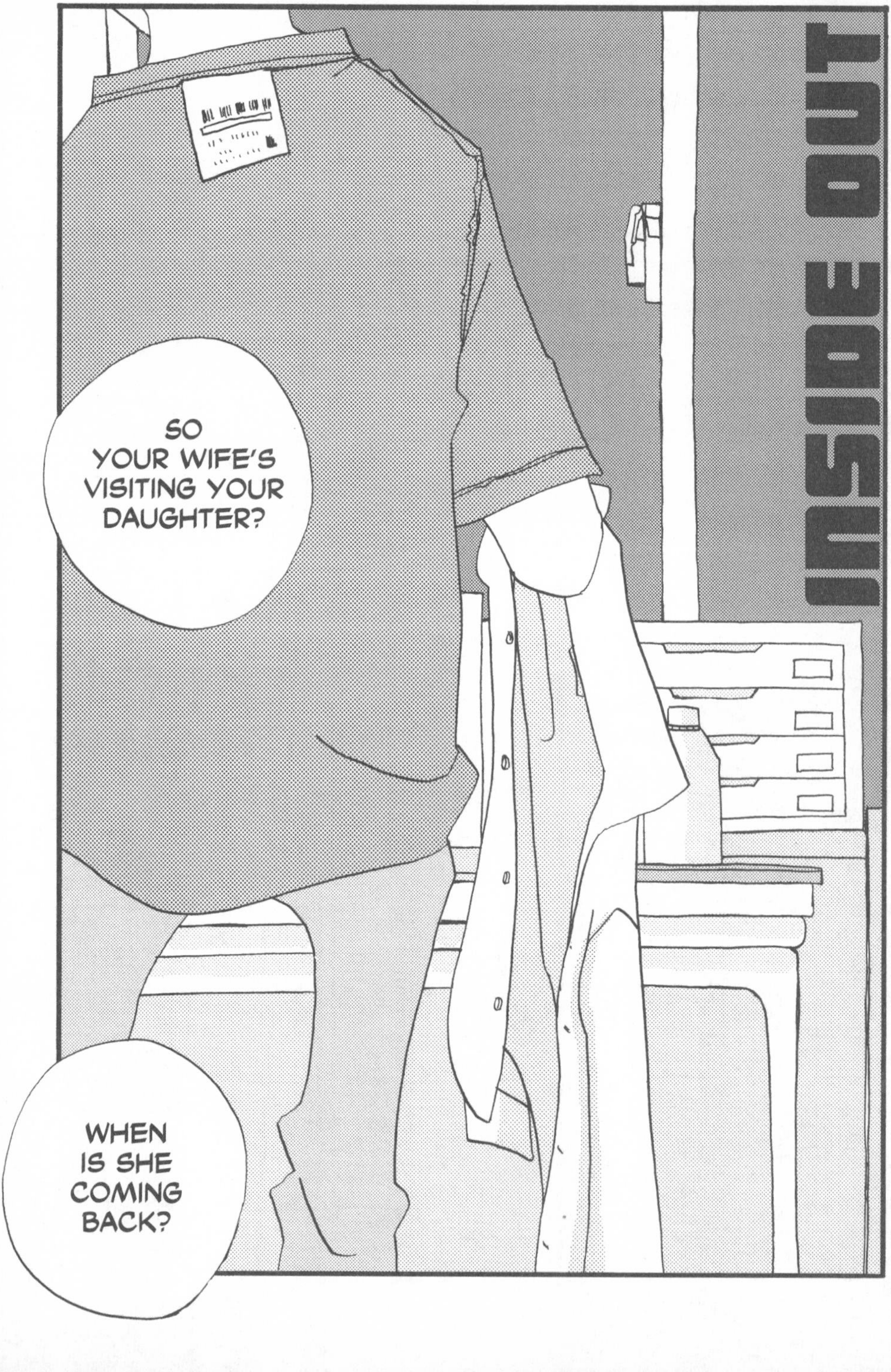
INSIDE OUT
SO YOUR WIFE'S VISITING YOUR DAUGHTER?
WHEN IS SHE COMING BACK?

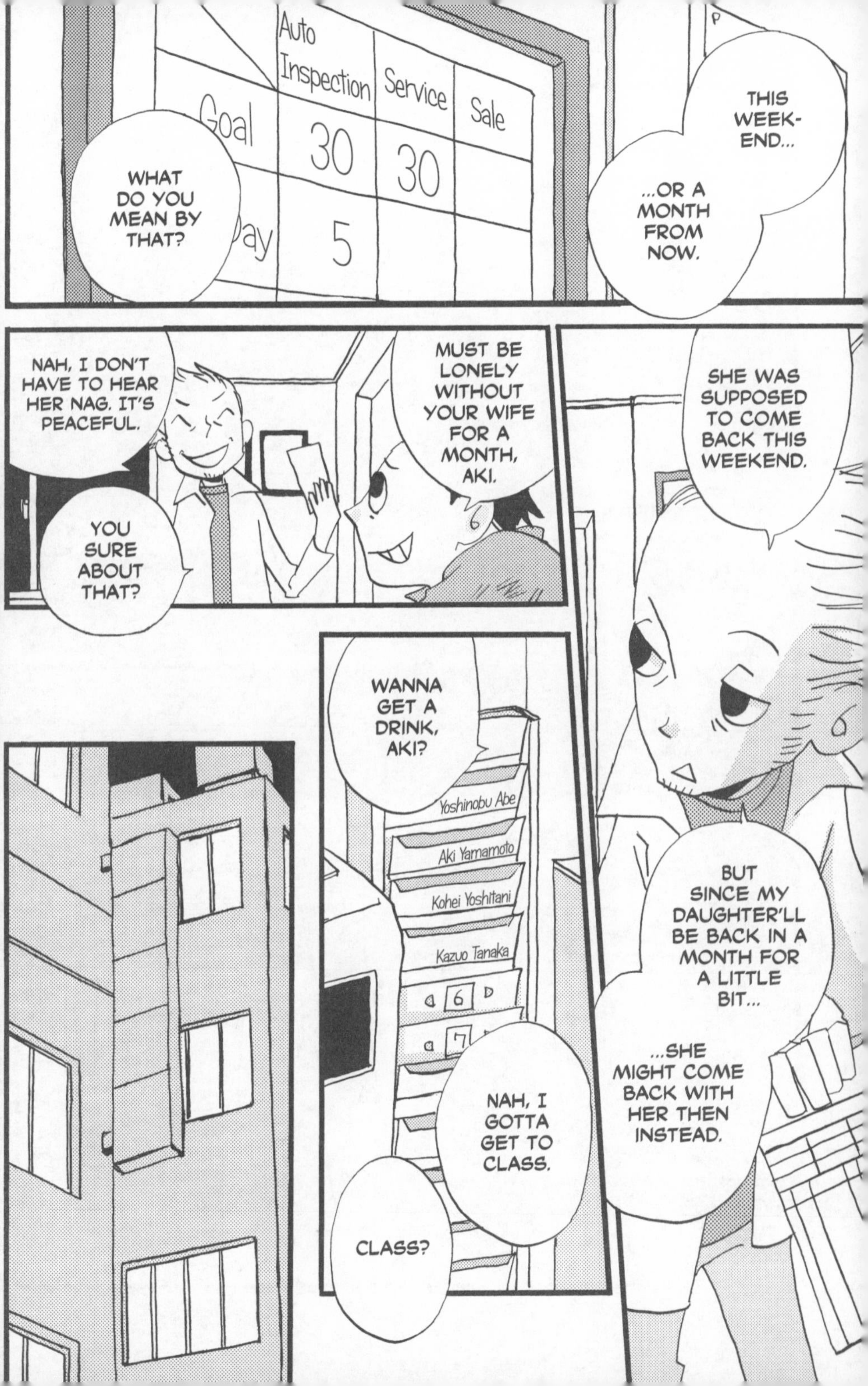
THIS WEEK-END...
...OR A MONTH FROM NOW.
Auto Inspection
Service
Sale
Goal
30
30
Day
5
WHAT DO YOU MEAN BY THAT?
SHE WAS SUPPOSED TO COME BACK THIS WEEKEND.
BUT SINCE MY DAUGHTER'LL BE BACK IN A MONTH FOR A LITTLE BIT...
...SHE MIGHT COME BACK WITH HER THEN INSTEAD.
MUST BE LONELY WITHOUT YOUR WIFE FOR A MONTH, AKI.
NAH, I DON'T HAVE TO HEAR HER NAG. IT'S PEACEFUL.
YOU SURE ABOUT THAT?
WANNA GET A DRINK, AKI?
Yoshinobu Abe
Aki Yamamoto
Kohei Yoshitani
Kazuo Tanaka
6
7
NAH, I GOTTA GET TO CLASS.
CLASS?

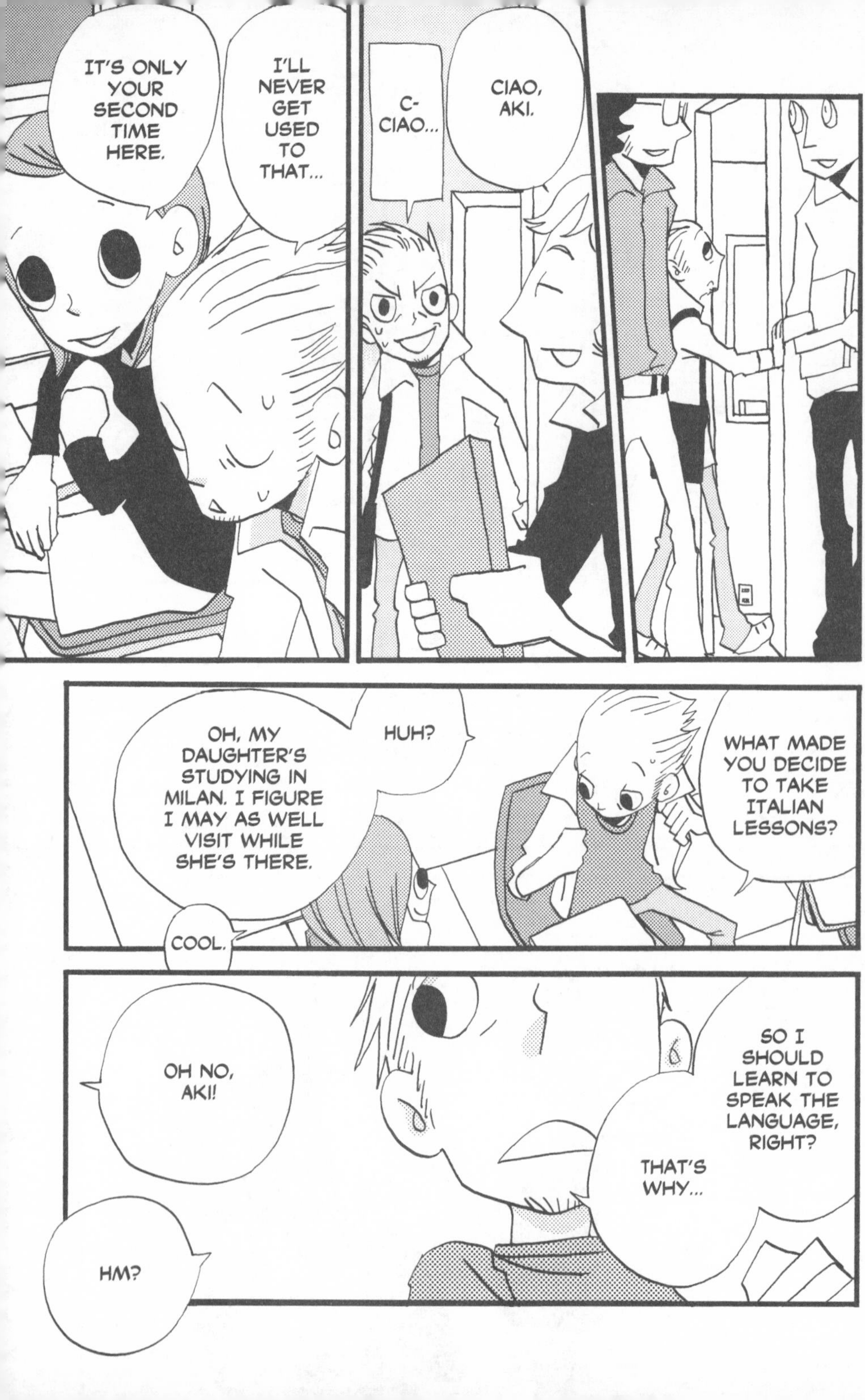
CIAO, AKI.
C-CIAO...
I'LL NEVER GET USED TO THAT...
IT'S ONLY YOUR SECOND TIME HERE.
WHAT MADE YOU DECIDE TO TAKE ITALIAN LESSONS?
HUH?
OH, MY DAUGHTER'S STUDYING IN MILAN. I FIGURE I MAY AS WELL VISIT WHILE SHE'S THERE.
COOL.
SO I SHOULD LEARN TO SPEAK THE LANGUAGE, RIGHT?
THAT'S WHY...
OH NO, AKI!
HM?

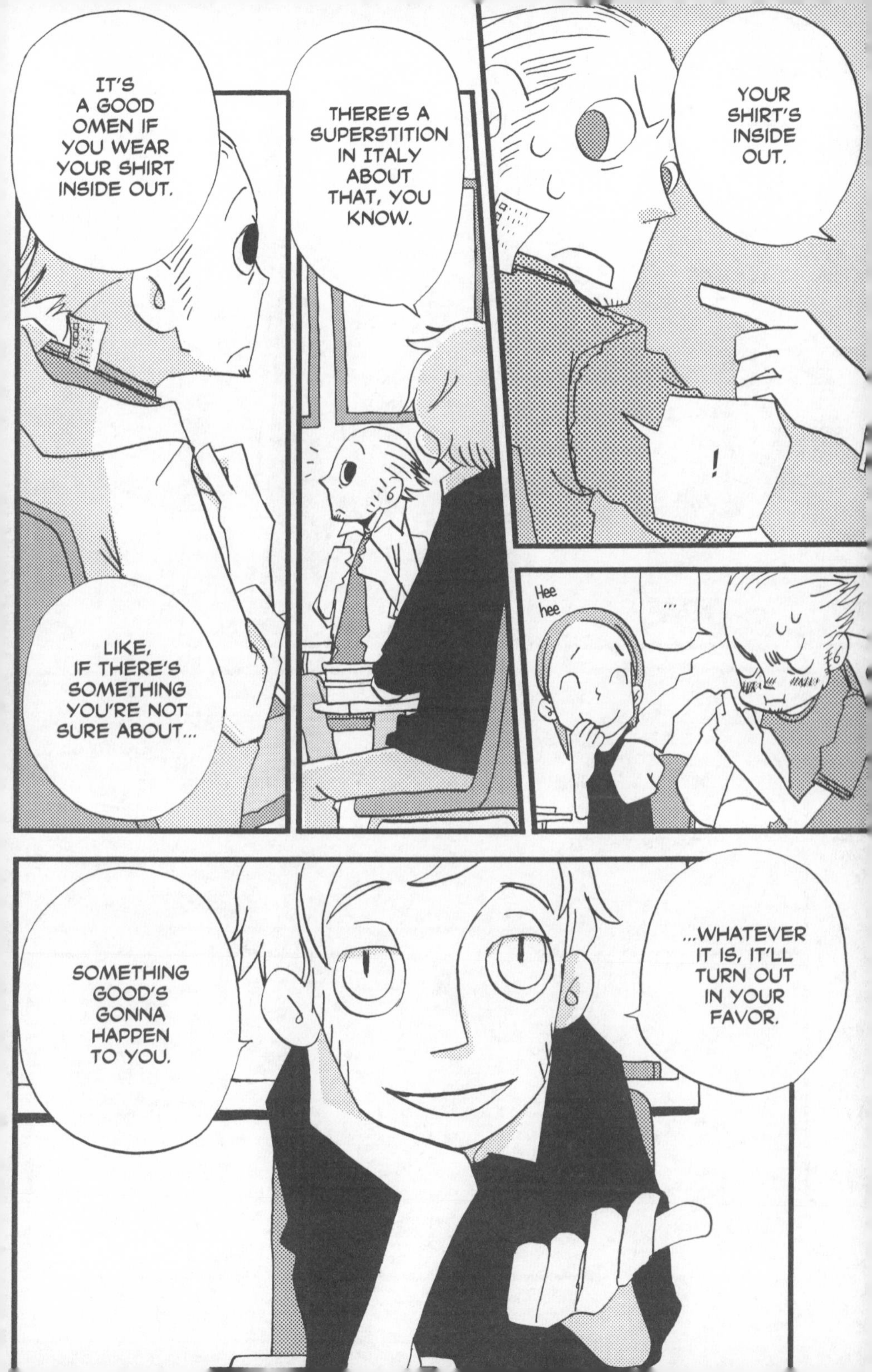

YOUR SHIRT'S INSIDE OUT.
!
Hee hee
...
THERE'S A SUPERSTITION IN ITALY ABOUT THAT, YOU KNOW.
IT'S A GOOD OMEN IF YOU WEAR YOUR SHIRT INSIDE OUT.
LIKE, IF THERE'S SOMETHING YOU'RE NOT SURE ABOUT...
...WHATEVER IT IS, IT'LL TURN OUT IN YOUR FAVOR.
SOMETHING GOOD'S GONNA HAPPEN TO YOU.

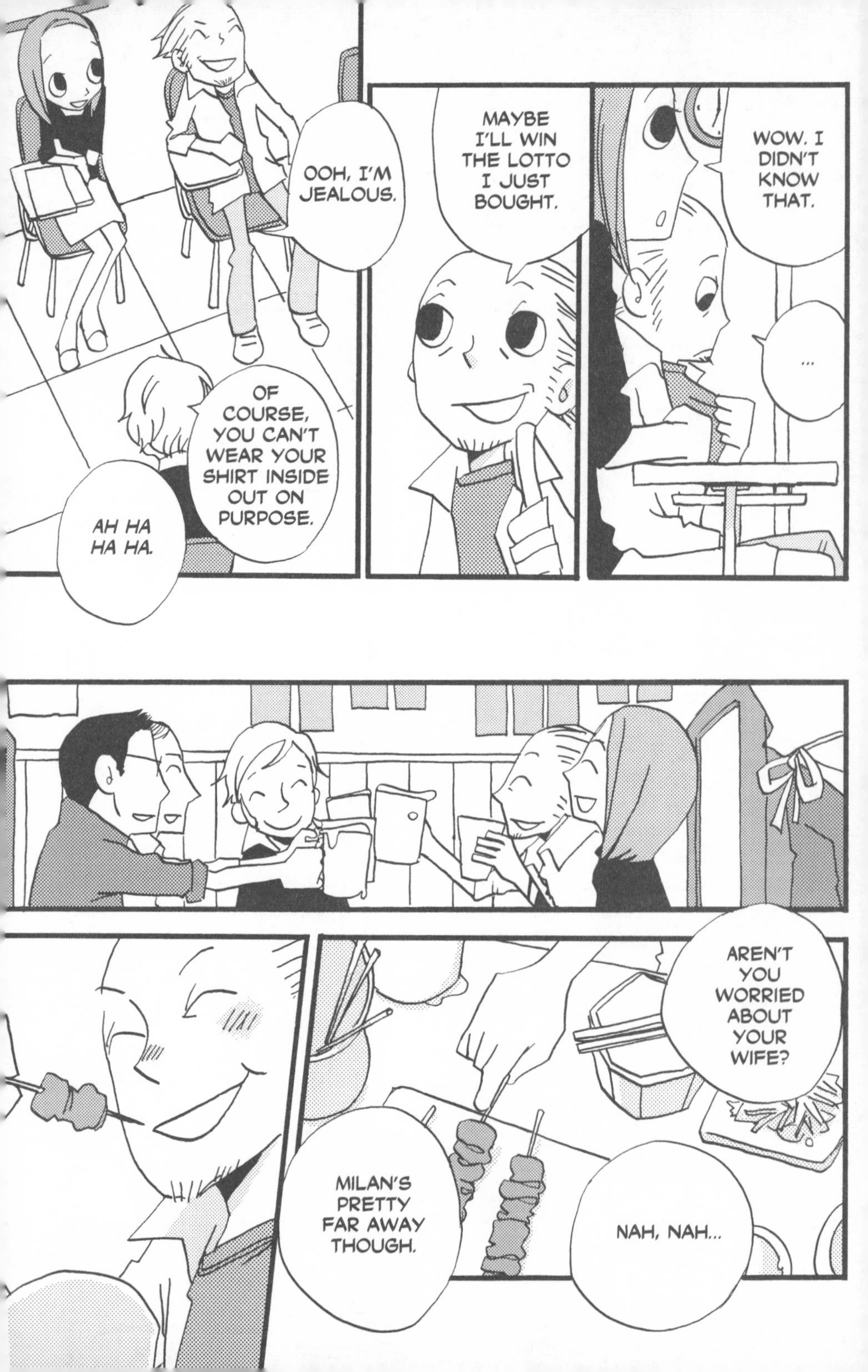
WOW. I DIDN'T KNOW THAT.
...
MAYBE I'LL WIN THE LOTTO I JUST BOUGHT.
OOH, I'M JEALOUS.
OF COURSE, YOU CAN'T WEAR YOUR SHIRT INSIDE OUT ON PURPOSE.
AH HA HA HA.
AREN'T YOU WORRIED ABOUT YOUR WIFE?
MILAN'S PRETTY FAR AWAY THOUGH.
NAH, NAH...

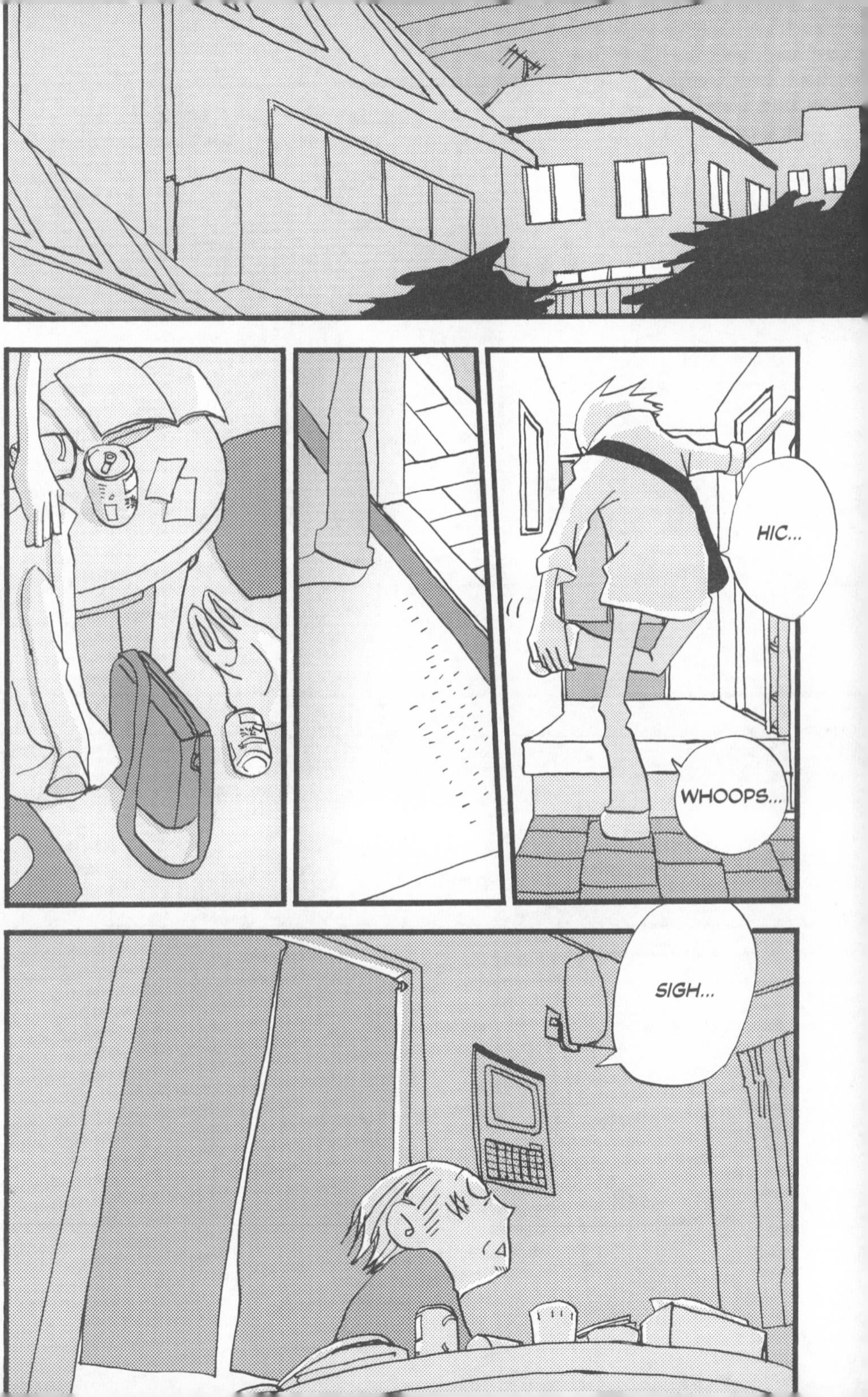
HIC...
WHOOPS...
SIGH...

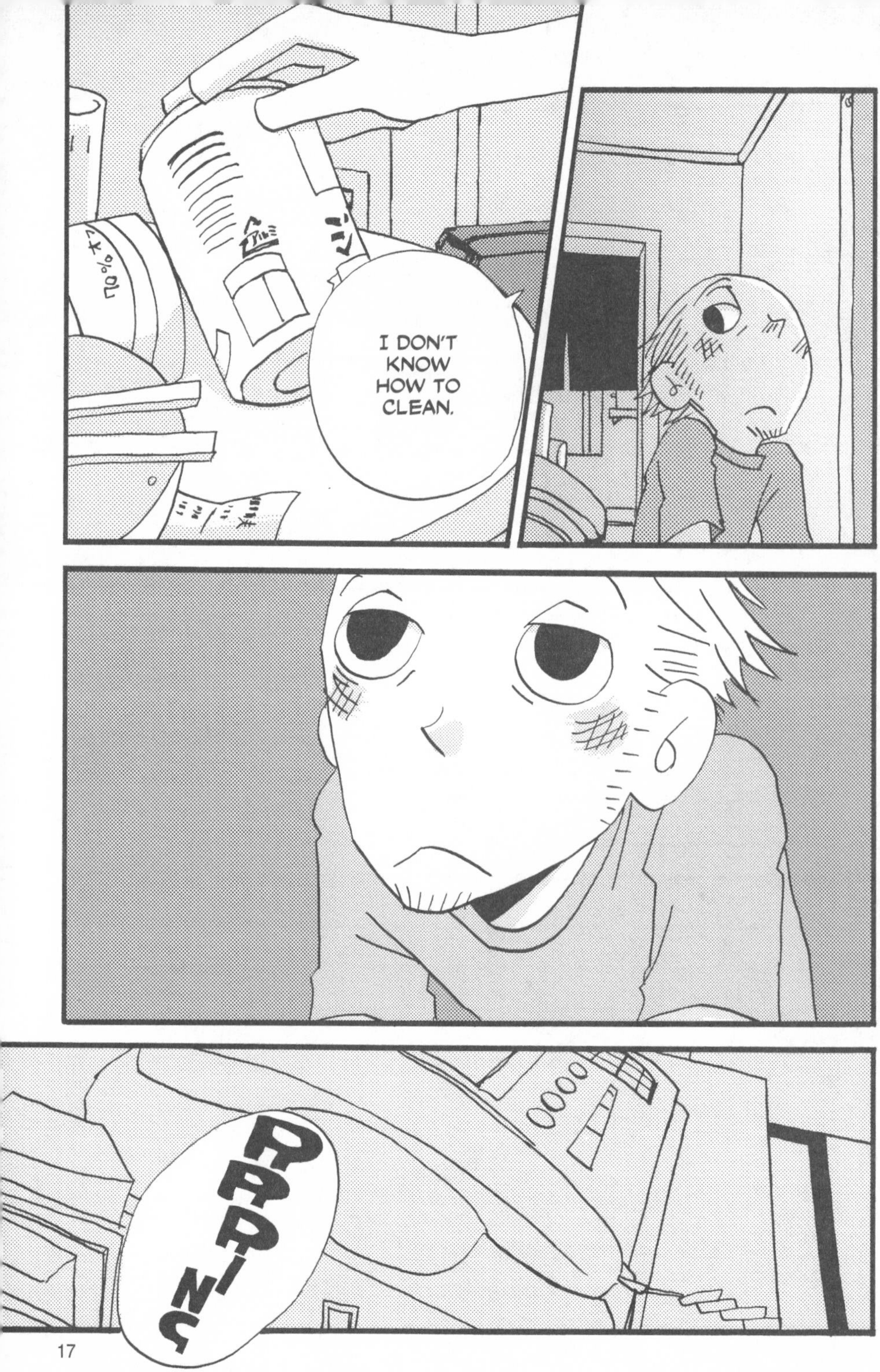
I DON'T KNOW HOW TO CLEAN.
PRRING

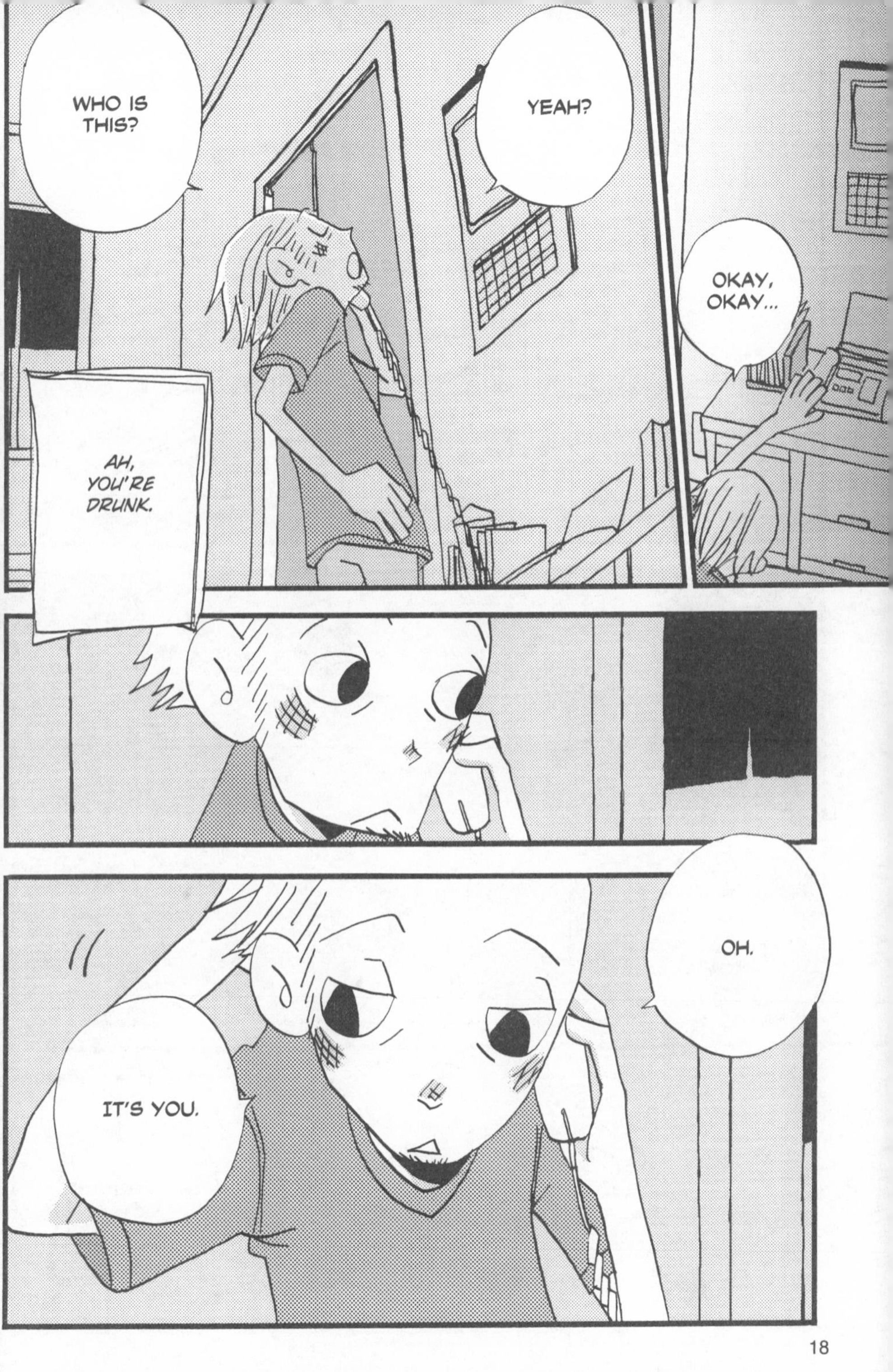
OKAY, OKAY...
YEAH?
WHO IS THIS?
AH, YOU'RE DRUNK.
OH.
IT'S YOU.

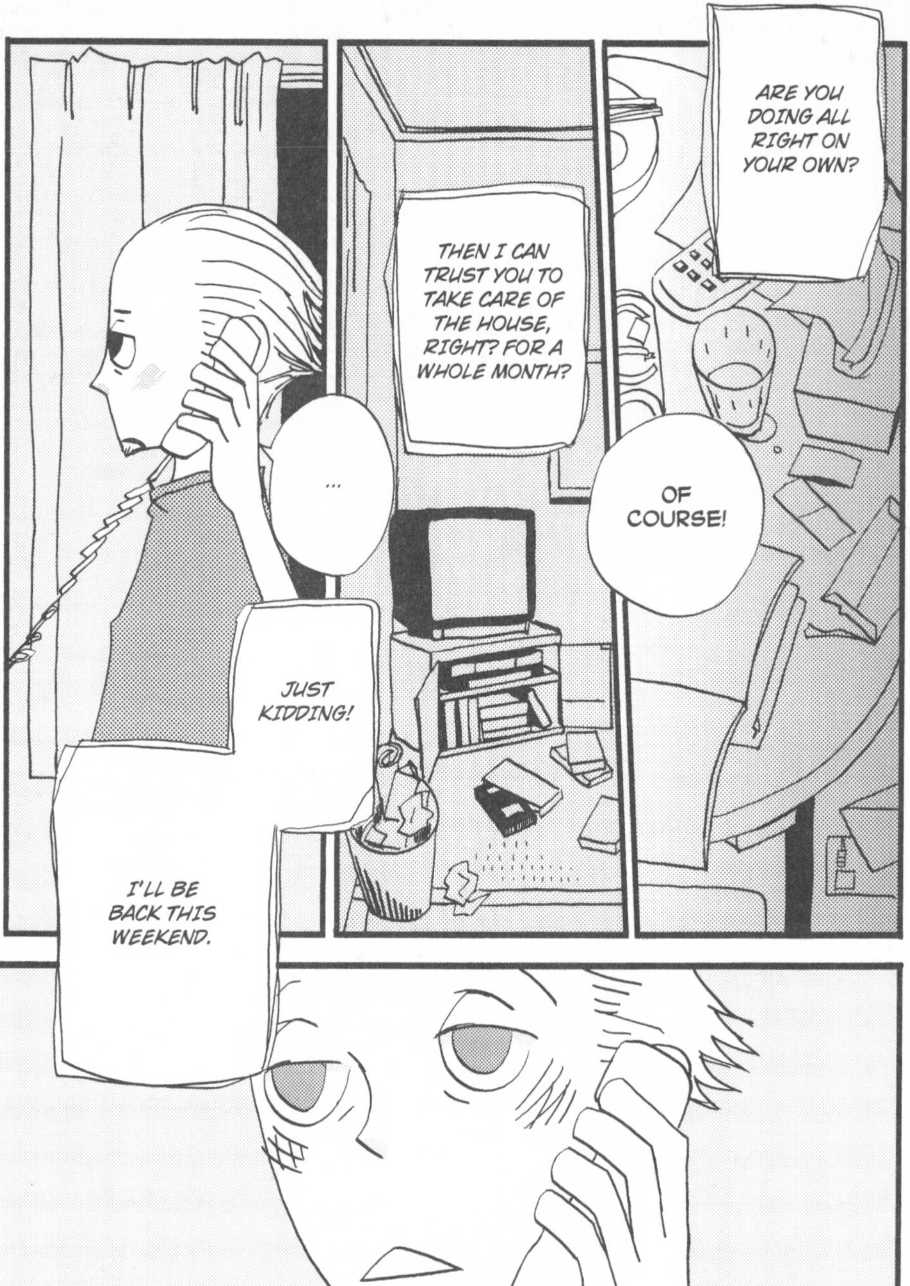
ARE YOU DOING ALL RIGHT ON YOUR OWN?
OF COURSE!
THEN I CAN TRUST YOU TO TAKE CARE OF THE HOUSE, RIGHT? FOR A WHOLE MONTH?
...
JUST KIDDING!
I'LL BE BACK THIS WEEKEND.

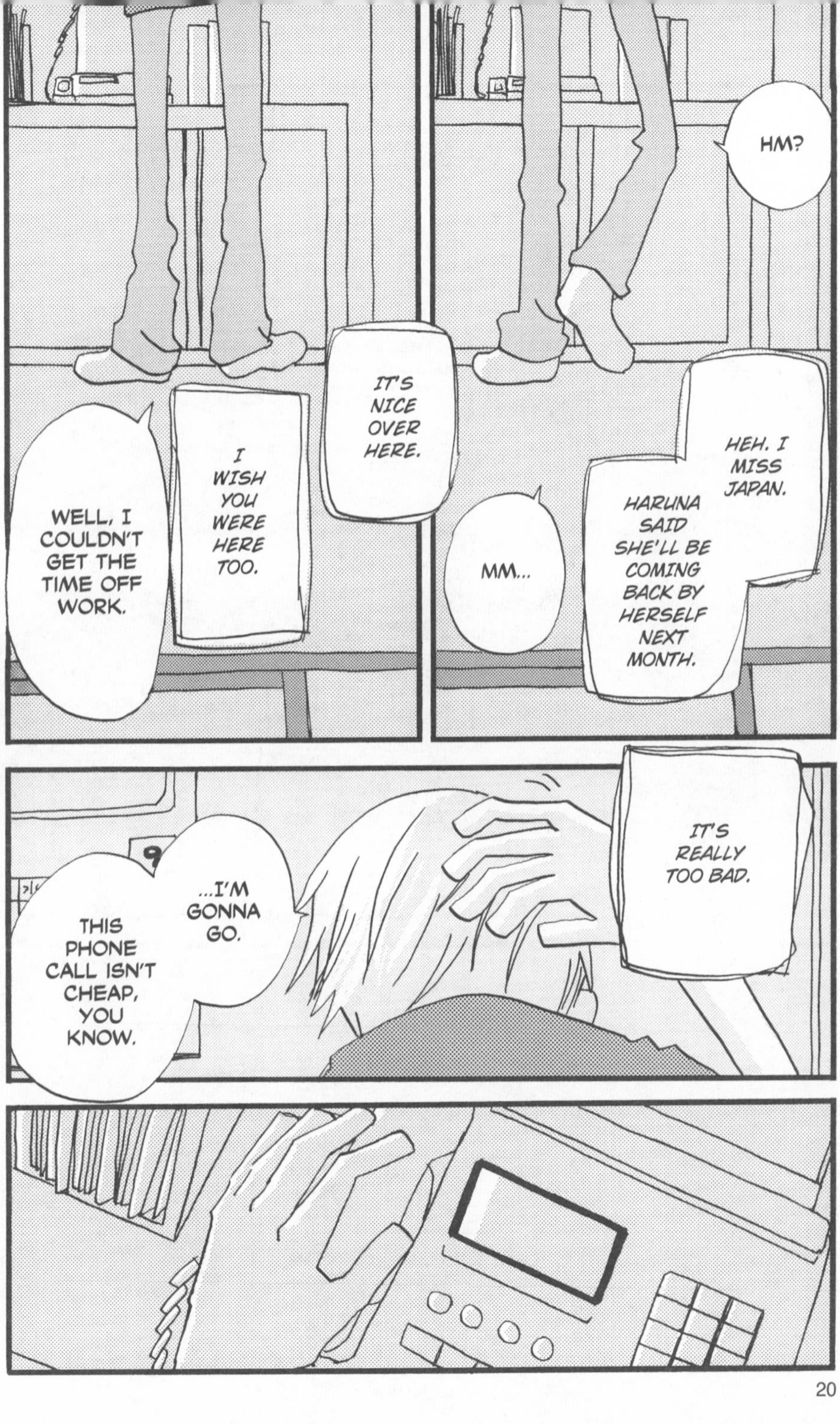
HM?
HEH. I MISS JAPAN.
HARUNA SAID SHE'LL BE COMING BACK BY HERSELF NEXT MONTH.
MM...
IT'S NICE OVER HERE.
I WISH YOU WERE HERE TOO.
WELL, I COULDN'T GET THE TIME OFF WORK.
IT'S REALLY TOO BAD.
...I'M GONNA GO.
THIS PHONE CALL ISN'T CHEAP, YOU KNOW.

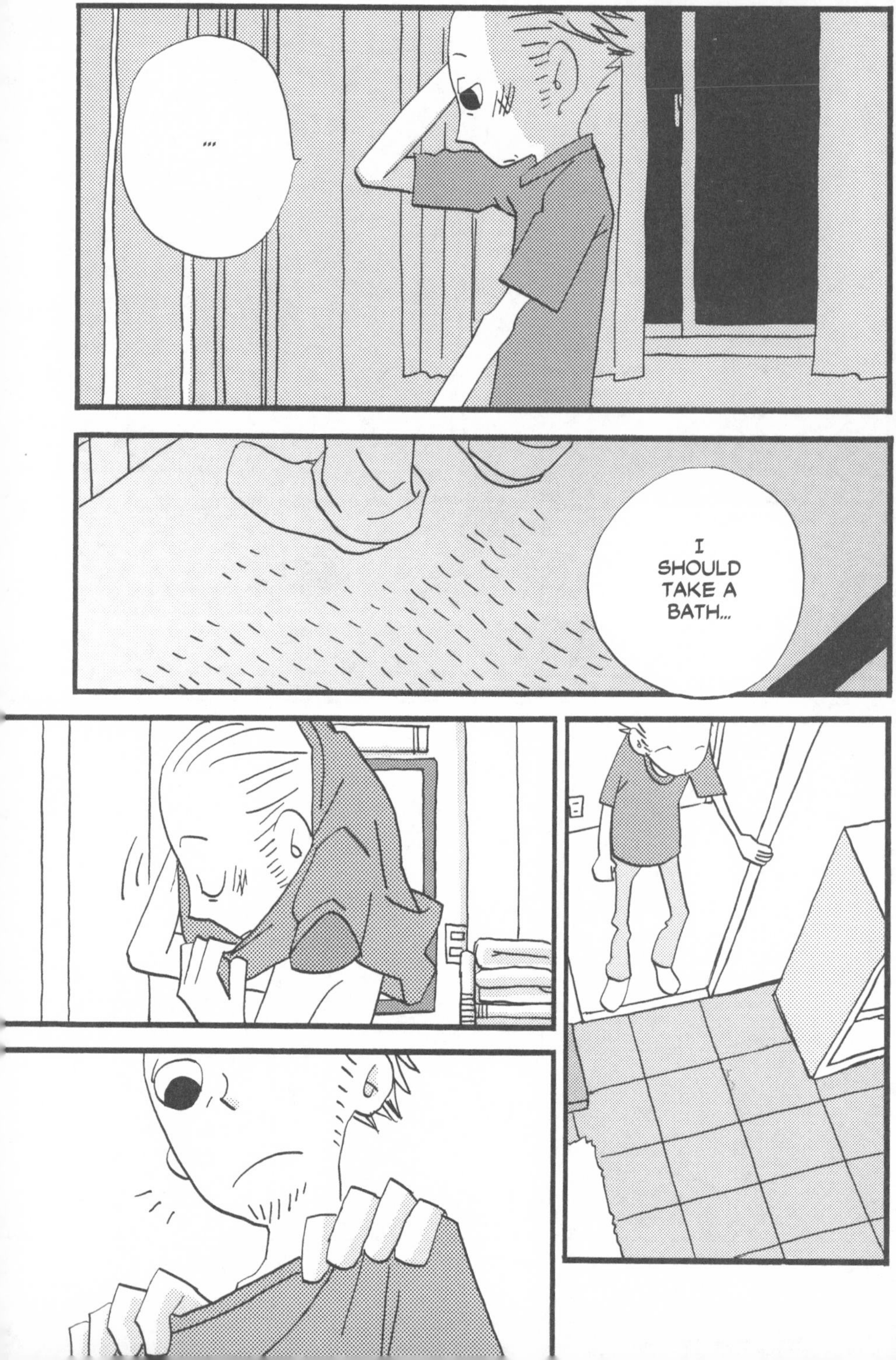
...
I SHOULD TAKE A BATH...

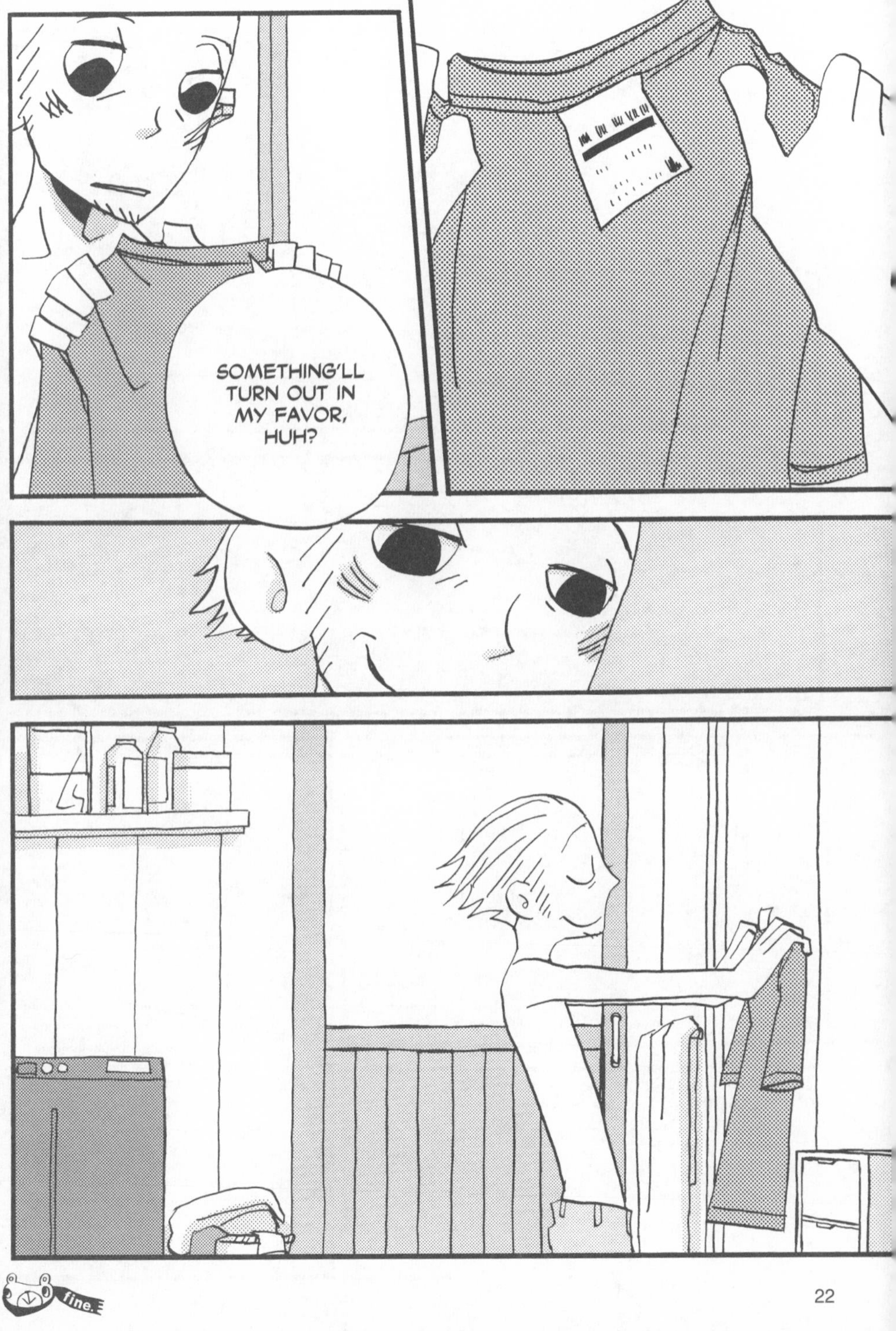
SOMETHING'LL TURN OUT IN MY FAVOR, HUH?
fine.

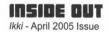

INSIDE OUT
Ikki - April 2005 Issue

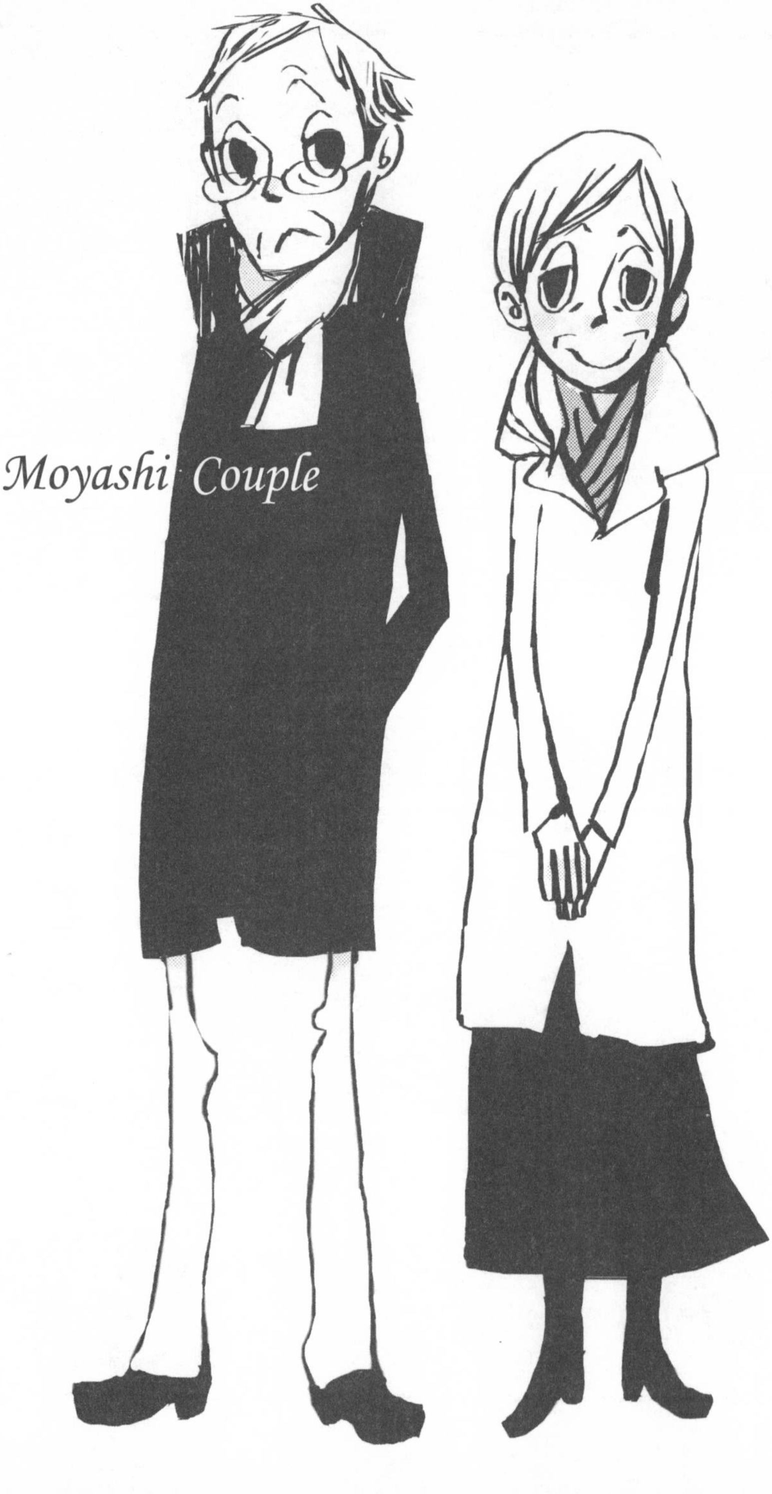
Moyashi Couple

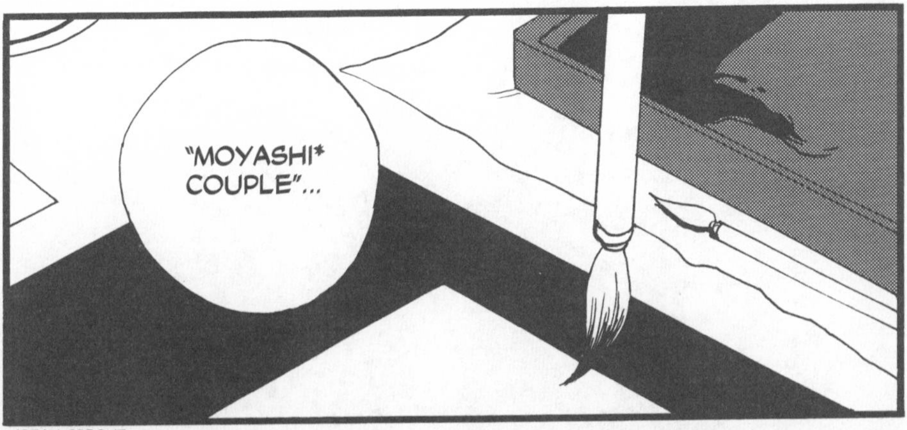
"MOYASHI*
COUPLE"...

*BEAN SPROUT

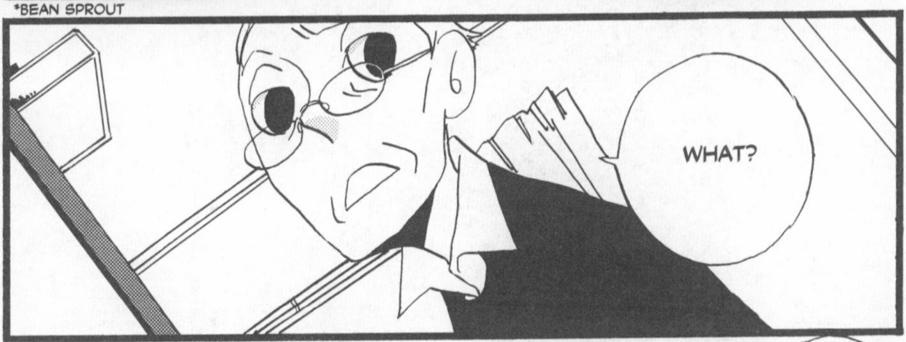
WHAT?

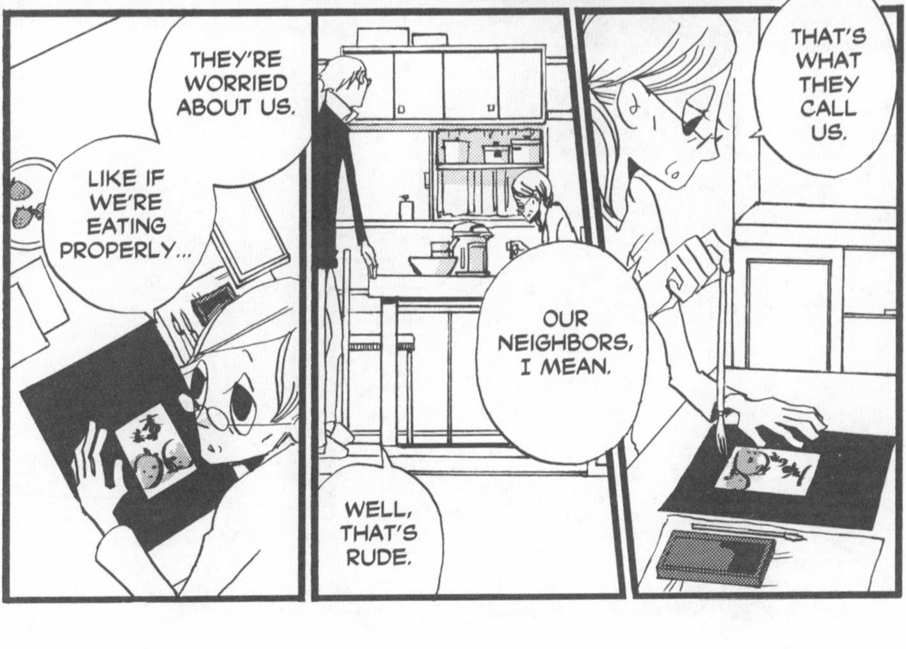
THAT'S WHAT THEY CALL US.
OUR NEIGHBORS, I MEAN.
WELL, THAT'S RUDE.
THEY'RE WORRIED ABOUT US.
LIKE IF WE'RE EATING PROPERLY...

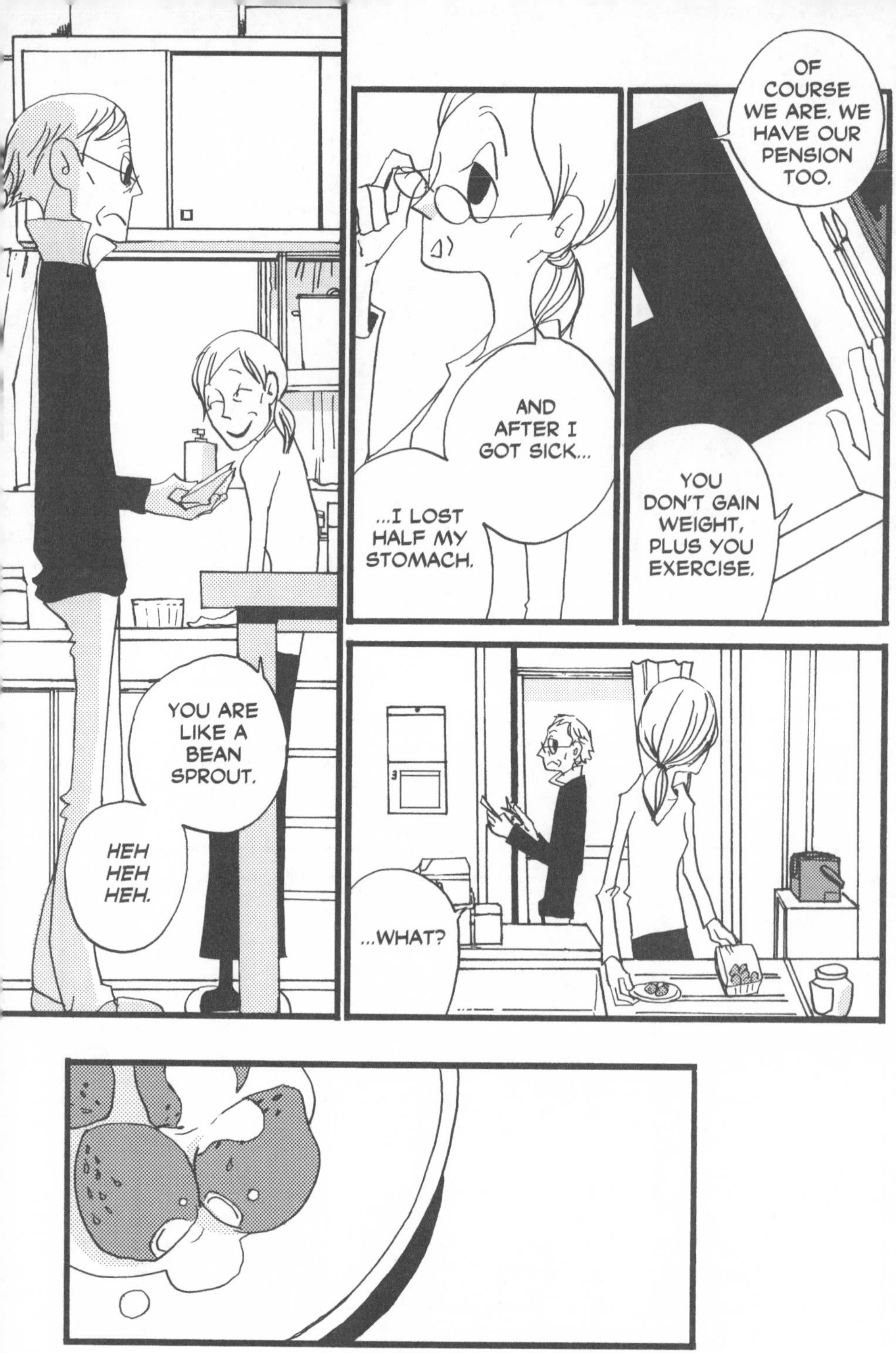
OF COURSE WE ARE. WE HAVE OUR PENSION TOO.
YOU DON'T GAIN WEIGHT, PLUS YOU EXERCISE.
AND AFTER I GOT SICK...
...I LOST HALF MY STOMACH.
...WHAT?
YOU ARE LIKE A BEAN SPROUT.
HEH HEH HEH.

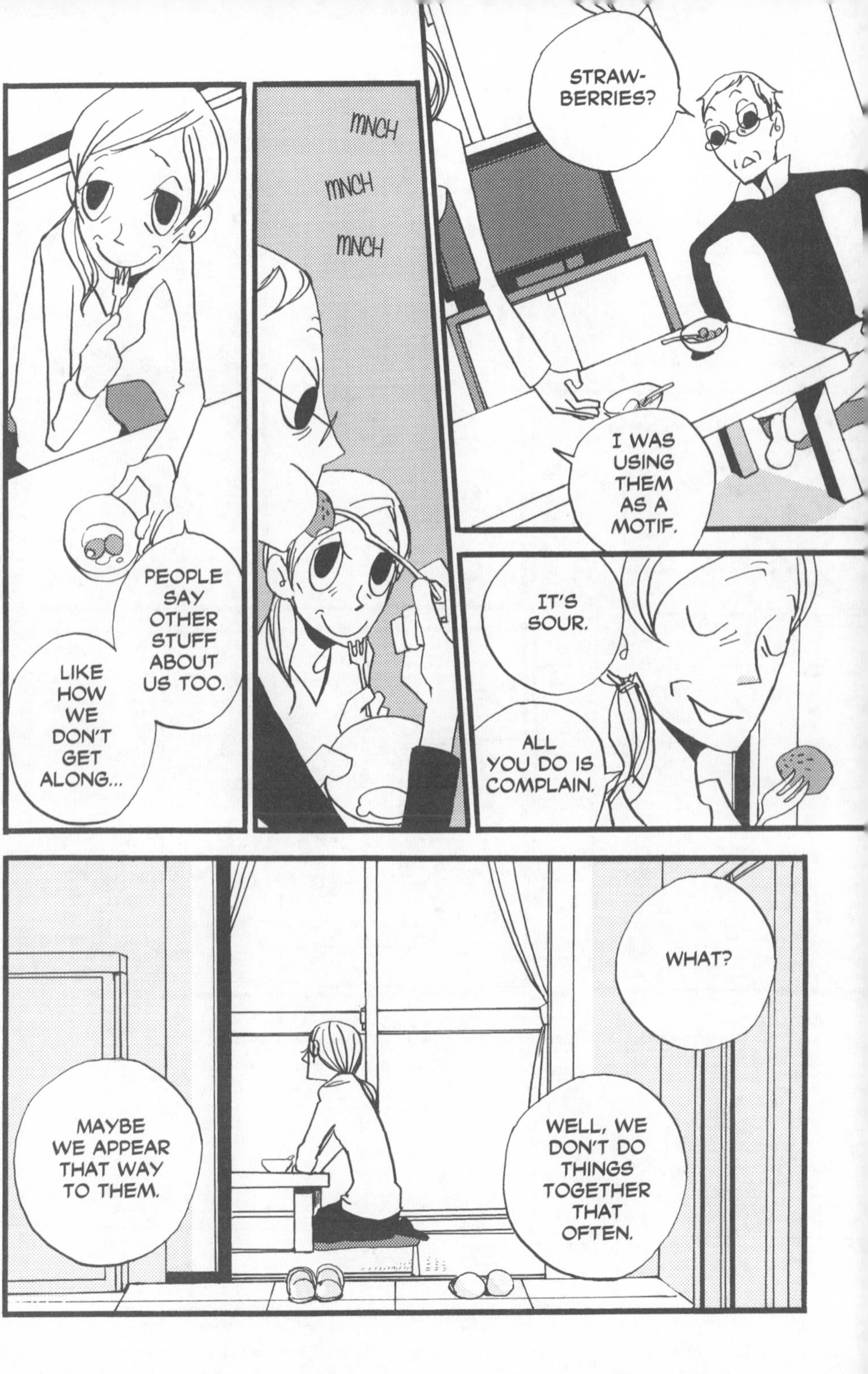
STRAW-BERRIES?
I WAS USING THEM AS A MOTIF.
IT'S SOUR.
ALL YOU DO IS COMPLAIN.
MNCH
MNCH
MNCH
PEOPLE SAY OTHER STUFF ABOUT US TOO.
LIKE HOW WE DON'T GET ALONG...
WHAT?
WELL, WE DON'T DO THINGS TOGETHER THAT OFTEN.
MAYBE WE APPEAR THAT WAY TO THEM.

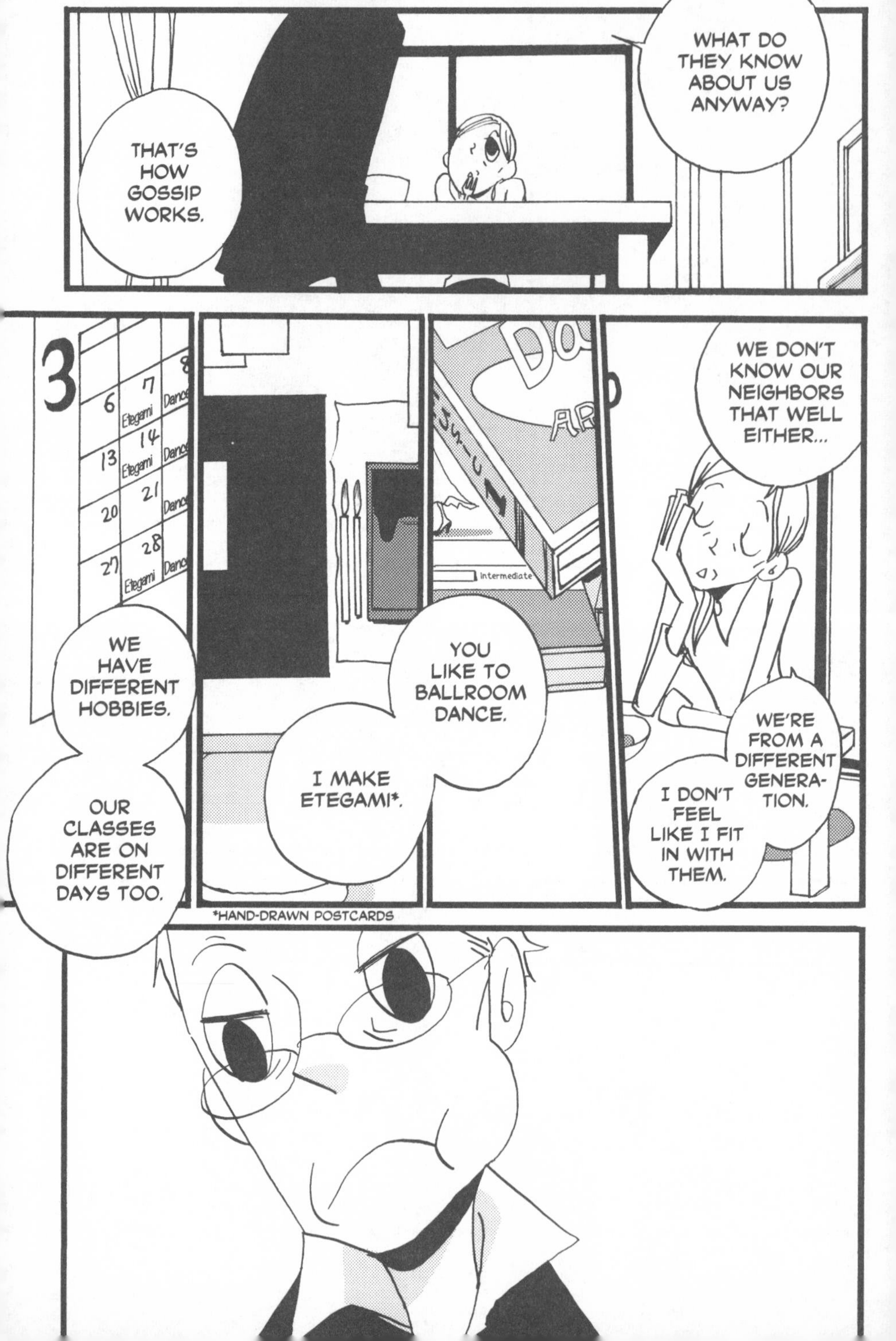
WHAT DO THEY KNOW ABOUT US ANYWAY?
THAT'S HOW GOSSIP WORKS.
WE DON'T KNOW OUR NEIGHBORS THAT WELL EITHER...
WE'RE FROM A DIFFERENT GENERATION.
I DON'T FEEL LIKE I FIT IN WITH THEM.
Intermediate
YOU LIKE TO BALLROOM DANCE.
I MAKE ETEGAMI*.
3
6
7 Etegami
8 Dance
13
14 Etegami
Dance
20
21
Dance
27
28 Etegami
Dance
WE HAVE DIFFERENT HOBBIES.
OUR CLASSES ARE ON DIFFERENT DAYS TOO.

*HAND-DRAWN POSTCARDS

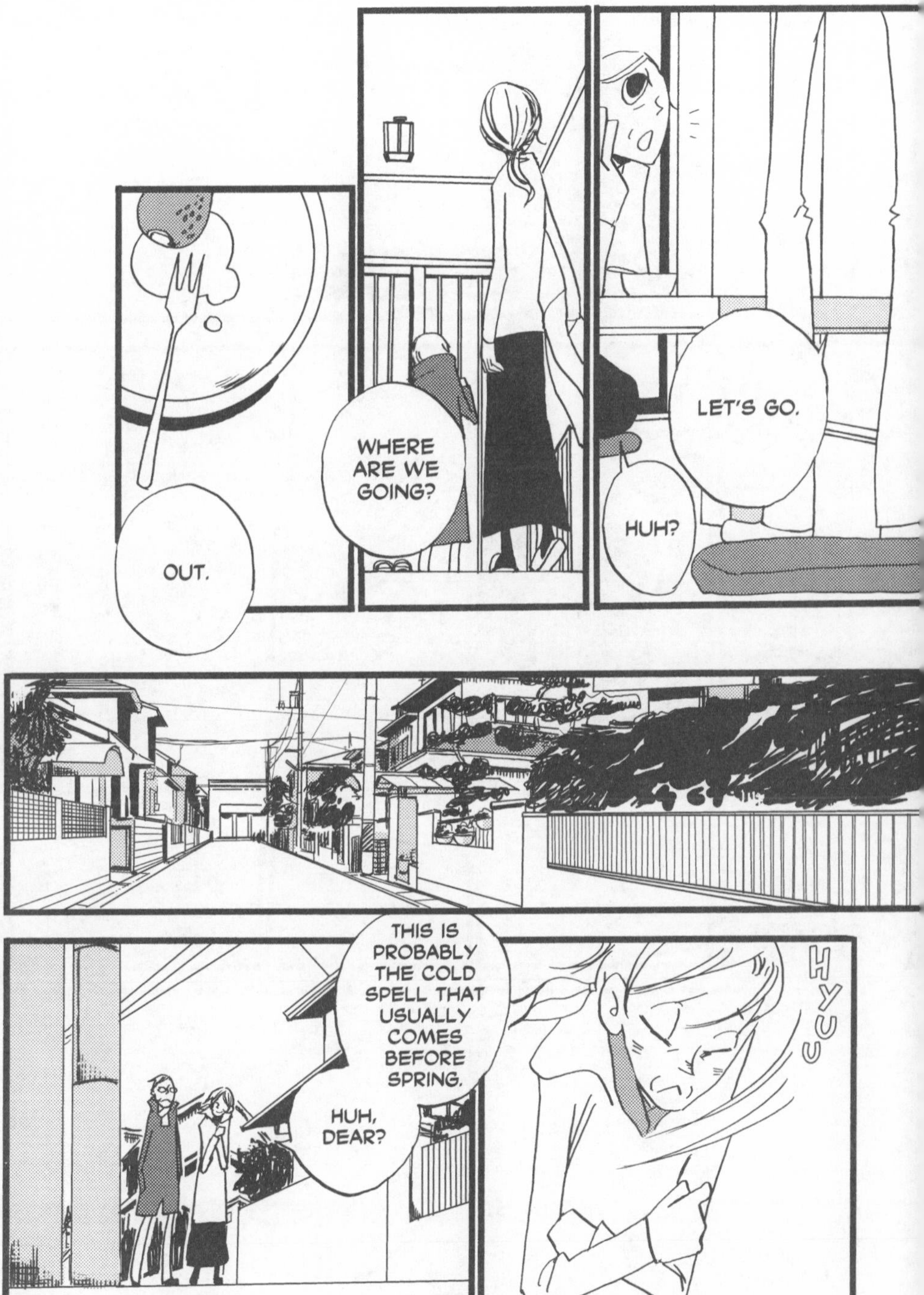
LET'S GO.
HUH?
WHERE ARE WE GOING?
OUT.
HYUUU
THIS IS PROBABLY THE COLD SPELL THAT USUALLY COMES BEFORE SPRING.
HUH, DEAR?

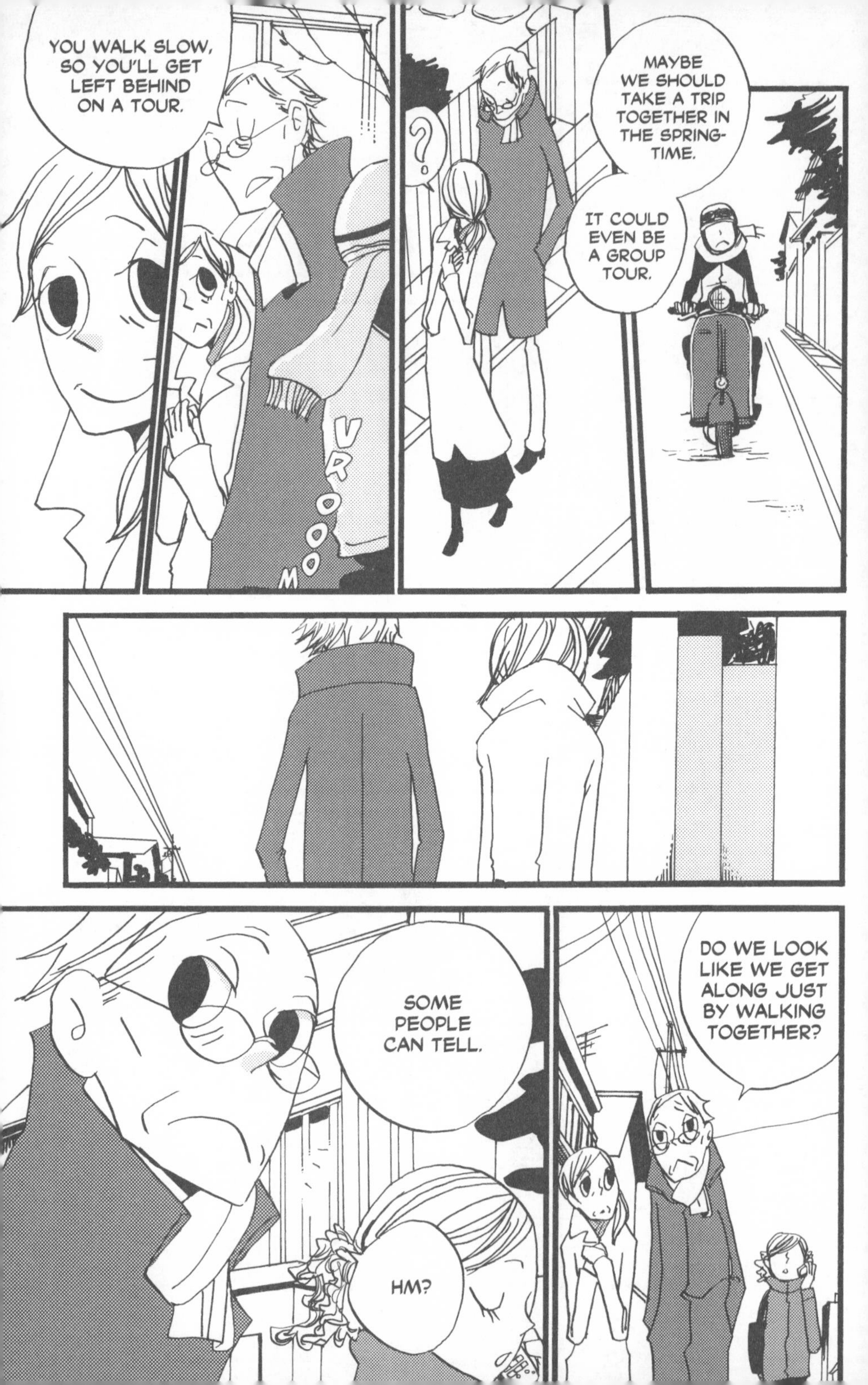
MAYBE WE SHOULD TAKE A TRIP TOGETHER IN THE SPRING-TIME.
IT COULD EVEN BE A GROUP TOUR.
?
VROOOOM
YOU WALK SLOW, SO YOU'LL GET LEFT BEHIND ON A TOUR.
DO WE LOOK LIKE WE GET ALONG JUST BY WALKING TOGETHER?
SOME PEOPLE CAN TELL.
HM?

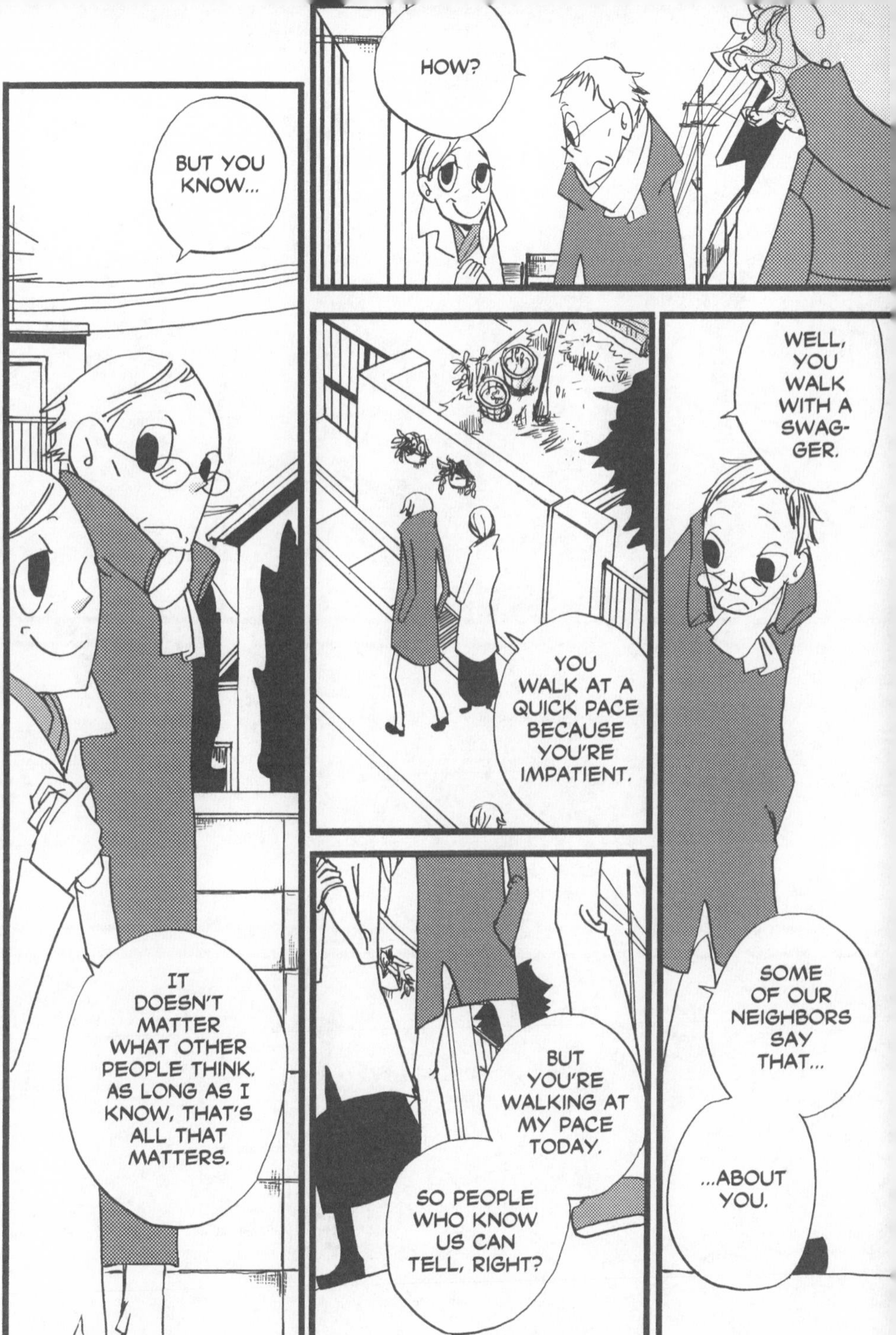
HOW?
WELL, YOU WALK WITH A SWAG-GER.
SOME OF OUR NEIGHBORS SAY THAT...
...ABOUT YOU.
YOU WALK AT A QUICK PACE BECAUSE YOU'RE IMPATIENT.
BUT YOU'RE WALKING AT MY PACE TODAY.
SO PEOPLE WHO KNOW US CAN TELL, RIGHT?
BUT YOU KNOW...
IT DOESN'T MATTER WHAT OTHER PEOPLE THINK. AS LONG AS I KNOW, THAT'S ALL THAT MATTERS.

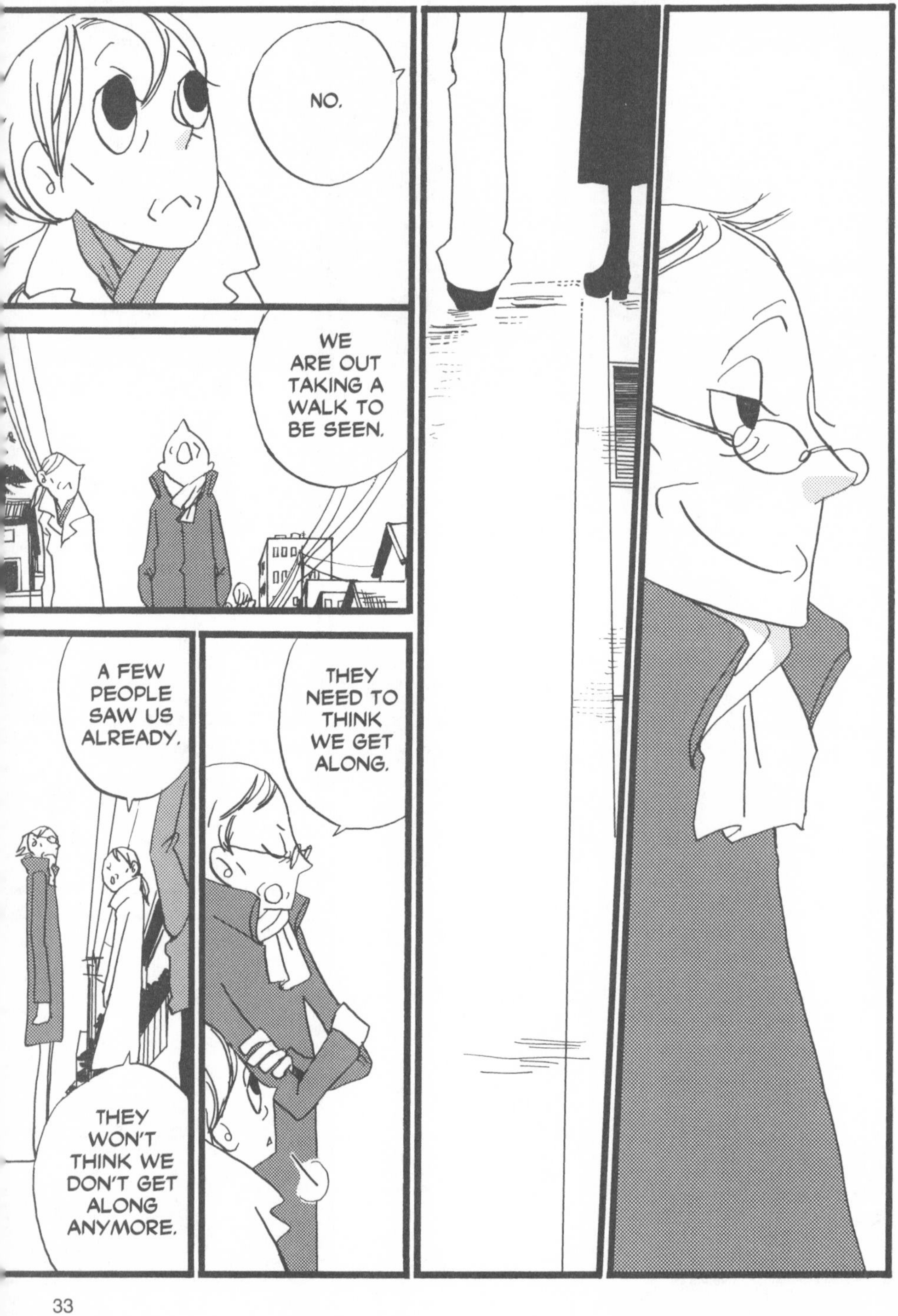
NO.
WE ARE OUT TAKING A WALK TO BE SEEN.
THEY NEED TO THINK WE GET ALONG.
A FEW PEOPLE SAW US ALREADY.
THEY WON'T THINK WE DON'T GET ALONG ANYMORE.

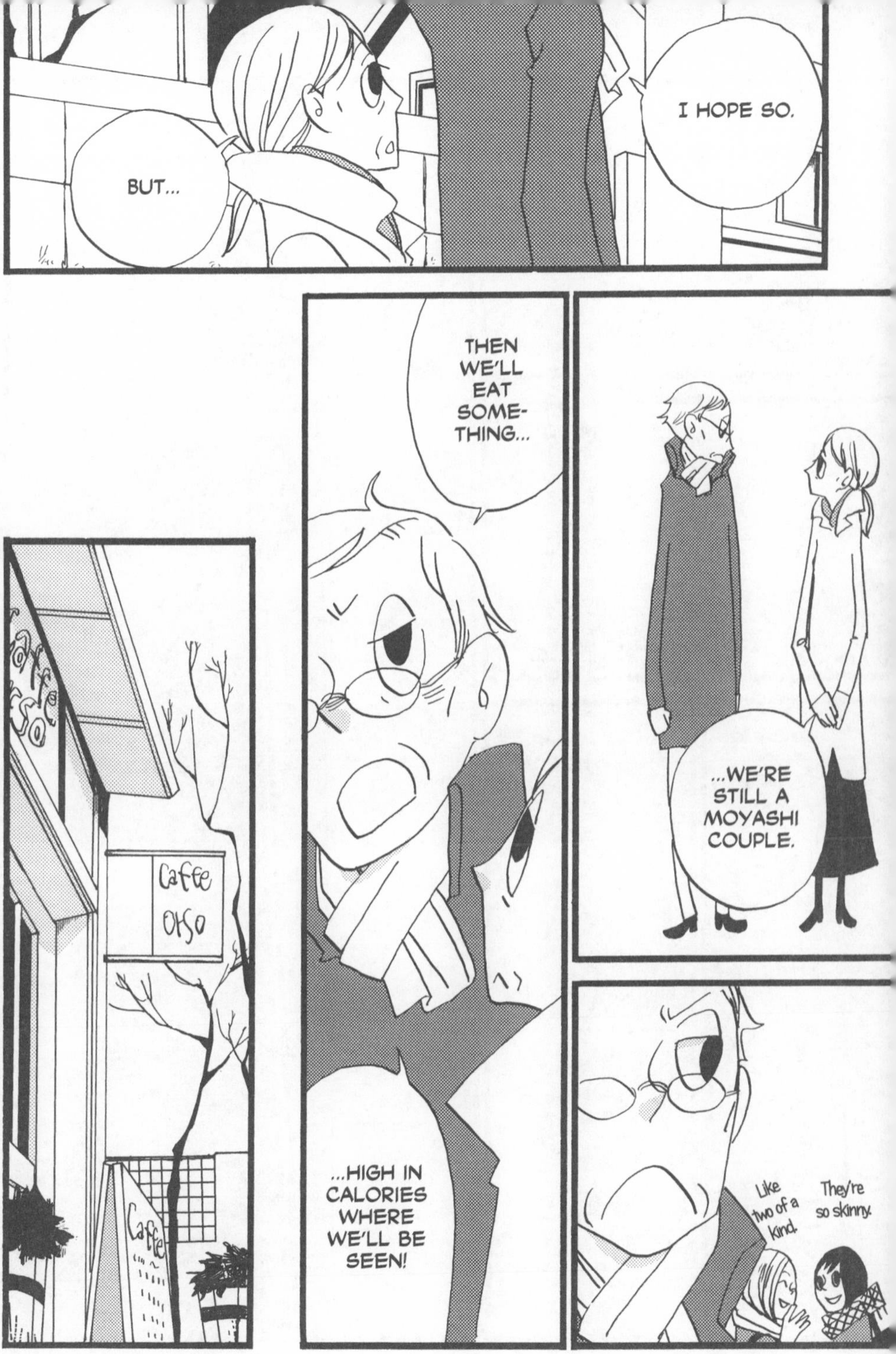
I HOPE SO.
BUT...
...WE'RE STILL A MOYASHI COUPLE.
They're so skinny.
Like two of a kind.
THEN WE'LL EAT SOME-THING...
...HIGH IN CALORIES WHERE WE'LL BE SEEN!
Caffe Orso
Caffe

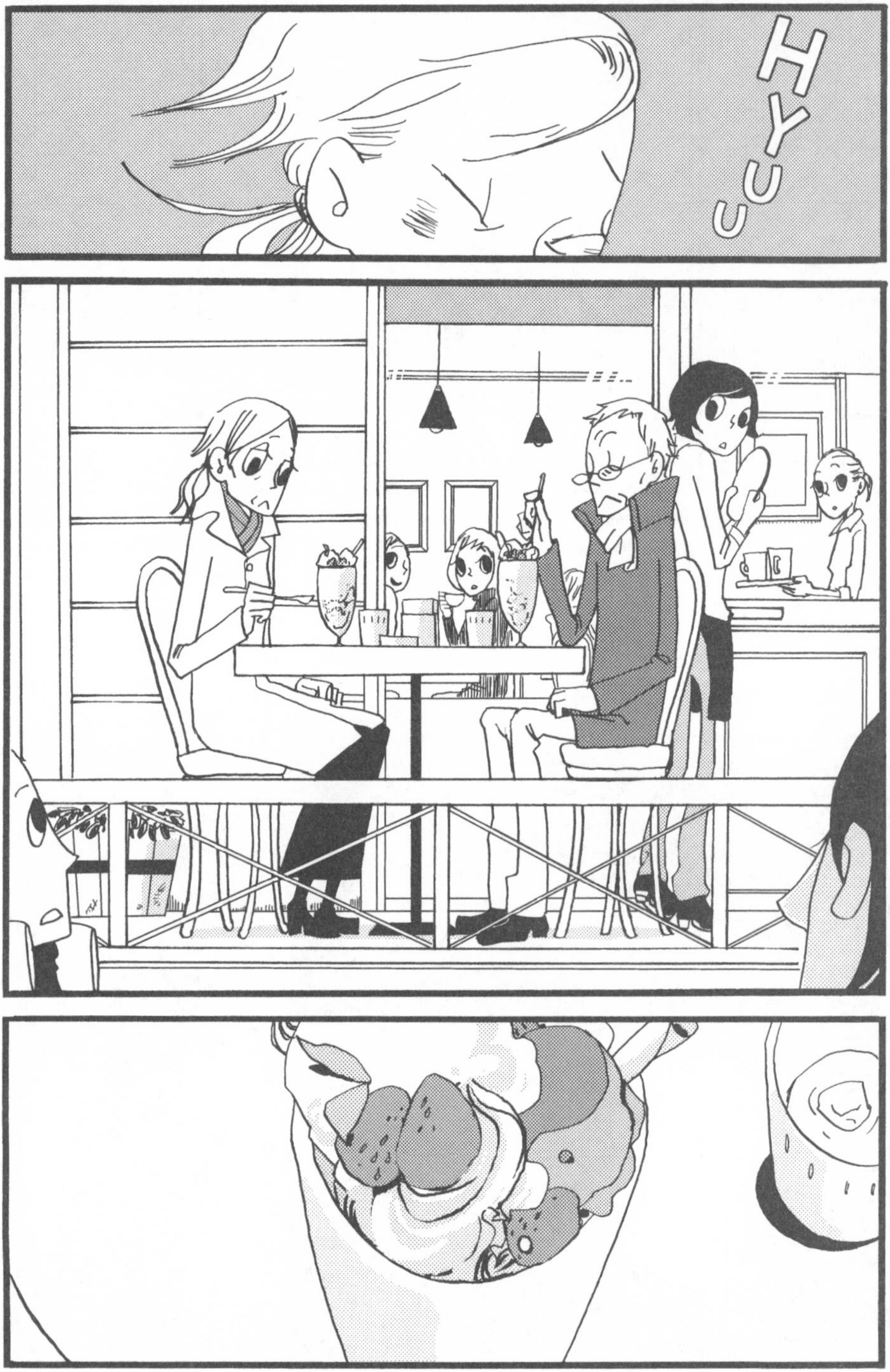
HYUUU

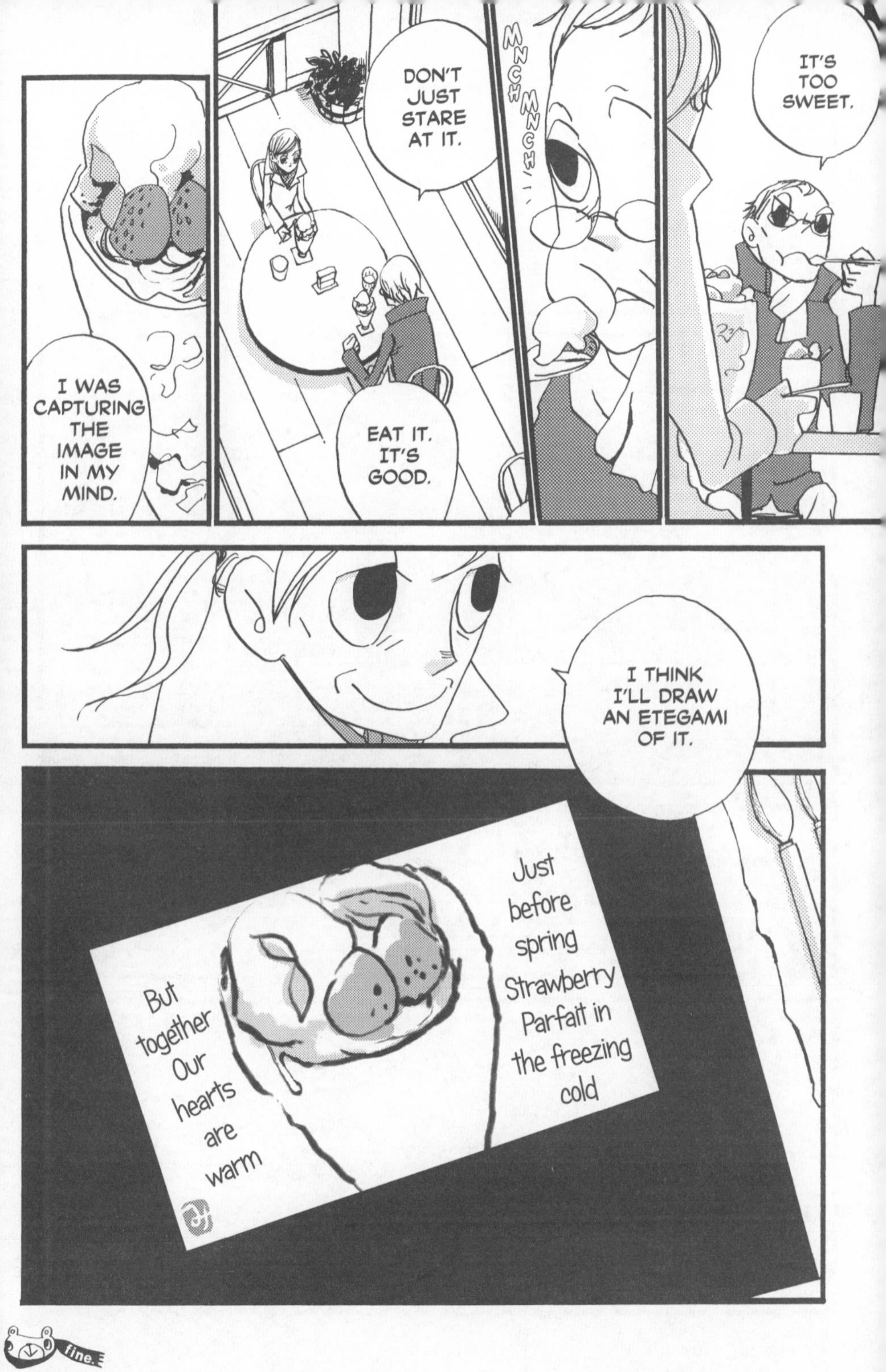
IT'S TOO SWEET.
MNCH MNCH!
DON'T JUST STARE AT IT.
EAT IT. IT'S GOOD.
I WAS CAPTURING THE IMAGE IN MY MIND.
I THINK I'LL DRAW AN ETEGAMI OF IT.
Just before spring
Strawberry Parfait in the freezing cold
But together Our hearts are warm
fine.

Moyashi Couple
Ikki - June 2005 Issue

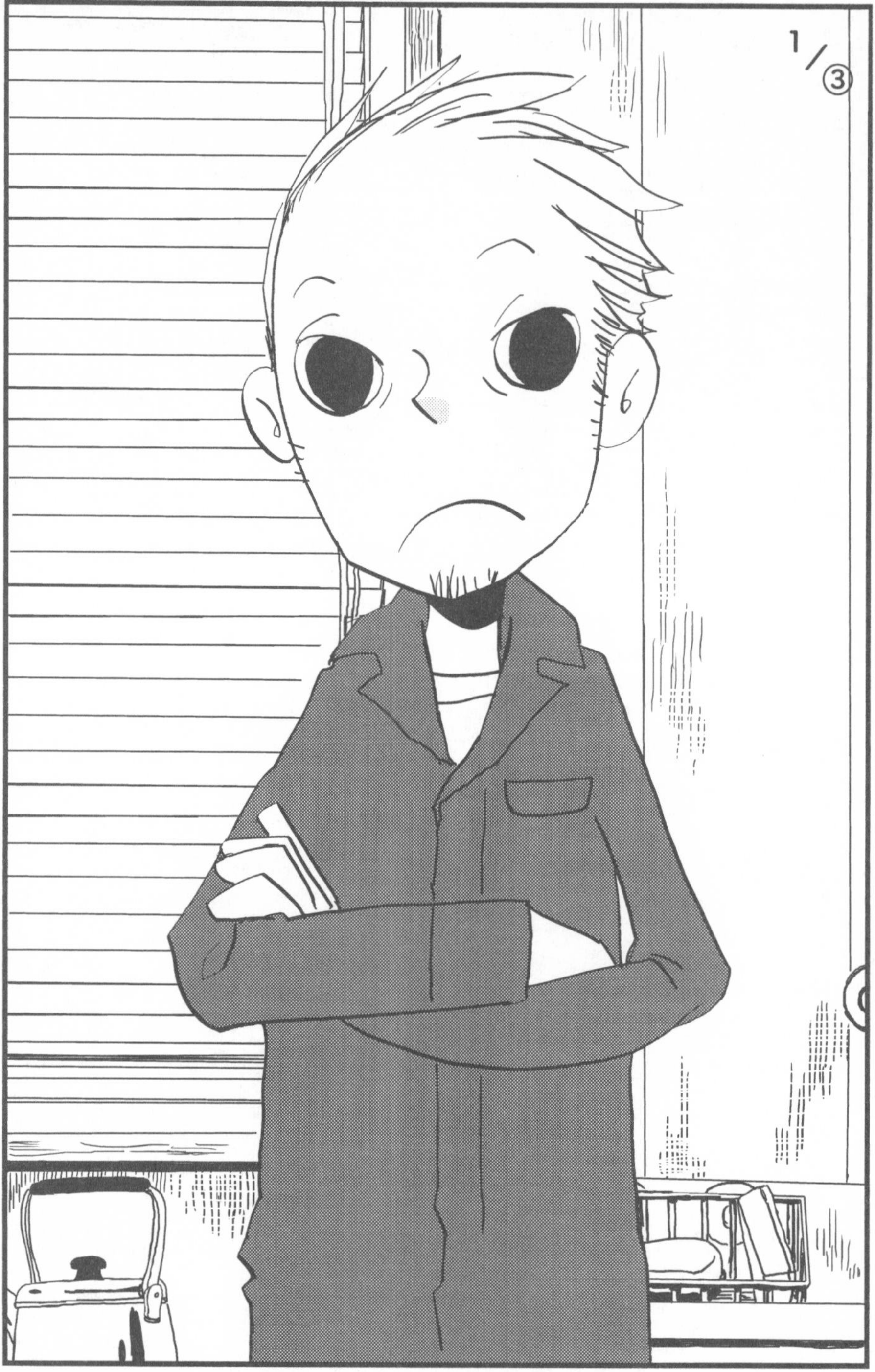
1/③

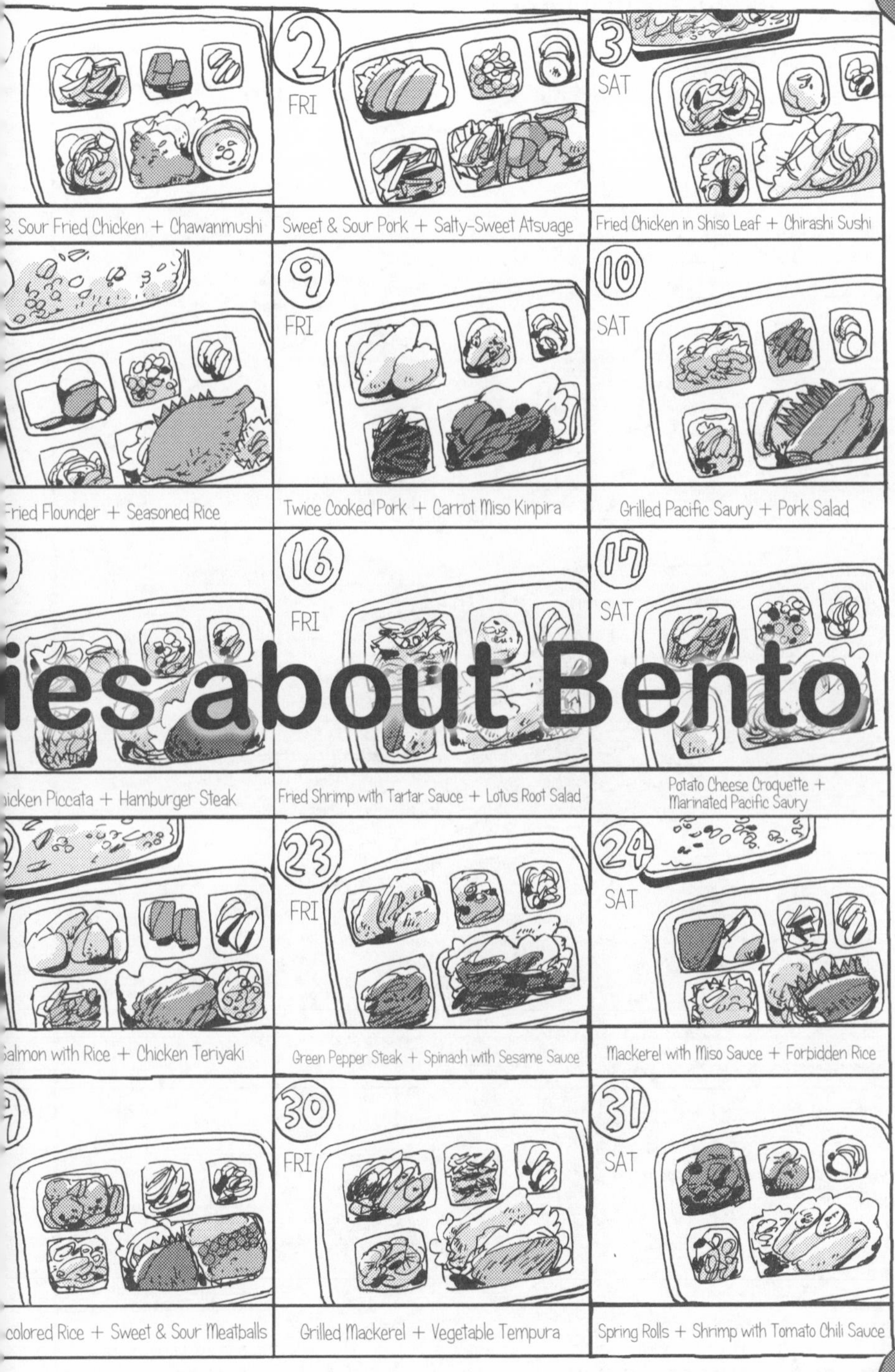
& Sour Fried Chicken + Chawanmushi
2
FRI
Sweet & Sour Pork + Salty-Sweet Atsuage
3
SAT
Fried Chicken in Shiso Leaf + Chirashi Sushi
Fried Flounder + Seasoned Rice
9
FRI
Twice Cooked Pork + Carrot Miso Kinpira
10
SAT
Grilled Pacific Saury + Pork Salad
ies about Bento
icken Piccata + Hamburger Steak
16
FRI
Fried Shrimp with Tartar Sauce + Lotus Root Salad
17
SAT
Potato Cheese Croquette + Marinated Pacific Saury
Salmon with Rice + Chicken Teriyaki
23
FRI
Green Pepper Steak + Spinach with Sesame Sauce
24
SAT
Mackerel with Miso Sauce + Forbidden Rice
colored Rice + Sweet & Sour Meatballs
30
FRI
Grilled Mackerel + Vegetable Tempura
31
SAT
Spring Rolls + Shrimp with Tomato Chili Sauce

Kumayama Bento
March Menu

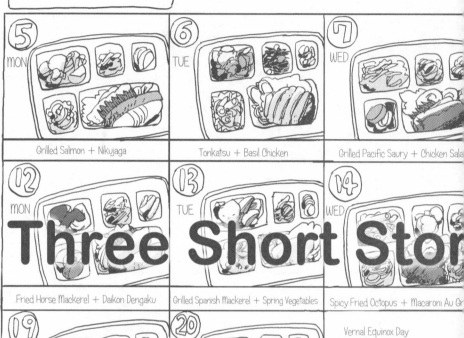

5 MON	6 TUE	7 WED
Grilled Salmon + Nikujaga	Tonkatsu + Basil Chicken	Grilled Pacific Saury + Chicken Salad
12 MON	13 TUE	14 WED
Fried Horse Mackerel + Daikon Dengaku	Grilled Spanish Mackerel + Spring Vegetables	Spicy Fried Octopus + Macaroni Au Gr...
19 MON	20 TUE	Vernal Equinox Day
Grilled Mackerel + Chinese Stir-Fry	Salmon Meuniere + Stir-fried Daikon and Atsuage	
26 MON	27 TUE	28 WED
Fried Stuffed Lotus Root + Mirin-Boshi Mackerel	Fried Sardines + Rapeseed with Mustard	Curry-Flavored Horse Mackerel + Bean S...

Three Short Stor...

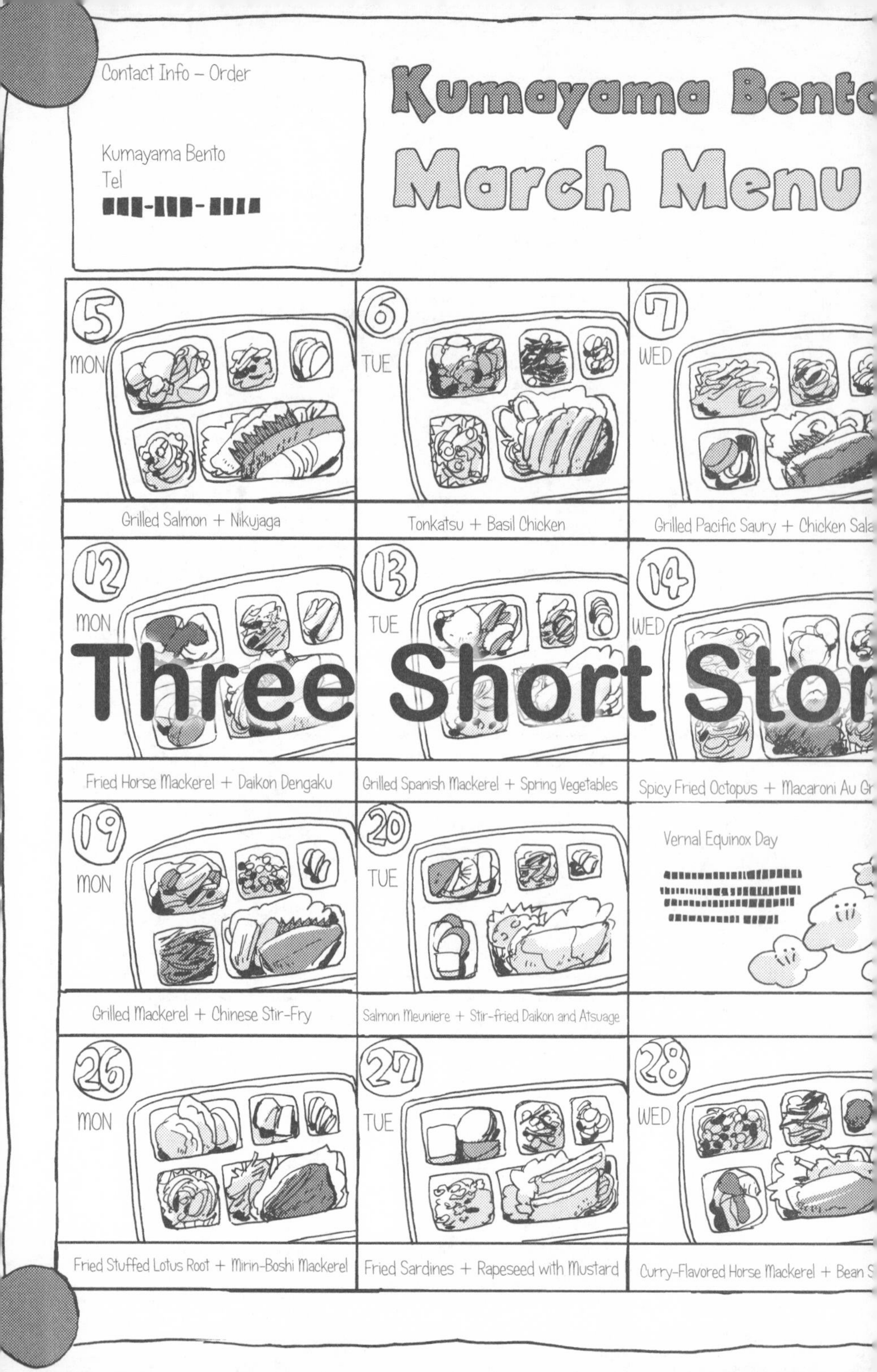

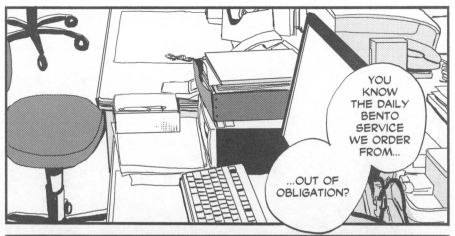

YOU KNOW THE DAILY BENTO SERVICE WE ORDER FROM...

...OUT OF OBLIGATION?

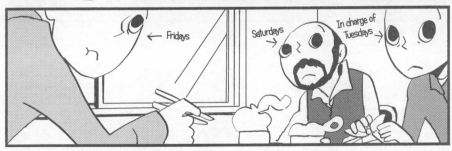

WE'VE BEEN TAKING TURNS EATING THEIR STUFF EVERY DAY FOR OVER TEN YEARS NOW.

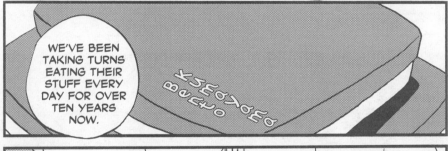

← Fridays

Saturdays →

In charge of Tuesdays →

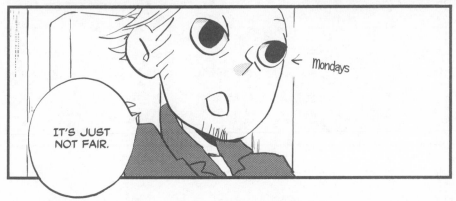

← Mondays

IT'S JUST NOT FAIR.

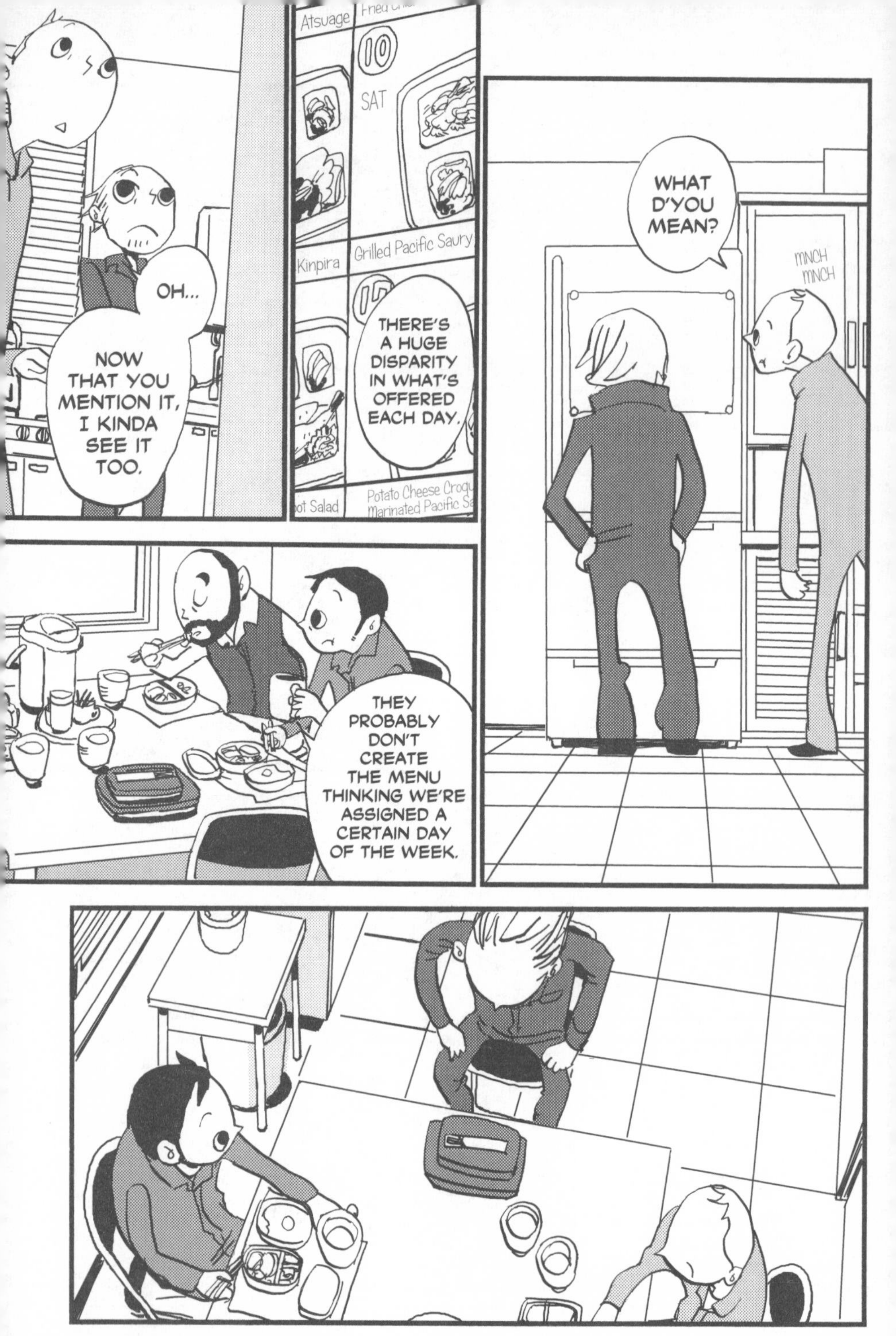
WHAT D'YOU MEAN?
MNCH MNCH
Atsuage
10
SAT
Kinpira
Grilled Pacific Saury
THERE'S A HUGE DISPARITY IN WHAT'S OFFERED EACH DAY.
OH...
NOW THAT YOU MENTION IT, I KINDA SEE IT TOO.
THEY PROBABLY DON'T CREATE THE MENU THINKING WE'RE ASSIGNED A CERTAIN DAY OF THE WEEK.

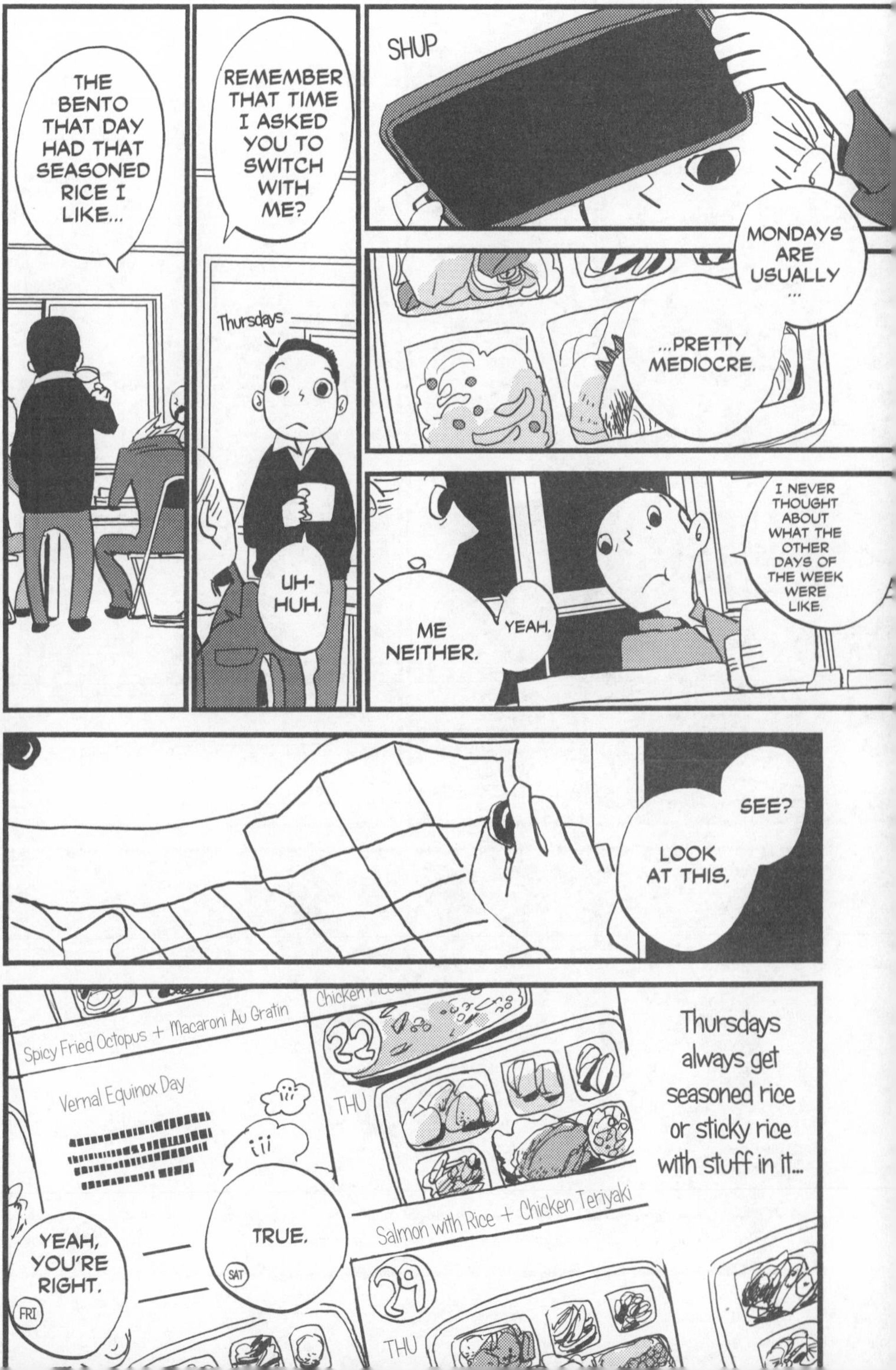
SHUP
MONDAYS ARE USUALLY...
...PRETTY MEDIOCRE.
I NEVER THOUGHT ABOUT WHAT THE OTHER DAYS OF THE WEEK WERE LIKE.
YEAH.
ME NEITHER.
REMEMBER THAT TIME I ASKED YOU TO SWITCH WITH ME?
Thursdays
UH-HUH.
THE BENTO THAT DAY HAD THAT SEASONED RICE I LIKE...
SEE?
LOOK AT THIS.
Thursdays always get seasoned rice or sticky rice with stuff in it...
22
THU
Spicy Fried Octopus + Macaroni Au Gratin
Vernal Equinox Day
Salmon with Rice + Chicken Teriyaki
29
THU
TRUE.
SAT
YEAH, YOU'RE RIGHT.
FRI

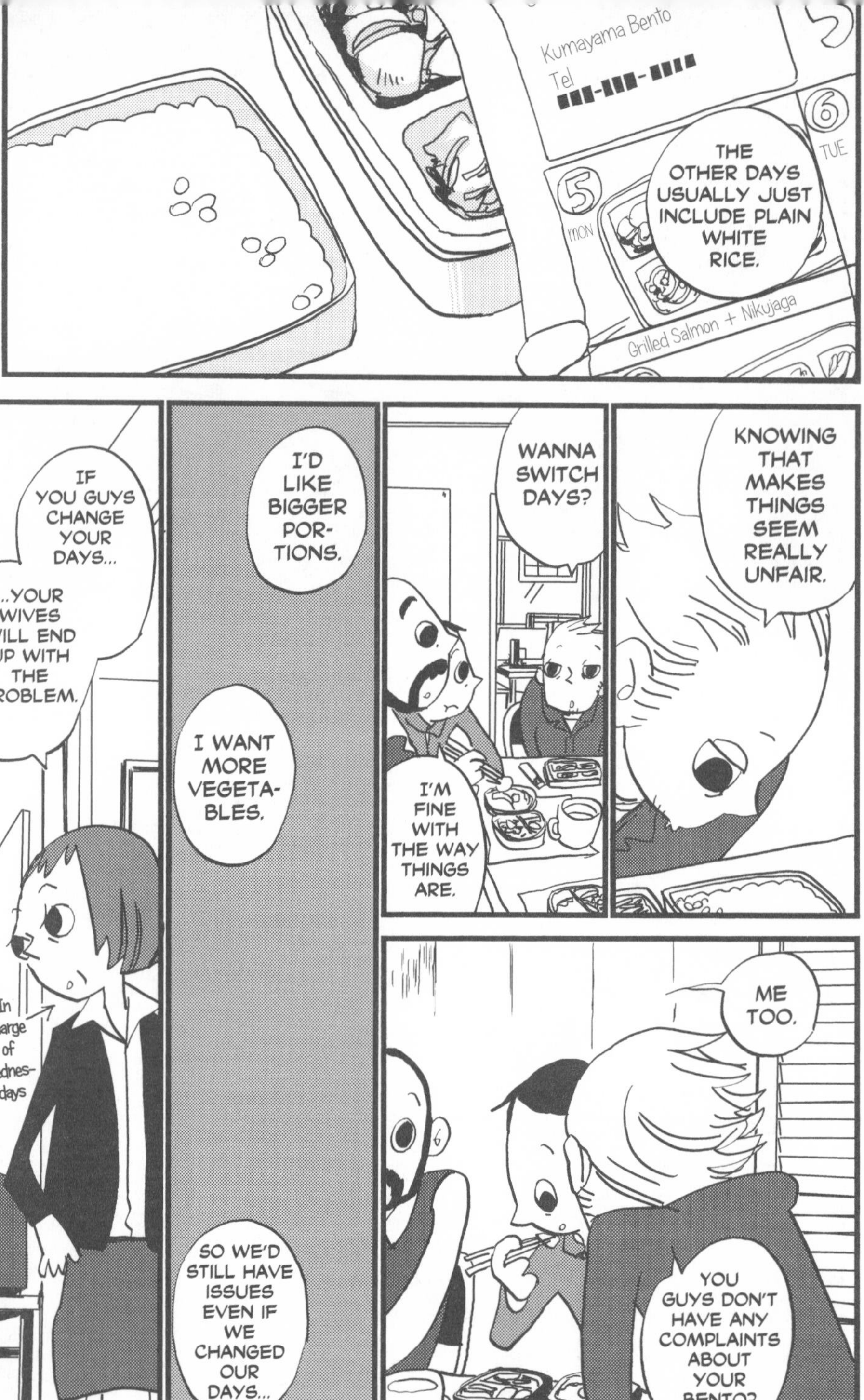
Kumayama Bento
Tel [redacted]
5
6
TUE
MON
THE OTHER DAYS USUALLY JUST INCLUDE PLAIN WHITE RICE.
Grilled Salmon + Nikujaga
KNOWING THAT MAKES THINGS SEEM REALLY UNFAIR.
WANNA SWITCH DAYS?
I'M FINE WITH THE WAY THINGS ARE.
ME TOO.
YOU GUYS DON'T HAVE ANY COMPLAINTS ABOUT YOUR BENTO?
I'D LIKE BIGGER POR-TIONS.
I WANT MORE VEGETA-BLES.
SO WE'D STILL HAVE ISSUES EVEN IF WE CHANGED OUR DAYS...
IF YOU GUYS CHANGE YOUR DAYS...
...YOUR WIVES WILL END UP WITH THE PROBLEM.
In charge of Wednes-days

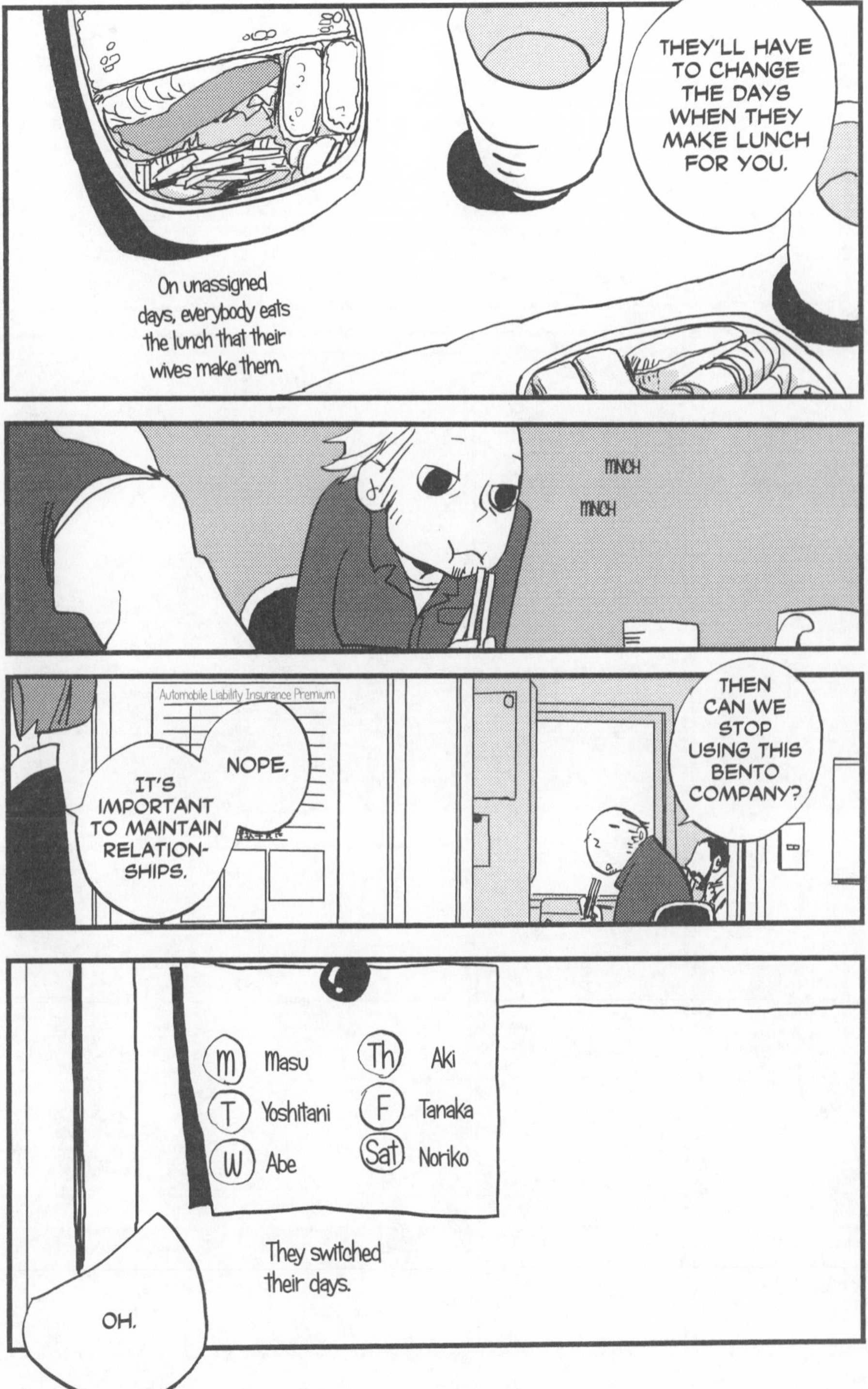

THEY'LL HAVE TO CHANGE THE DAYS WHEN THEY MAKE LUNCH FOR YOU.
On unassigned days, everybody eats the lunch that their wives make them.
MNCH
MNCH
THEN CAN WE STOP USING THIS BENTO COMPANY?
Automobile Liability Insurance Premium
NOPE.
IT'S IMPORTANT TO MAINTAIN RELATION-SHIPS.
M Masu
T Yoshitani
W Abe
Th Aki
F Tanaka
Sat Noriko
They switched their days.
OH.

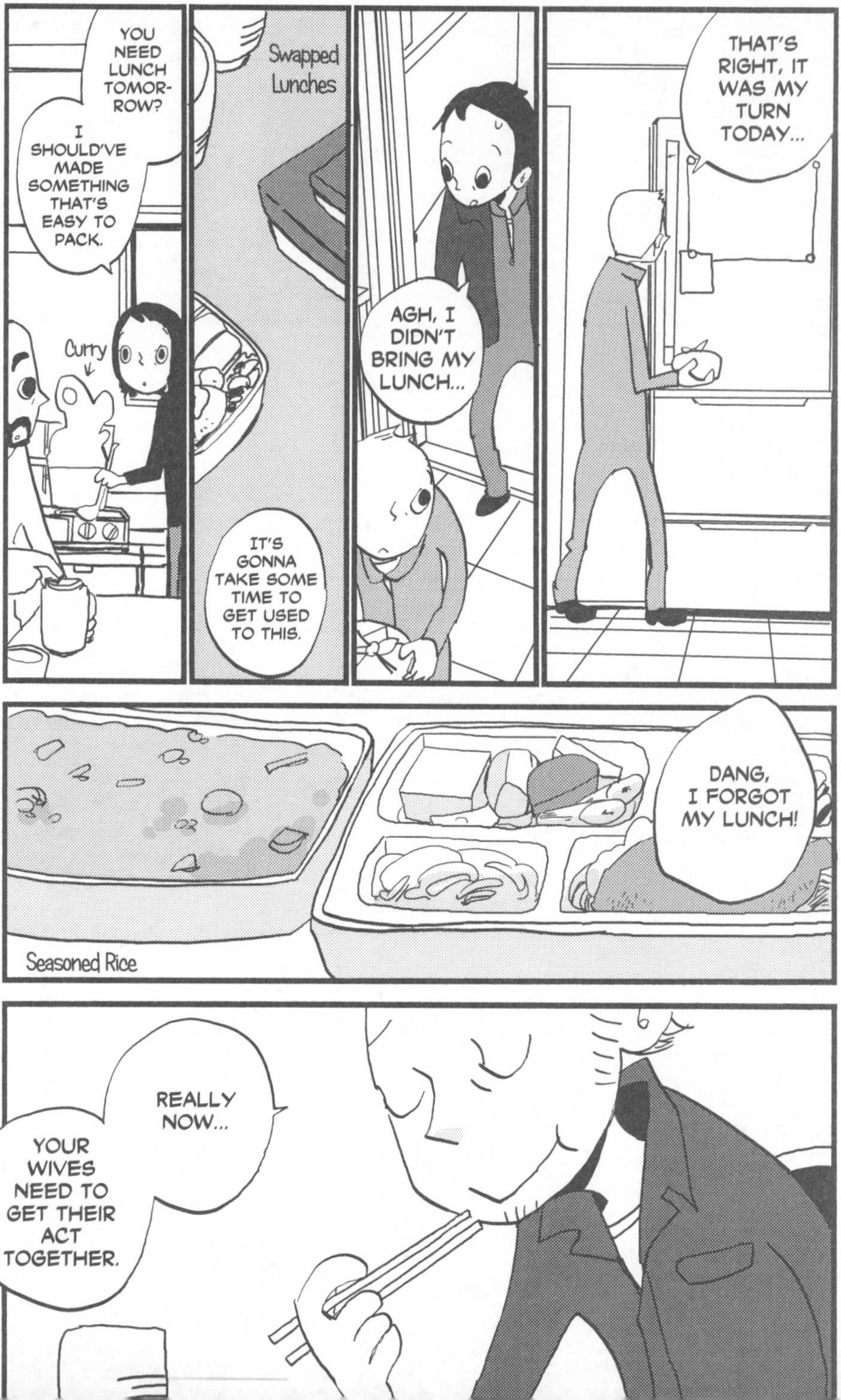
THAT'S RIGHT, IT WAS MY TURN TODAY...
AGH, I DIDN'T BRING MY LUNCH...
Swapped Lunches
IT'S GONNA TAKE SOME TIME TO GET USED TO THIS.
YOU NEED LUNCH TOMOR-ROW?
I SHOULD'VE MADE SOMETHING THAT'S EASY TO PACK.
Curry
DANG, I FORGOT MY LUNCH!
Seasoned Rice
REALLY NOW...
YOUR WIVES NEED TO GET THEIR ACT TOGETHER.

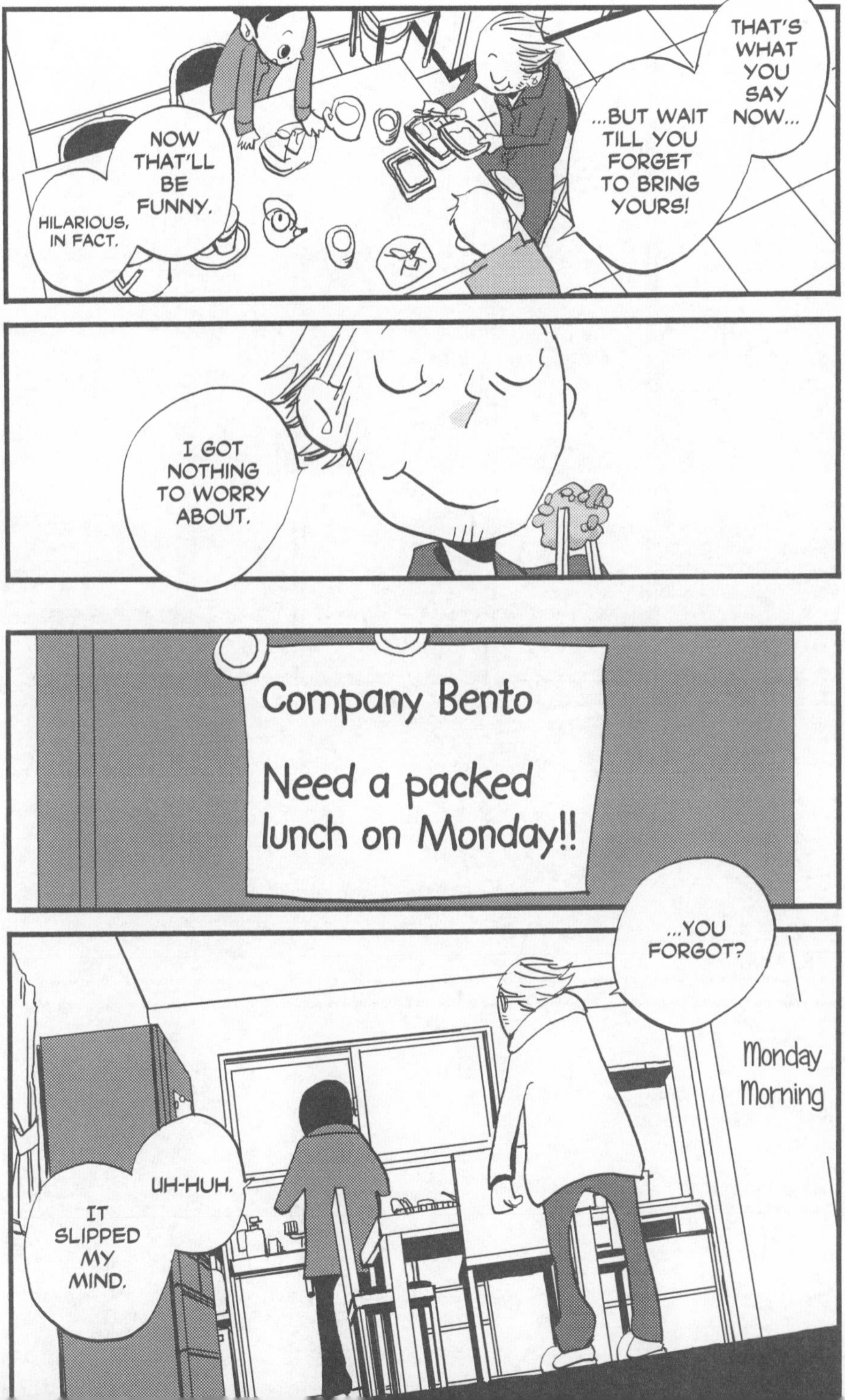
THAT'S WHAT YOU SAY NOW...
...BUT WAIT TILL YOU FORGET TO BRING YOURS!
NOW THAT'LL BE FUNNY.
HILARIOUS, IN FACT.
I GOT NOTHING TO WORRY ABOUT.
Company Bento
Need a packed lunch on Monday!!
Monday Morning
...YOU FORGOT?
UH-HUH.
IT SLIPPED MY MIND.

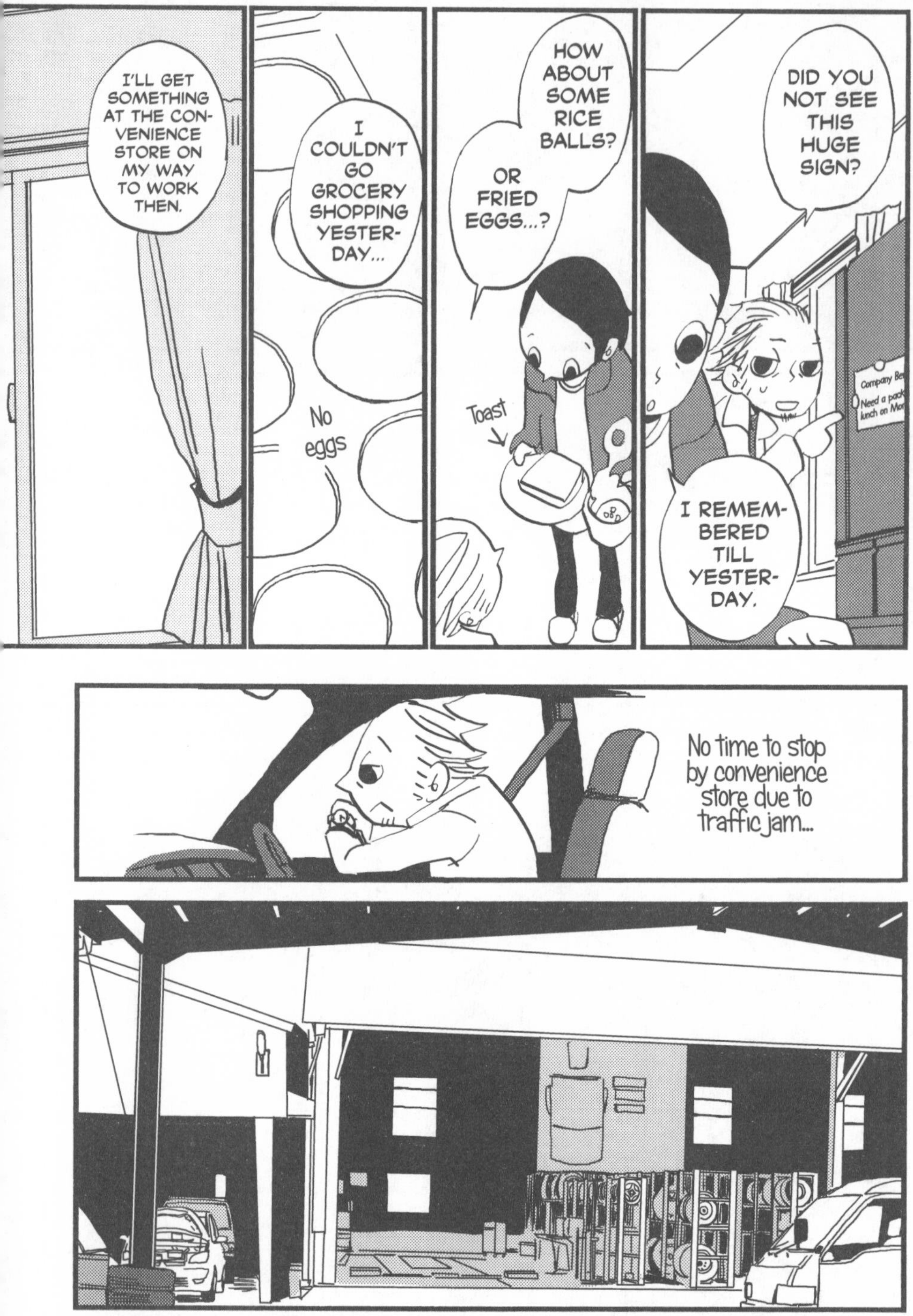
DID YOU NOT SEE THIS HUGE SIGN?
I REMEMBERED TILL YESTERDAY.
HOW ABOUT SOME RICE BALLS?
OR FRIED EGGS...?
Toast
I COULDN'T GO GROCERY SHOPPING YESTERDAY...
No eggs
I'LL GET SOMETHING AT THE CONVENIENCE STORE ON MY WAY TO WORK THEN.
No time to stop by convenience store due to traffic jam...

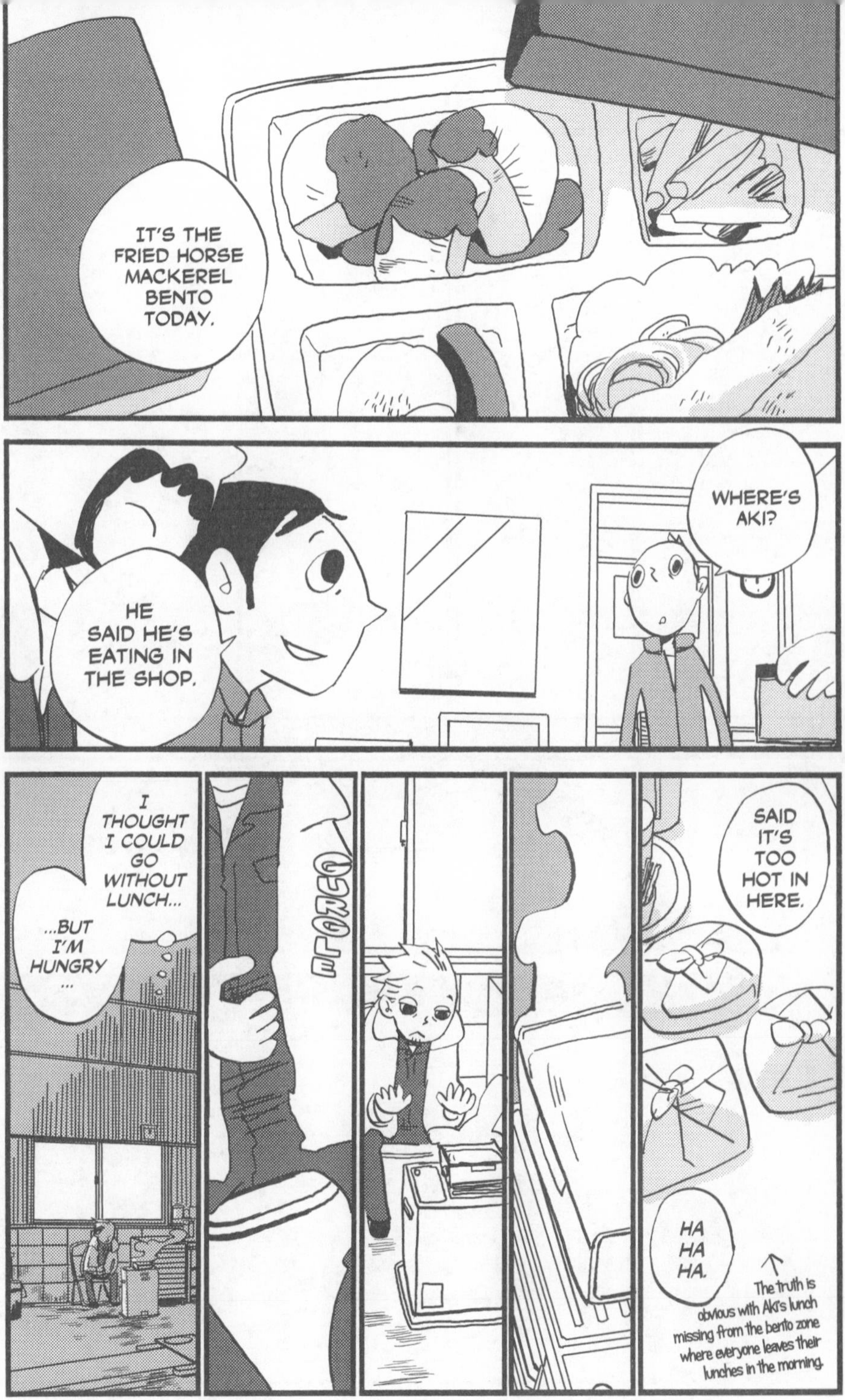
IT'S THE FRIED HORSE MACKEREL BENTO TODAY.
WHERE'S AKI?
HE SAID HE'S EATING IN THE SHOP.
SAID IT'S TOO HOT IN HERE.
HA HA HA.
The truth is obvious with Aki's lunch missing from the bento zone where everyone leaves their lunches in the morning.
GURGLE
I THOUGHT I COULD GO WITHOUT LUNCH...
...BUT I'M HUNGRY ...

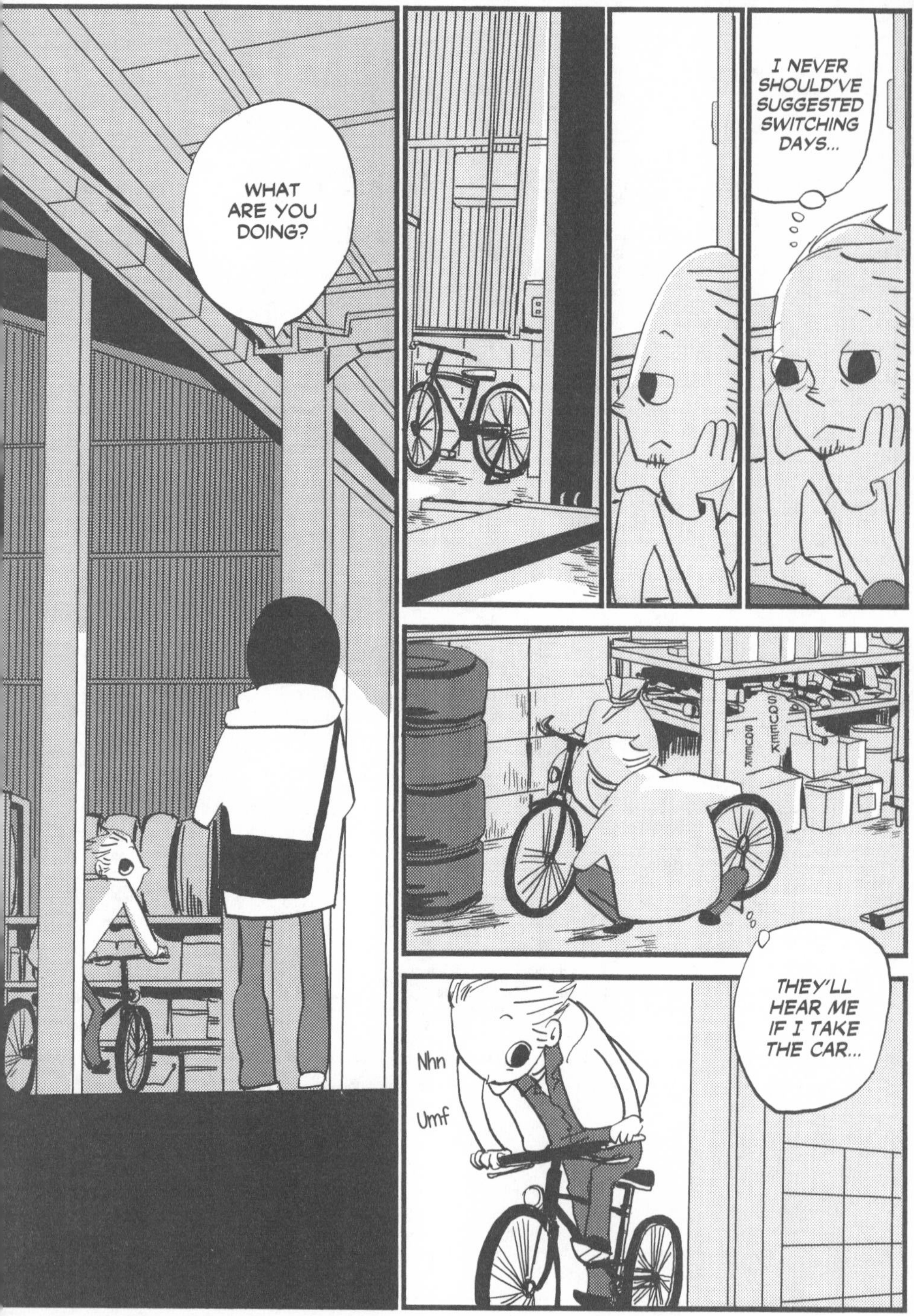
I NEVER SHOULD'VE SUGGESTED SWITCHING DAYS...
SQUEEK
SQUEEK
THEY'LL HEAR ME IF I TAKE THE CAR...
Nhn
Umf
WHAT ARE YOU DOING?

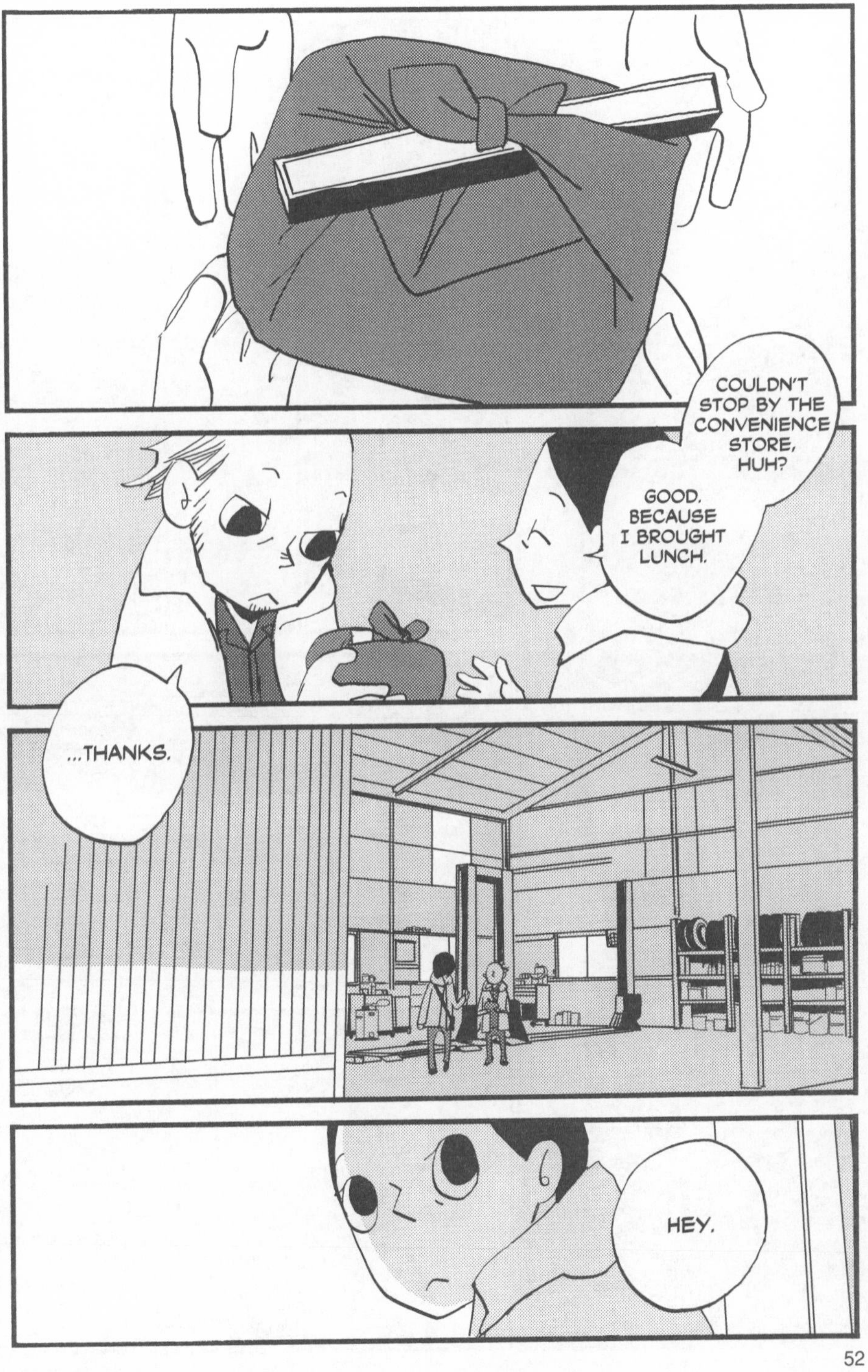
COULDN'T STOP BY THE CONVENIENCE STORE, HUH?
GOOD. BECAUSE I BROUGHT LUNCH.
...THANKS.
HEY.

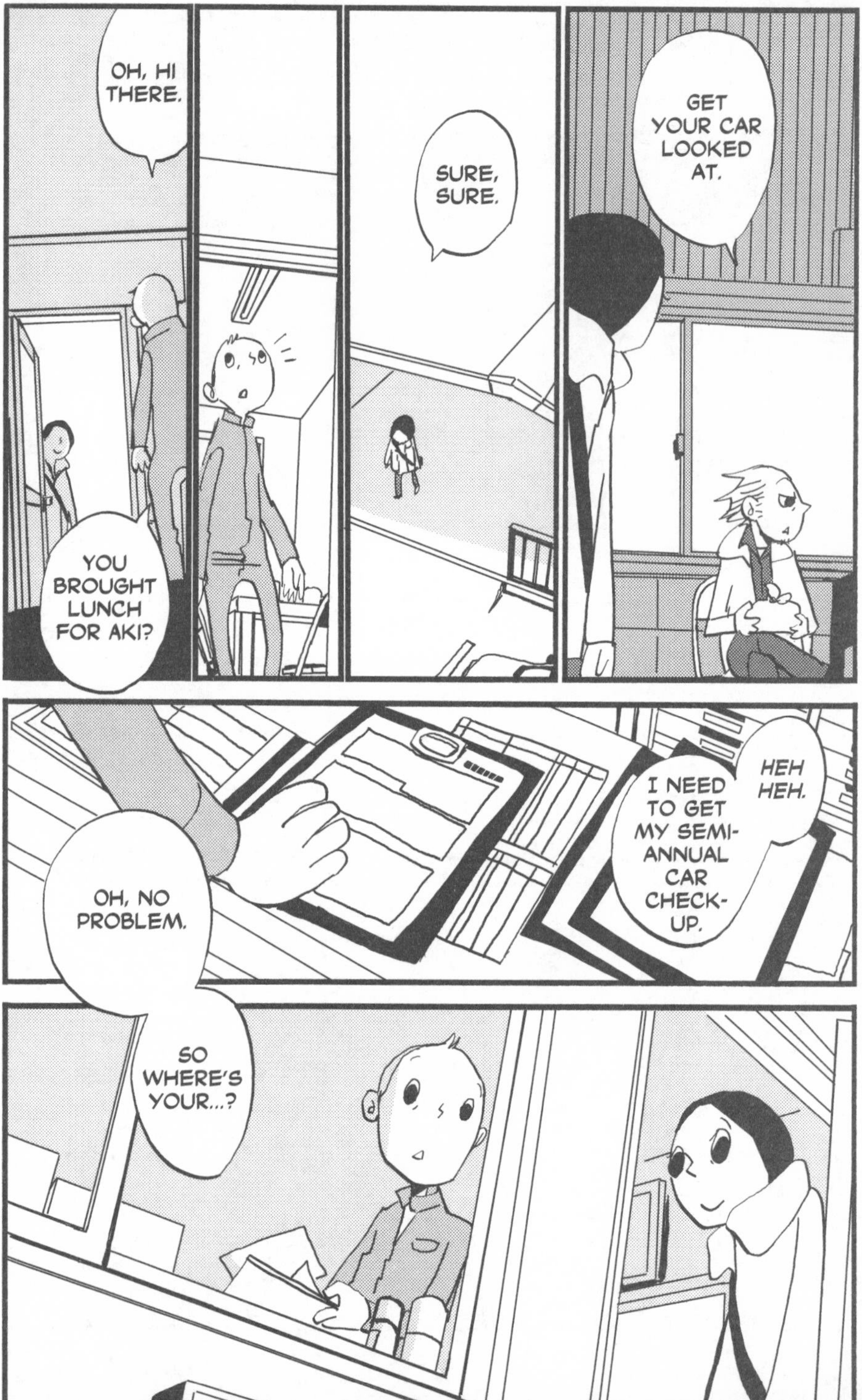
GET YOUR CAR LOOKED AT.
SURE, SURE.
OH, HI THERE.
YOU BROUGHT LUNCH FOR AKI?
HEH HEH.
I NEED TO GET MY SEMI-ANNUAL CAR CHECK-UP.
OH, NO PROBLEM.
SO WHERE'S YOUR...?

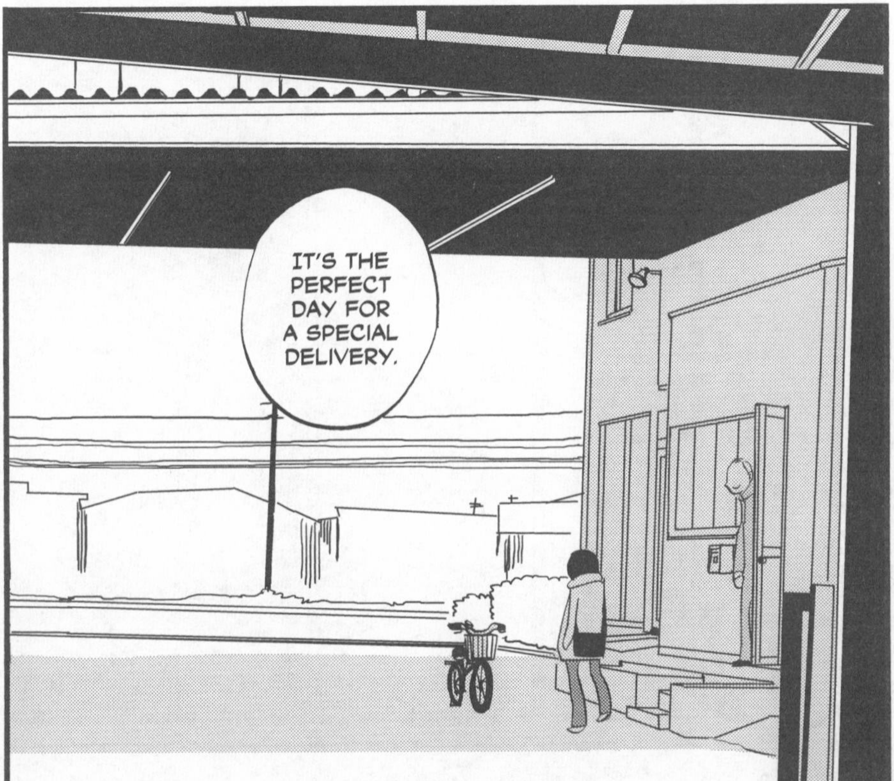
IT'S THE PERFECT DAY FOR A SPECIAL DELIVERY.
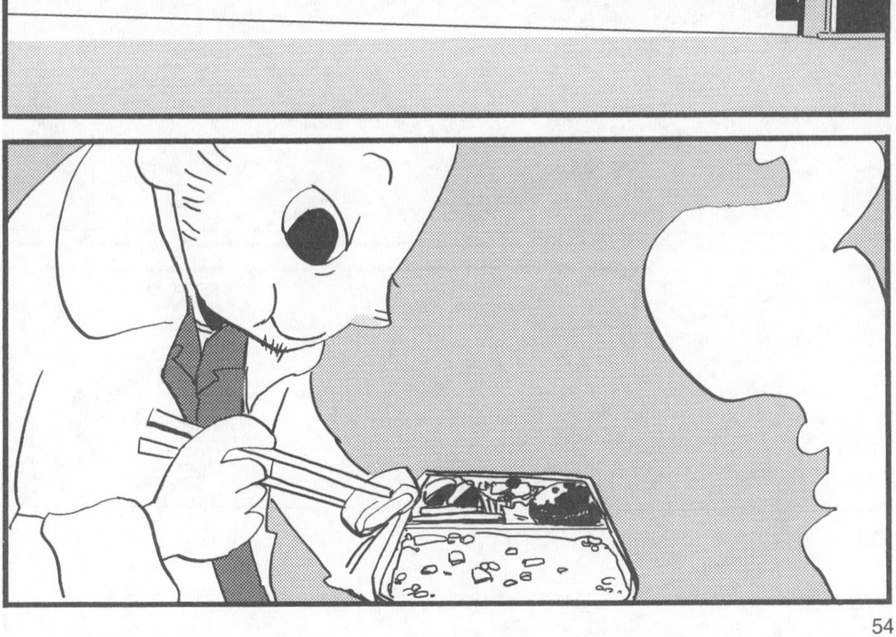

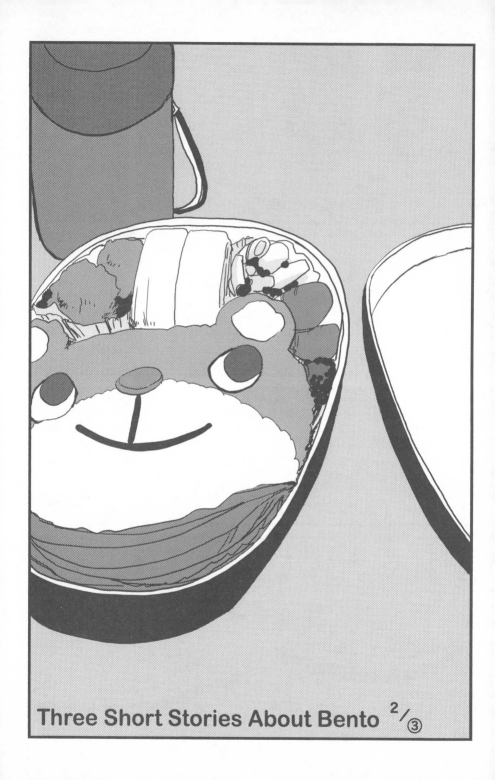

Three Short Stories About Bento $^2/_{③}$

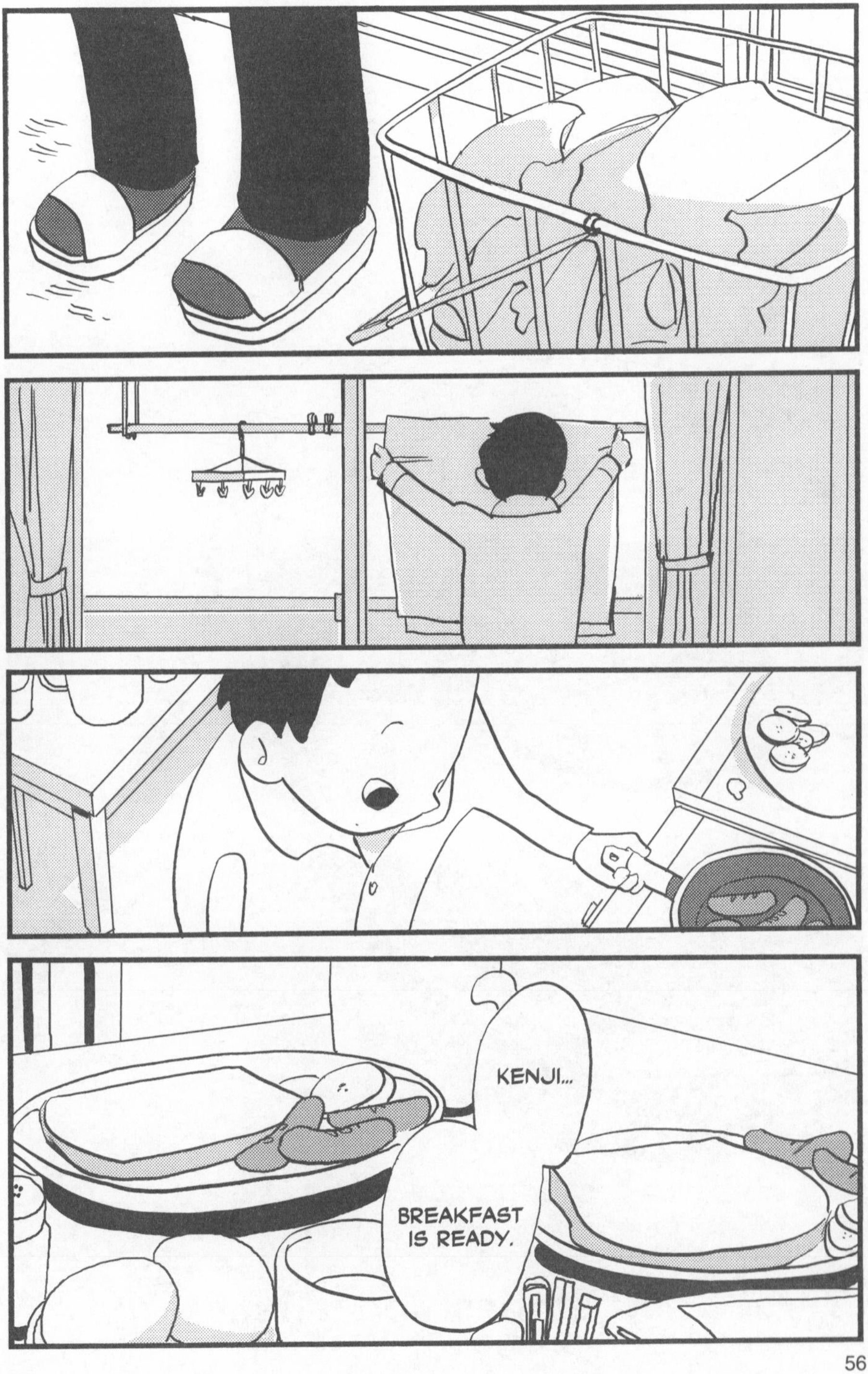
KENJI...
BREAKFAST IS READY.

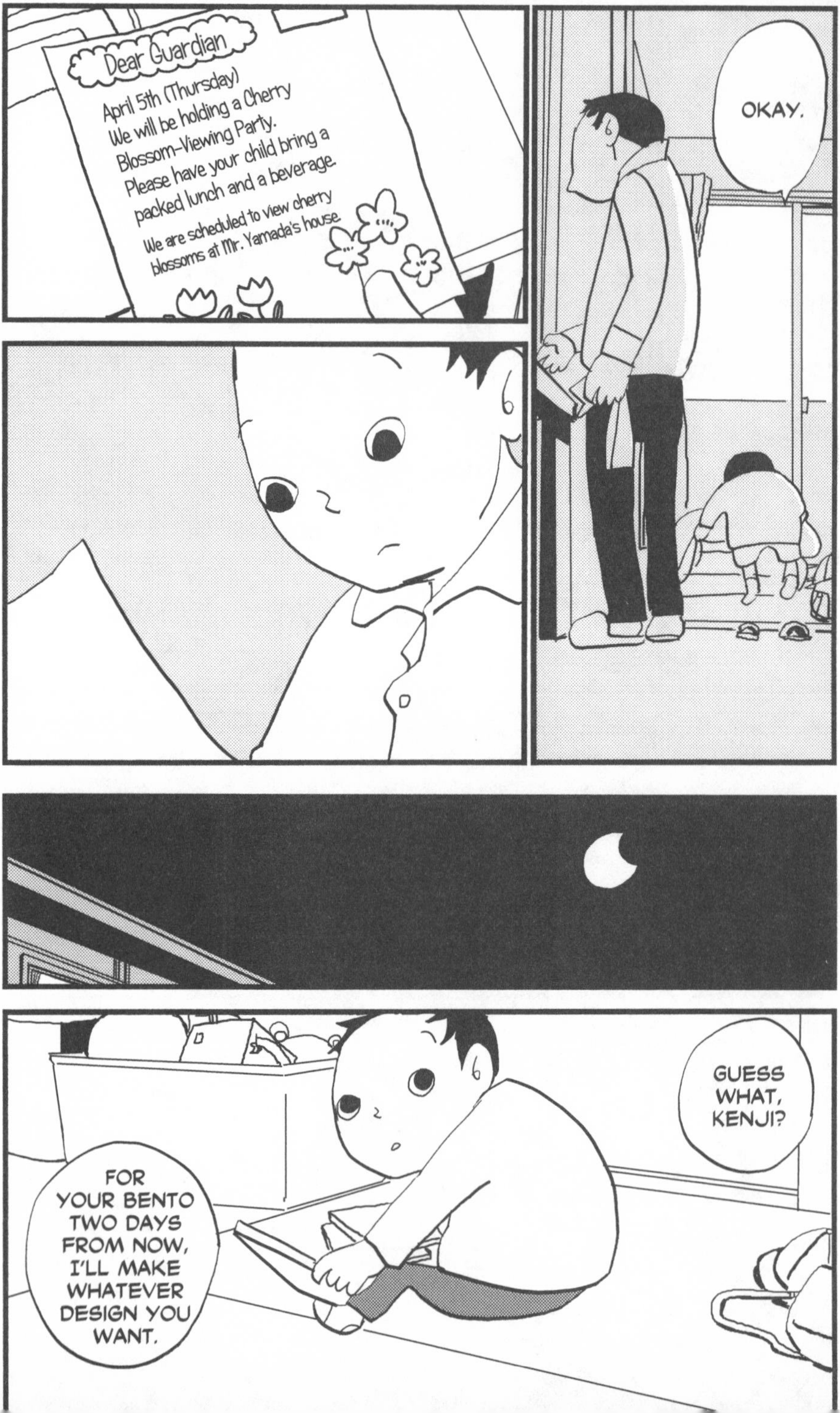
OKAY.
Dear Guardian
April 5th (Thursday)
We will be holding a Cherry Blossom-Viewing Party.
Please have your child bring a packed lunch and a beverage.
We are scheduled to view cherry blossoms at Mr. Yamada's house.
GUESS WHAT, KENJI?
FOR YOUR BENTO TWO DAYS FROM NOW, I'LL MAKE WHATEVER DESIGN YOU WANT.

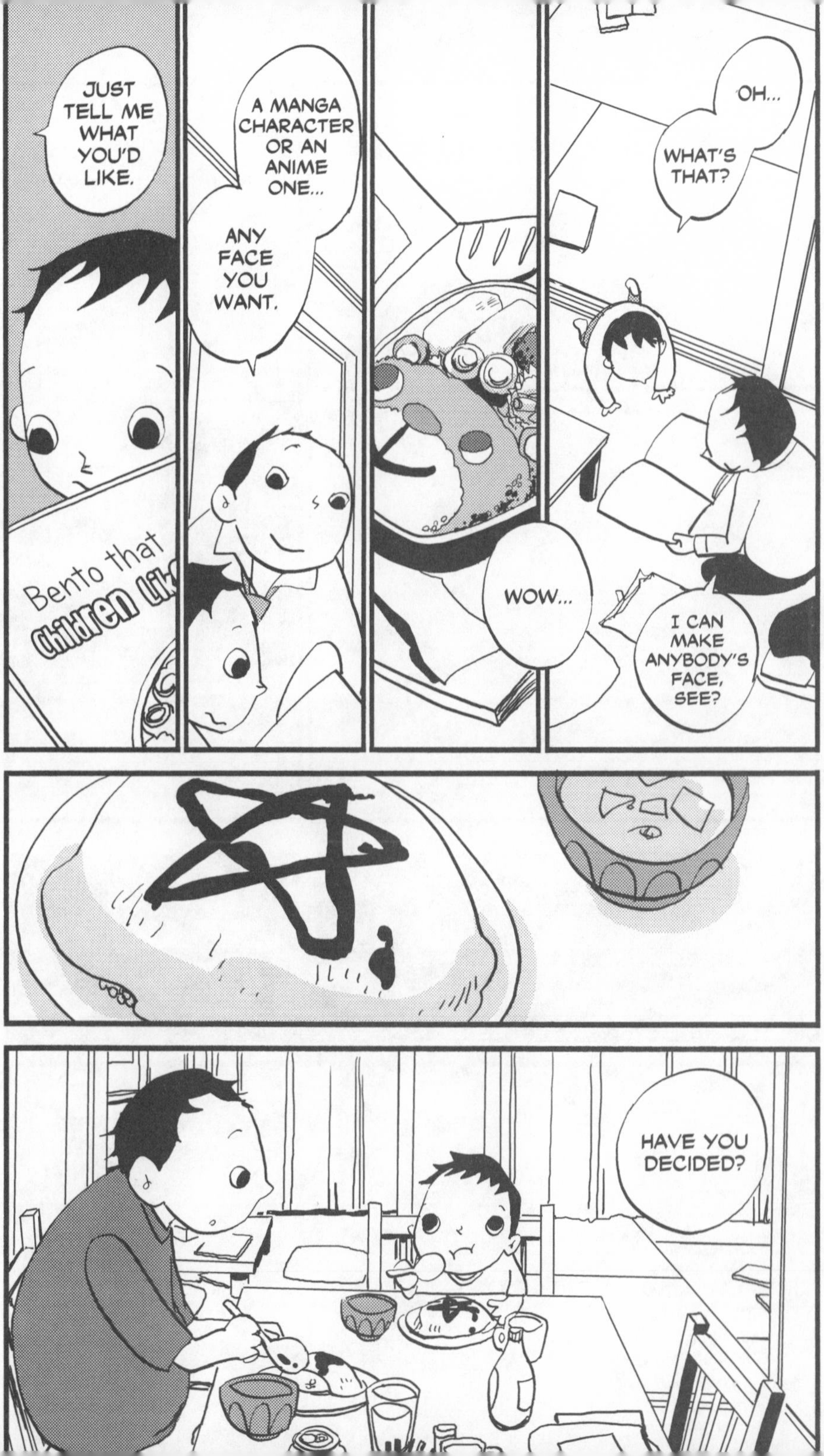
OH...
WHAT'S THAT?
I CAN MAKE ANYBODY'S FACE, SEE?
WOW...
A MANGA CHARACTER OR AN ANIME ONE...
ANY FACE YOU WANT.
JUST TELL ME WHAT YOU'D LIKE.
Bento that Children
HAVE YOU DECIDED?

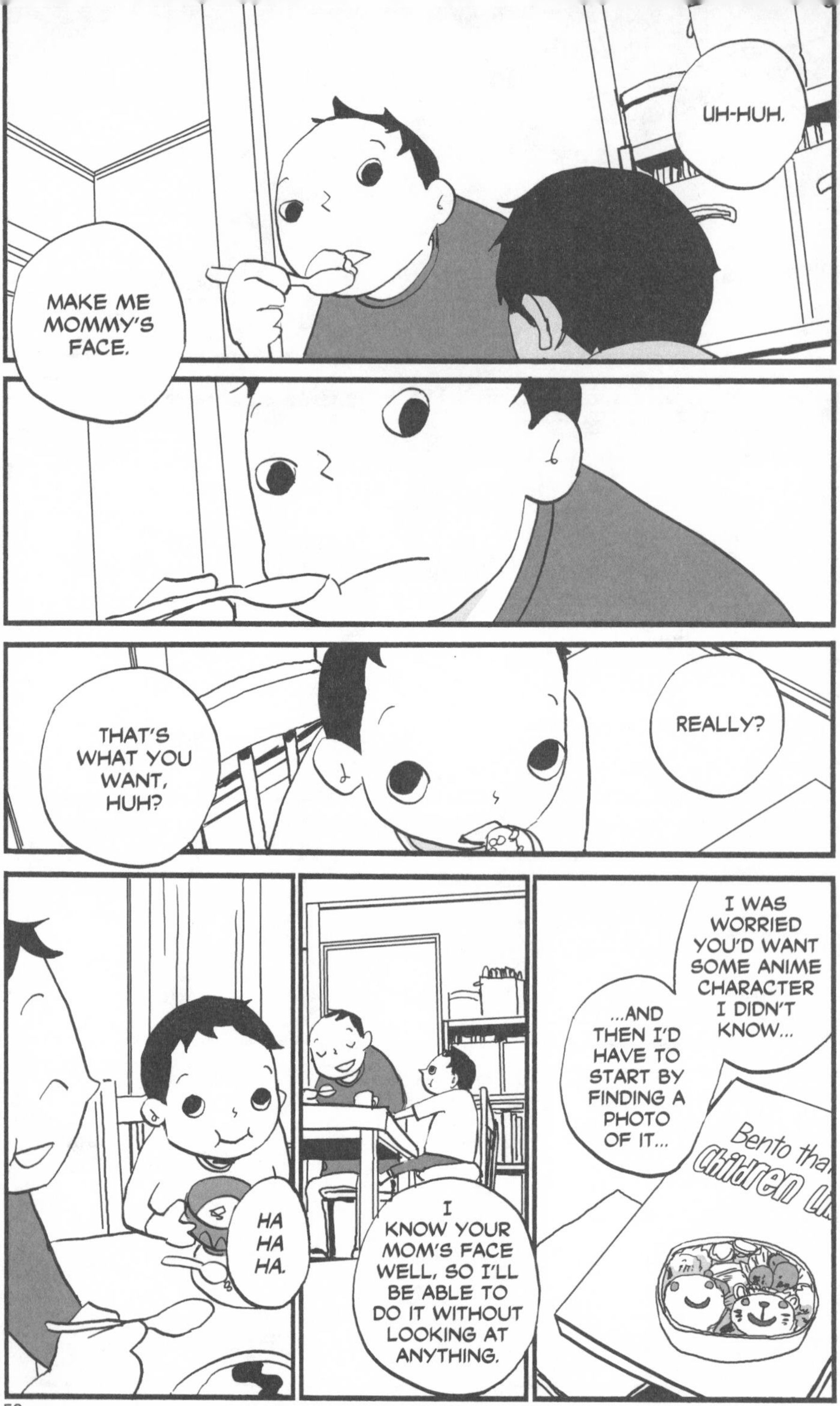
UH-HUH.
MAKE ME MOMMY'S FACE.
REALLY?
THAT'S WHAT YOU WANT, HUH?
I WAS WORRIED YOU'D WANT SOME ANIME CHARACTER I DIDN'T KNOW...
...AND THEN I'D HAVE TO START BY FINDING A PHOTO OF IT...
I KNOW YOUR MOM'S FACE WELL, SO I'LL BE ABLE TO DO IT WITHOUT LOOKING AT ANYTHING.
HA HA HA.

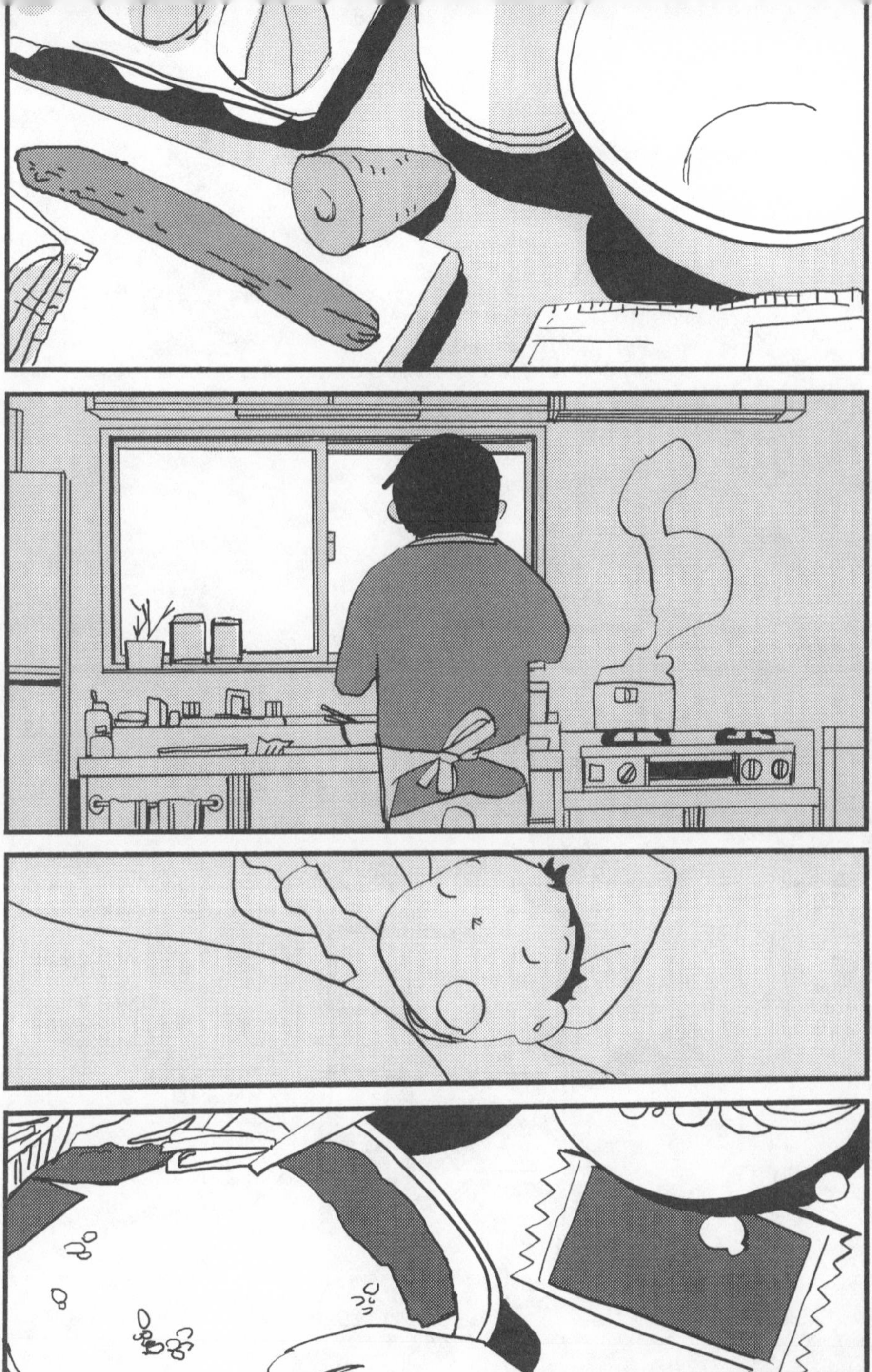

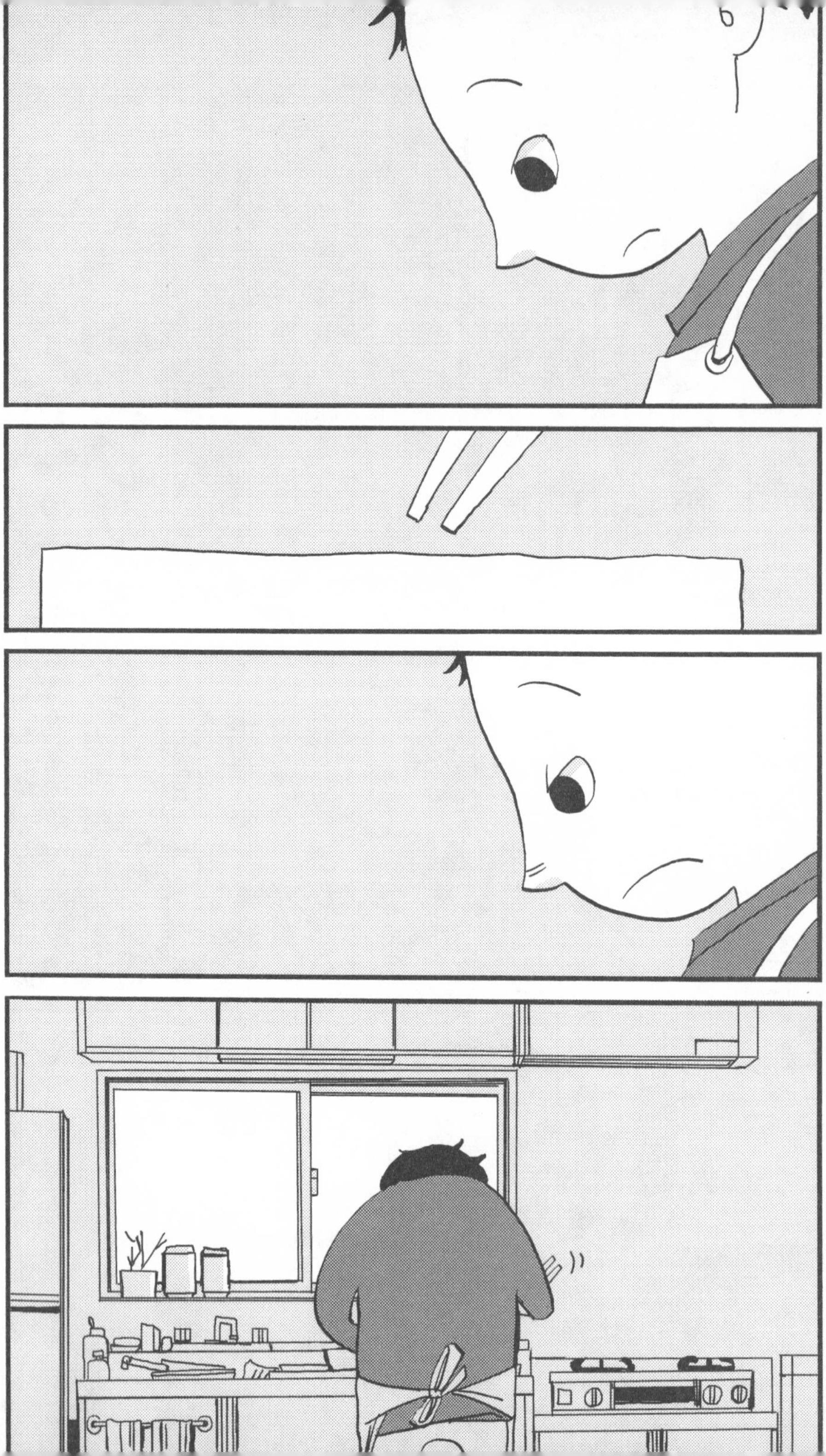

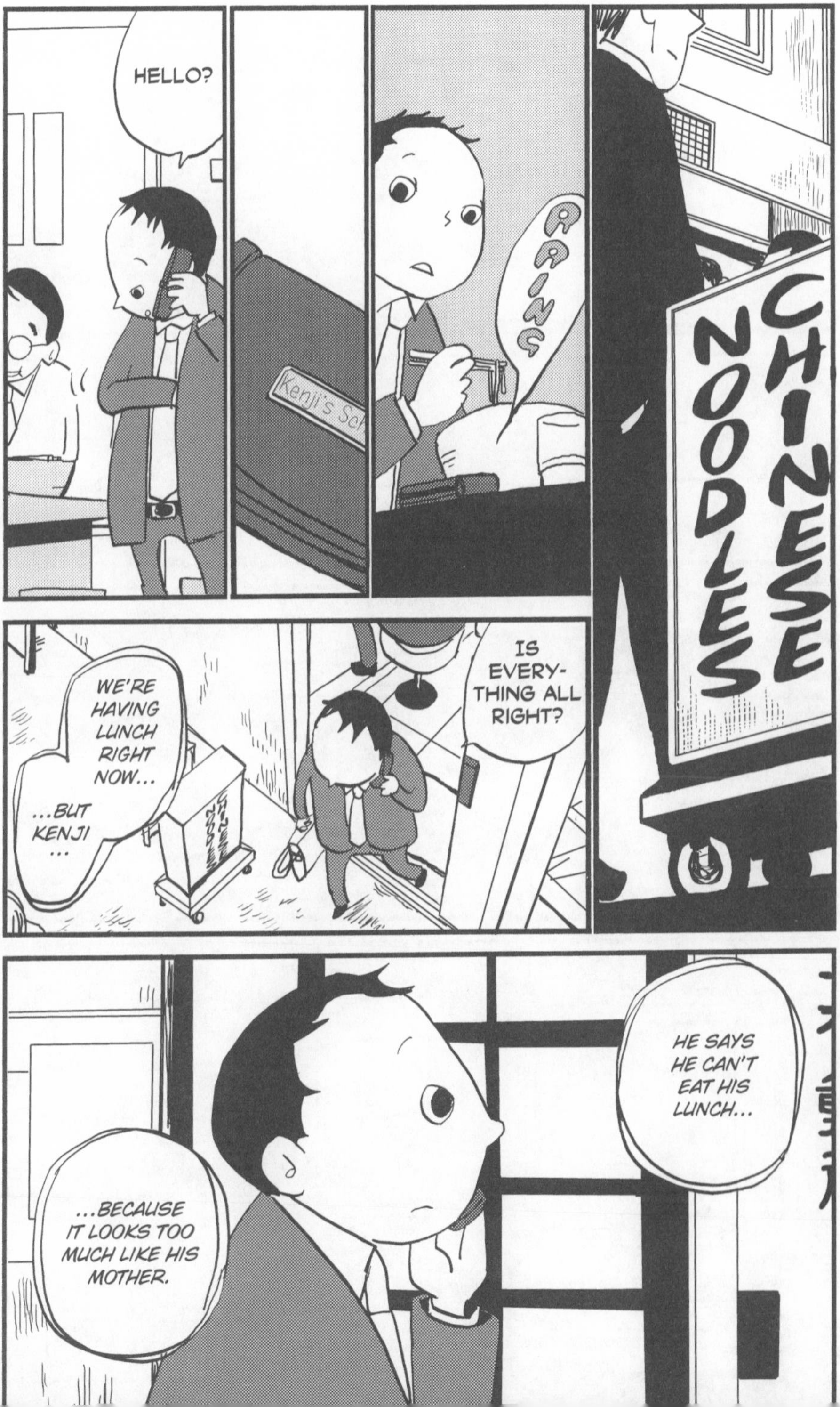
CHINESE NOODLES
RRING
Kenji's Sch
HELLO?
IS EVERY-THING ALL RIGHT?
WE'RE HAVING LUNCH RIGHT NOW...
...BUT KENJI ...
HE SAYS HE CAN'T EAT HIS LUNCH...
...BECAUSE IT LOOKS TOO MUCH LIKE HIS MOTHER.

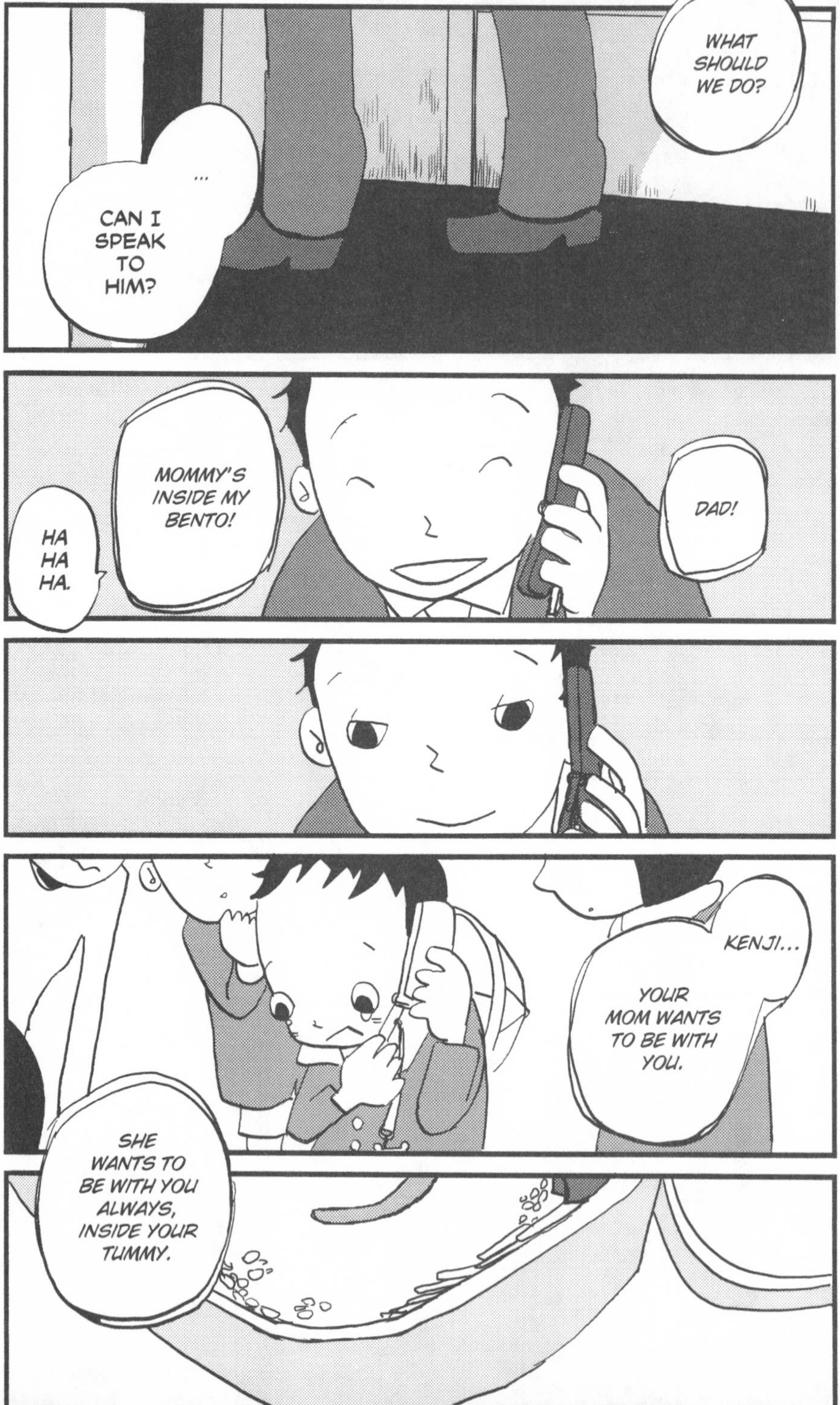
WHAT SHOULD WE DO?
... CAN I SPEAK TO HIM?
DAD!
MOMMY'S INSIDE MY BENTO!
HA HA HA.
KENJI... YOUR MOM WANTS TO BE WITH YOU.
SHE WANTS TO BE WITH YOU ALWAYS, INSIDE YOUR TUMMY.

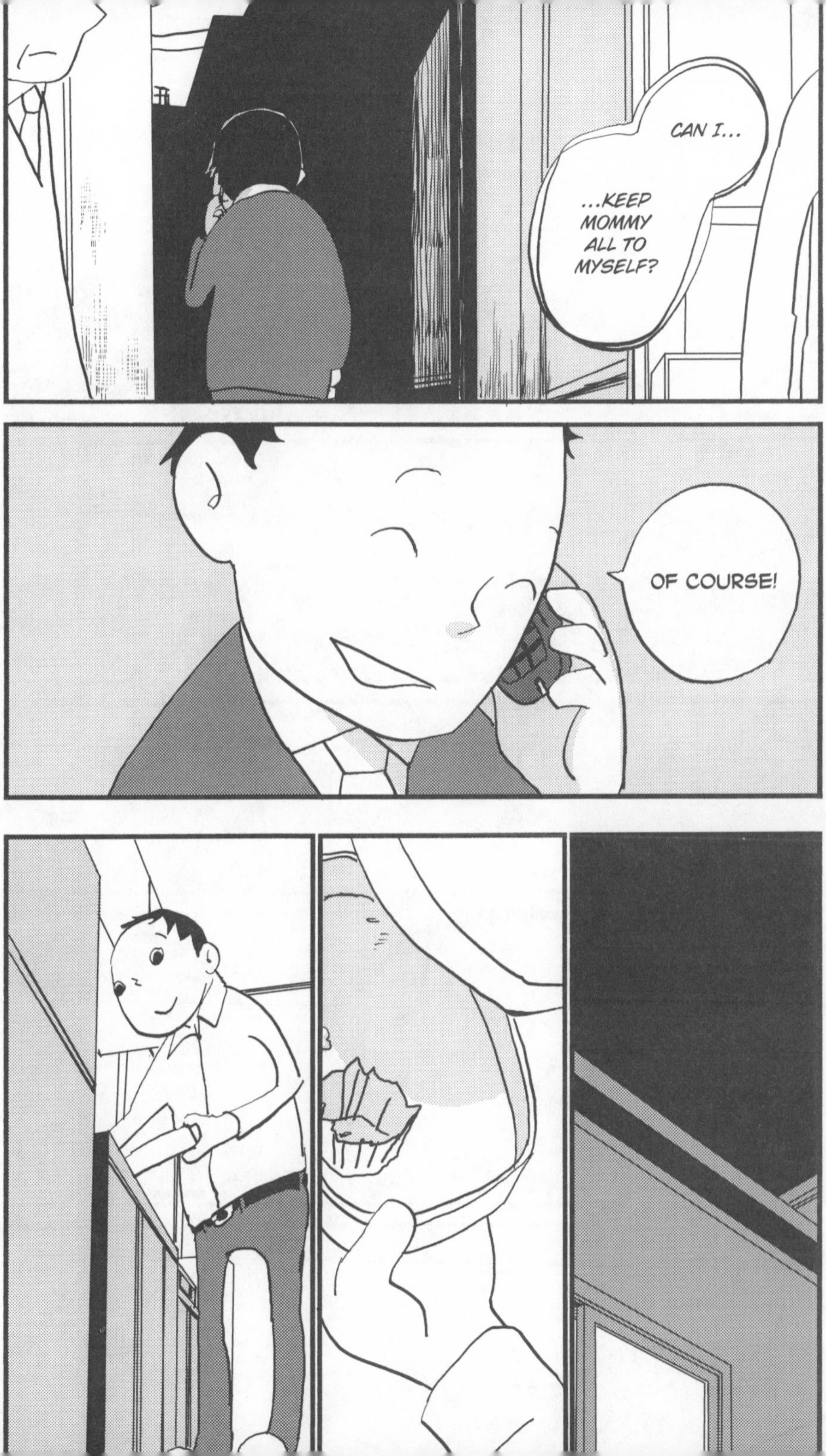
CAN I...
...KEEP MOMMY ALL TO MYSELF?
OF COURSE!

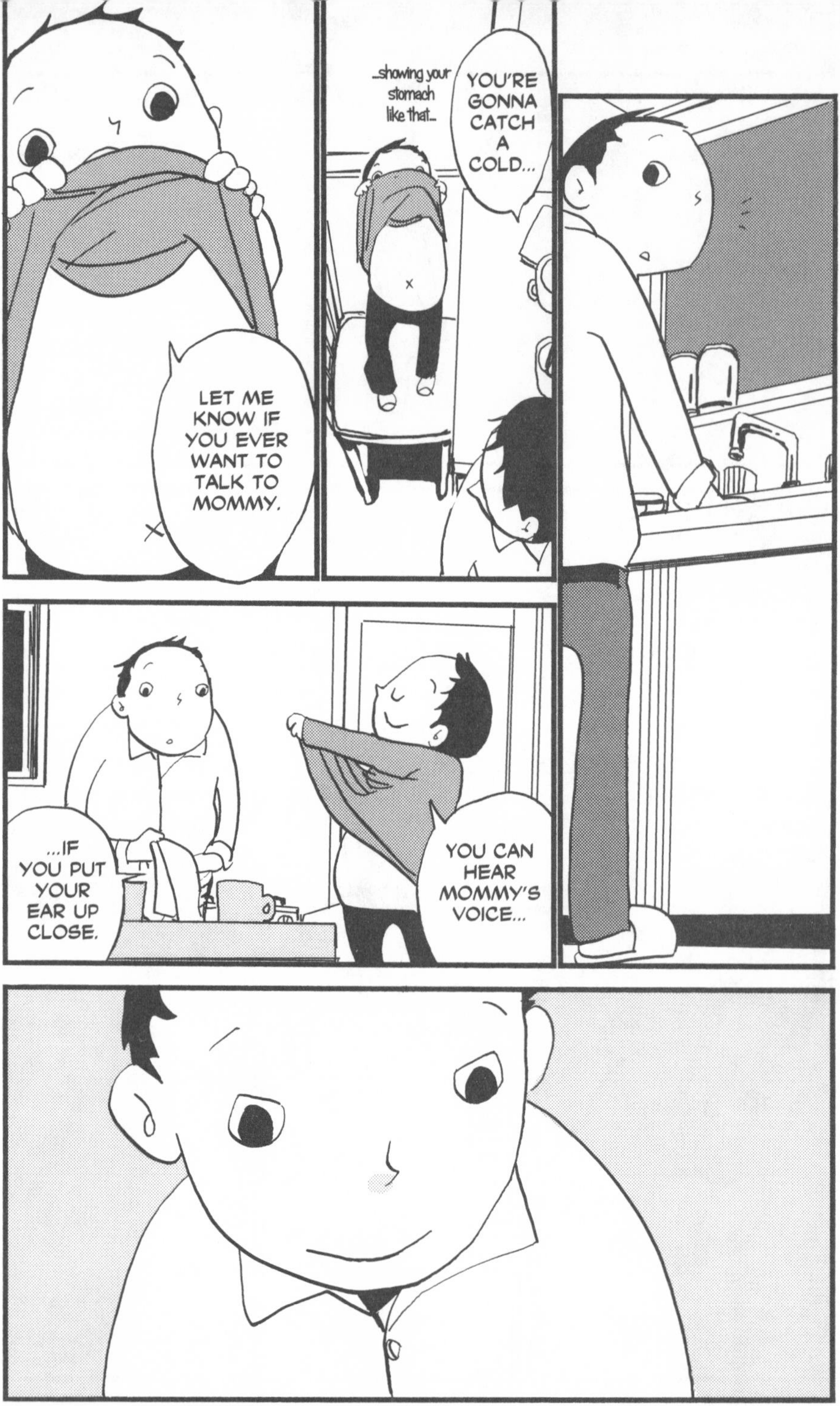
YOU'RE GONNA CATCH A COLD...
...showing your stomach like that...
LET ME KNOW IF YOU EVER WANT TO TALK TO MOMMY.
YOU CAN HEAR MOMMY'S VOICE...
...IF YOU PUT YOUR EAR UP CLOSE.

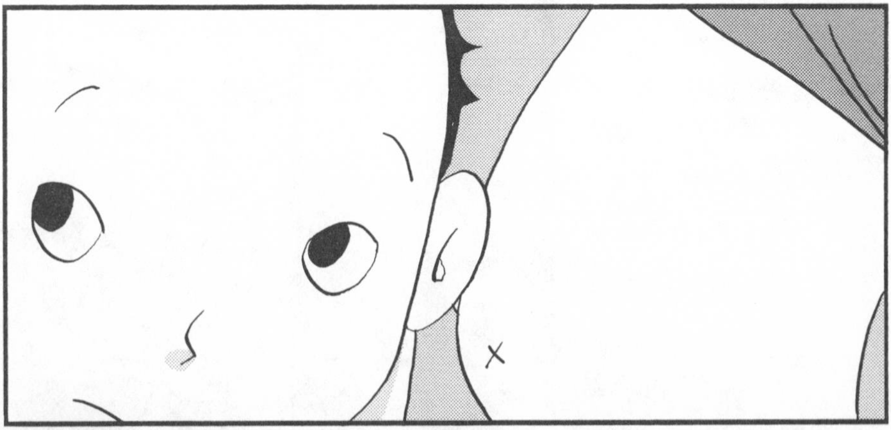

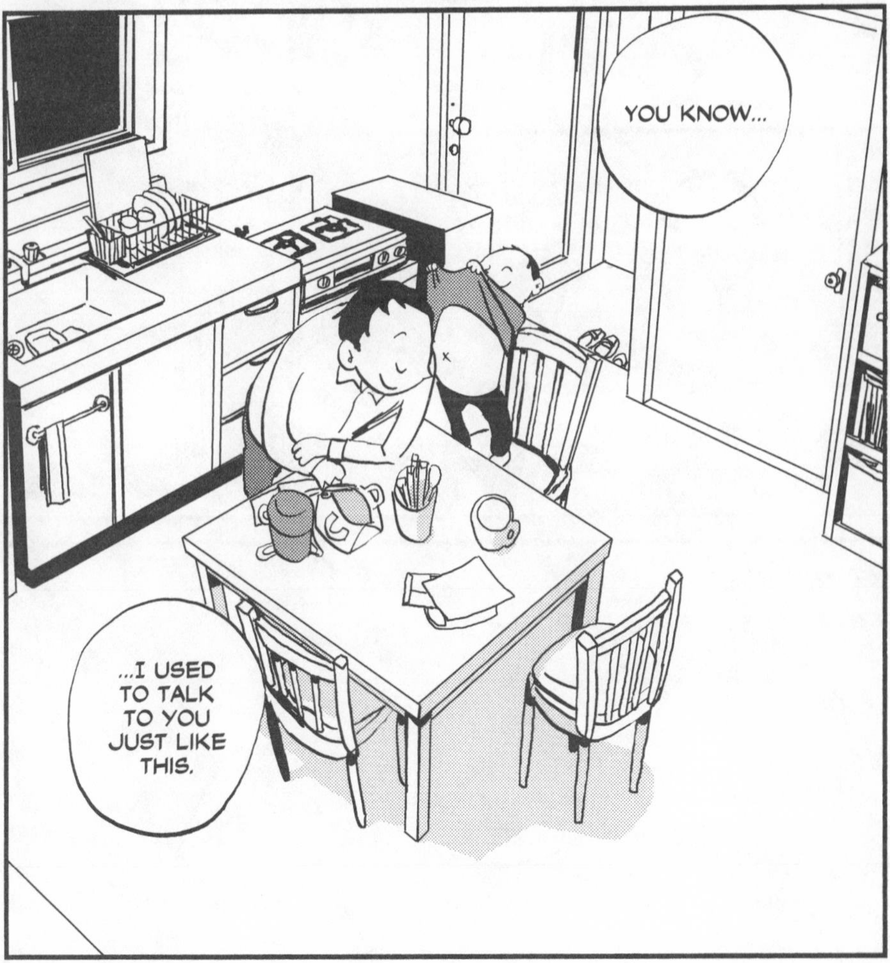
YOU KNOW...
...I USED TO TALK TO YOU JUST LIKE THIS.

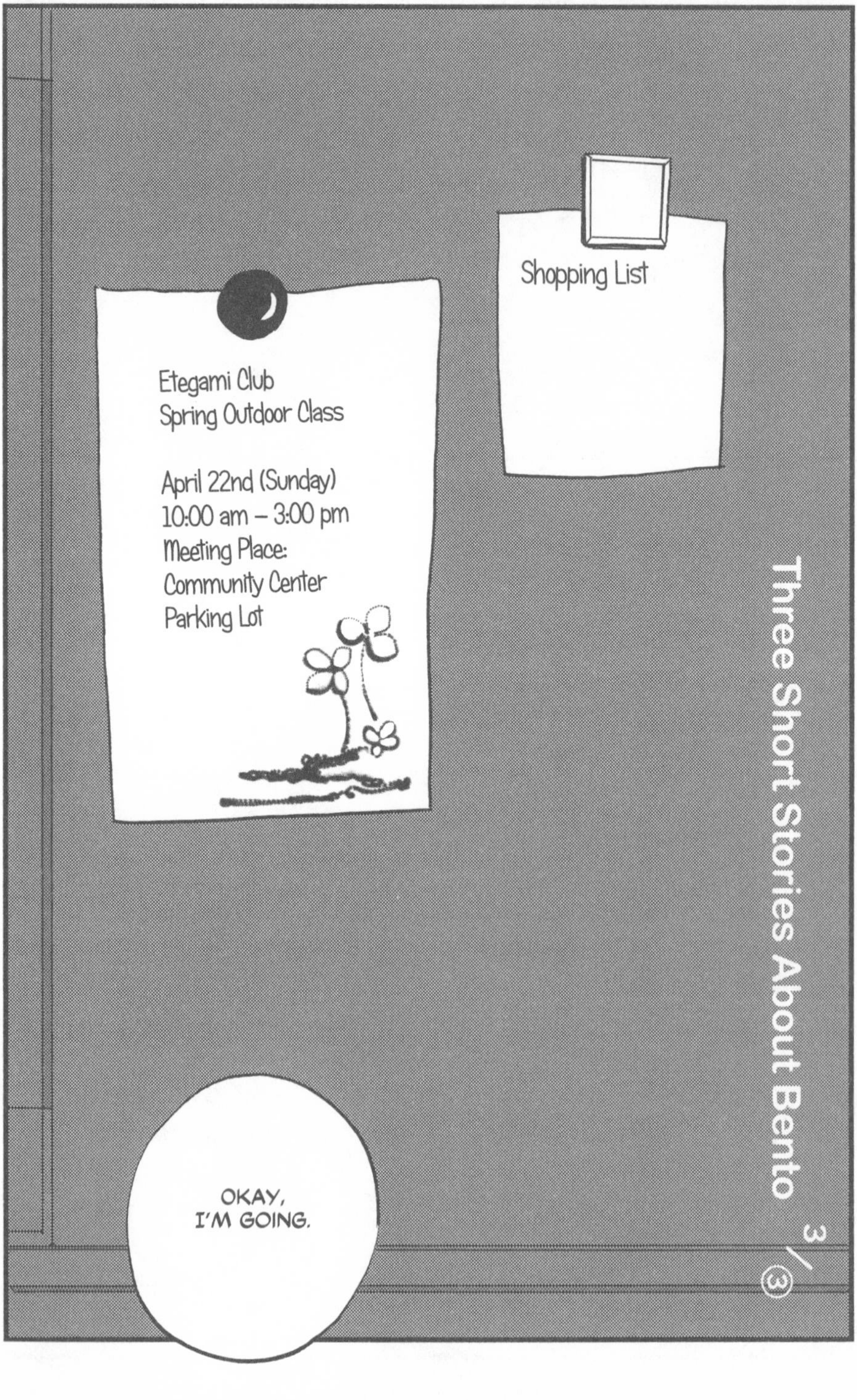
Three Short Stories About Bento
3/③
Shopping List
Etegami Club
Spring Outdoor Class
April 22nd (Sunday)
10:00 am – 3:00 pm
Meeting Place:
Community Center
Parking Lot
OKAY, I'M GOING.

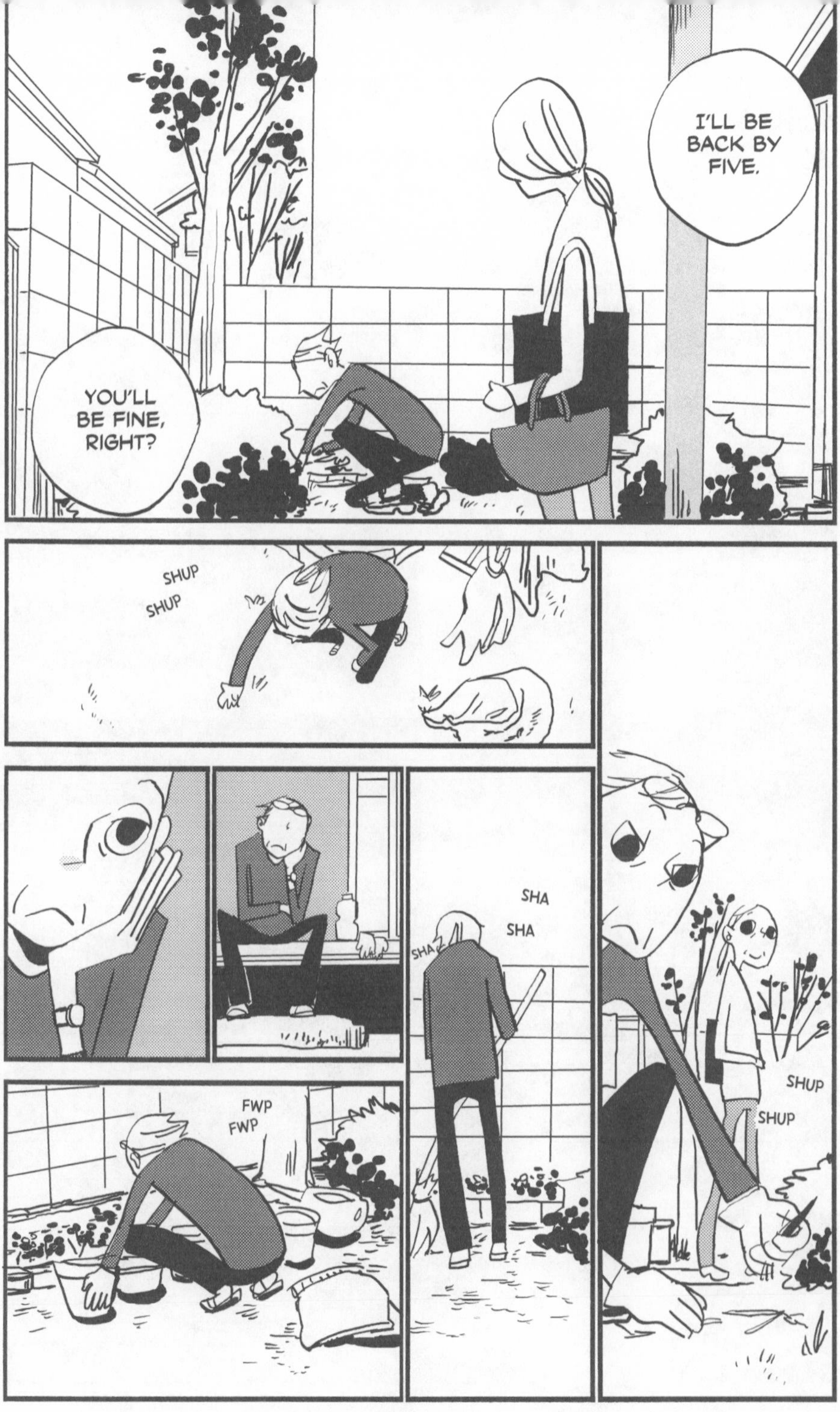
I'LL BE BACK BY FIVE.
YOU'LL BE FINE, RIGHT?
SHUP SHUP
SHUP SHUP
SHA SHA SHA
FWP FWP

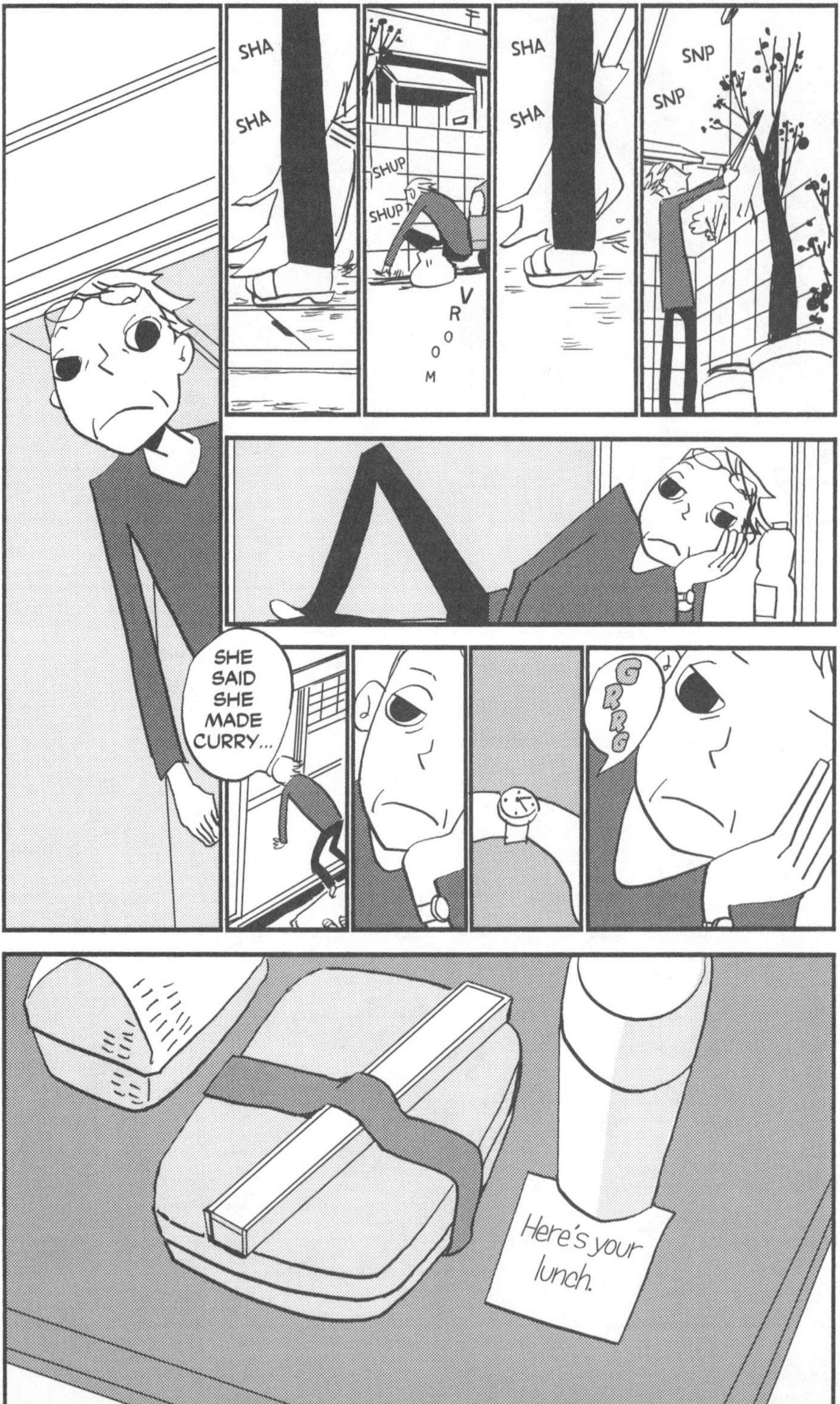
SNP
SNP
SHA
SHA
SHUP
SHUP
VROOM
SHA
SHA
GRRG
SHE SAID SHE MADE CURRY...
Here's your lunch.

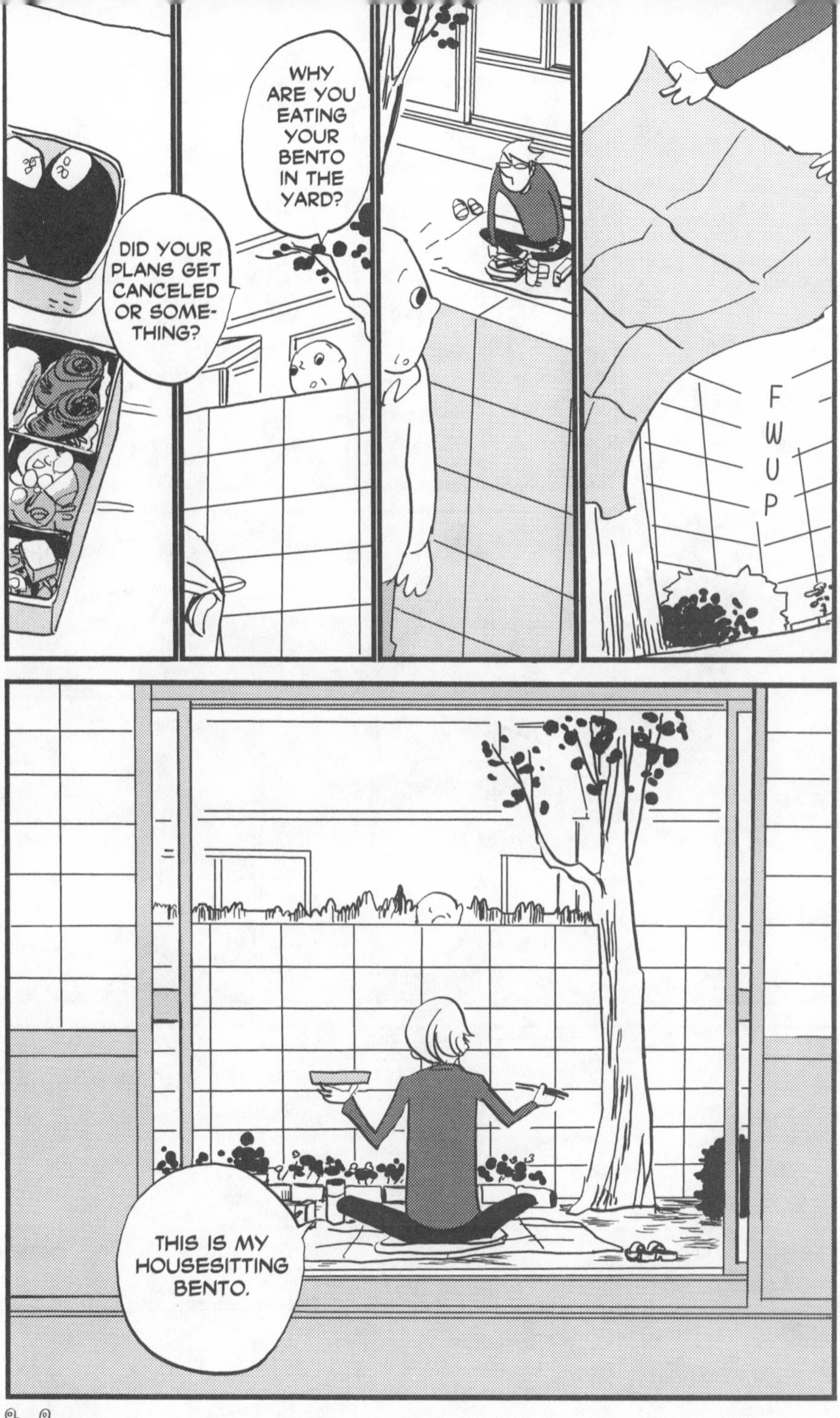
FWUP
WHY ARE YOU EATING YOUR BENTO IN THE YARD?
DID YOUR PLANS GET CANCELED OR SOMETHING?
THIS IS MY HOUSESITTING BENTO.

fine.

Three Short Stories About Bento

Ikki - July 2008 Issue

Natsume Ono

Tesoro 2

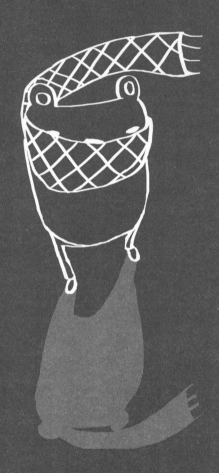

Eva's Memory

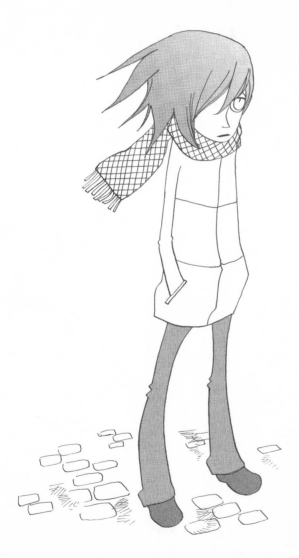

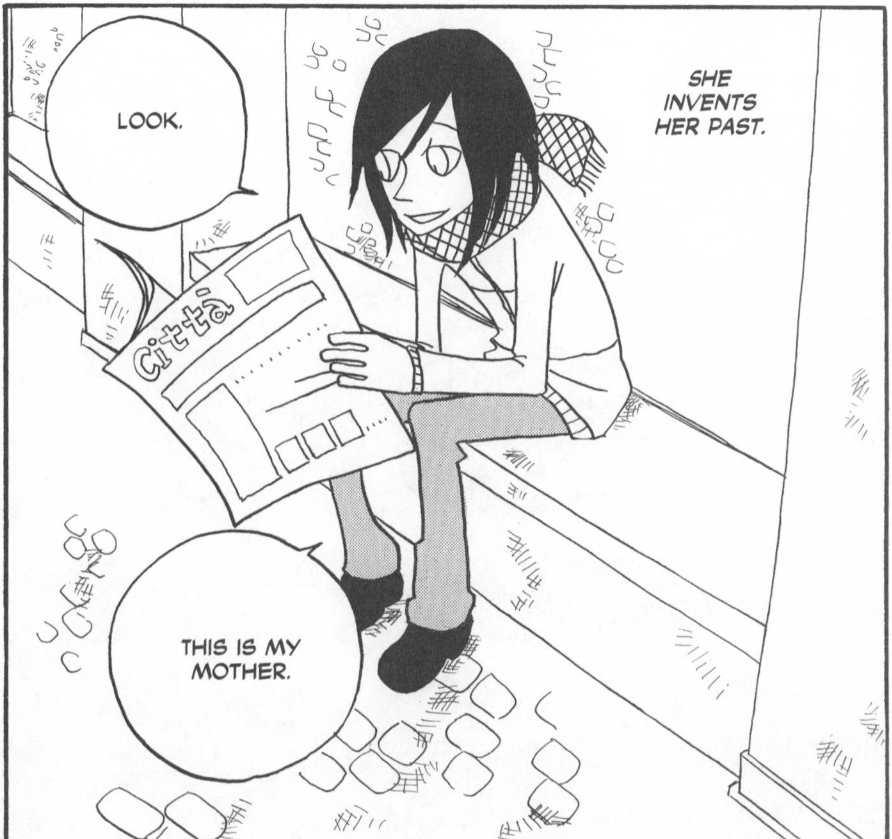
SHE INVENTS HER PAST.
LOOK.
THIS IS MY MOTHER.

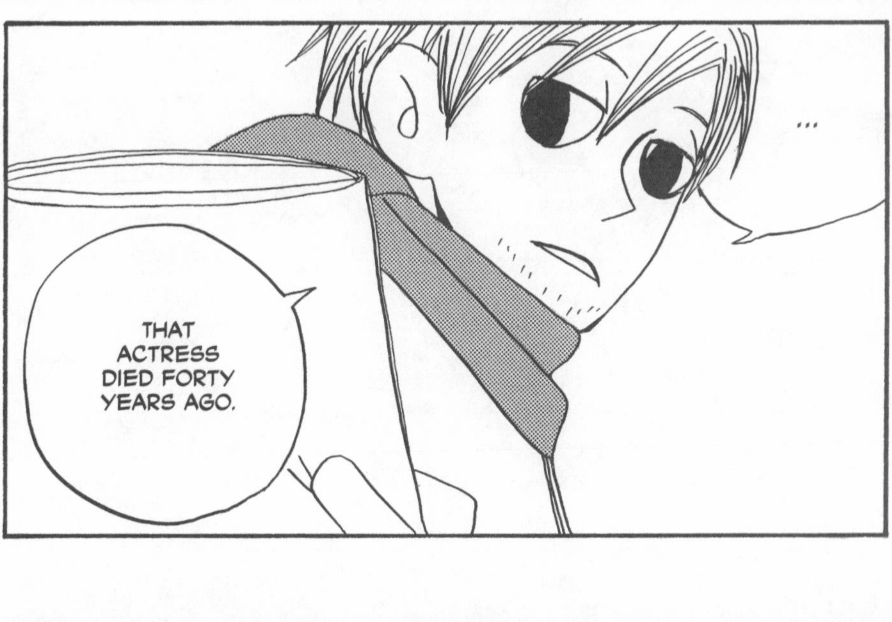
...
THAT ACTRESS DIED FORTY YEARS AGO.

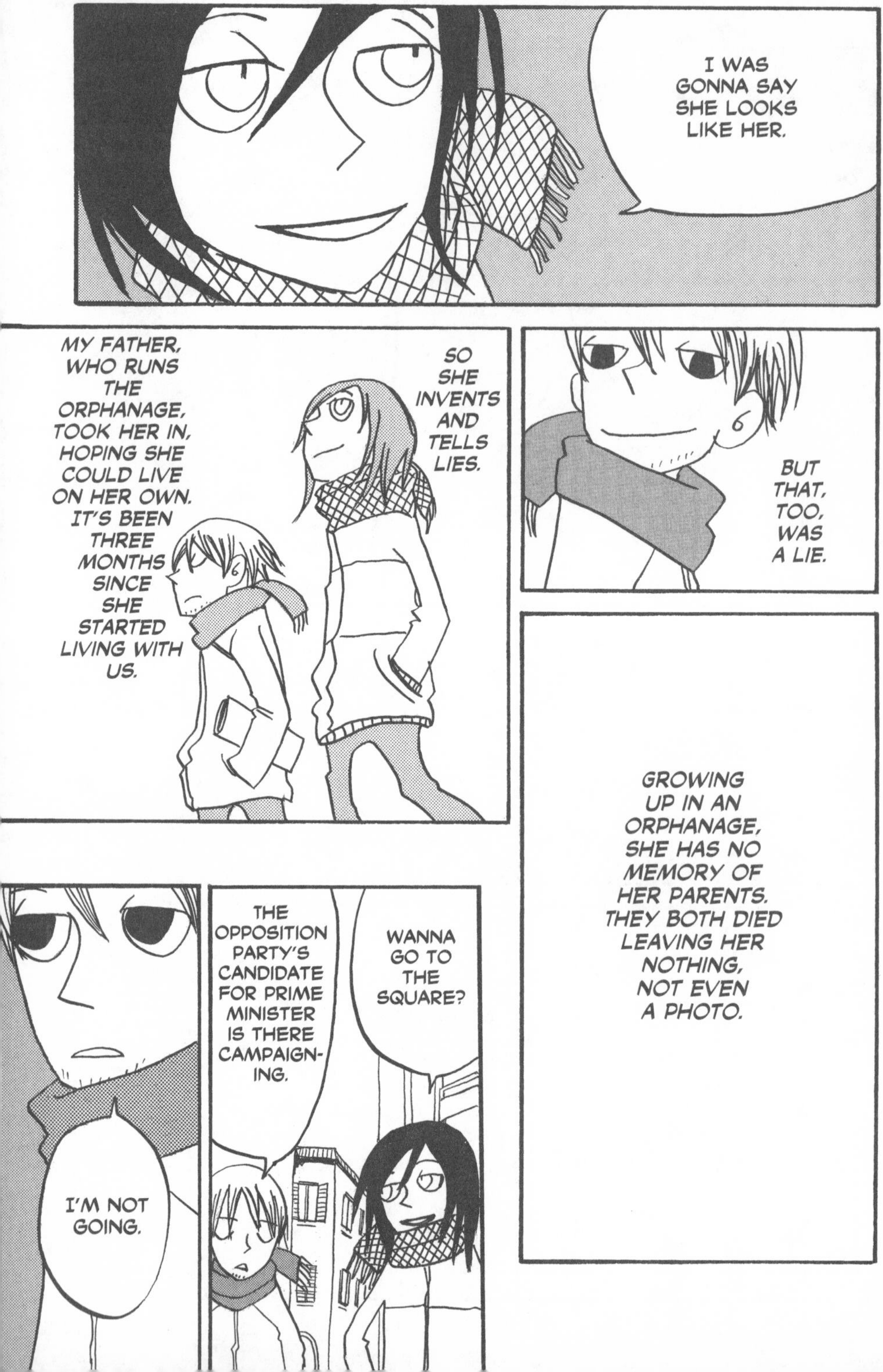
I WAS GONNA SAY SHE LOOKS LIKE HER.
BUT THAT, TOO, WAS A LIE.
GROWING UP IN AN ORPHANAGE, SHE HAS NO MEMORY OF HER PARENTS. THEY BOTH DIED LEAVING HER NOTHING, NOT EVEN A PHOTO.
SO SHE INVENTS AND TELLS LIES.
MY FATHER, WHO RUNS THE ORPHANAGE, TOOK HER IN, HOPING SHE COULD LIVE ON HER OWN. IT'S BEEN THREE MONTHS SINCE SHE STARTED LIVING WITH US.
WANNA GO TO THE SQUARE?
THE OPPOSITION PARTY'S CANDIDATE FOR PRIME MINISTER IS THERE CAMPAIGN-ING.
I'M NOT GOING.

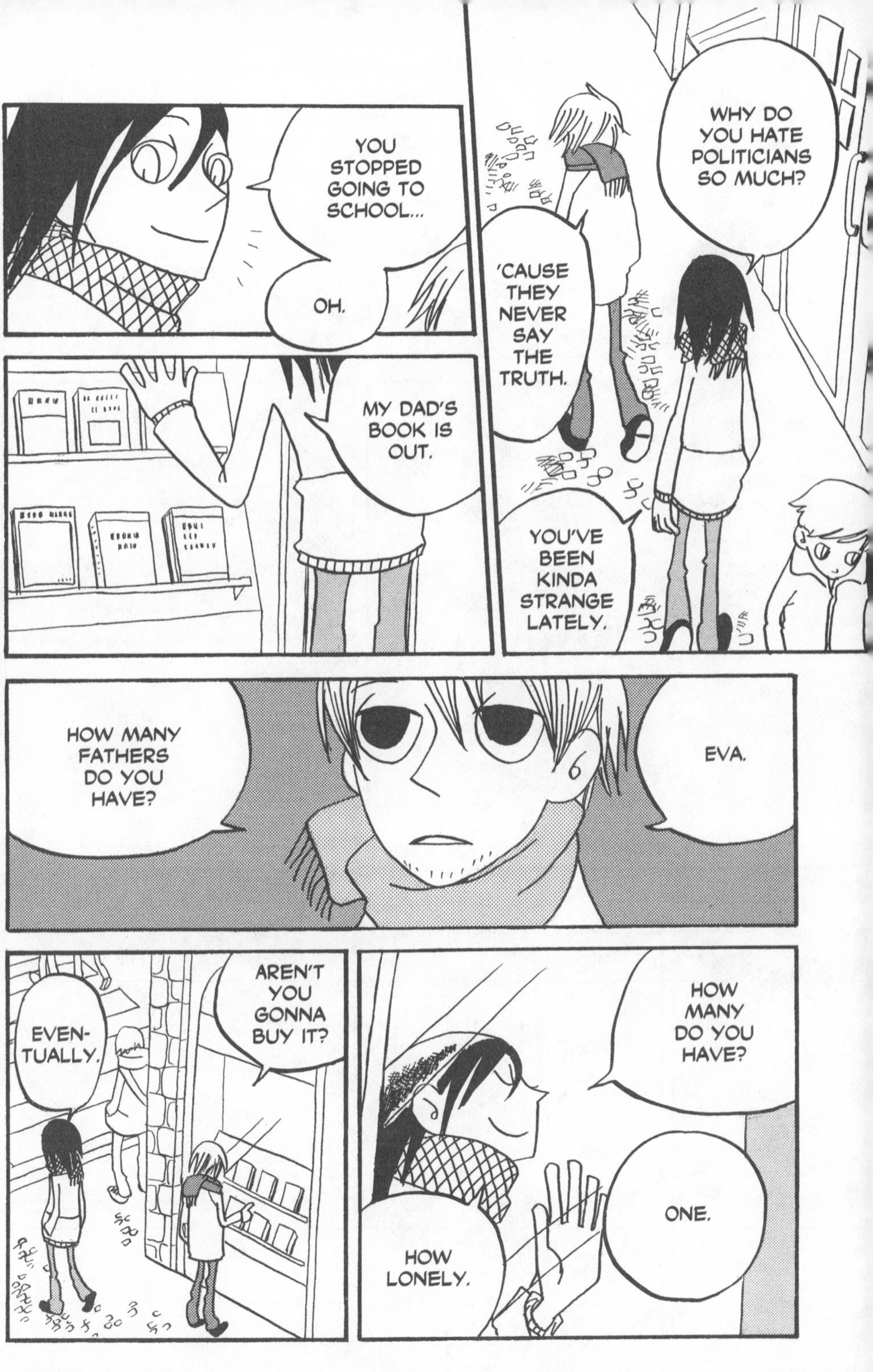
WHY DO YOU HATE POLITICIANS SO MUCH?
'CAUSE THEY NEVER SAY THE TRUTH.
YOU'VE BEEN KINDA STRANGE LATELY.
YOU STOPPED GOING TO SCHOOL...
OH.
MY DAD'S BOOK IS OUT.
EVA.
HOW MANY FATHERS DO YOU HAVE?
HOW MANY DO YOU HAVE?
ONE.
HOW LONELY.
AREN'T YOU GONNA BUY IT?
EVEN-TUALLY.

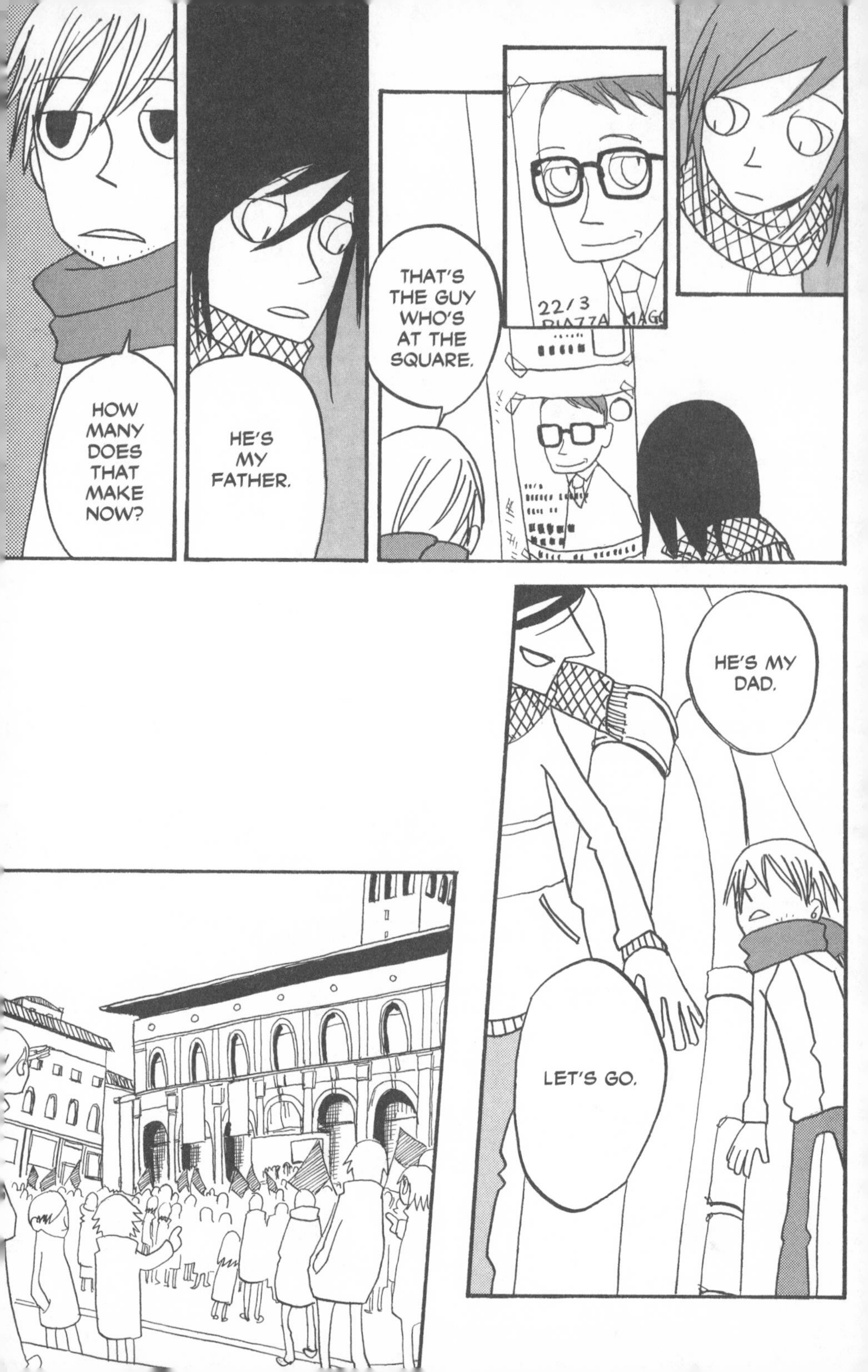
22/3
THAT'S THE GUY WHO'S AT THE SQUARE.
HE'S MY FATHER.
HOW MANY DOES THAT MAKE NOW?
HE'S MY DAD.
LET'S GO.

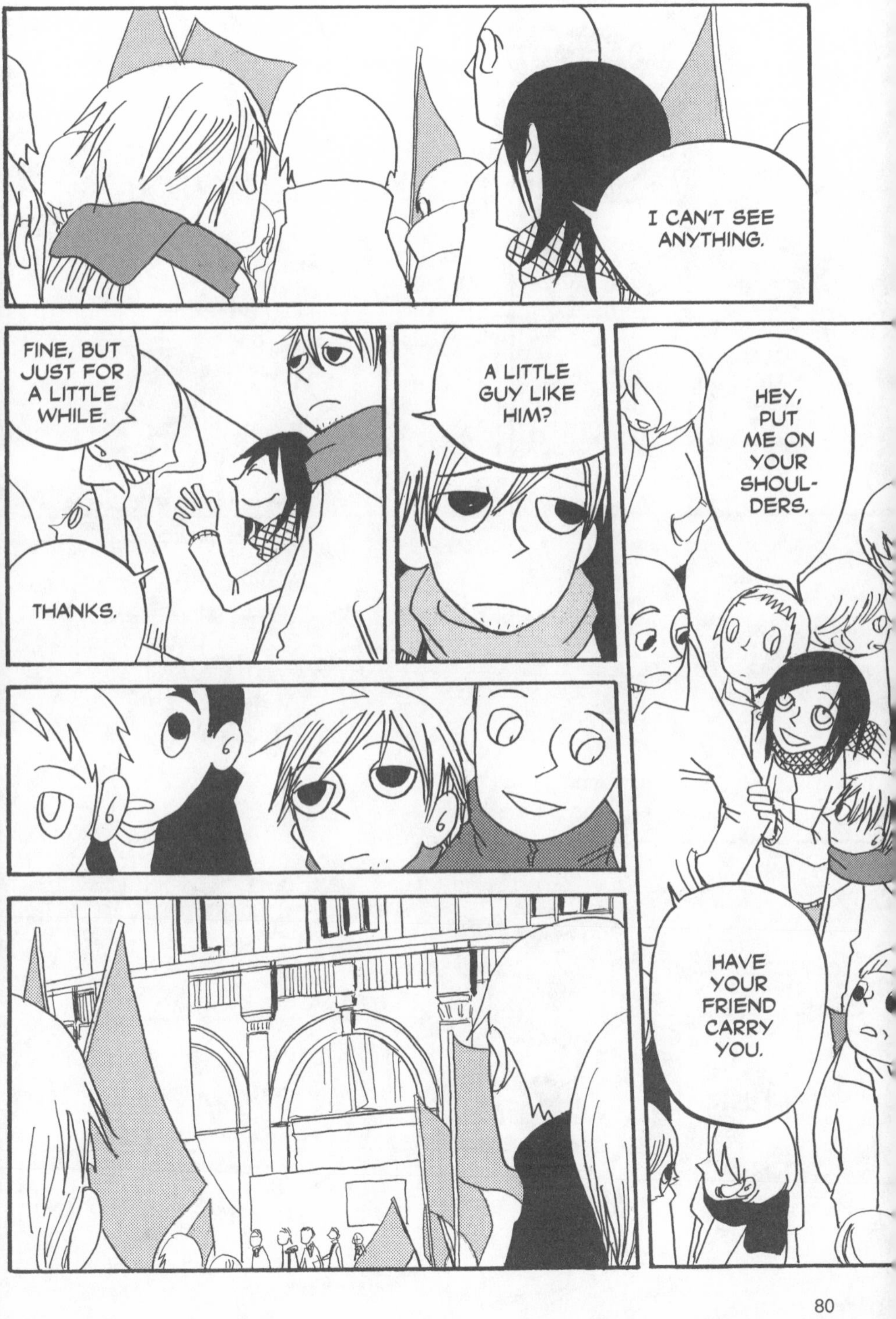
I CAN'T SEE ANYTHING.
HEY, PUT ME ON YOUR SHOULDERS.
HAVE YOUR FRIEND CARRY YOU.
A LITTLE GUY LIKE HIM?
FINE, BUT JUST FOR A LITTLE WHILE.
THANKS.

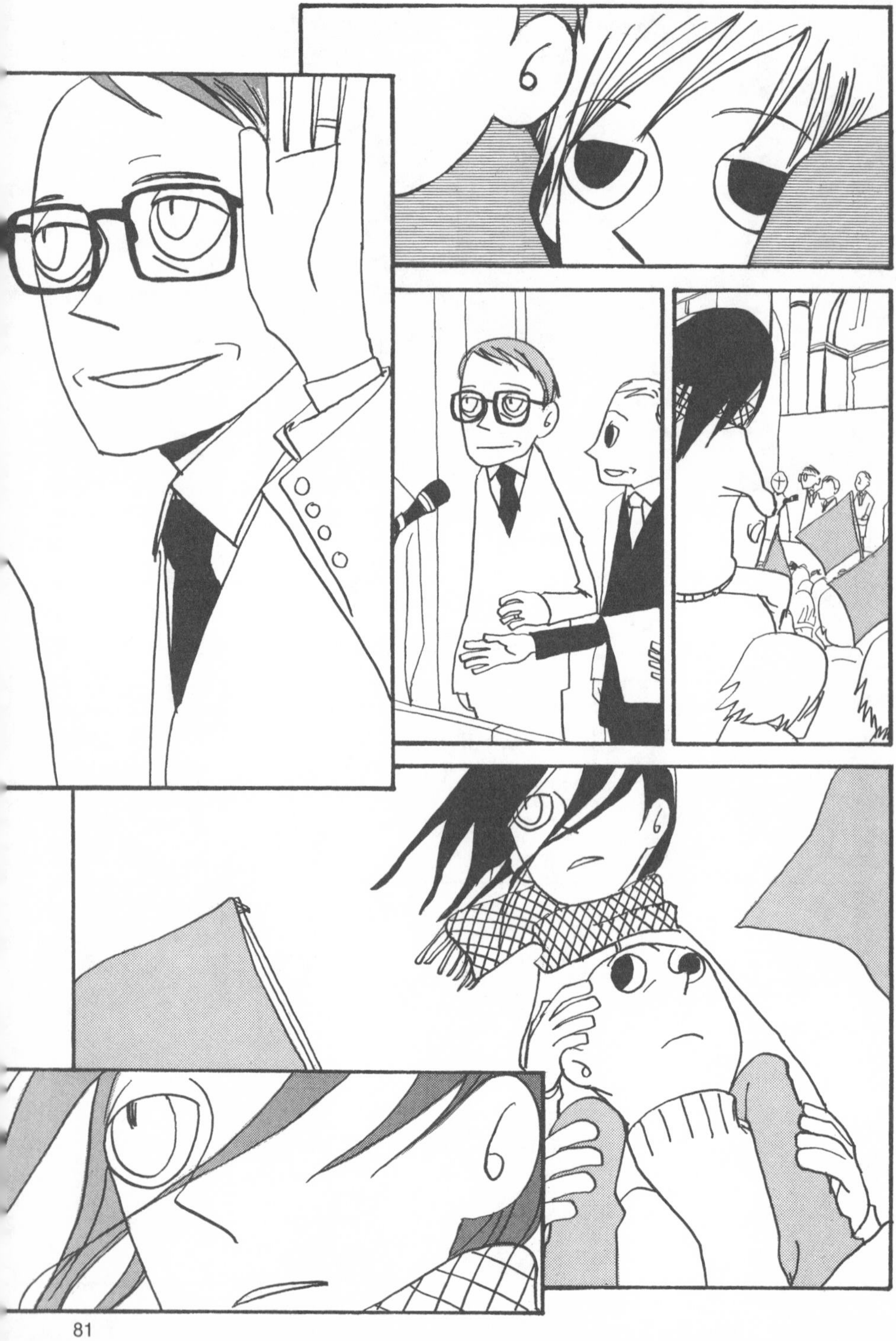

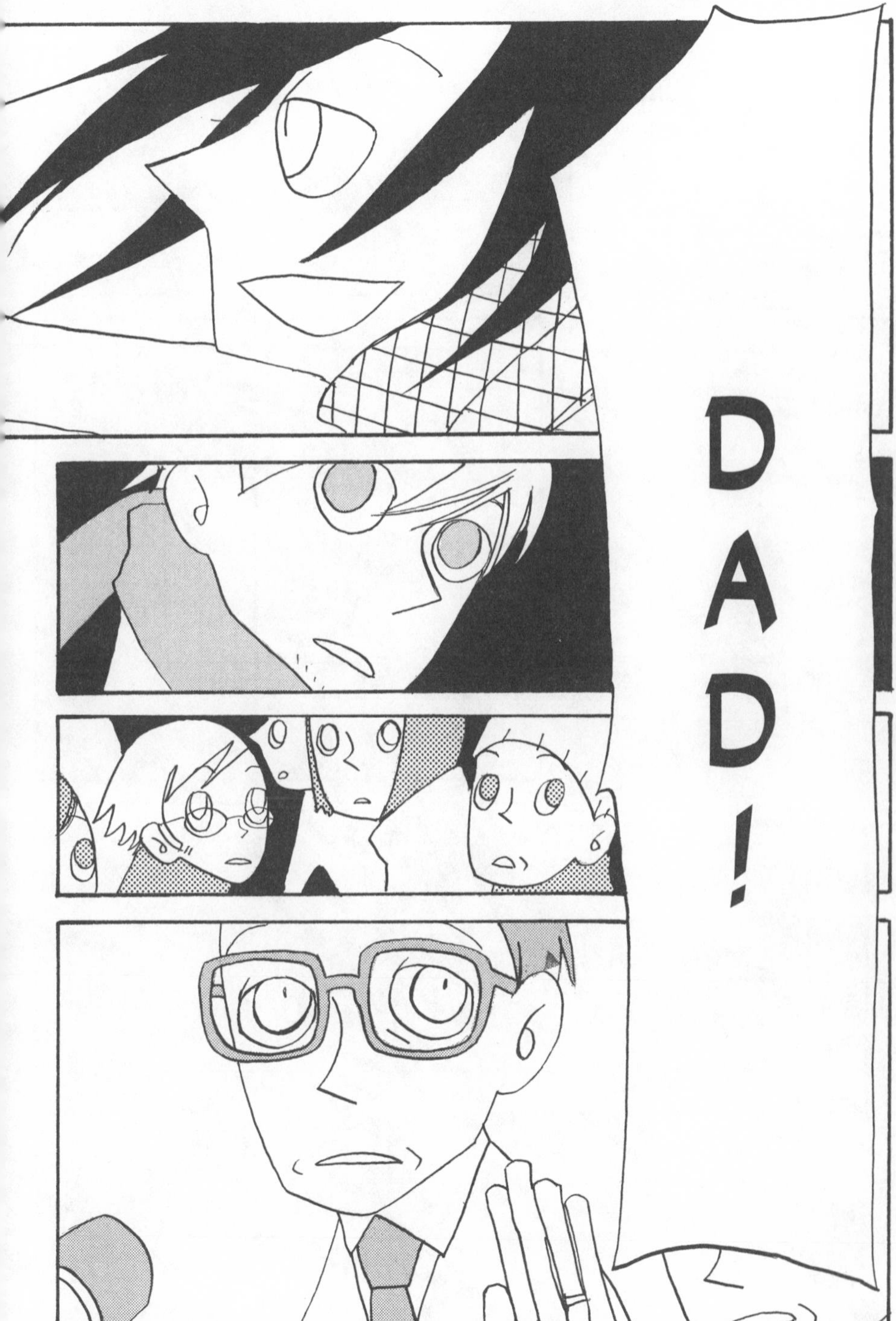
DAD!

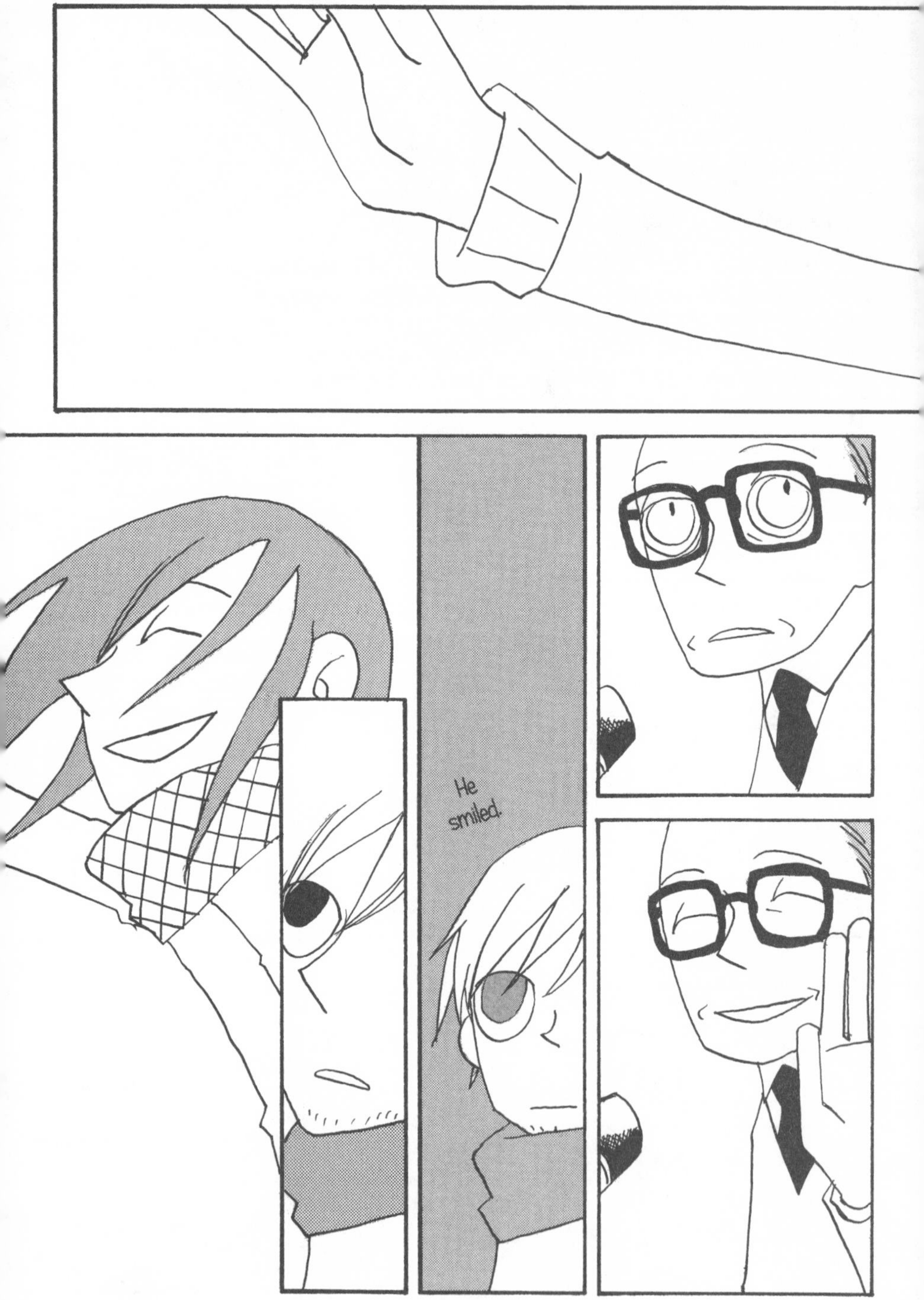
He smiled.

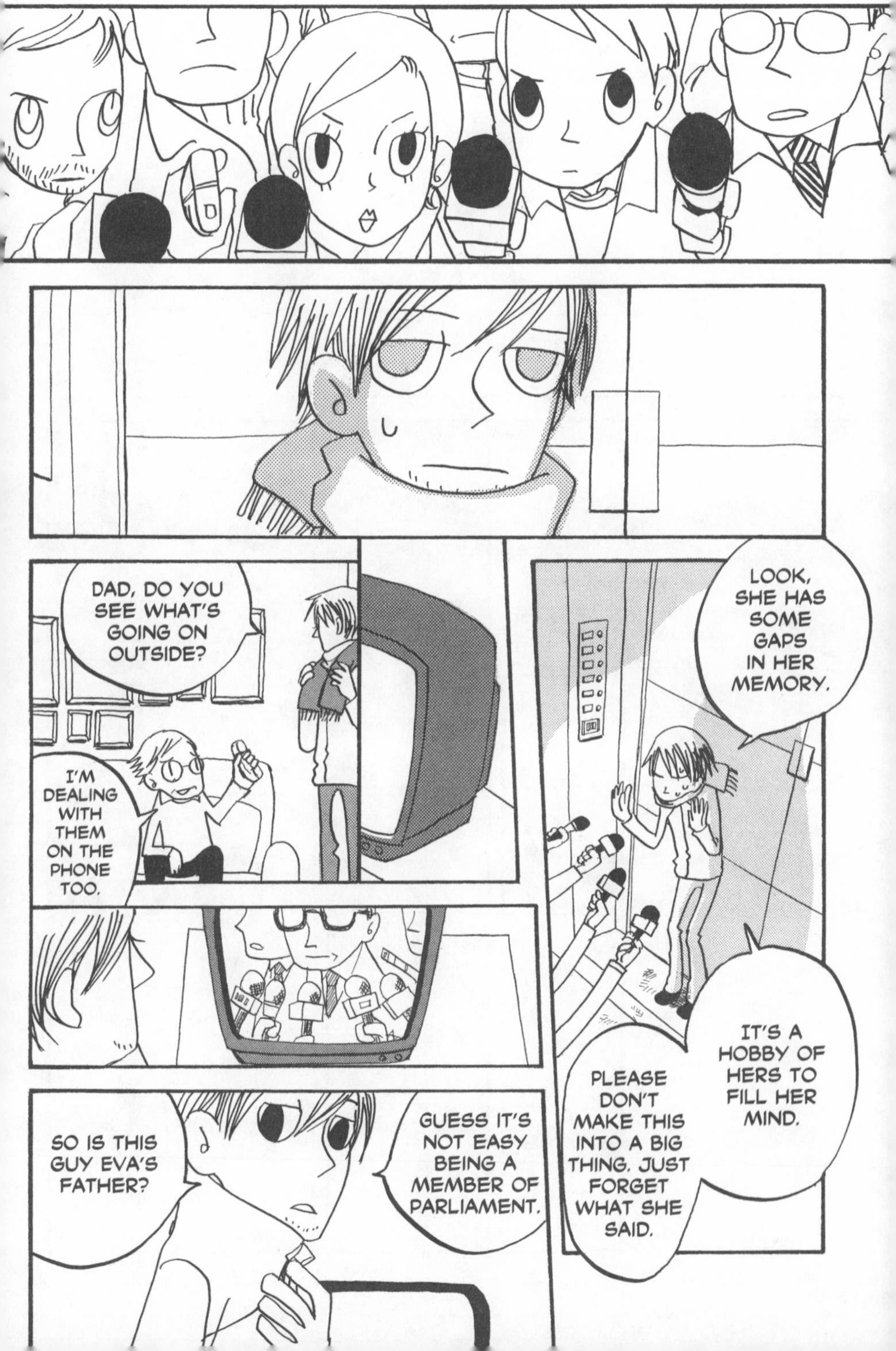
LOOK, SHE HAS SOME GAPS IN HER MEMORY.
IT'S A HOBBY OF HERS TO FILL HER MIND.
PLEASE DON'T MAKE THIS INTO A BIG THING. JUST FORGET WHAT SHE SAID.
DAD, DO YOU SEE WHAT'S GOING ON OUTSIDE?
I'M DEALING WITH THEM ON THE PHONE TOO.
GUESS IT'S NOT EASY BEING A MEMBER OF PARLIAMENT.
SO IS THIS GUY EVA'S FATHER?

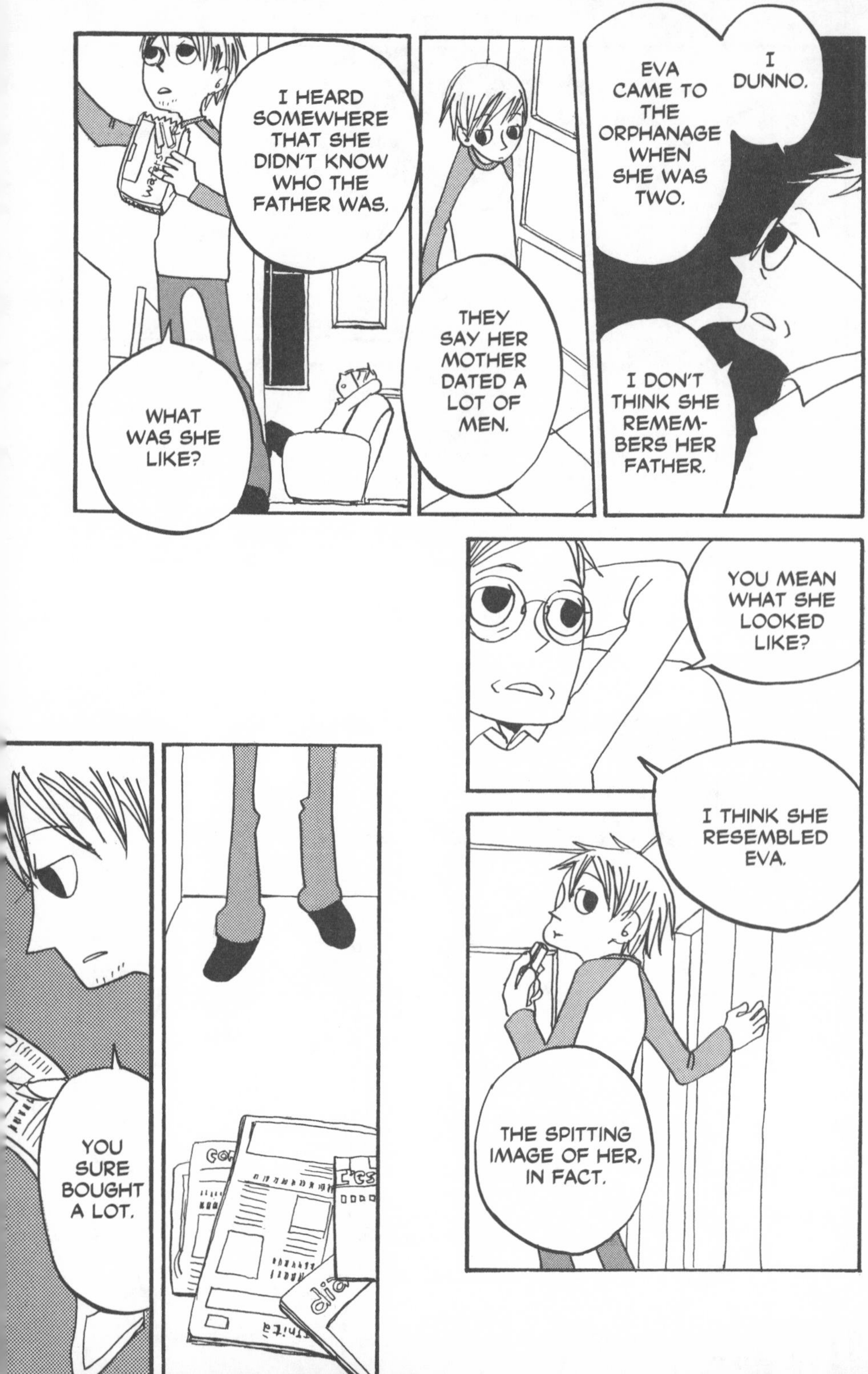
I DUNNO.
EVA CAME TO THE ORPHANAGE WHEN SHE WAS TWO.
I DON'T THINK SHE REMEMBERS HER FATHER.
THEY SAY HER MOTHER DATED A LOT OF MEN.
I HEARD SOMEWHERE THAT SHE DIDN'T KNOW WHO THE FATHER WAS.
WHAT WAS SHE LIKE?
YOU MEAN WHAT SHE LOOKED LIKE?
I THINK SHE RESEMBLED EVA.
THE SPITTING IMAGE OF HER, IN FACT.
YOU SURE BOUGHT A LOT.

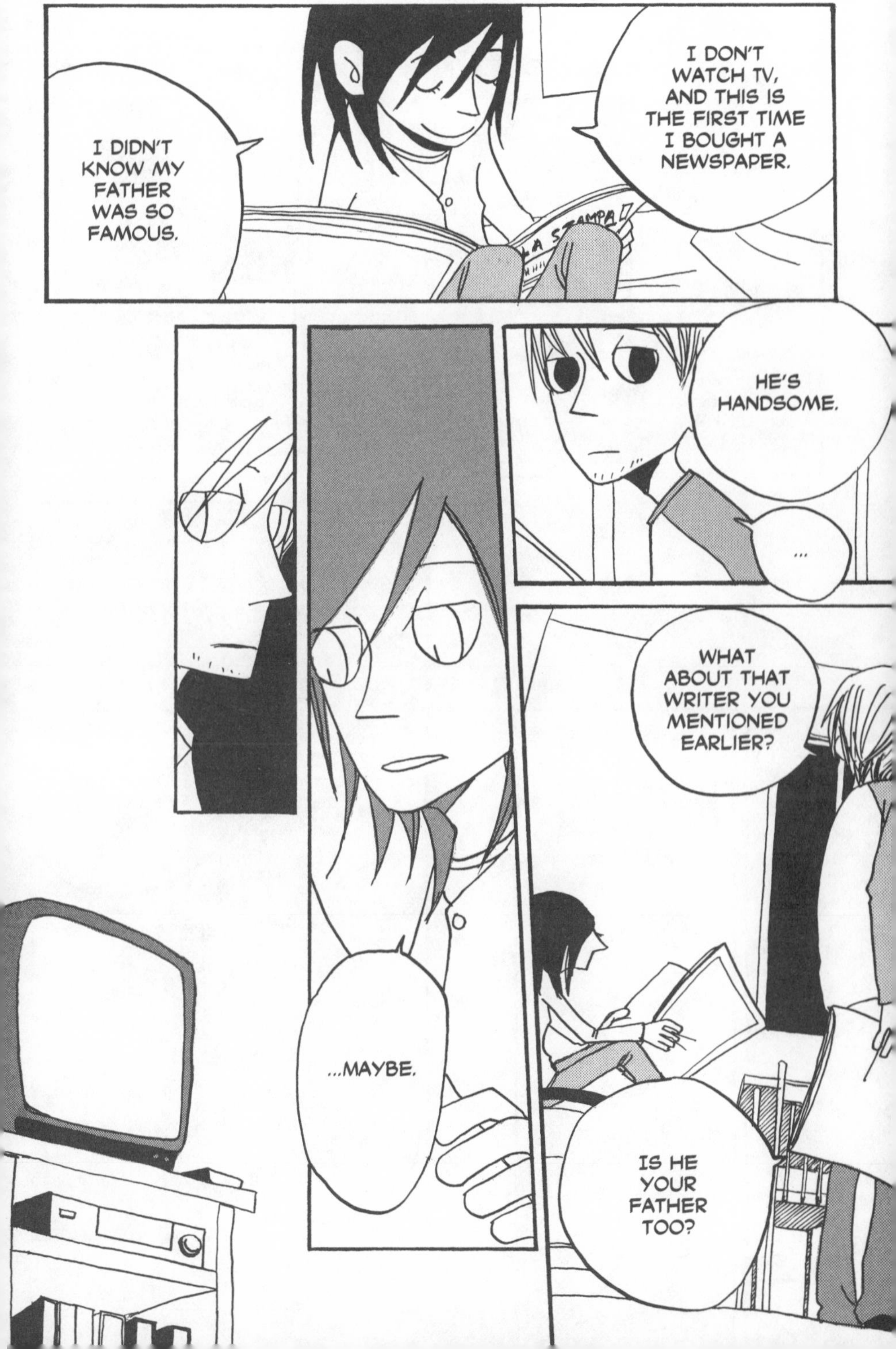
I DON'T WATCH TV, AND THIS IS THE FIRST TIME I BOUGHT A NEWSPAPER.
LA STAMPA
I DIDN'T KNOW MY FATHER WAS SO FAMOUS.
HE'S HANDSOME.
...
WHAT ABOUT THAT WRITER YOU MENTIONED EARLIER?
IS HE YOUR FATHER TOO?
...MAYBE.

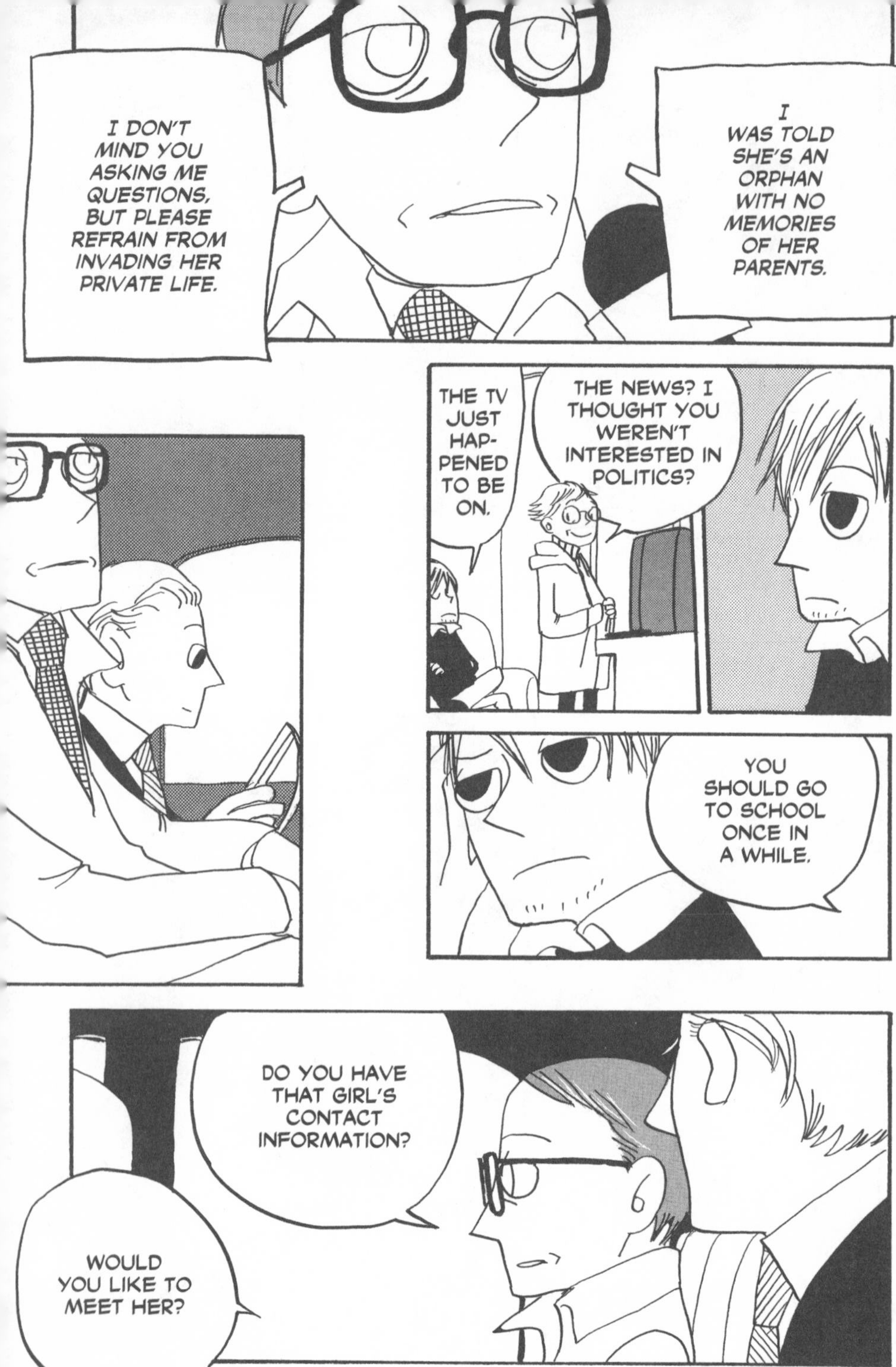
I WAS TOLD SHE'S AN ORPHAN WITH NO MEMORIES OF HER PARENTS.
I DON'T MIND YOU ASKING ME QUESTIONS, BUT PLEASE REFRAIN FROM INVADING HER PRIVATE LIFE.
THE NEWS? I THOUGHT YOU WEREN'T INTERESTED IN POLITICS?
THE TV JUST HAP-PENED TO BE ON.
YOU SHOULD GO TO SCHOOL ONCE IN A WHILE.
DO YOU HAVE THAT GIRL'S CONTACT INFORMATION?
WOULD YOU LIKE TO MEET HER?

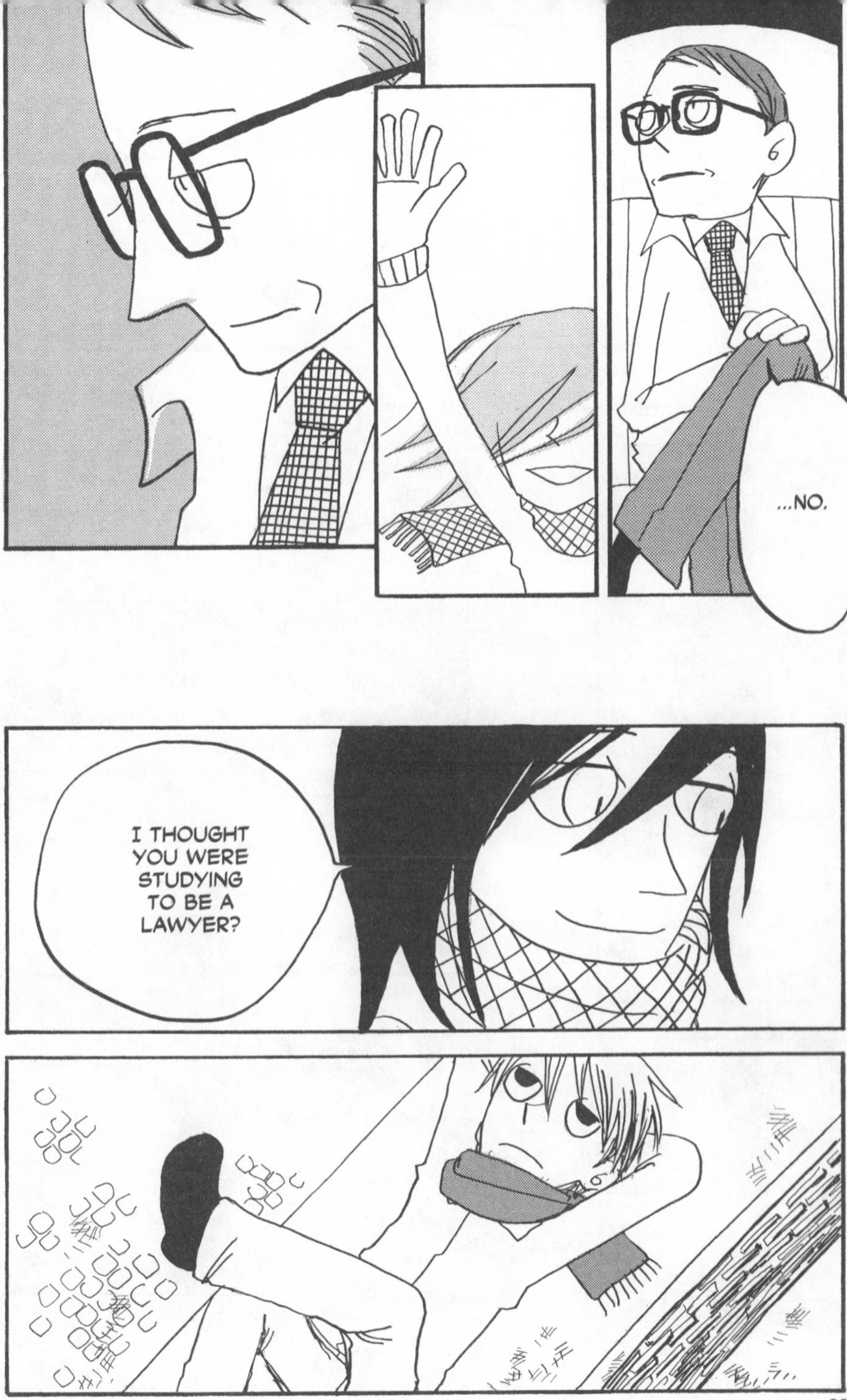
...NO.
I THOUGHT YOU WERE STUDYING TO BE A LAWYER?

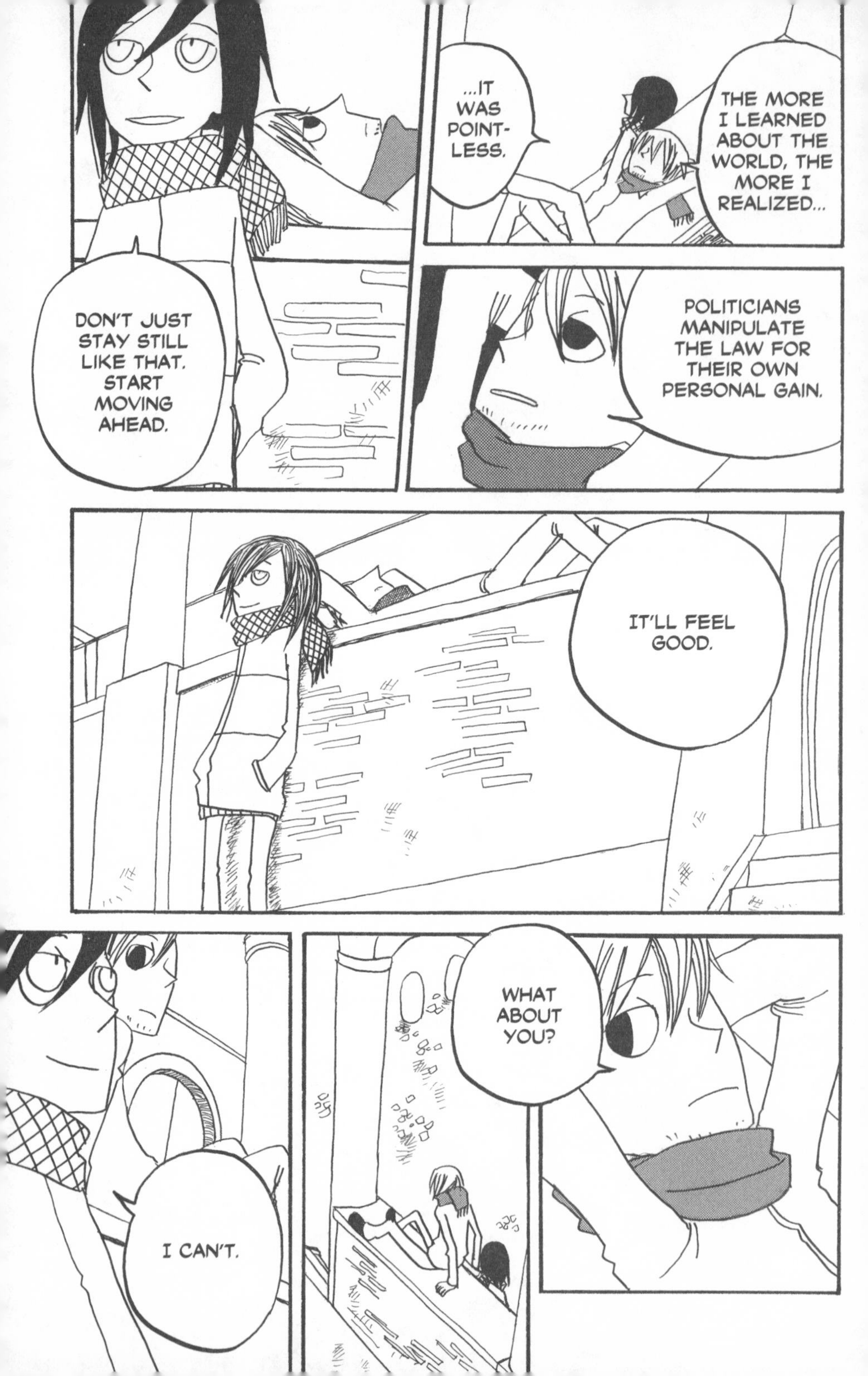
THE MORE I LEARNED ABOUT THE WORLD, THE MORE I REALIZED...
...IT WAS POINT-LESS.
POLITICIANS MANIPULATE THE LAW FOR THEIR OWN PERSONAL GAIN.
DON'T JUST STAY STILL LIKE THAT. START MOVING AHEAD.
IT'LL FEEL GOOD.
WHAT ABOUT YOU?
I CAN'T.

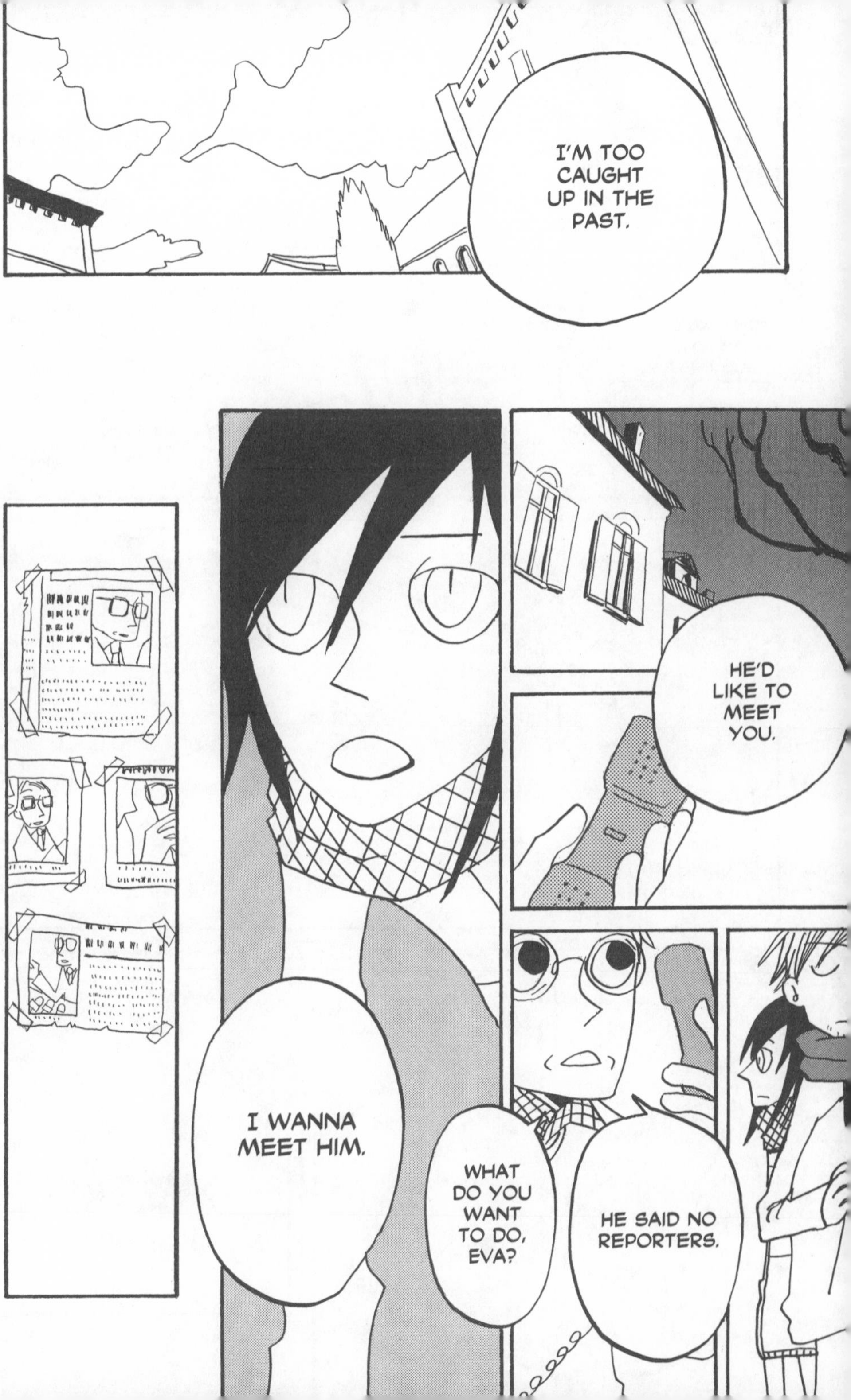
I'M TOO CAUGHT UP IN THE PAST.
HE'D LIKE TO MEET YOU.
HE SAID NO REPORTERS.
WHAT DO YOU WANT TO DO, EVA?
I WANNA MEET HIM.

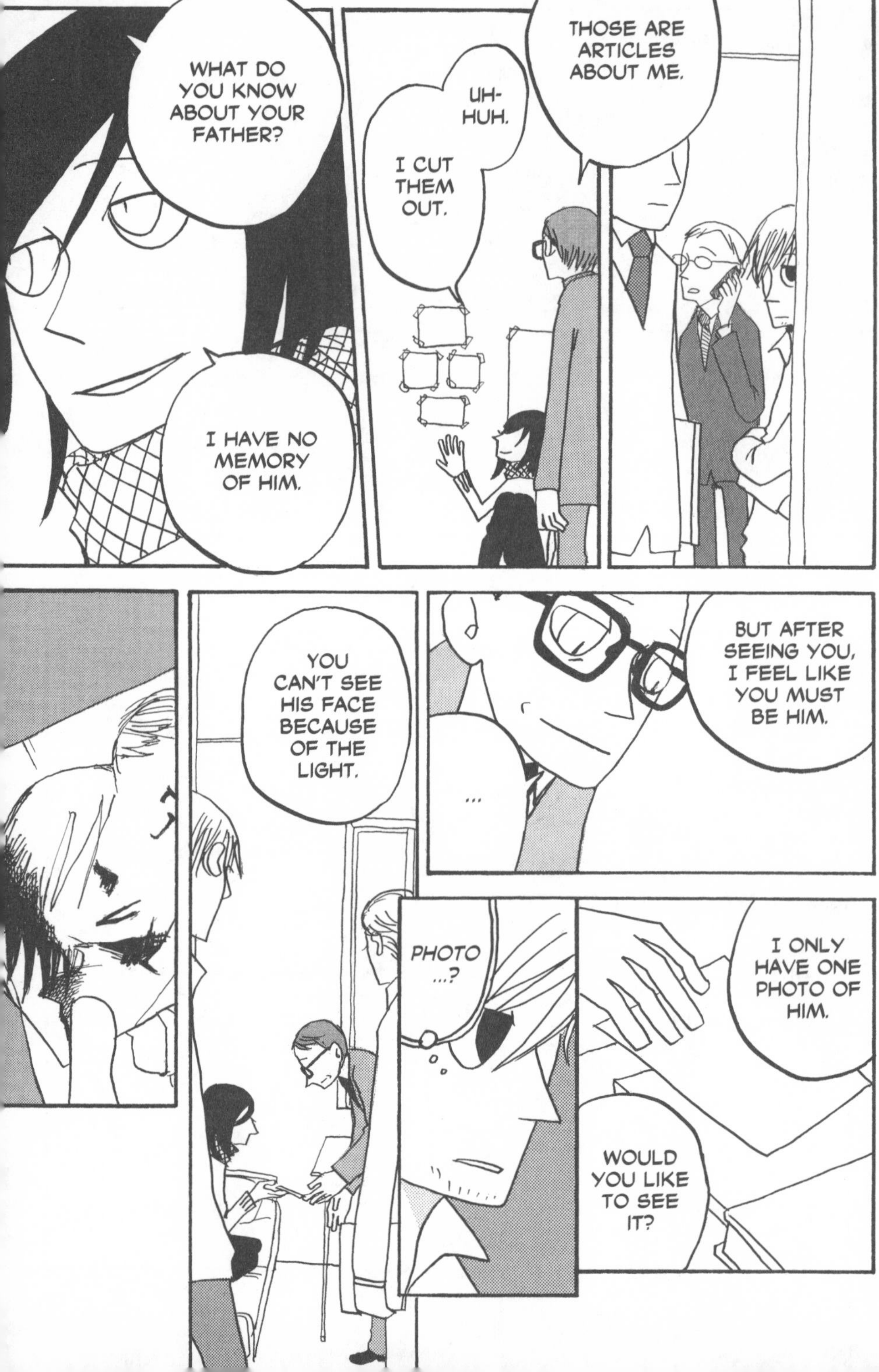
THOSE ARE ARTICLES ABOUT ME.
UH-HUH.
I CUT THEM OUT.
WHAT DO YOU KNOW ABOUT YOUR FATHER?
I HAVE NO MEMORY OF HIM.
BUT AFTER SEEING YOU, I FEEL LIKE YOU MUST BE HIM.
...
I ONLY HAVE ONE PHOTO OF HIM.
WOULD YOU LIKE TO SEE IT?
PHOTO ...?
YOU CAN'T SEE HIS FACE BECAUSE OF THE LIGHT.

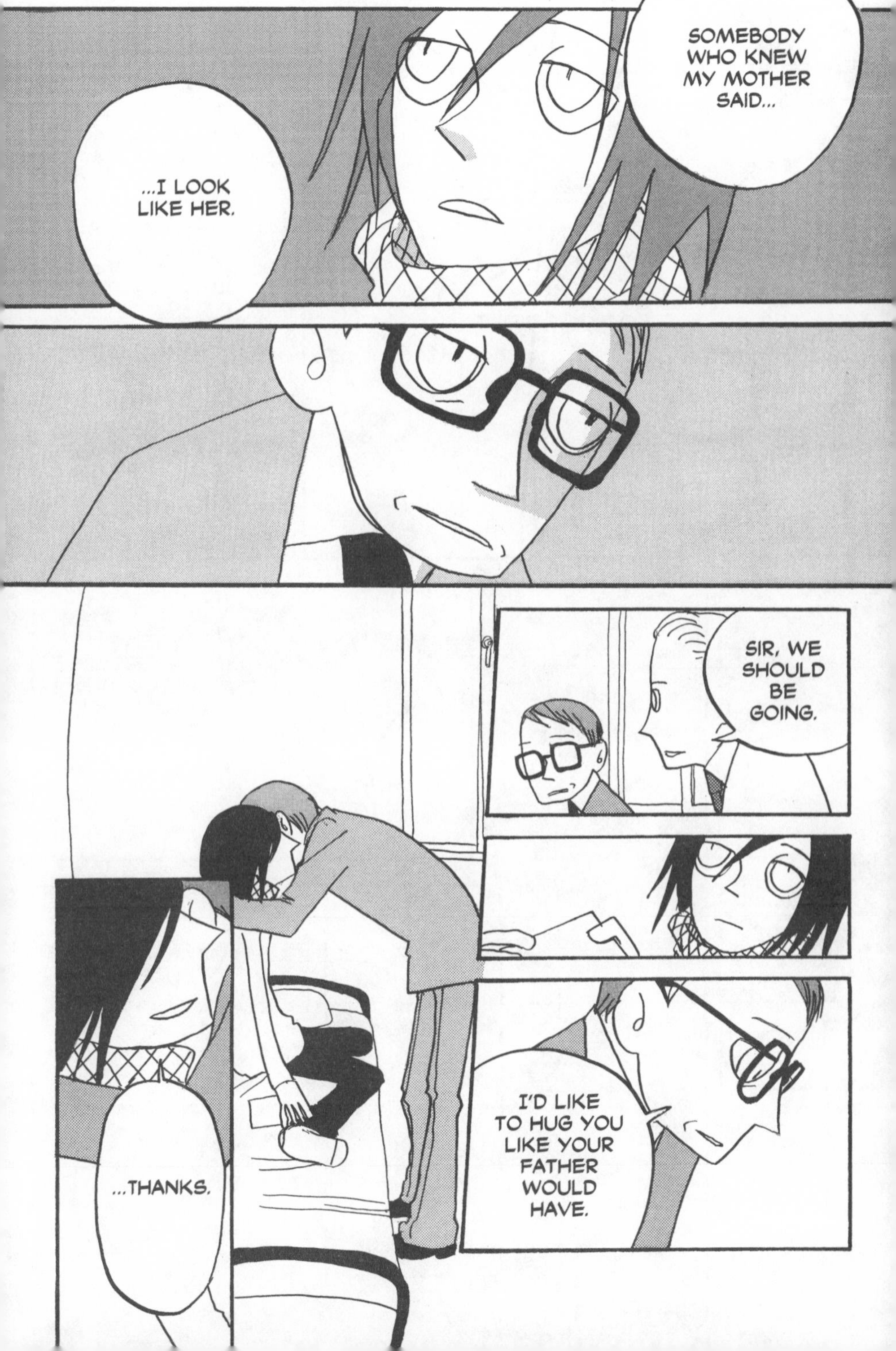
SOMEBODY WHO KNEW MY MOTHER SAID...
...I LOOK LIKE HER.
SIR, WE SHOULD BE GOING.
I'D LIKE TO HUG YOU LIKE YOUR FATHER WOULD HAVE.
...THANKS.

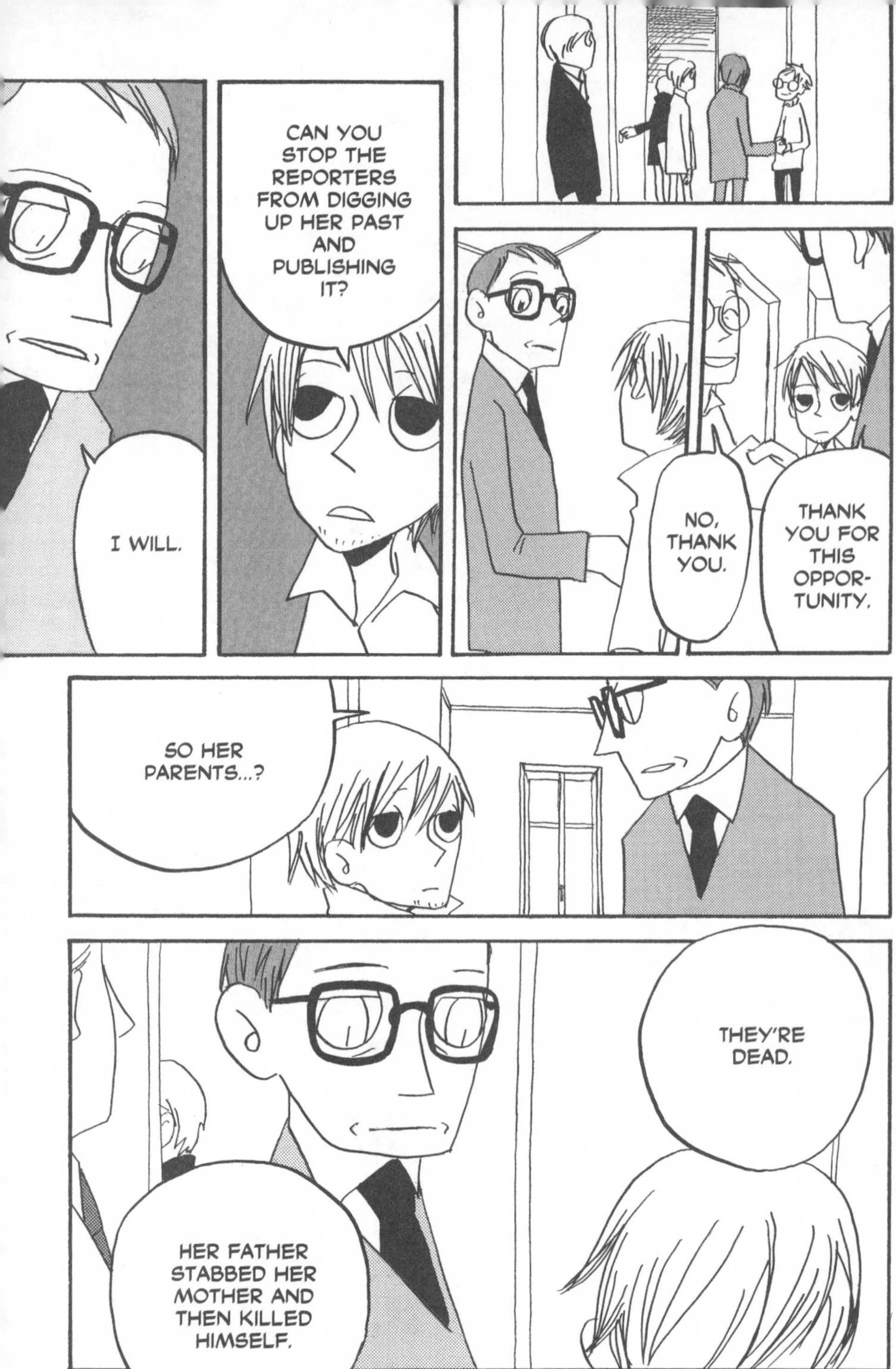
CAN YOU STOP THE REPORTERS FROM DIGGING UP HER PAST AND PUBLISHING IT?
I WILL.
THANK YOU FOR THIS OPPOR-TUNITY.
NO, THANK YOU.
SO HER PARENTS...?
THEY'RE DEAD.
HER FATHER STABBED HER MOTHER AND THEN KILLED HIMSELF.

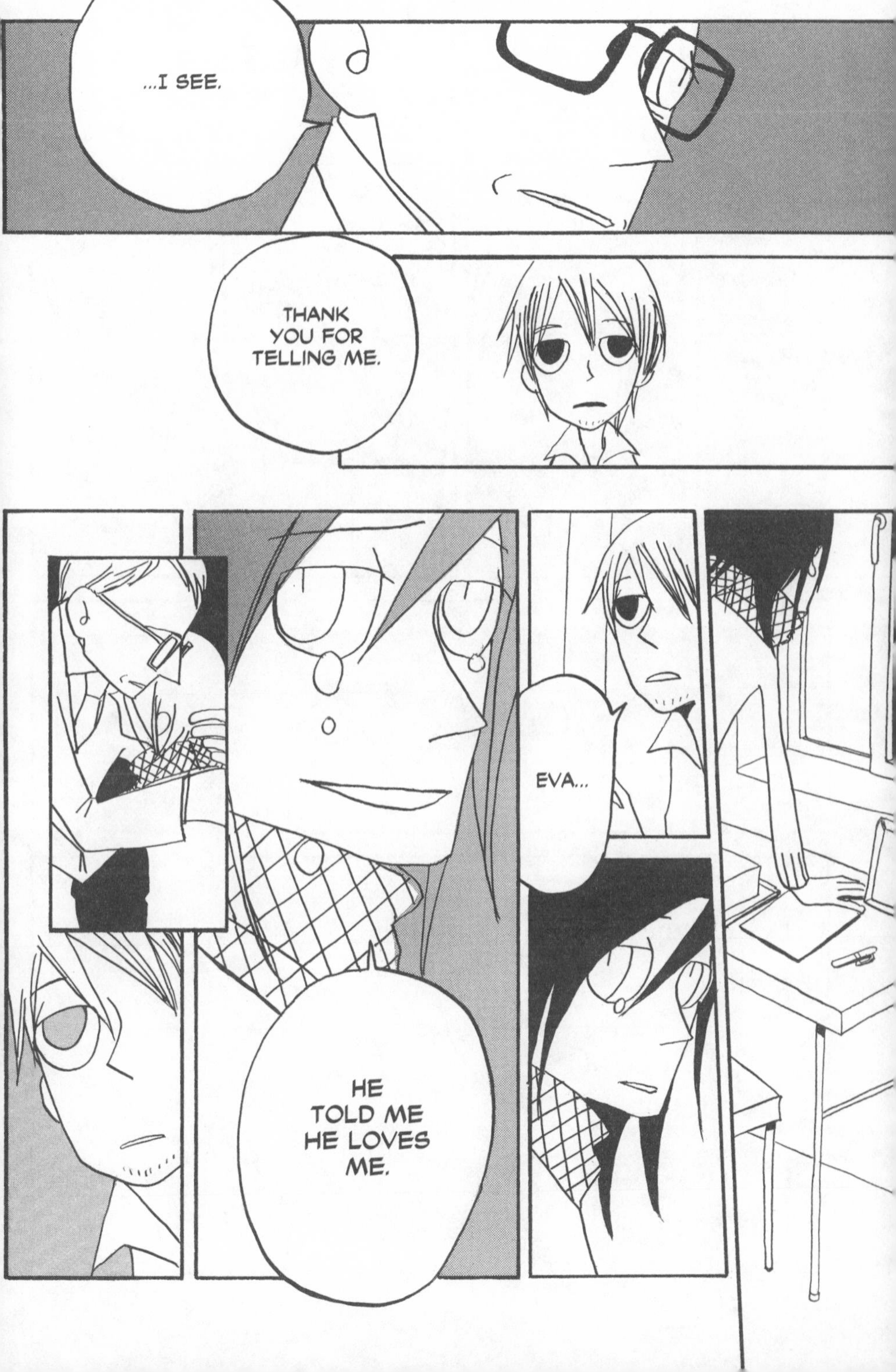
...I SEE.
THANK YOU FOR TELLING ME.
EVA...
HE TOLD ME HE LOVES ME.

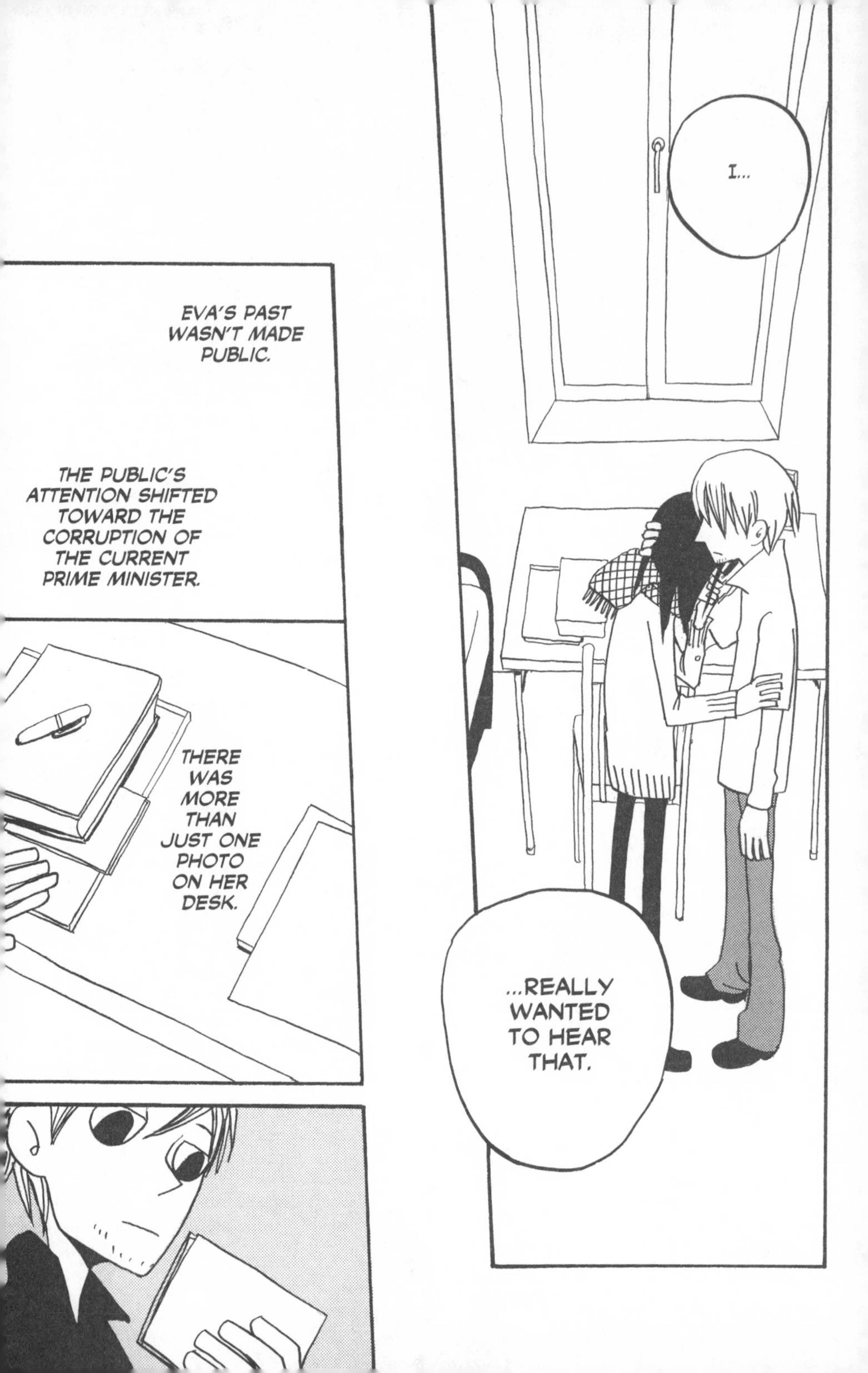
I...
...REALLY WANTED TO HEAR THAT.
EVA'S PAST WASN'T MADE PUBLIC.
THE PUBLIC'S ATTENTION SHIFTED TOWARD THE CORRUPTION OF THE CURRENT PRIME MINISTER.
THERE WAS MORE THAN JUST ONE PHOTO ON HER DESK.

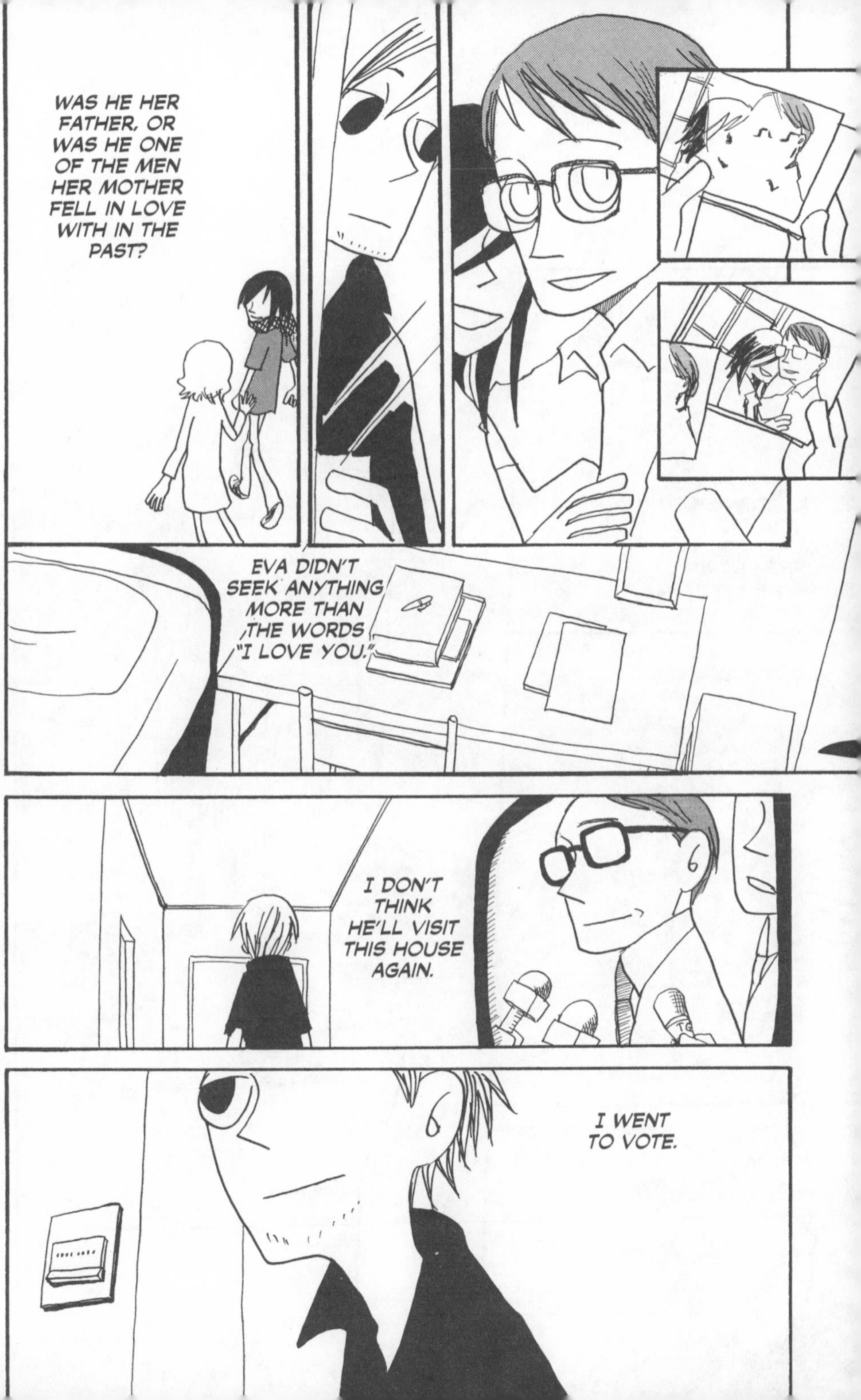
WAS HE HER FATHER, OR WAS HE ONE OF THE MEN HER MOTHER FELL IN LOVE WITH IN THE PAST?
EVA DIDN'T SEEK ANYTHING MORE THAN THE WORDS "I LOVE YOU."
I DON'T THINK HE'LL VISIT THIS HOUSE AGAIN.
I WENT TO VOTE.

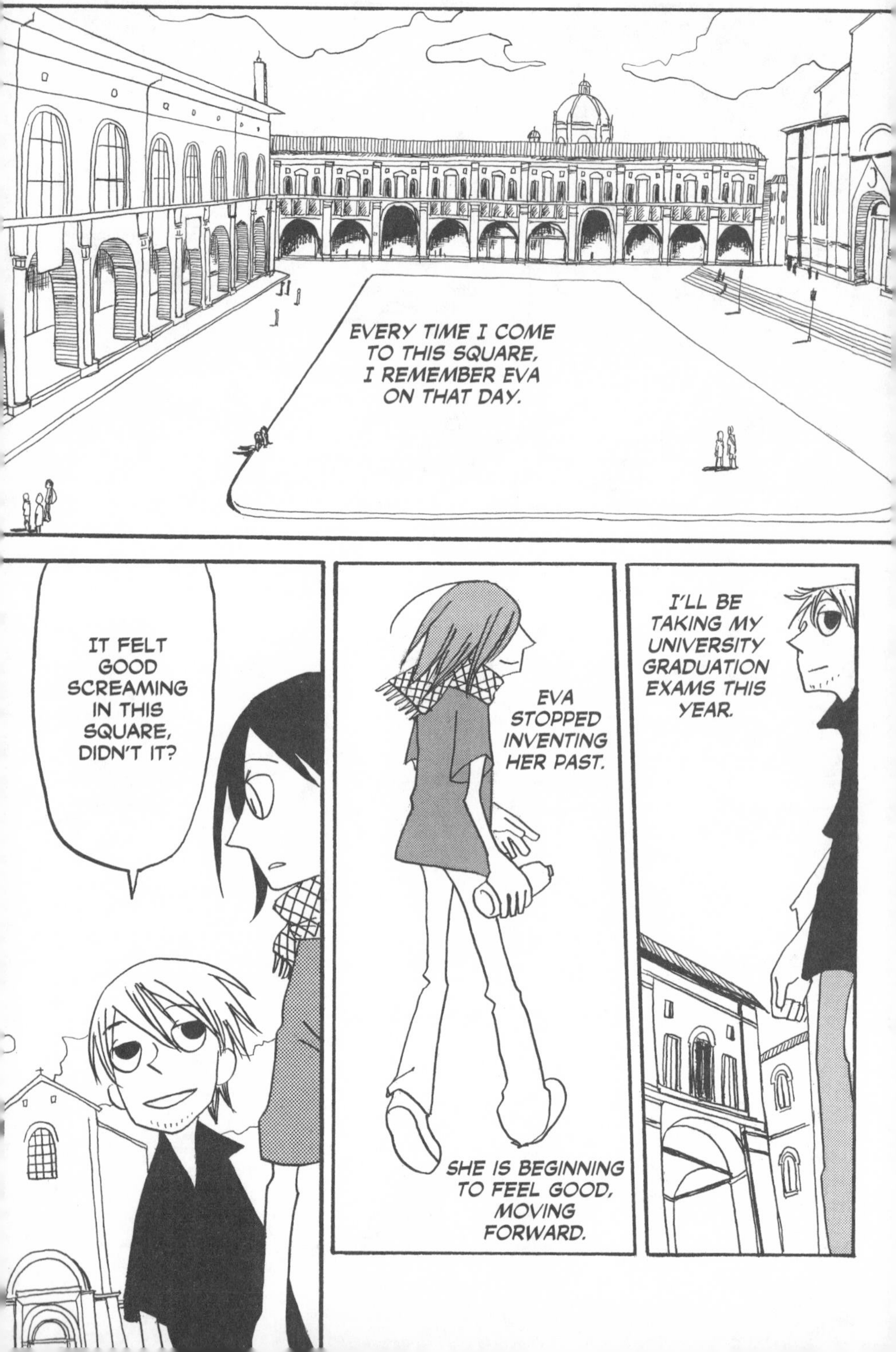
EVERY TIME I COME TO THIS SQUARE, I REMEMBER EVA ON THAT DAY.
I'LL BE TAKING MY UNIVERSITY GRADUATION EXAMS THIS YEAR.
EVA STOPPED INVENTING HER PAST.
SHE IS BEGINNING TO FEEL GOOD, MOVING FORWARD.
IT FELT GOOD SCREAMING IN THIS SQUARE, DIDN'T IT?

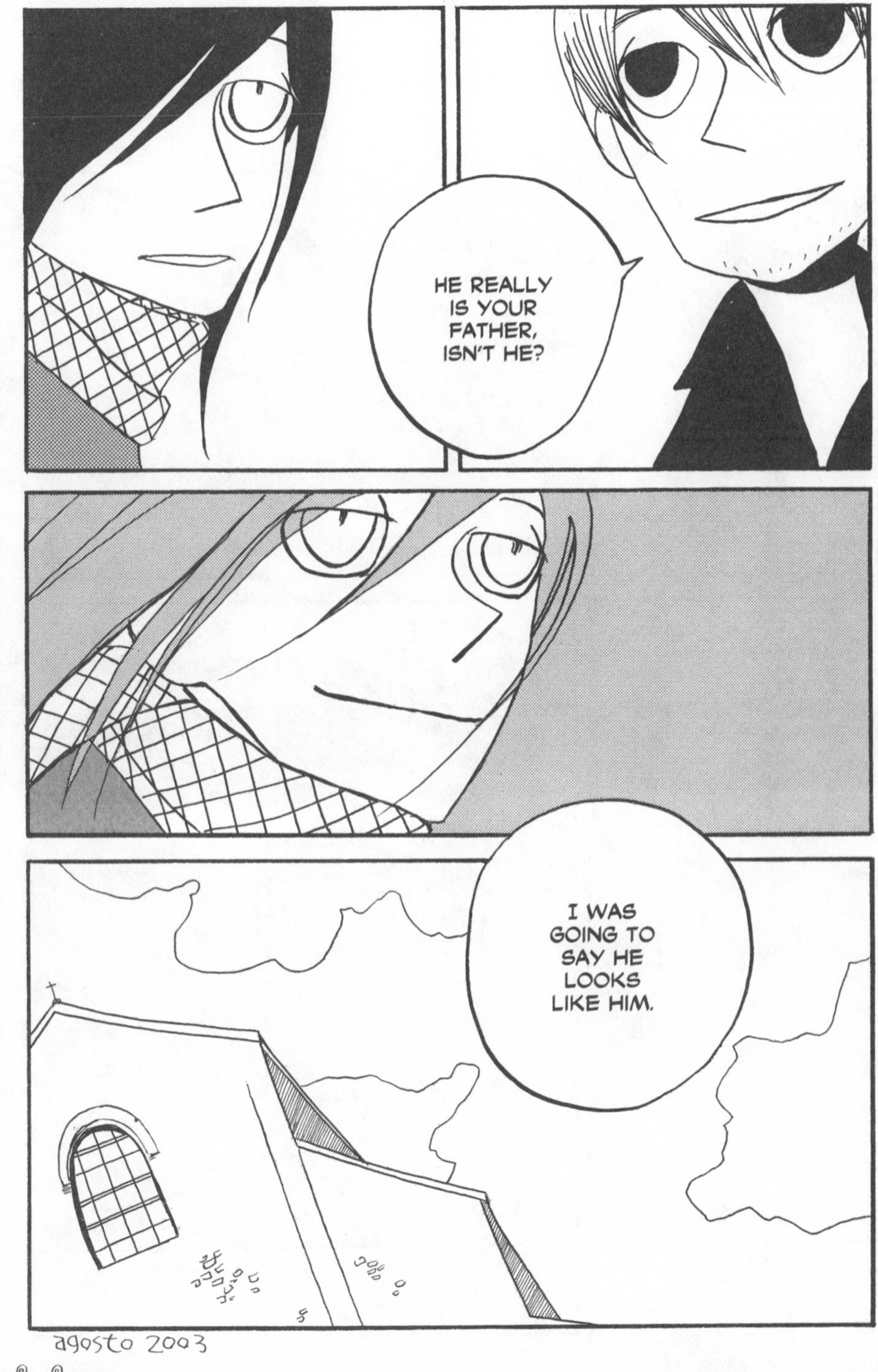
HE REALLY IS YOUR FATHER, ISN'T HE?
I WAS GOING TO SAY HE LOOKS LIKE HIM.
agosto 2003
fine.

Eva's Memory
Eva's Memory (Dojinshi)
Published in November 2004

2004

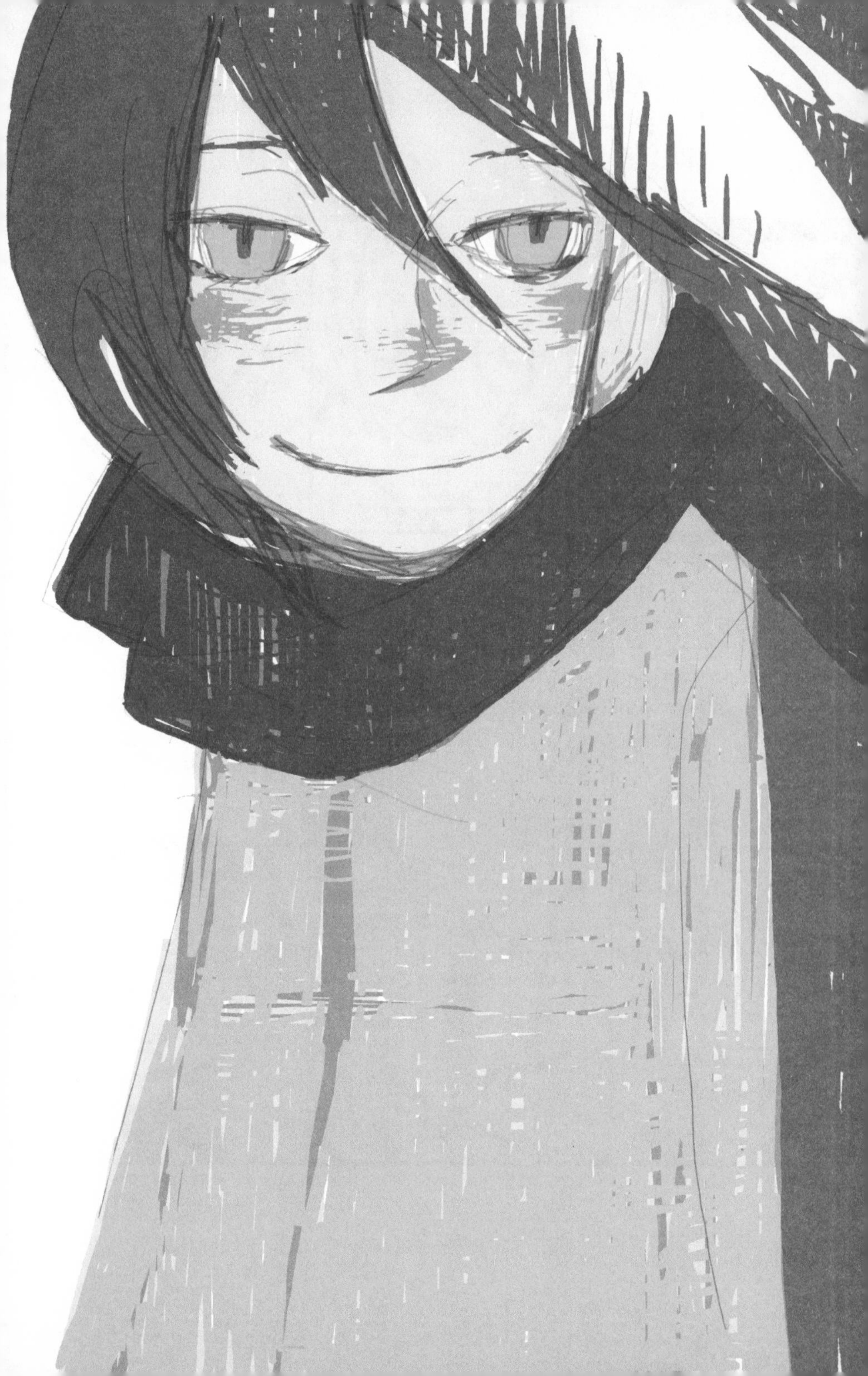

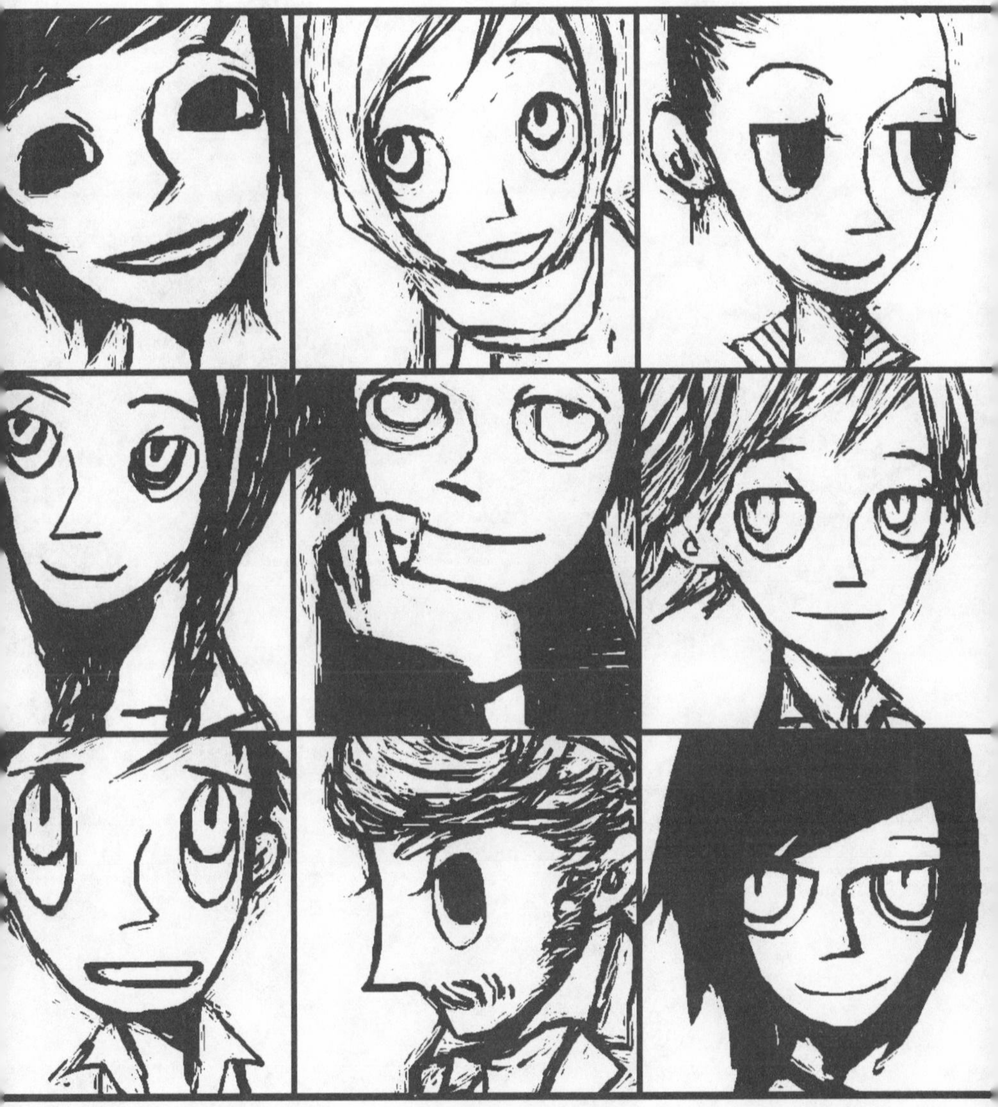

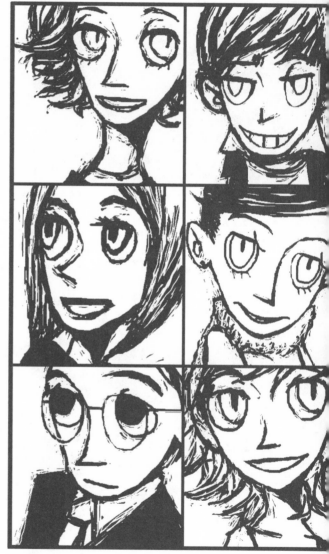

2003

Natsume Ono

Tesoro 3

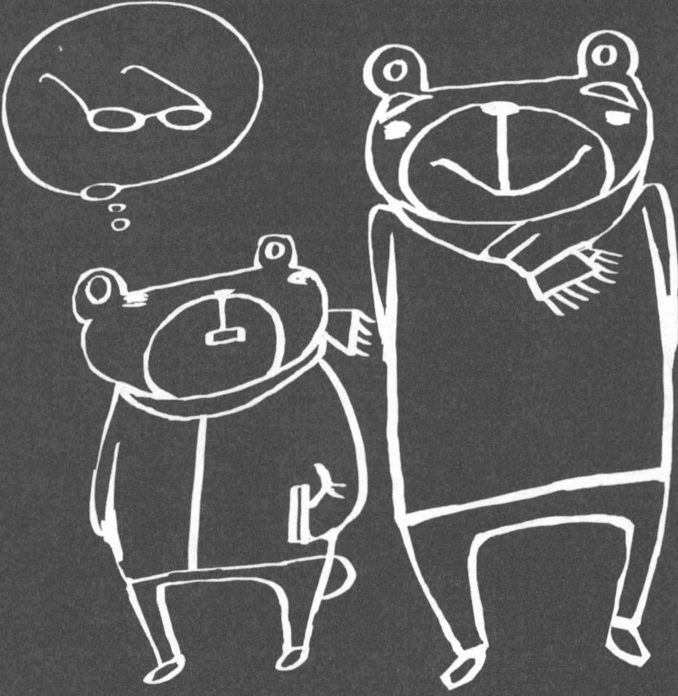

senza titolo #1

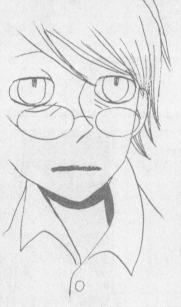

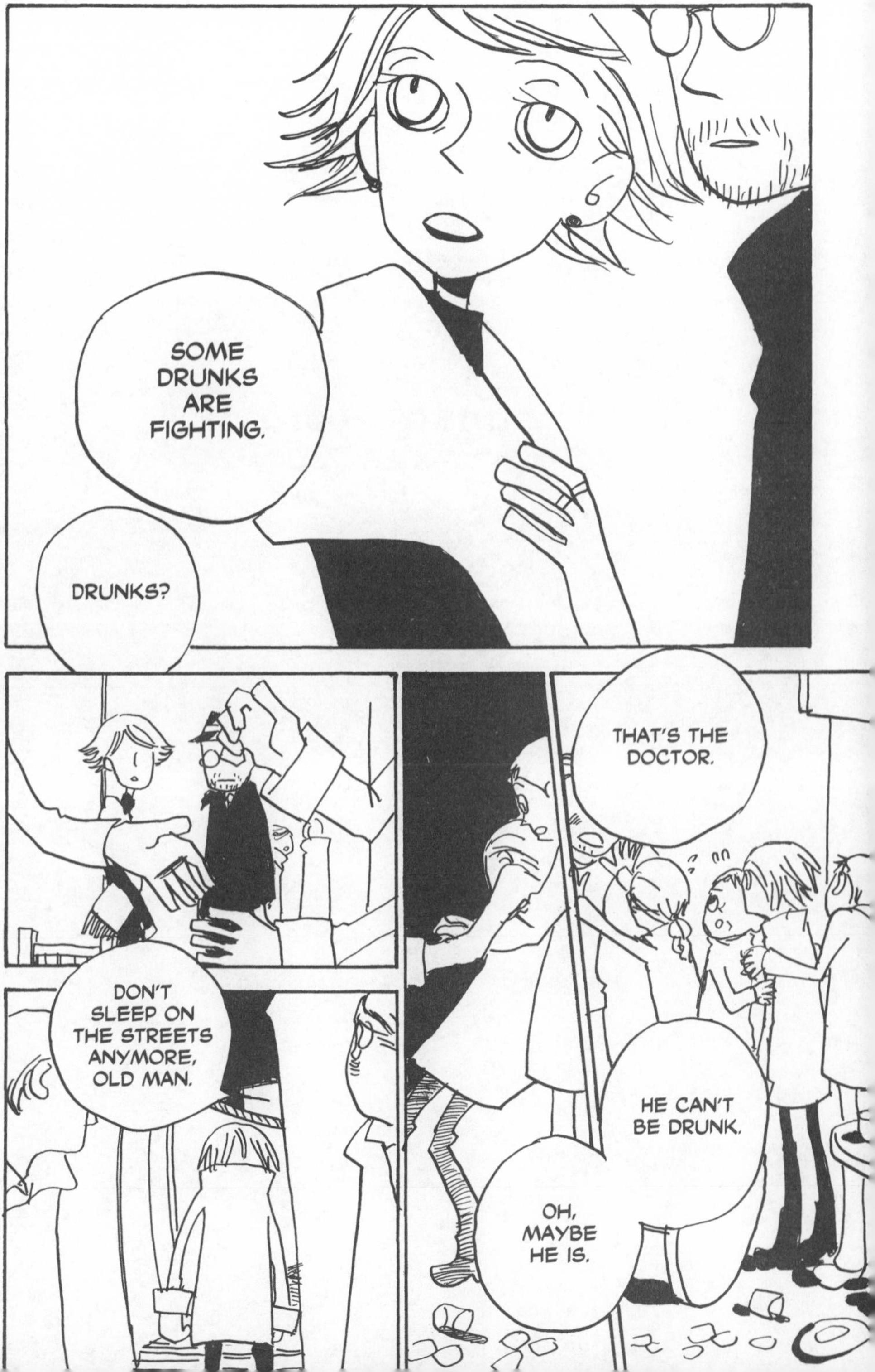
SOME DRUNKS ARE FIGHTING.
DRUNKS?
THAT'S THE DOCTOR.
HE CAN'T BE DRUNK.
OH, MAYBE HE IS.
DON'T SLEEP ON THE STREETS ANYMORE, OLD MAN.

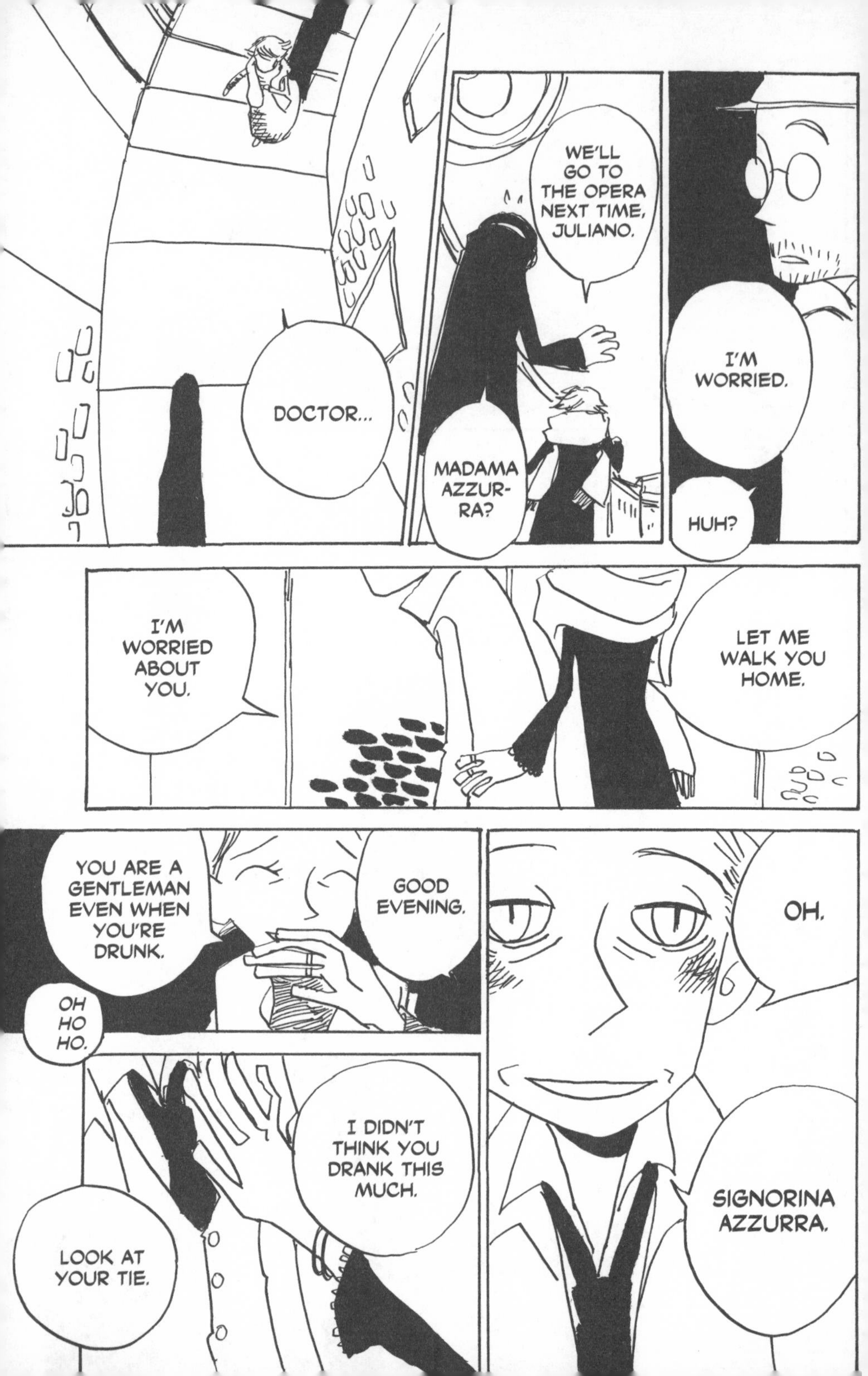
I'M WORRIED.
HUH?
WE'LL GO TO THE OPERA NEXT TIME, JULIANO.
MADAMA AZZUR-RA?
DOCTOR...
LET ME WALK YOU HOME.
I'M WORRIED ABOUT YOU.
OH.
SIGNORINA AZZURRA.
GOOD EVENING.
YOU ARE A GENTLEMAN EVEN WHEN YOU'RE DRUNK.
OH HO HO.
I DIDN'T THINK YOU DRANK THIS MUCH.
LOOK AT YOUR TIE.

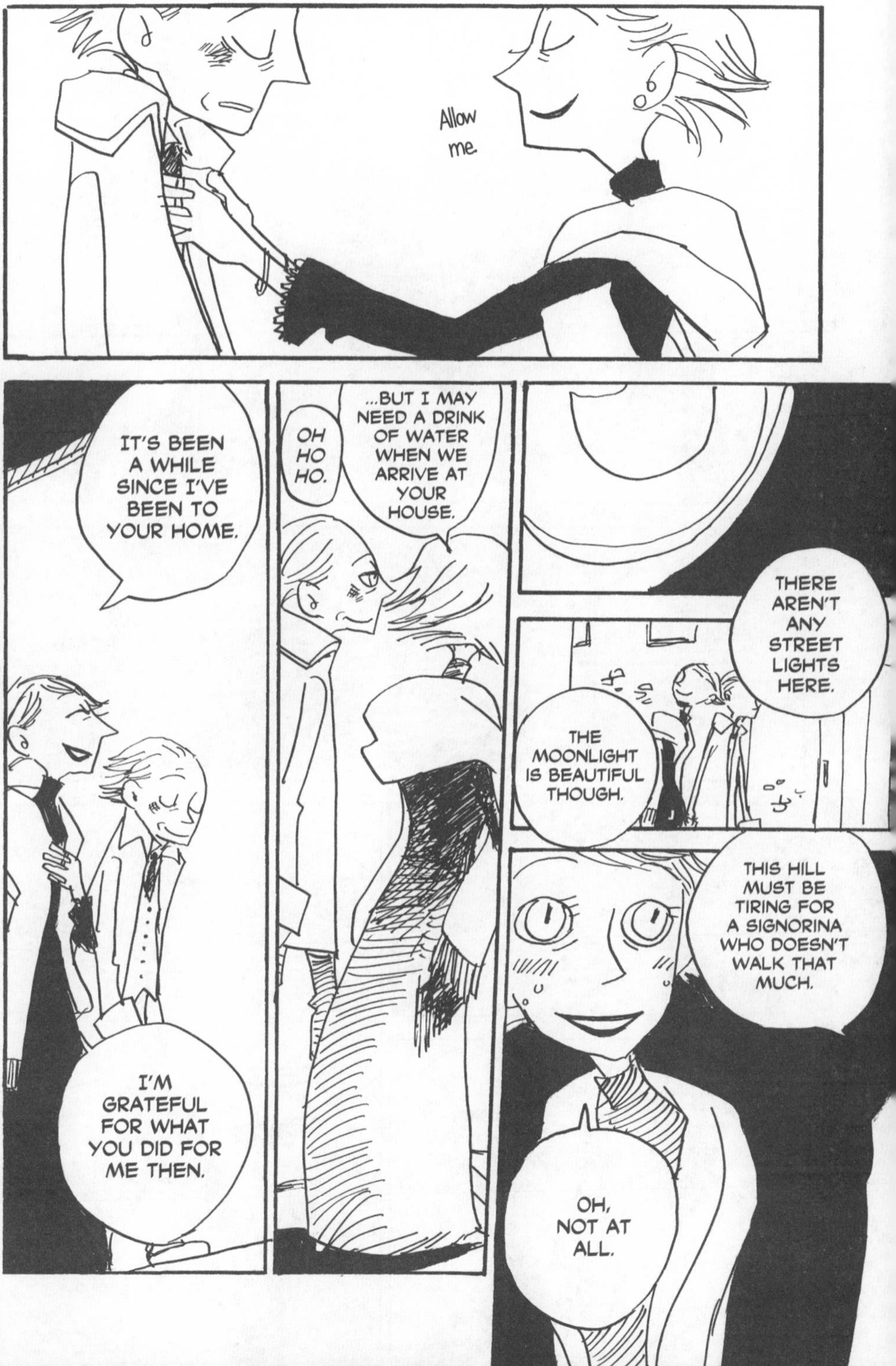
Allow me.
THERE AREN'T ANY STREET LIGHTS HERE.
THE MOONLIGHT IS BEAUTIFUL THOUGH.
THIS HILL MUST BE TIRING FOR A SIGNORINA WHO DOESN'T WALK THAT MUCH.
OH, NOT AT ALL.
...BUT I MAY NEED A DRINK OF WATER WHEN WE ARRIVE AT YOUR HOUSE.
OH HO HO.
IT'S BEEN A WHILE SINCE I'VE BEEN TO YOUR HOME.
I'M GRATEFUL FOR WHAT YOU DID FOR ME THEN.

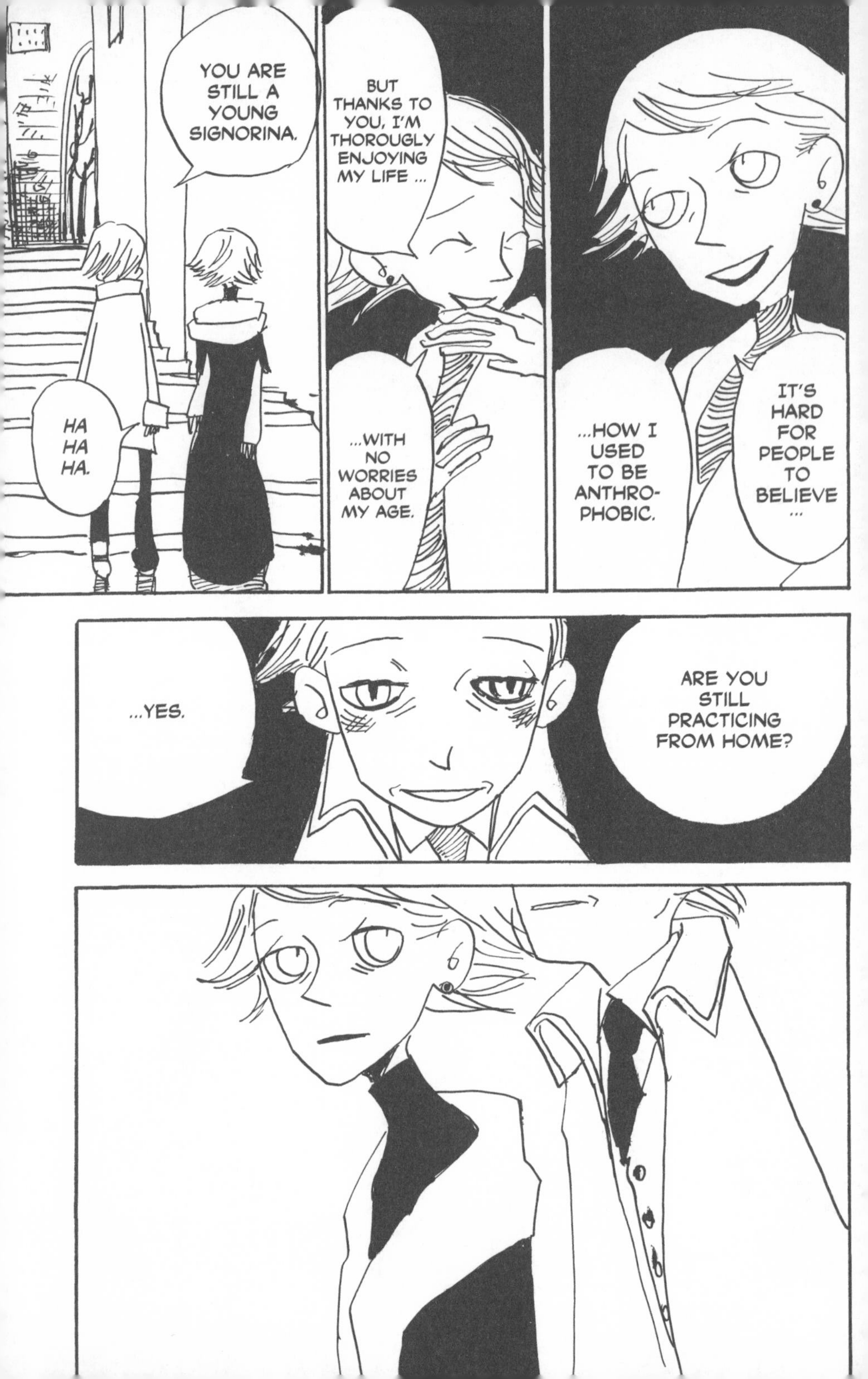
YOU ARE STILL A YOUNG SIGNORINA.
HA HA HA.
BUT THANKS TO YOU, I'M THOROUGLY ENJOYING MY LIFE ...
...WITH NO WORRIES ABOUT MY AGE.
IT'S HARD FOR PEOPLE TO BELIEVE ...
...HOW I USED TO BE ANTHRO-PHOBIC.
ARE YOU STILL PRACTICING FROM HOME?
...YES.

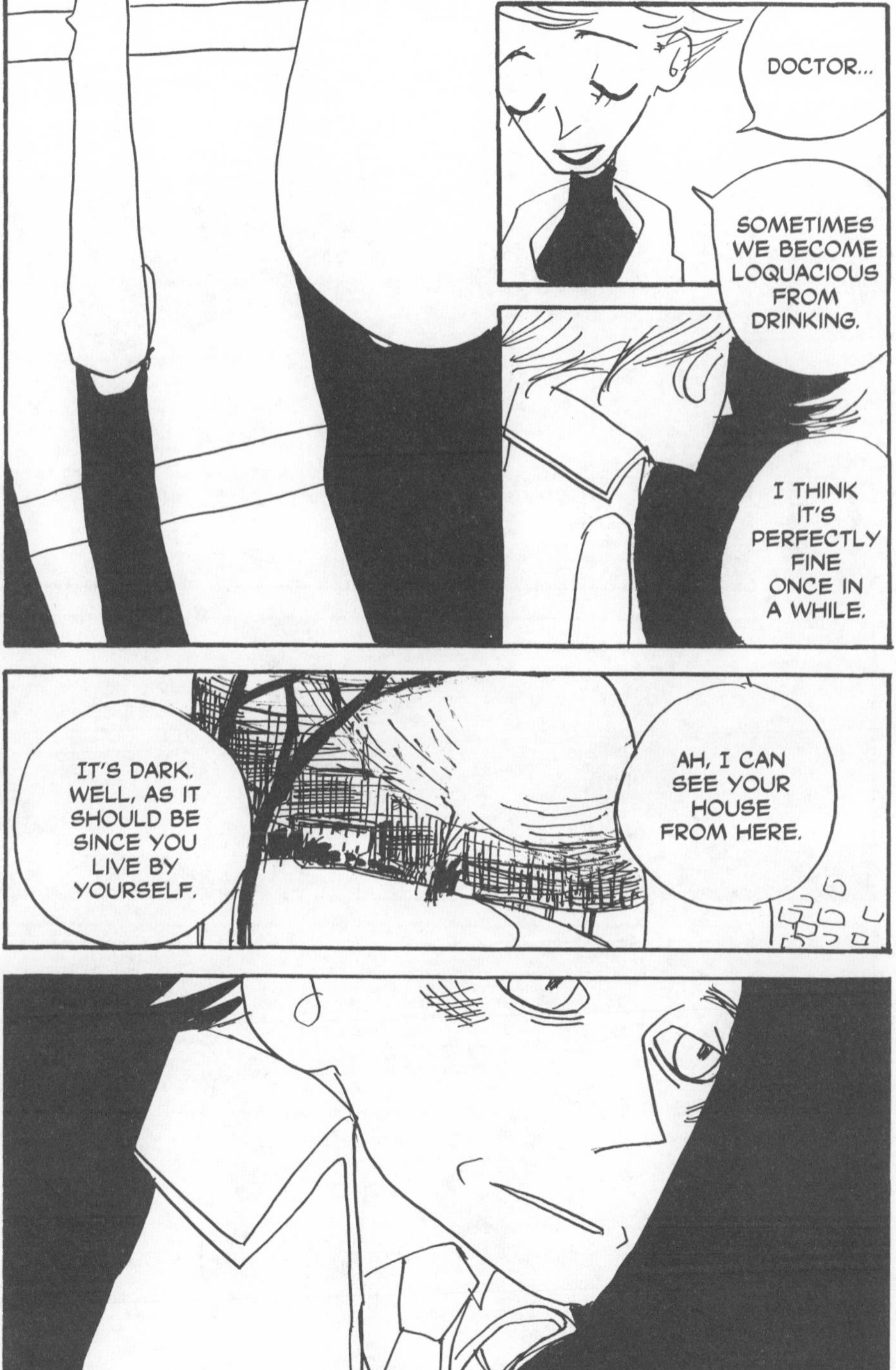
DOCTOR...
SOMETIMES WE BECOME LOQUACIOUS FROM DRINKING.
I THINK IT'S PERFECTLY FINE ONCE IN A WHILE.
AH, I CAN SEE YOUR HOUSE FROM HERE.
IT'S DARK. WELL, AS IT SHOULD BE SINCE YOU LIVE BY YOURSELF.

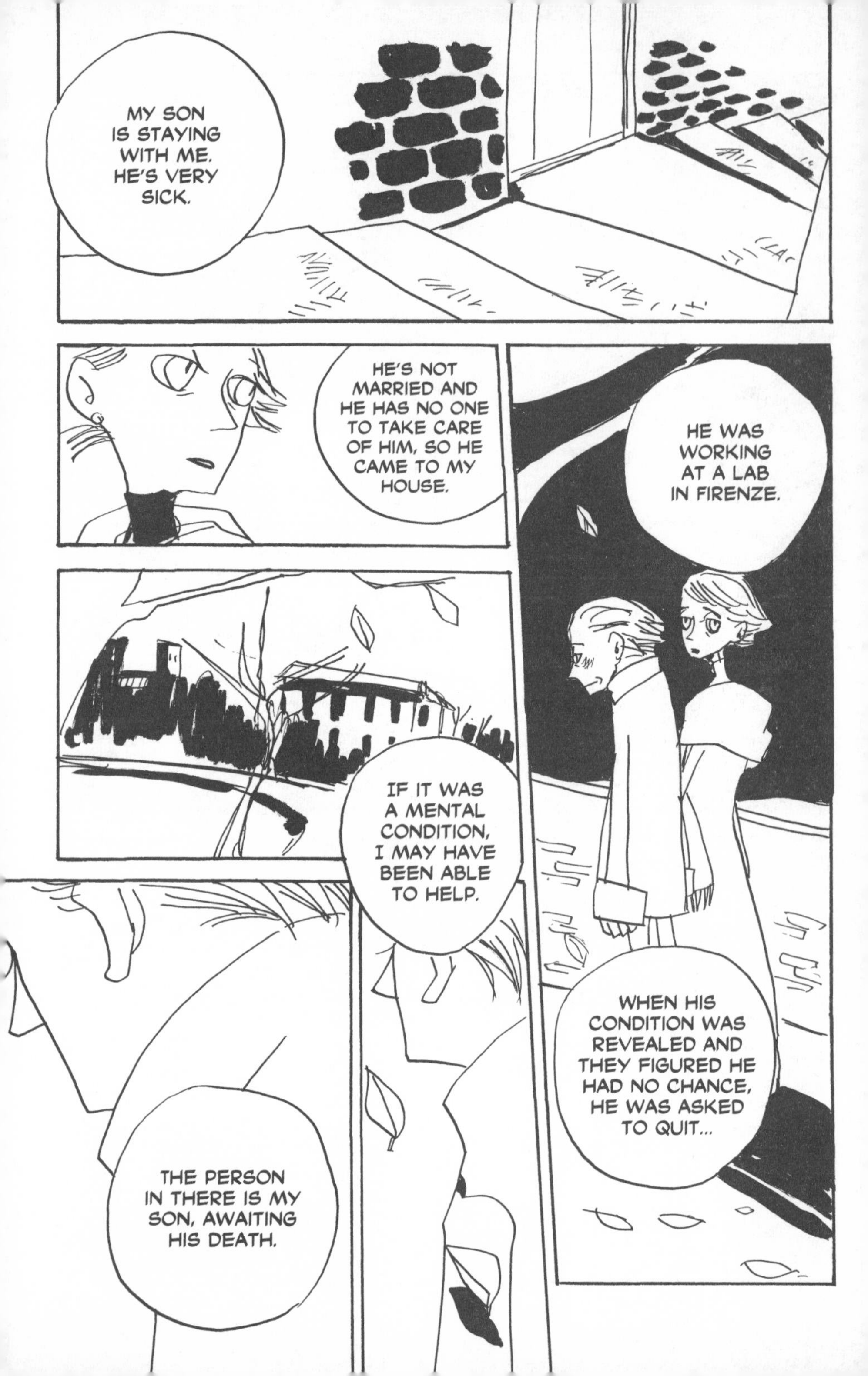
MY SON IS STAYING WITH ME. HE'S VERY SICK.
HE WAS WORKING AT A LAB IN FIRENZE.
WHEN HIS CONDITION WAS REVEALED AND THEY FIGURED HE HAD NO CHANCE, HE WAS ASKED TO QUIT...
HE'S NOT MARRIED AND HE HAS NO ONE TO TAKE CARE OF HIM, SO HE CAME TO MY HOUSE.
IF IT WAS A MENTAL CONDITION, I MAY HAVE BEEN ABLE TO HELP.
THE PERSON IN THERE IS MY SON, AWAITING HIS DEATH.

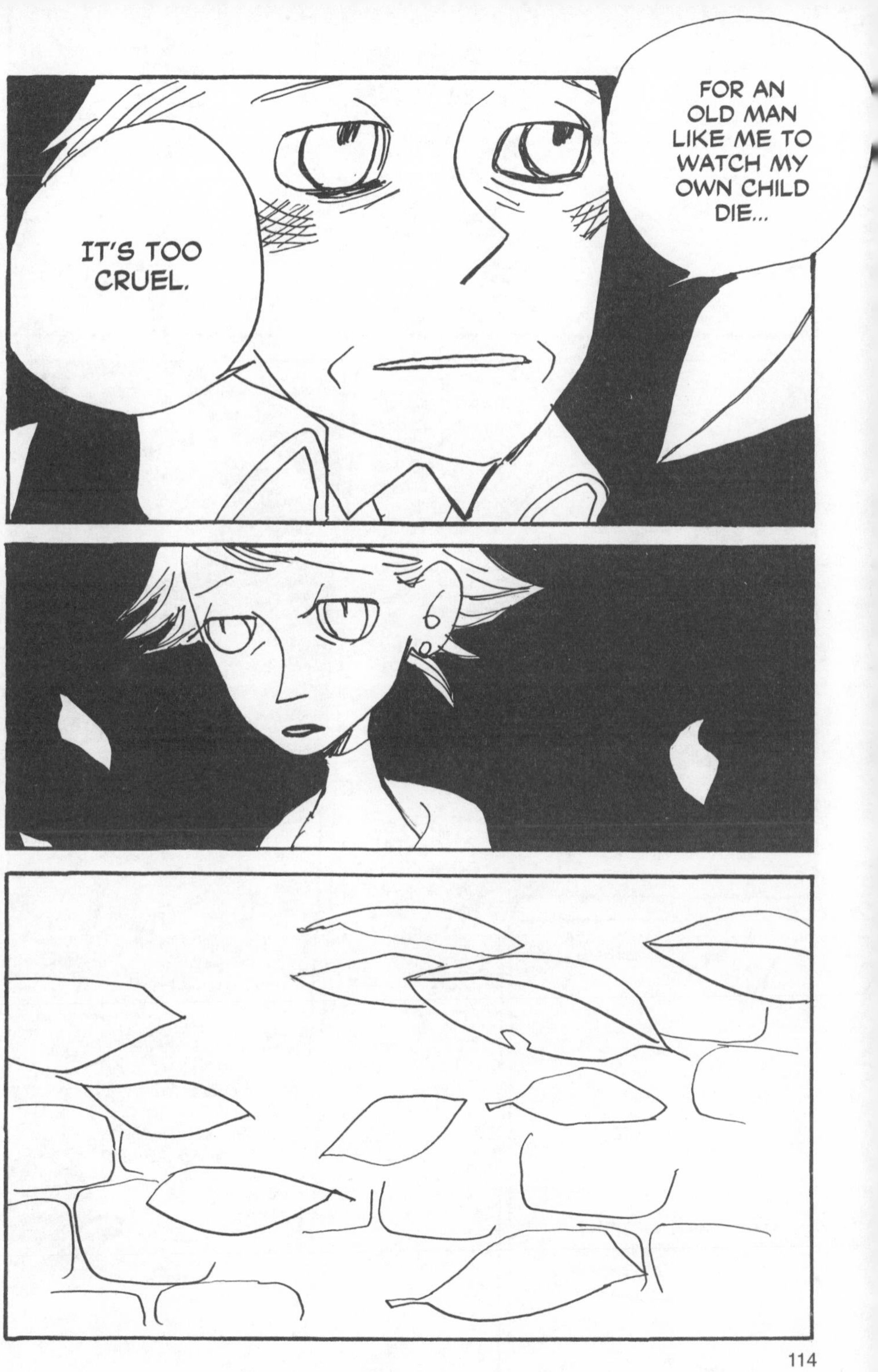
FOR AN OLD MAN LIKE ME TO WATCH MY OWN CHILD DIE...
IT'S TOO CRUEL.

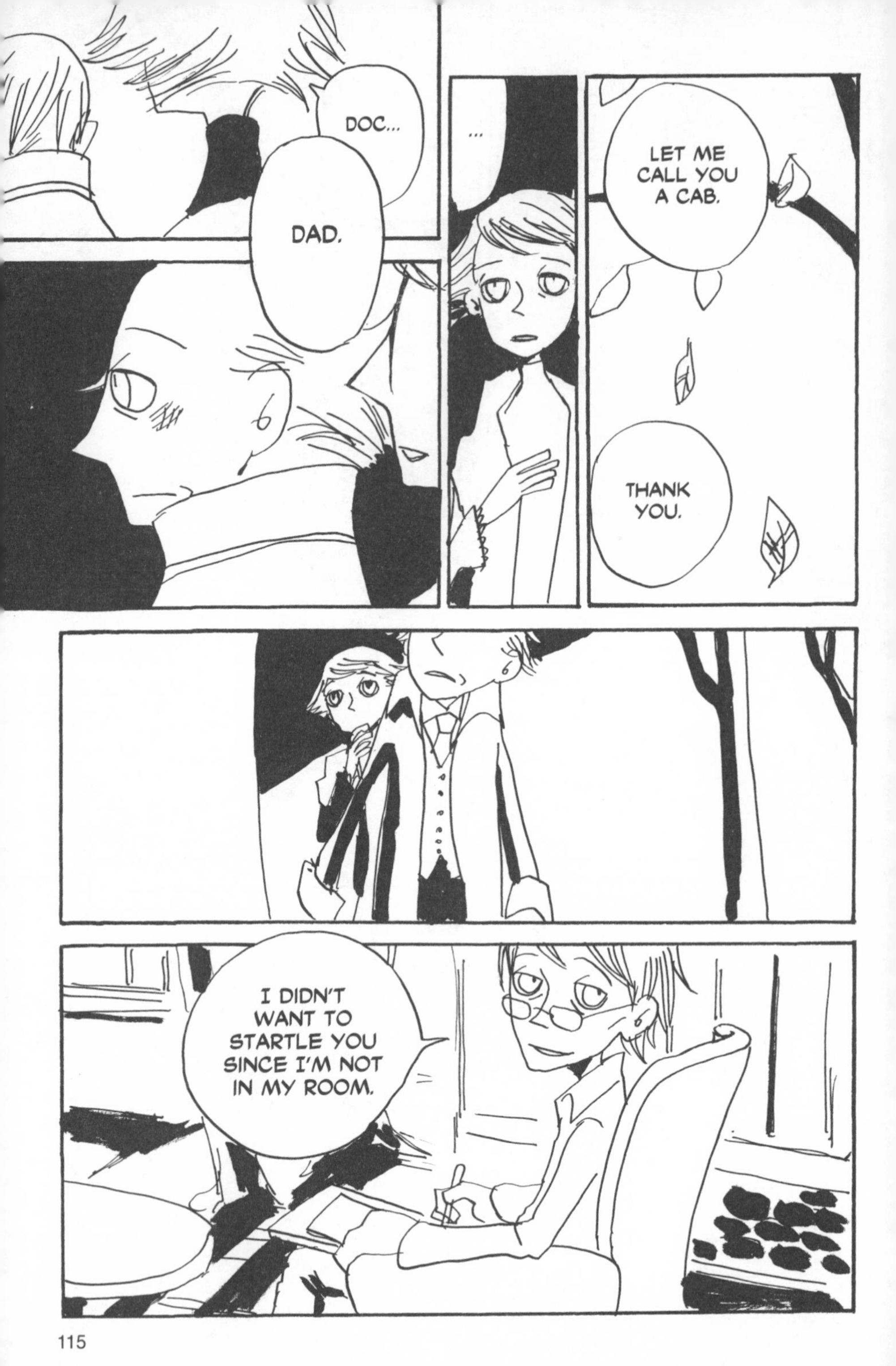
LET ME CALL YOU A CAB.
THANK YOU.
...
DOC...
DAD.
I DIDN'T WANT TO STARTLE YOU SINCE I'M NOT IN MY ROOM.

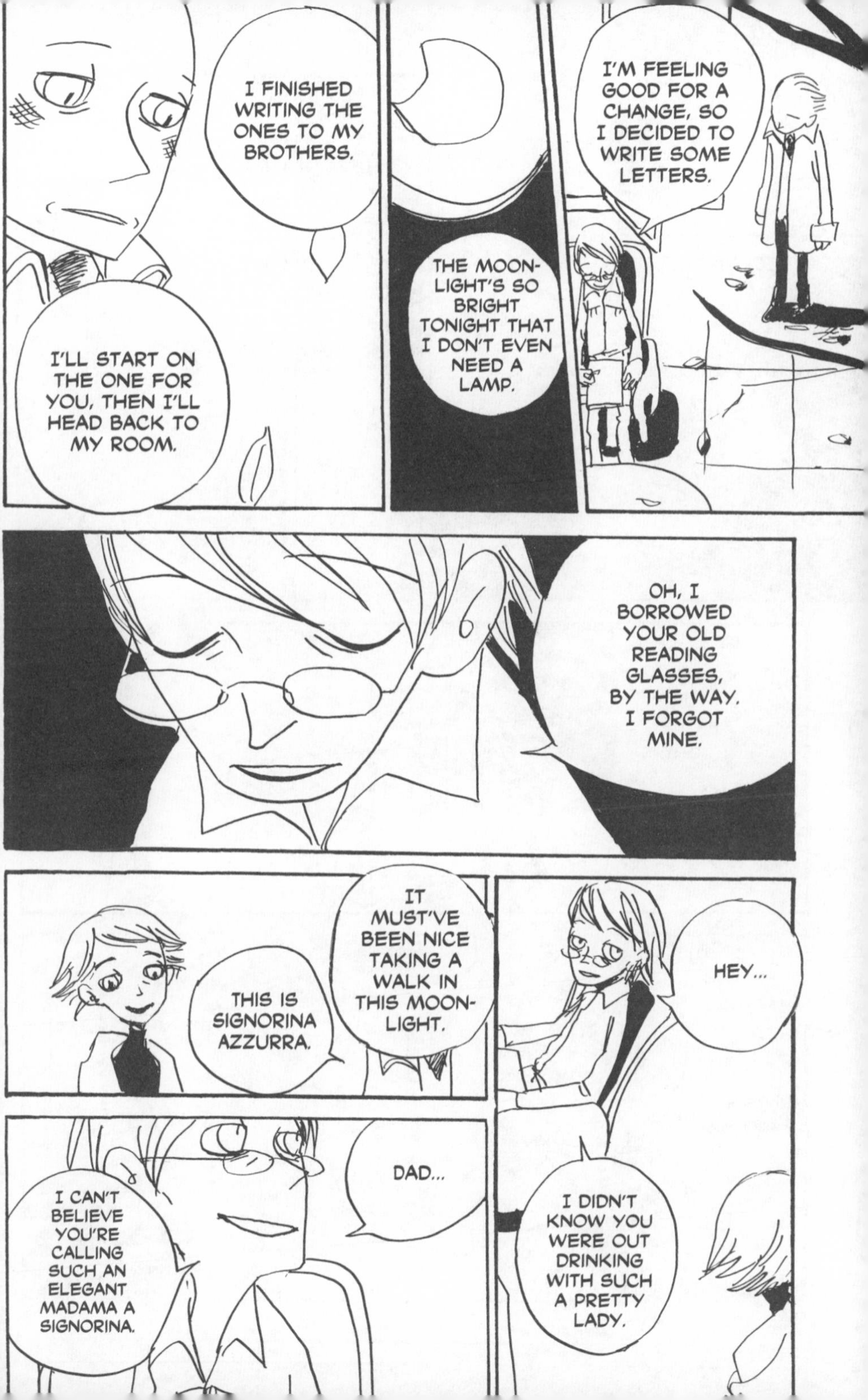
I'M FEELING GOOD FOR A CHANGE, SO I DECIDED TO WRITE SOME LETTERS.
THE MOON-LIGHT'S SO BRIGHT TONIGHT THAT I DON'T EVEN NEED A LAMP.
I FINISHED WRITING THE ONES TO MY BROTHERS.
I'LL START ON THE ONE FOR YOU, THEN I'LL HEAD BACK TO MY ROOM.
OH, I BORROWED YOUR OLD READING GLASSES, BY THE WAY. I FORGOT MINE.
HEY...
I DIDN'T KNOW YOU WERE OUT DRINKING WITH SUCH A PRETTY LADY.
IT MUST'VE BEEN NICE TAKING A WALK IN THIS MOON-LIGHT.
THIS IS SIGNORINA AZZURRA.
DAD...
I CAN'T BELIEVE YOU'RE CALLING SUCH AN ELEGANT MADAMA A SIGNORINA.

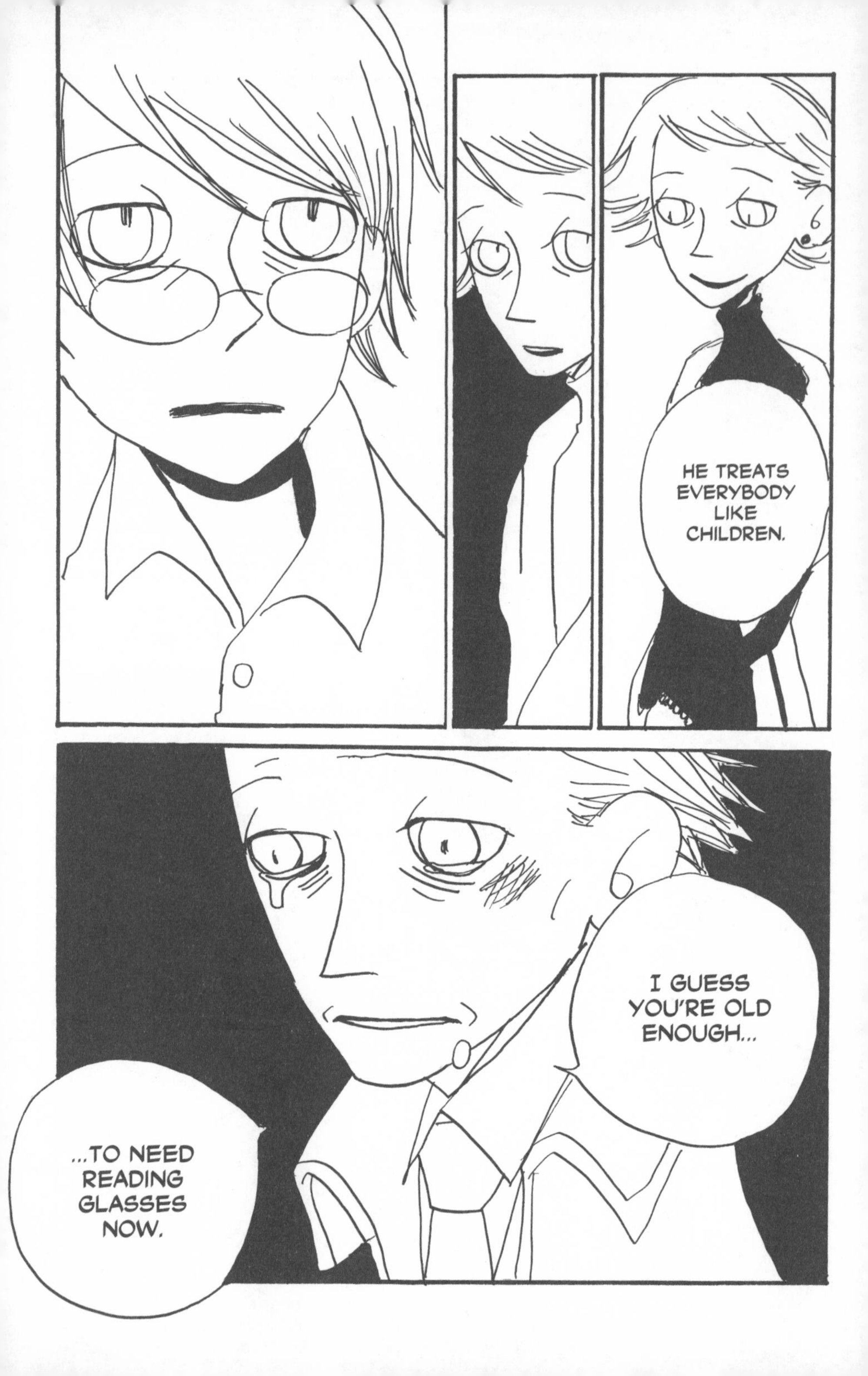
HE TREATS EVERYBODY LIKE CHILDREN.
I GUESS YOU'RE OLD ENOUGH...
...TO NEED READING GLASSES NOW.

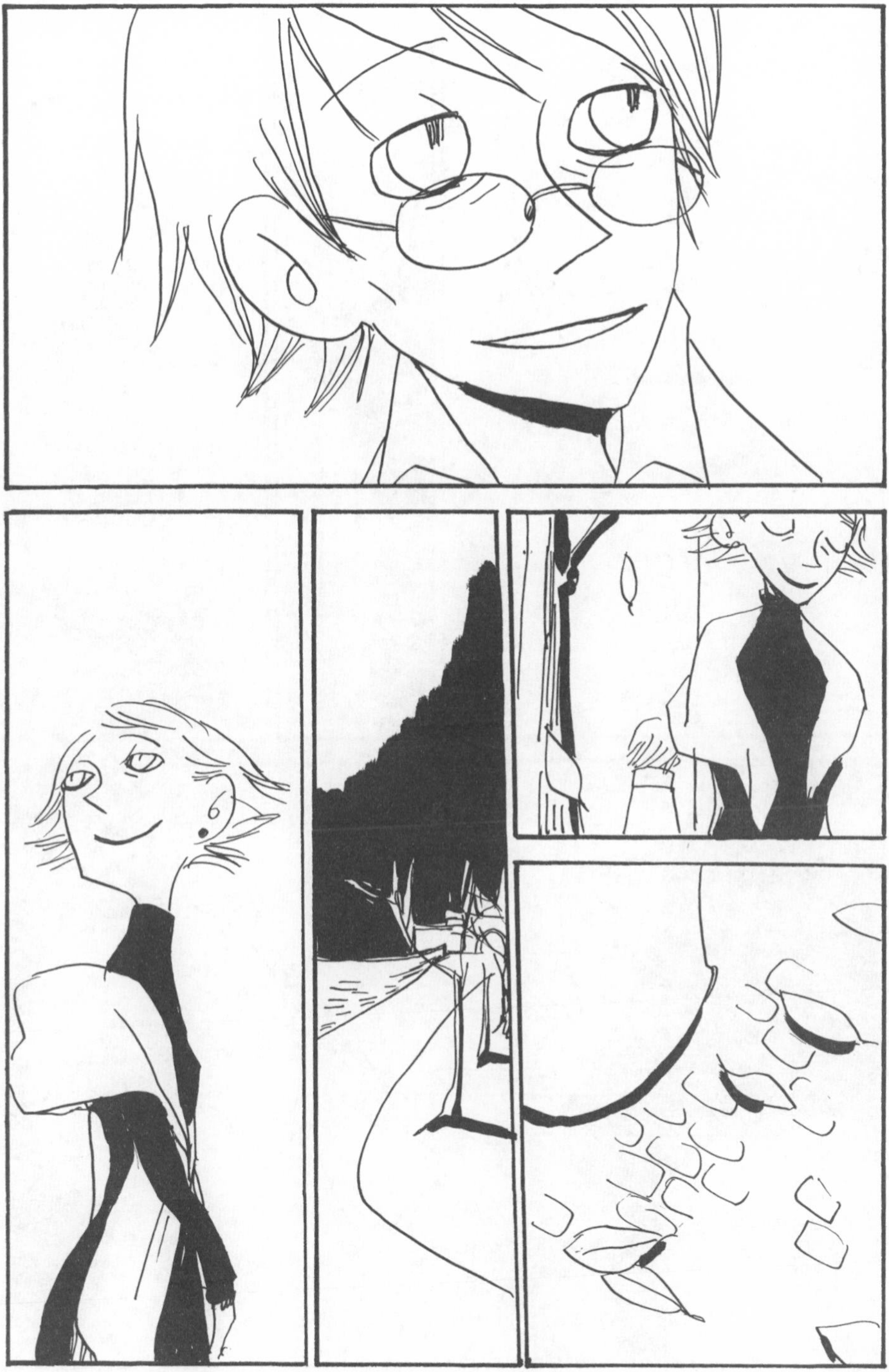

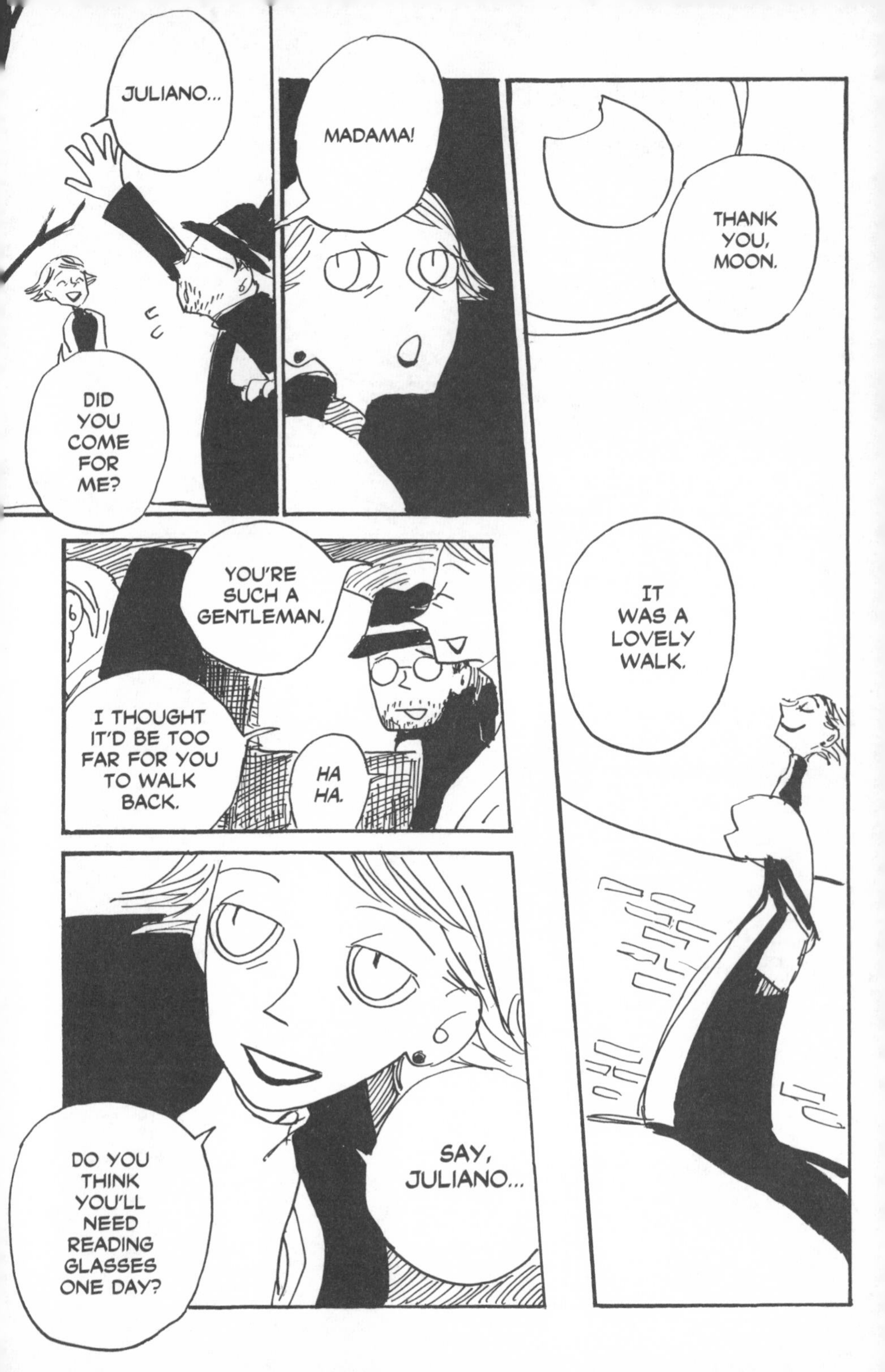
THANK YOU, MOON.
IT WAS A LOVELY WALK.
MADAMA!
JULIANO...
DID YOU COME FOR ME?
I THOUGHT IT'D BE TOO FAR FOR YOU TO WALK BACK.
YOU'RE SUCH A GENTLEMAN.
HA HA.
SAY, JULIANO...
DO YOU THINK YOU'LL NEED READING GLASSES ONE DAY?

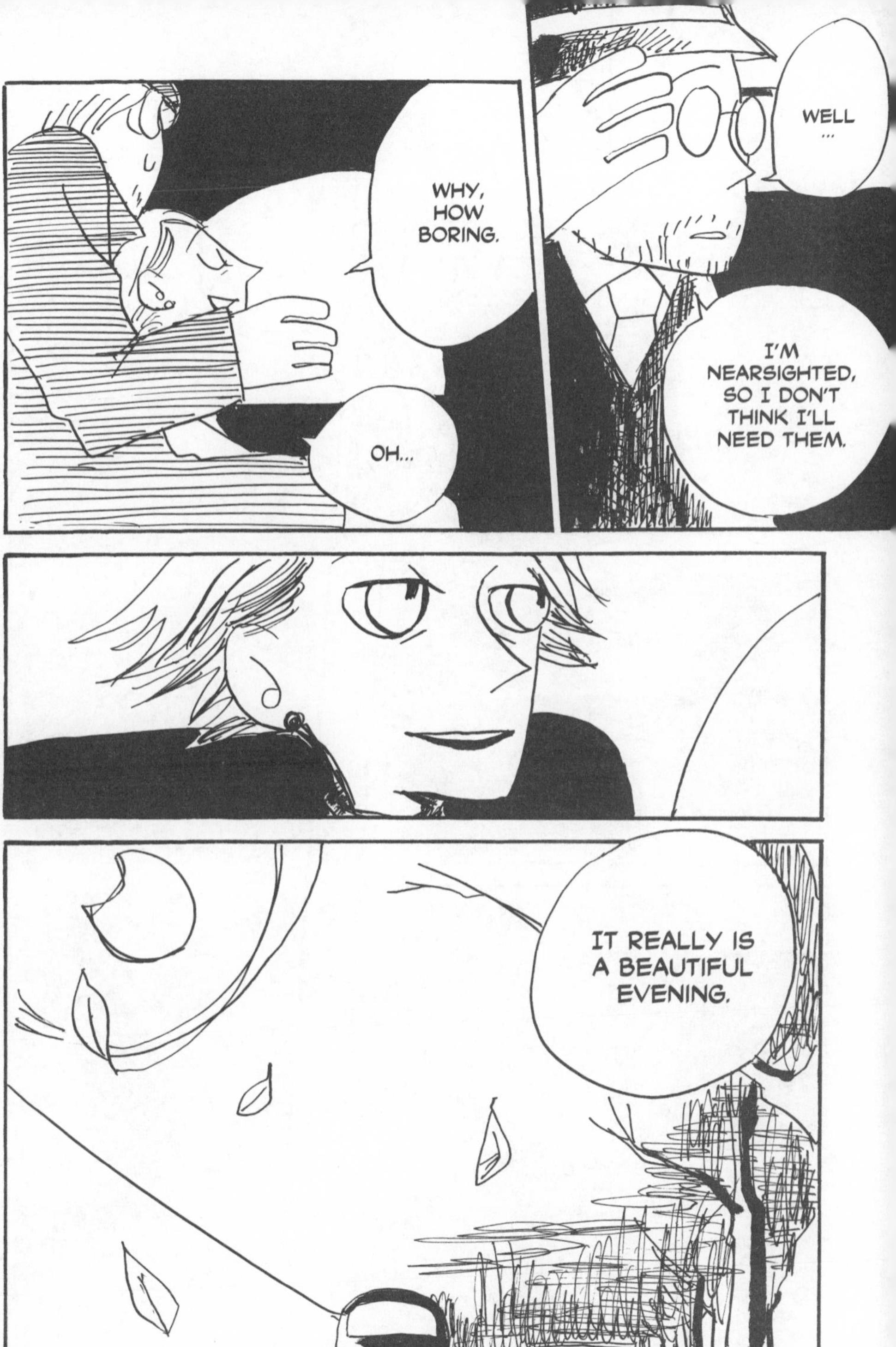
WELL ...
I'M NEARSIGHTED, SO I DON'T THINK I'LL NEED THEM.
WHY, HOW BORING.
OH...
IT REALLY IS A BEAUTIFUL EVENING.

fine.

***senza titolo* #1**
GENTILUOMO (Dojinshi)
Published in November 2003

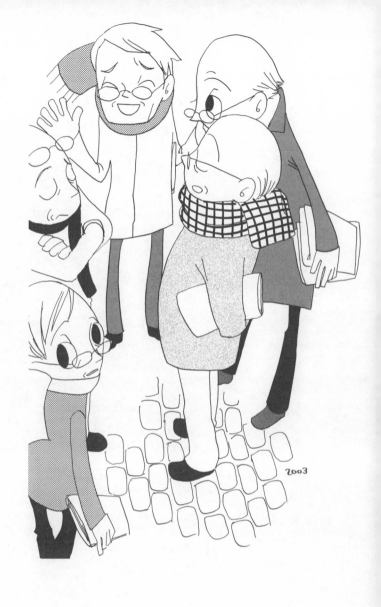

senza titolo #2

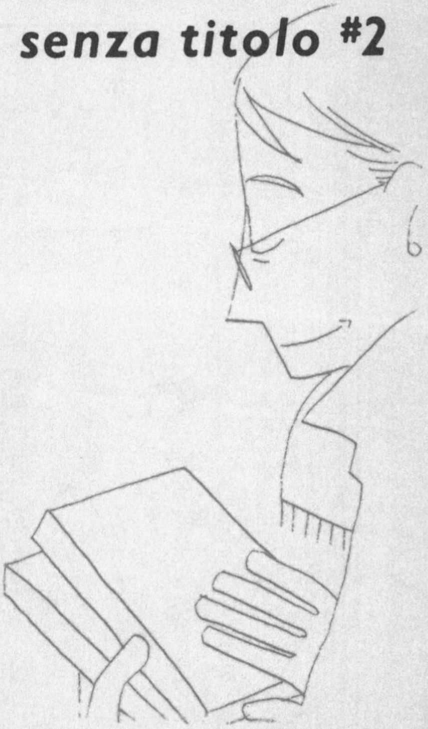

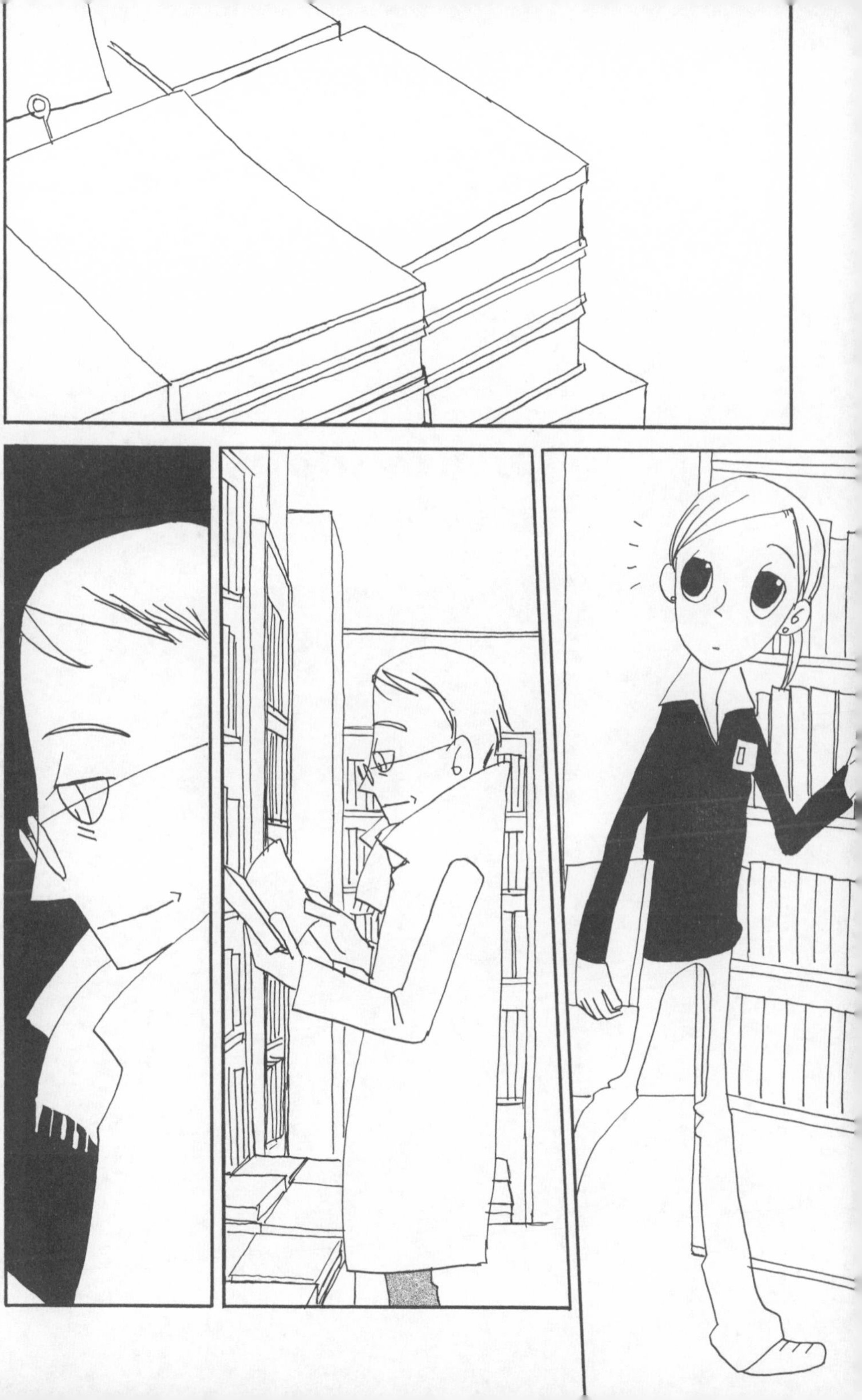

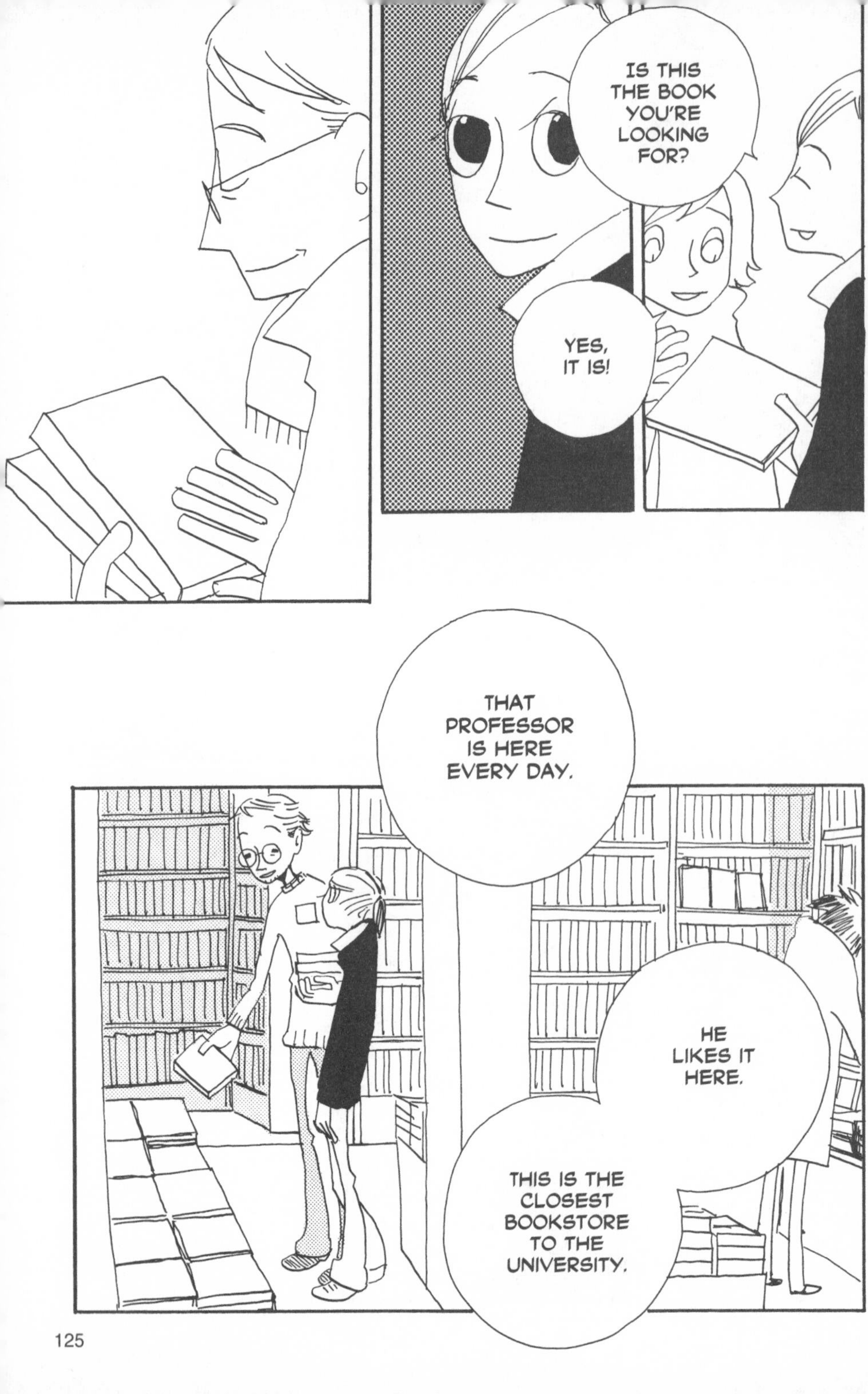
IS THIS THE BOOK YOU'RE LOOKING FOR?
YES, IT IS!
THAT PROFESSOR IS HERE EVERY DAY.
HE LIKES IT HERE.
THIS IS THE CLOSEST BOOKSTORE TO THE UNIVERSITY.

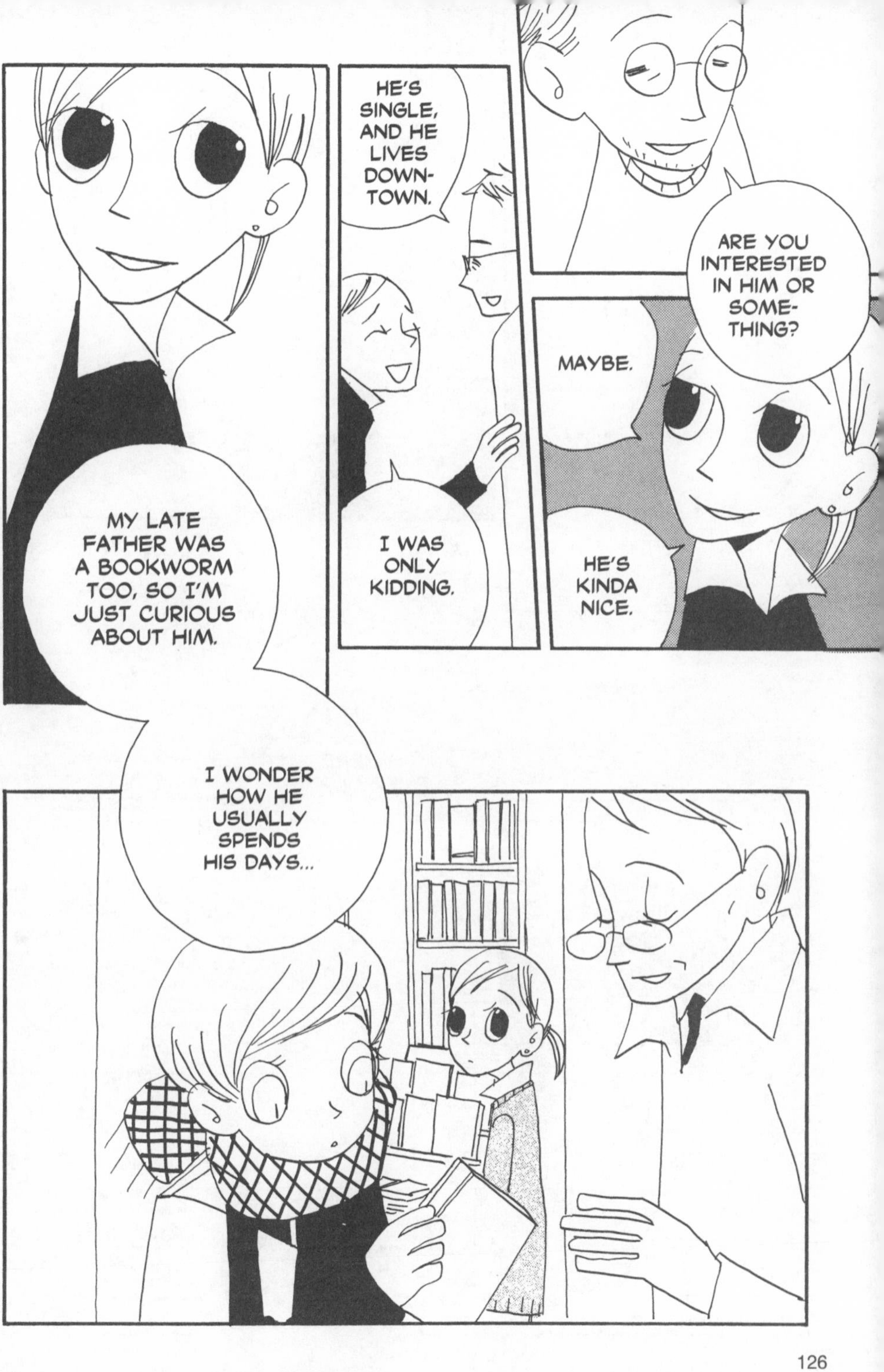
ARE YOU INTERESTED IN HIM OR SOME-THING?
MAYBE.
HE'S KINDA NICE.
HE'S SINGLE, AND HE LIVES DOWN-TOWN.
I WAS ONLY KIDDING.
MY LATE FATHER WAS A BOOKWORM TOO, SO I'M JUST CURIOUS ABOUT HIM.
I WONDER HOW HE USUALLY SPENDS HIS DAYS...

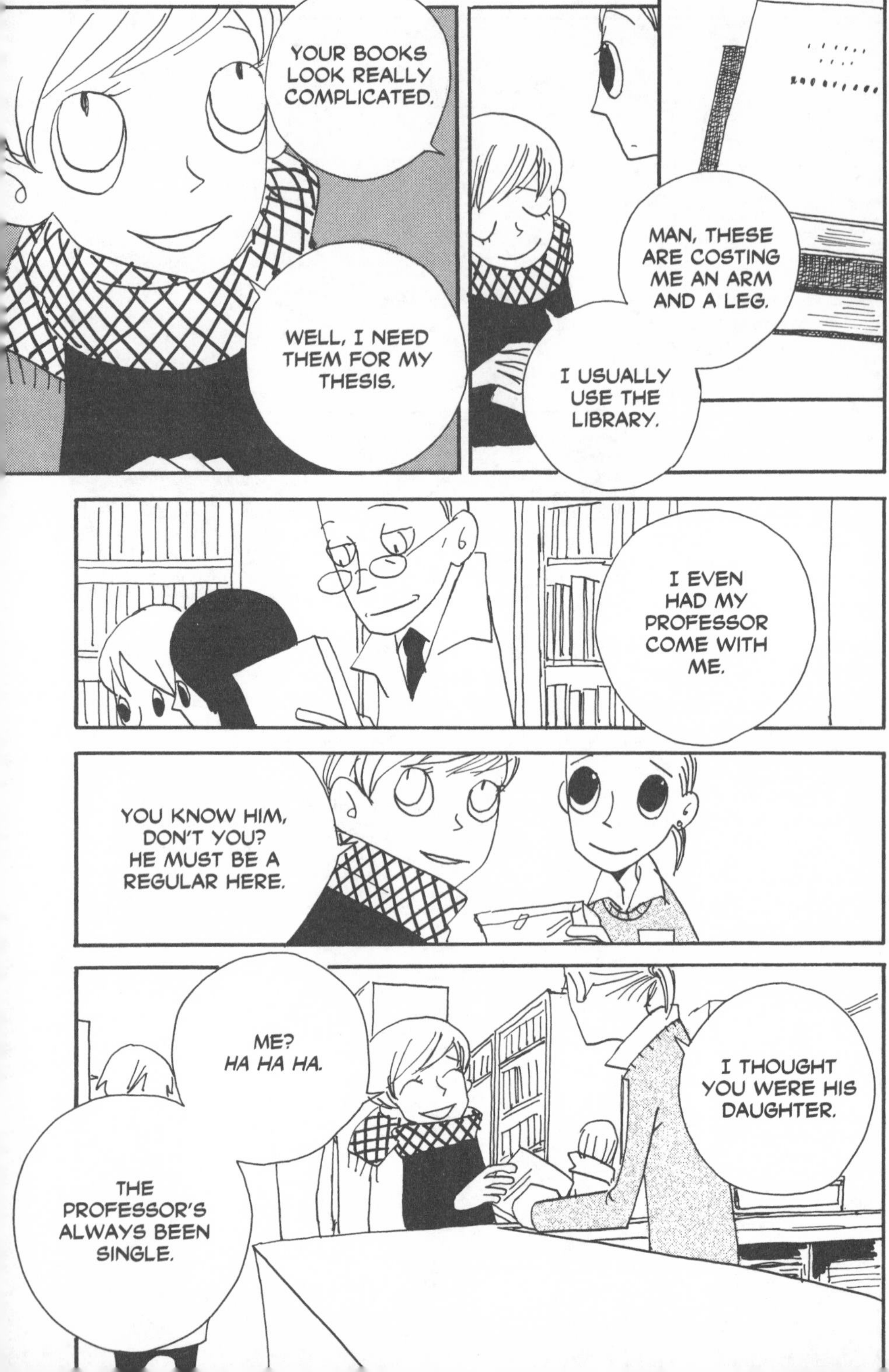
MAN, THESE ARE COSTING ME AN ARM AND A LEG.
I USUALLY USE THE LIBRARY.
YOUR BOOKS LOOK REALLY COMPLICATED.
WELL, I NEED THEM FOR MY THESIS.
I EVEN HAD MY PROFESSOR COME WITH ME.
YOU KNOW HIM, DON'T YOU? HE MUST BE A REGULAR HERE.
I THOUGHT YOU WERE HIS DAUGHTER.
ME? *HA HA HA.*
THE PROFESSOR'S ALWAYS BEEN SINGLE.

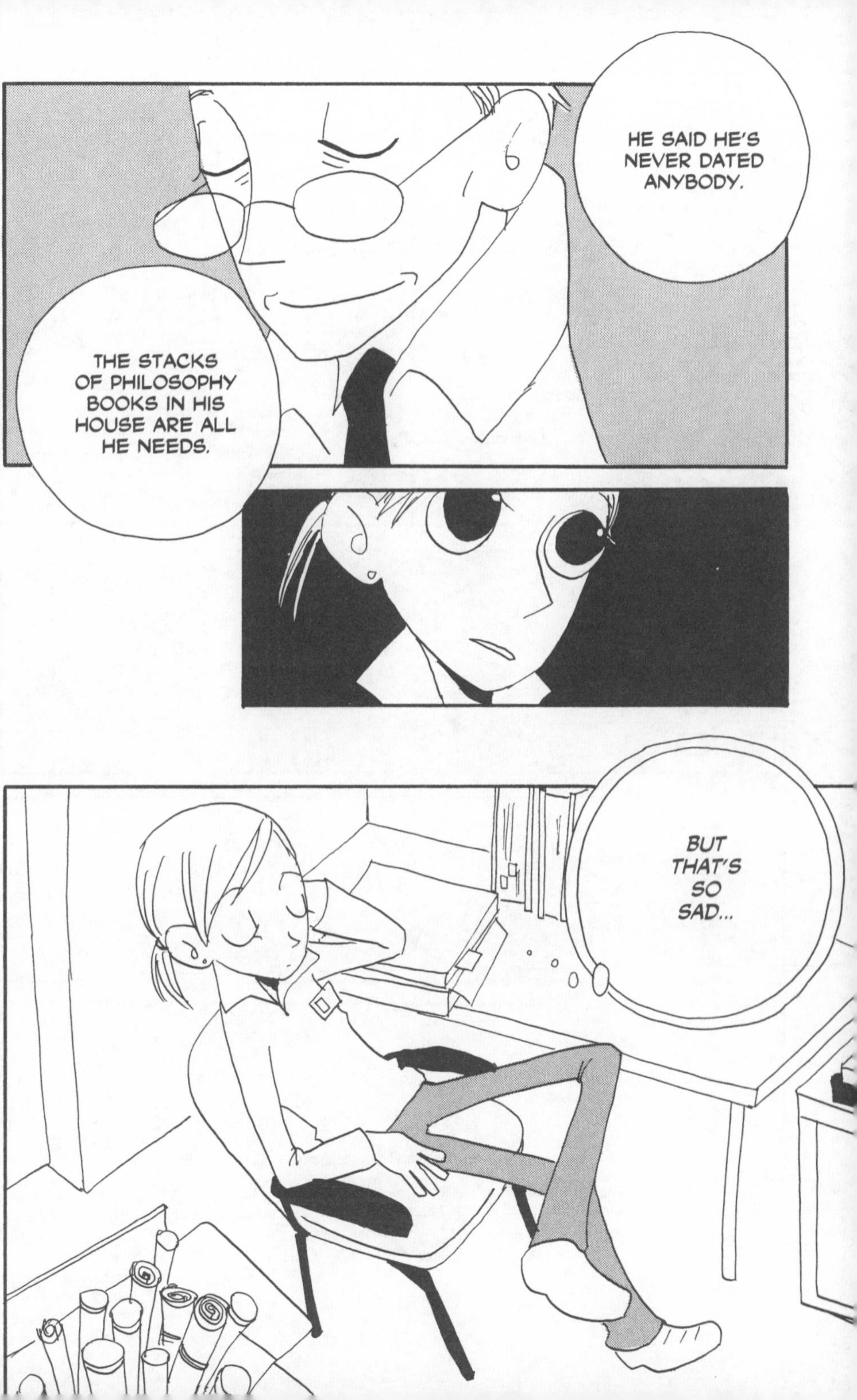
HE SAID HE'S NEVER DATED ANYBODY.
THE STACKS OF PHILOSOPHY BOOKS IN HIS HOUSE ARE ALL HE NEEDS.
BUT THAT'S SO SAD...

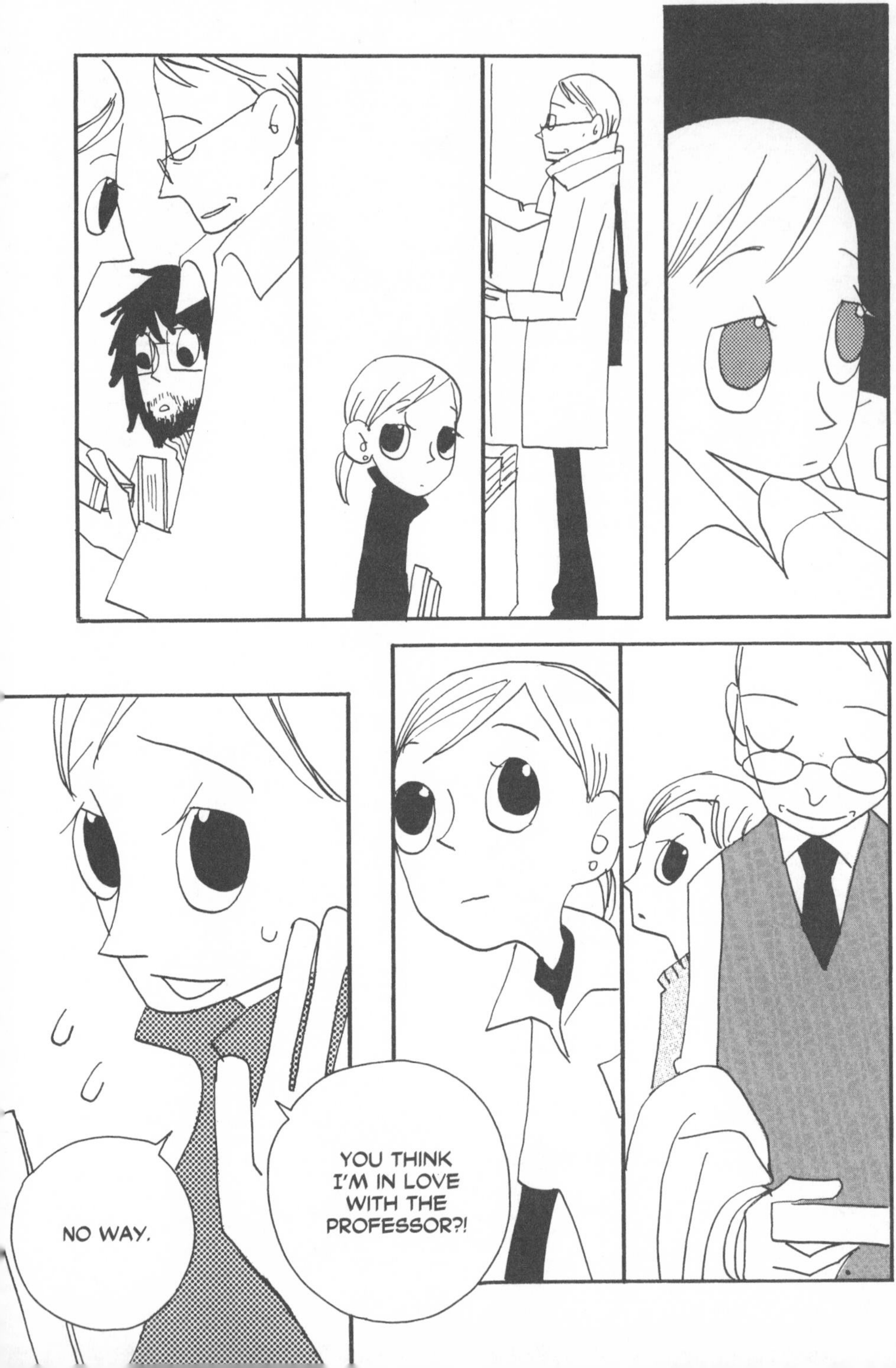
YOU THINK I'M IN LOVE WITH THE PROFESSOR?!
NO WAY.

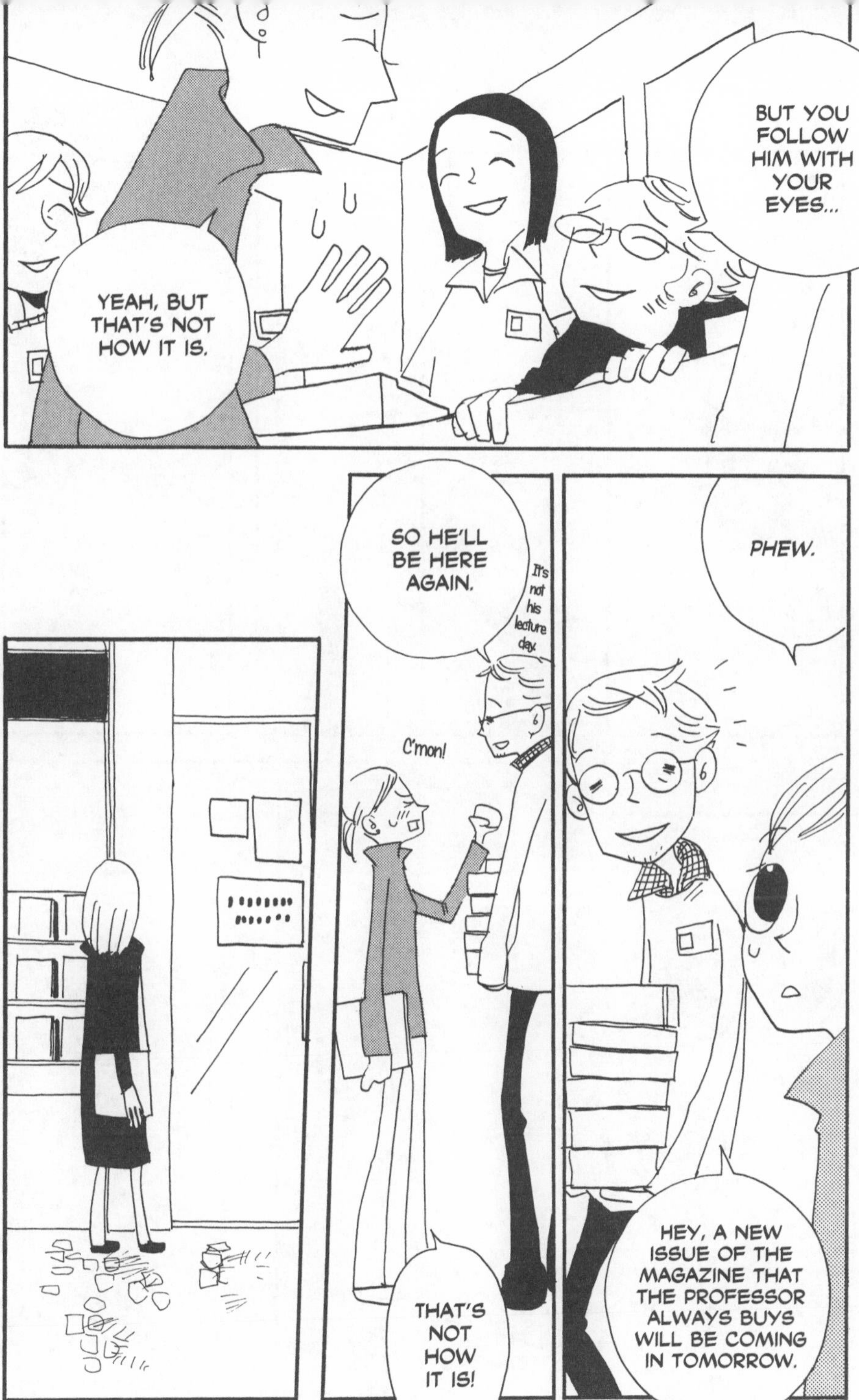
BUT YOU FOLLOW HIM WITH YOUR EYES...
YEAH, BUT THAT'S NOT HOW IT IS.
PHEW.
HEY, A NEW ISSUE OF THE MAGAZINE THAT THE PROFESSOR ALWAYS BUYS WILL BE COMING IN TOMORROW.
SO HE'LL BE HERE AGAIN.
It's not his lecture day.
C'mon!
THAT'S NOT HOW IT IS!

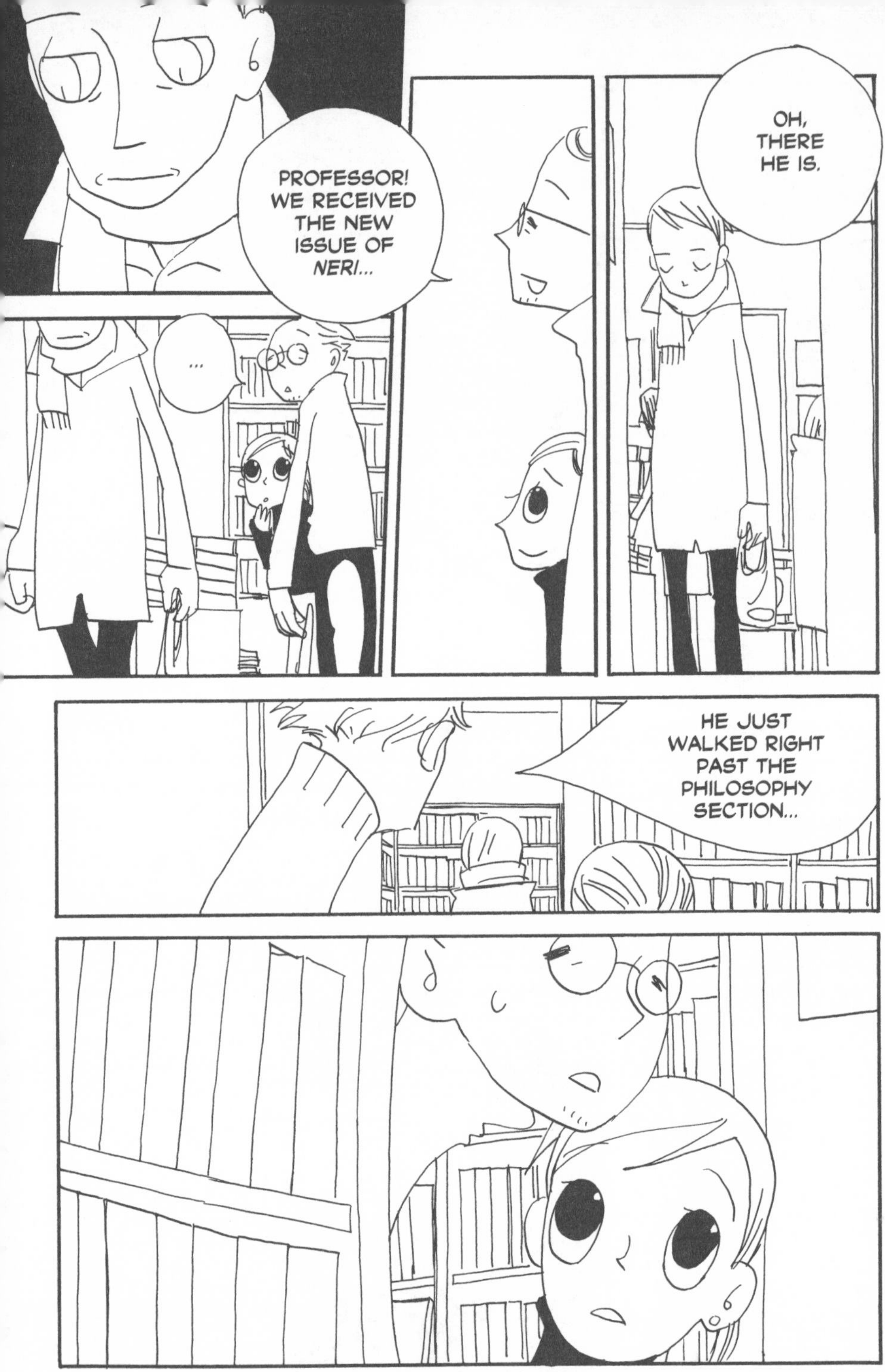
OH, THERE HE IS.
PROFESSOR! WE RECEIVED THE NEW ISSUE OF *NERI*...
...
HE JUST WALKED RIGHT PAST THE PHILOSOPHY SECTION...

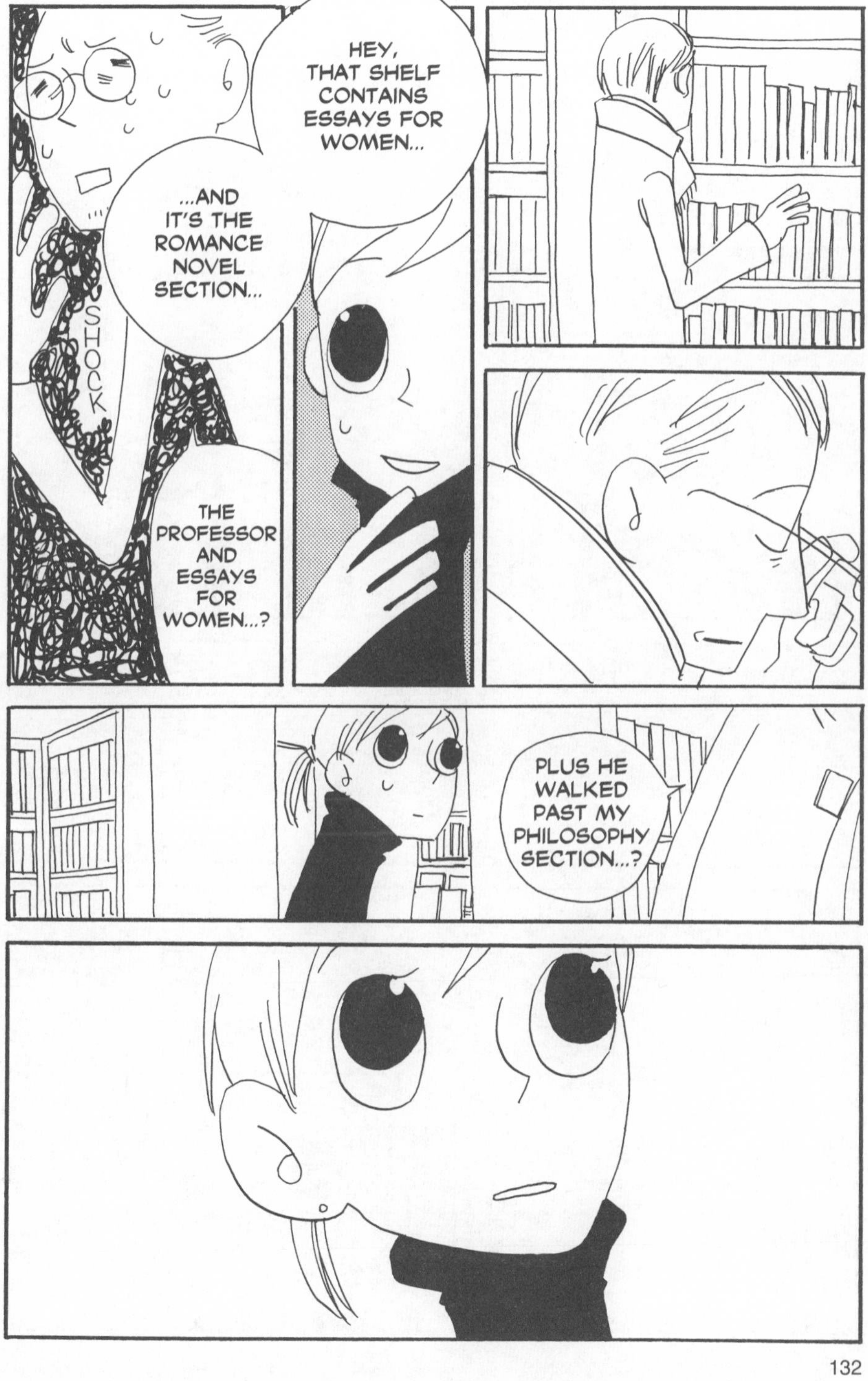
HEY, THAT SHELF CONTAINS ESSAYS FOR WOMEN...
...AND IT'S THE ROMANCE NOVEL SECTION...
SHOCK
THE PROFESSOR AND ESSAYS FOR WOMEN...?
PLUS HE WALKED PAST MY PHILOSOPHY SECTION...?

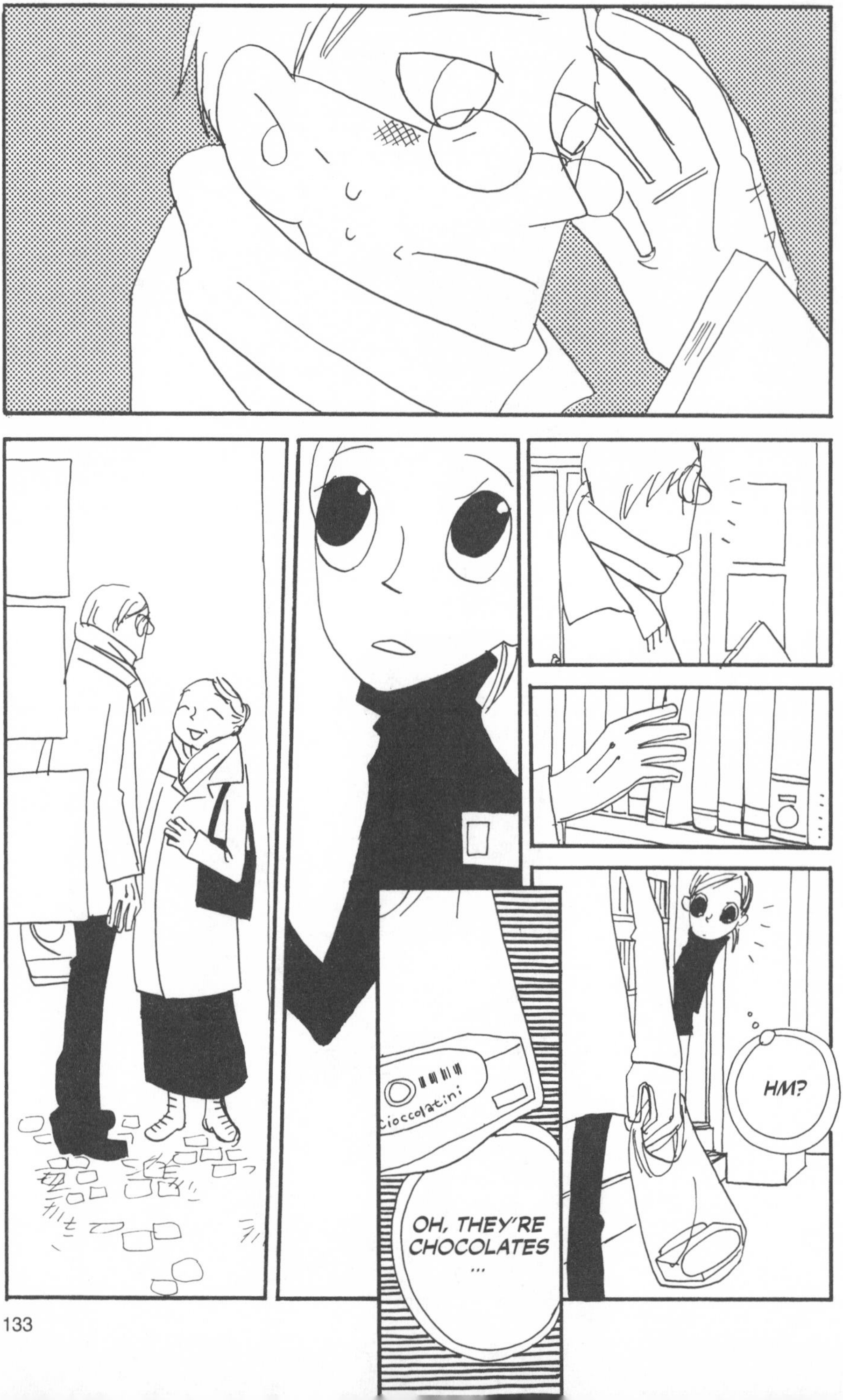
HM?
OH, THEY'RE CHOCOLATES ...
cioccolatini

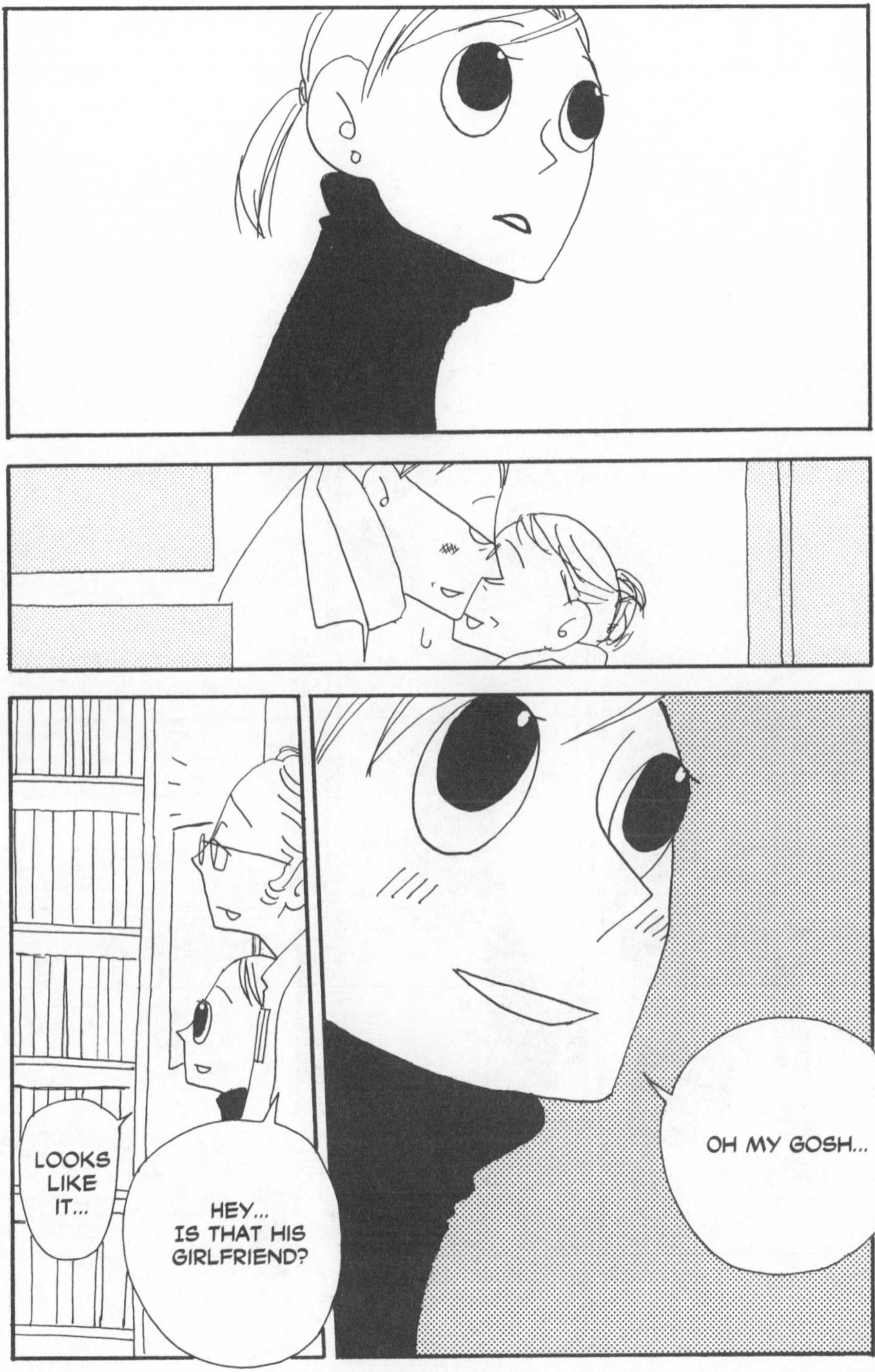
OH MY GOSH...
HEY... IS THAT HIS GIRLFRIEND?
LOOKS LIKE IT...

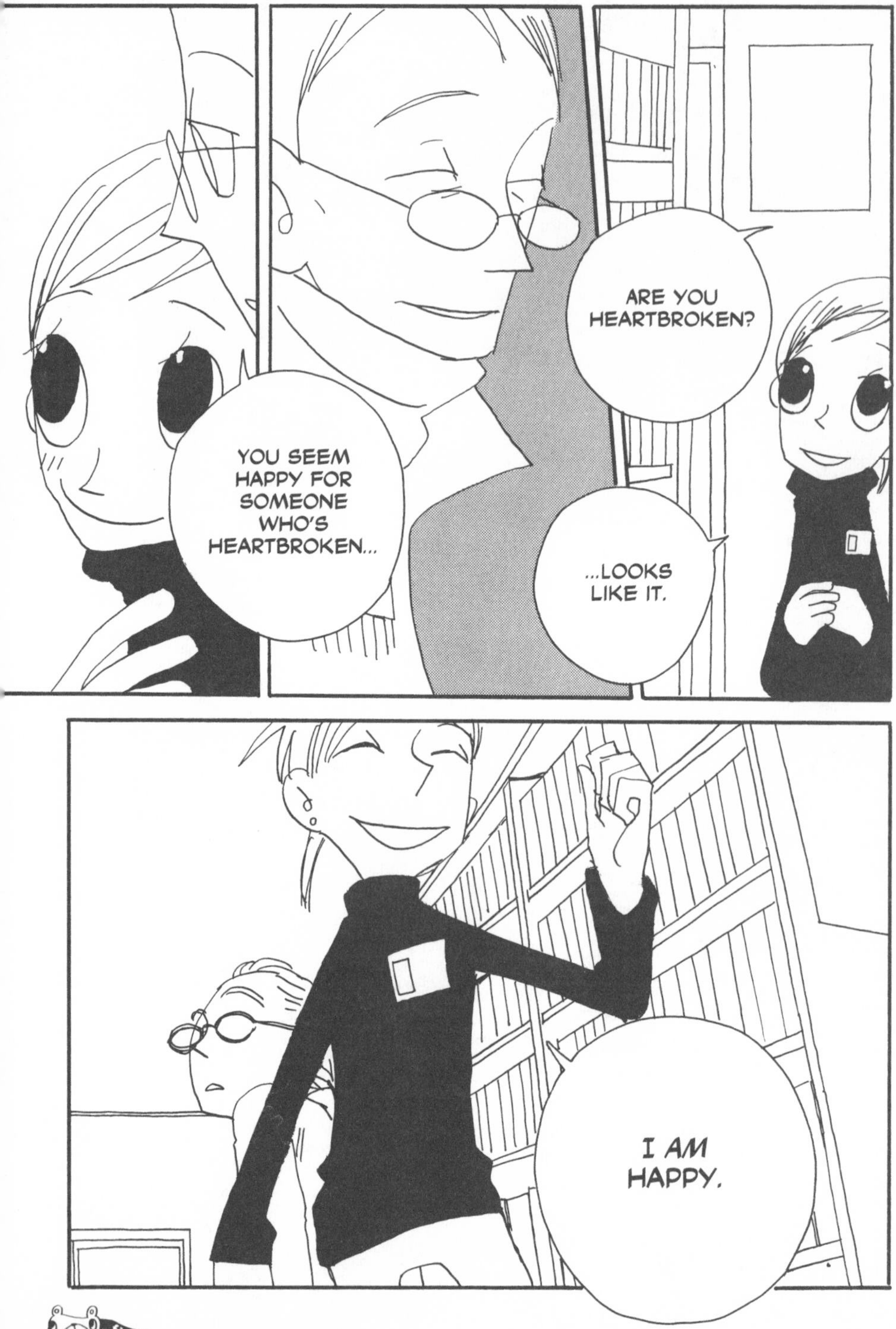
ARE YOU HEARTBROKEN?
...LOOKS LIKE IT.
YOU SEEM HAPPY FOR SOMEONE WHO'S HEARTBROKEN...
I AM HAPPY.
fine.

senza titolo #2
GENTILUOMO (Dojinshi)
Published in November 2003

Natsume Ono

Tesoro 4

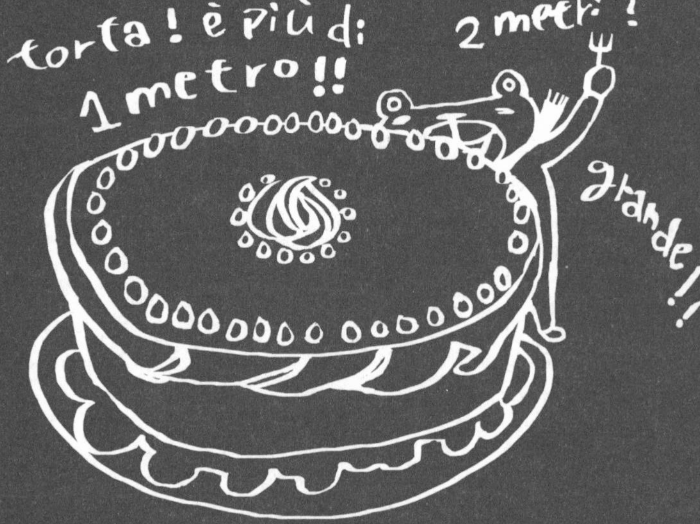
torta! è più di 1 metro!!
2 metri?
grande!!

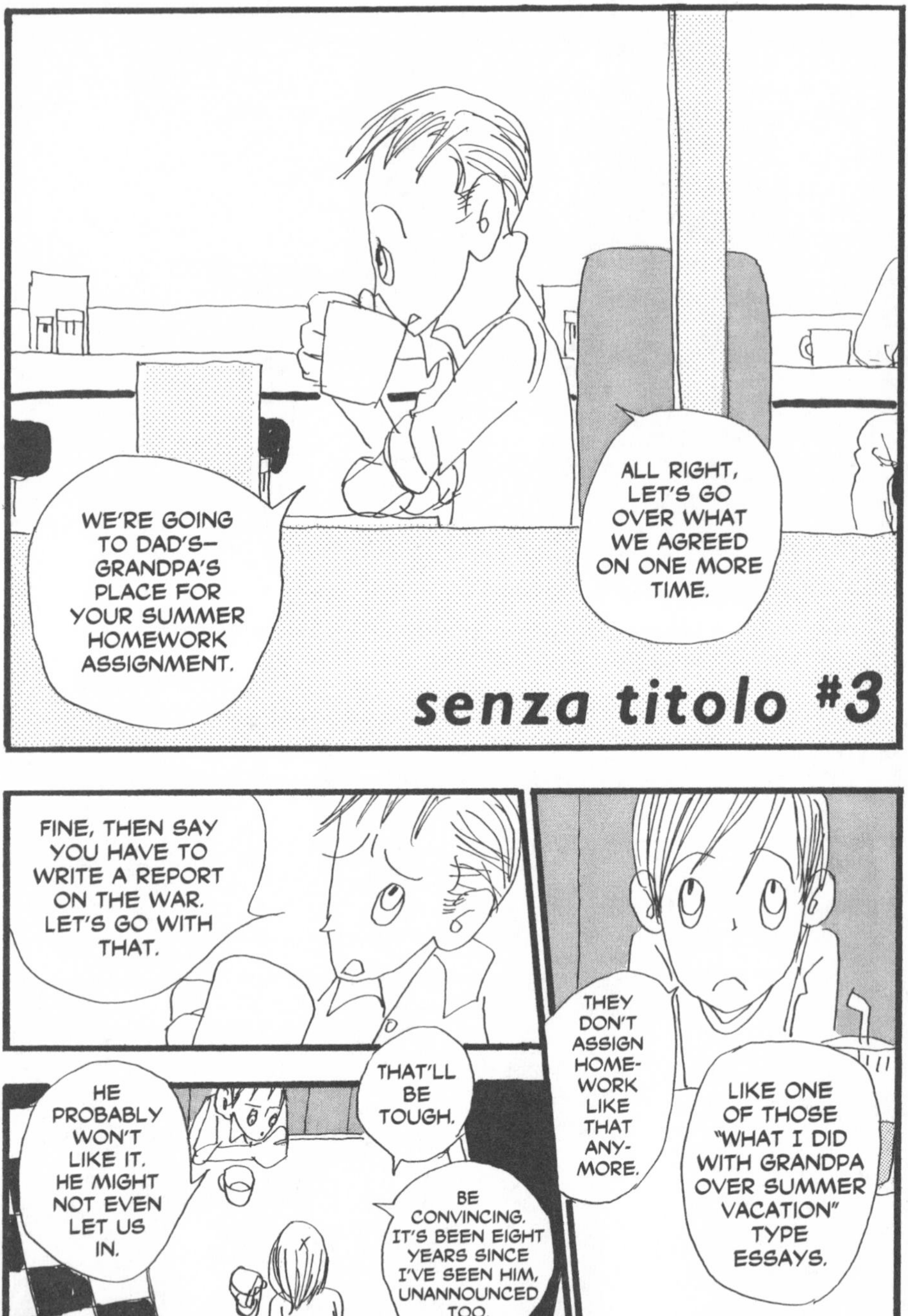
ALL RIGHT, LET'S GO OVER WHAT WE AGREED ON ONE MORE TIME.
WE'RE GOING TO DAD'S— GRANDPA'S PLACE FOR YOUR SUMMER HOMEWORK ASSIGNMENT.
senza titolo #3
LIKE ONE OF THOSE "WHAT I DID WITH GRANDPA OVER SUMMER VACATION" TYPE ESSAYS.
THEY DON'T ASSIGN HOME-WORK LIKE THAT ANY-MORE.
FINE, THEN SAY YOU HAVE TO WRITE A REPORT ON THE WAR. LET'S GO WITH THAT.
THAT'LL BE TOUGH.
HE PROBABLY WON'T LIKE IT. HE MIGHT NOT EVEN LET US IN.
BE CONVINCING. IT'S BEEN EIGHT YEARS SINCE I'VE SEEN HIM, UNANNOUNCED TOO.

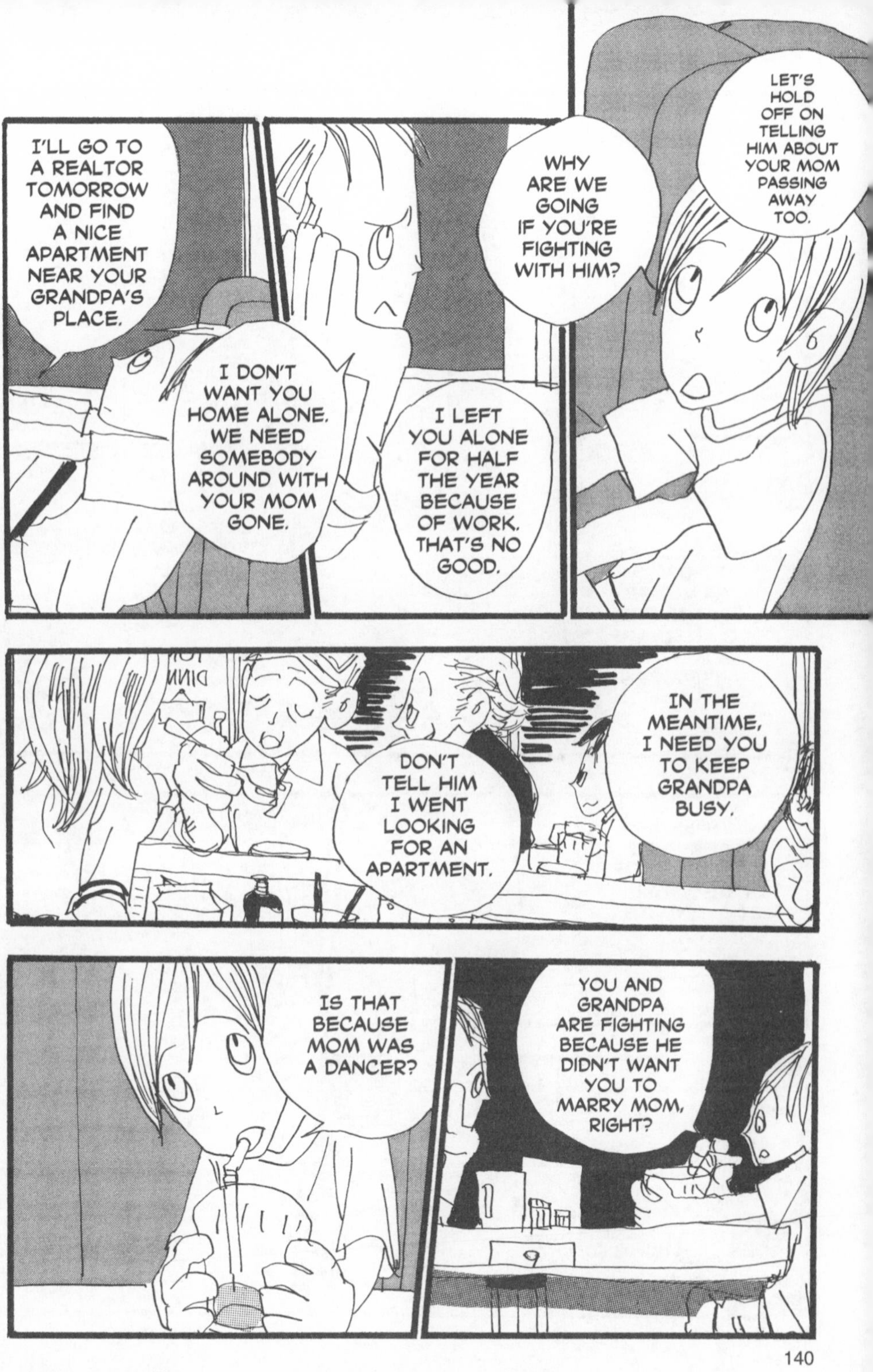
LET'S HOLD OFF ON TELLING HIM ABOUT YOUR MOM PASSING AWAY TOO.
WHY ARE WE GOING IF YOU'RE FIGHTING WITH HIM?
I LEFT YOU ALONE FOR HALF THE YEAR BECAUSE OF WORK. THAT'S NO GOOD.
I DON'T WANT YOU HOME ALONE. WE NEED SOMEBODY AROUND WITH YOUR MOM GONE.
I'LL GO TO A REALTOR TOMORROW AND FIND A NICE APARTMENT NEAR YOUR GRANDPA'S PLACE.
IN THE MEANTIME, I NEED YOU TO KEEP GRANDPA BUSY.
DON'T TELL HIM I WENT LOOKING FOR AN APARTMENT.
YOU AND GRANDPA ARE FIGHTING BECAUSE HE DIDN'T WANT YOU TO MARRY MOM, RIGHT?
IS THAT BECAUSE MOM WAS A DANCER?

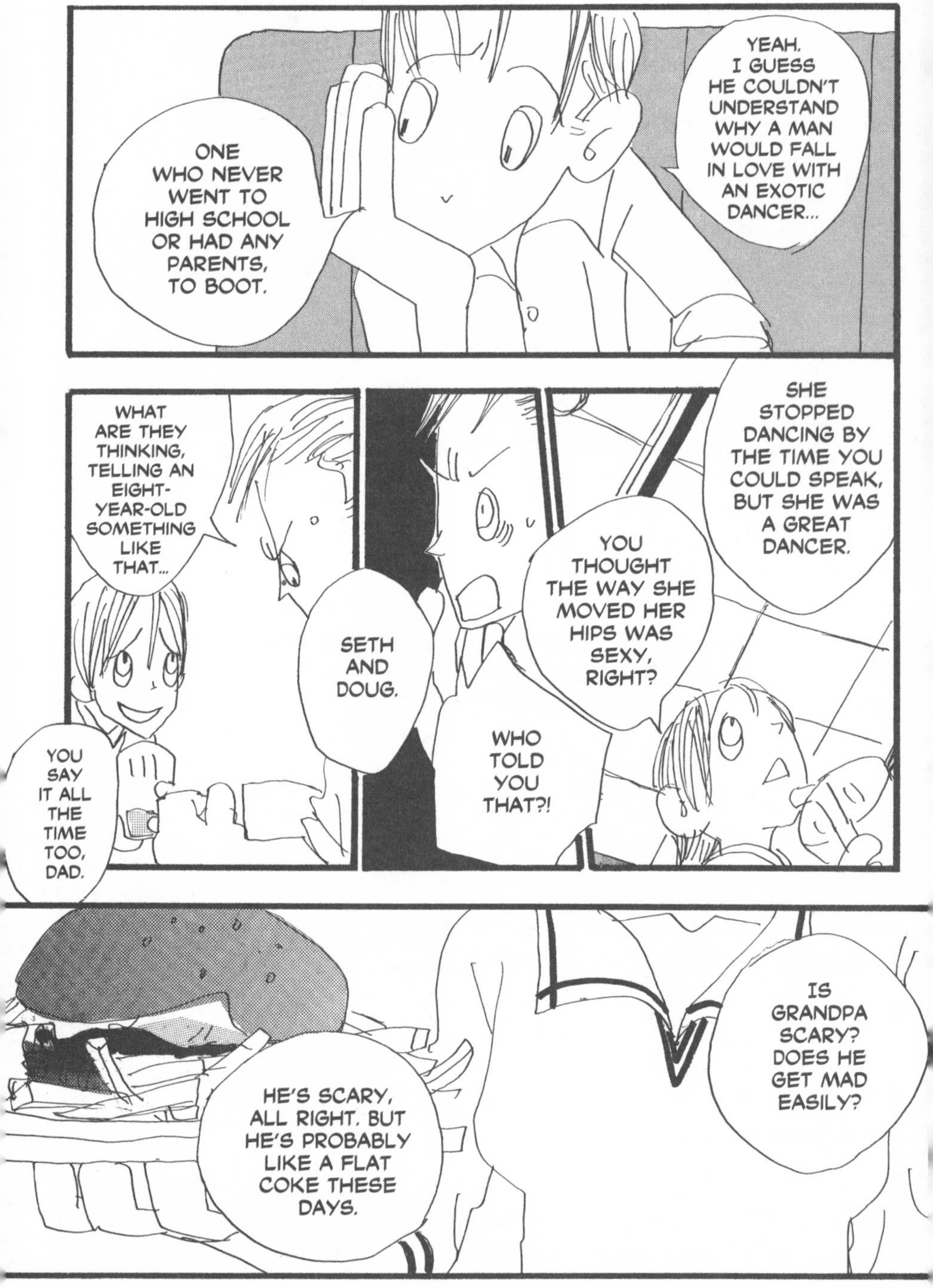
YEAH. I GUESS HE COULDN'T UNDERSTAND WHY A MAN WOULD FALL IN LOVE WITH AN EXOTIC DANCER...
ONE WHO NEVER WENT TO HIGH SCHOOL OR HAD ANY PARENTS, TO BOOT.
SHE STOPPED DANCING BY THE TIME YOU COULD SPEAK, BUT SHE WAS A GREAT DANCER.
YOU THOUGHT THE WAY SHE MOVED HER HIPS WAS SEXY, RIGHT?
WHO TOLD YOU THAT?!
SETH AND DOUG.
WHAT ARE THEY THINKING, TELLING AN EIGHT-YEAR-OLD SOMETHING LIKE THAT...
YOU SAY IT ALL THE TIME TOO, DAD.
IS GRANDPA SCARY? DOES HE GET MAD EASILY?
HE'S SCARY, ALL RIGHT. BUT HE'S PROBABLY LIKE A FLAT COKE THESE DAYS.

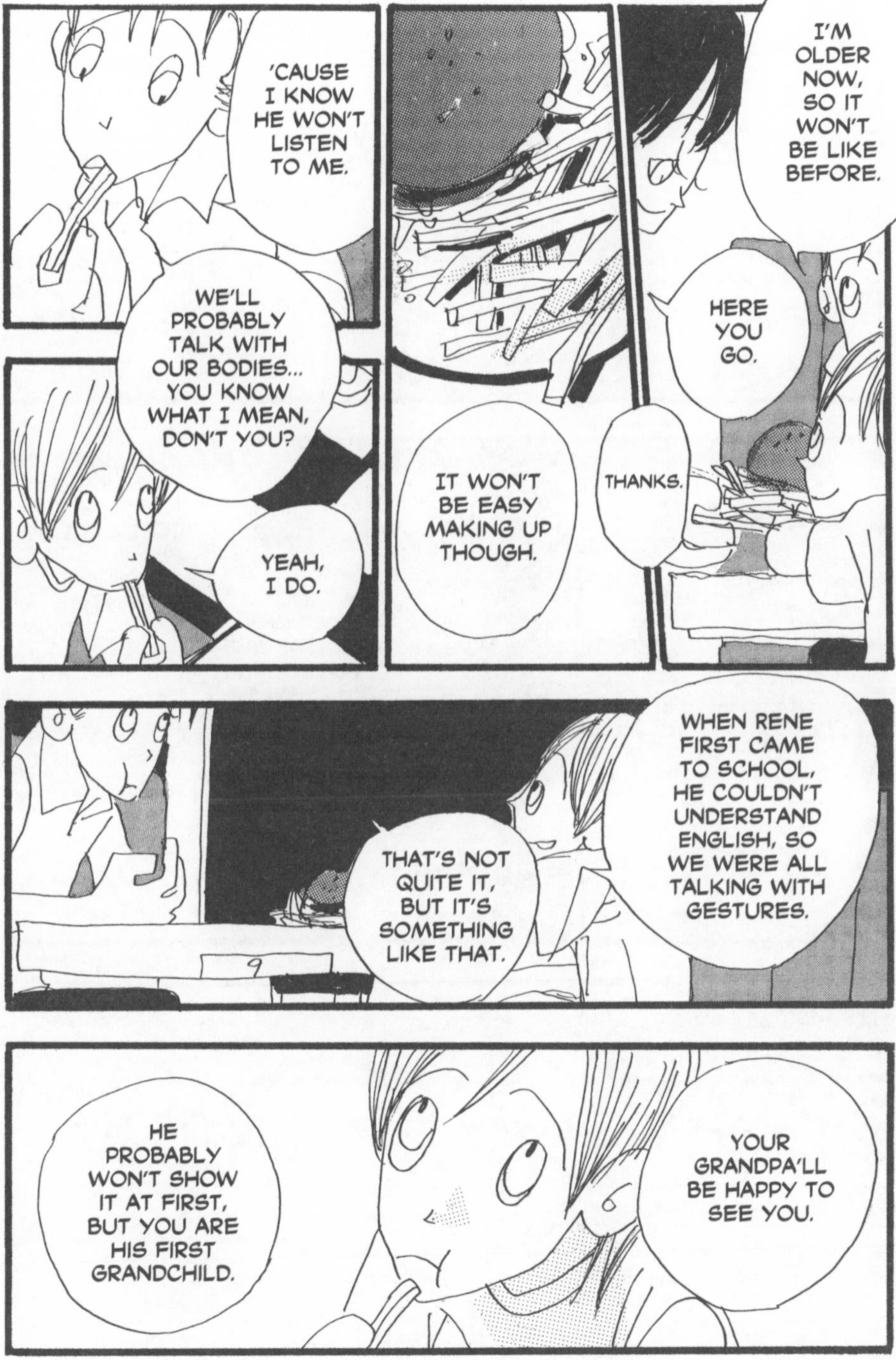
I'M OLDER NOW, SO IT WON'T BE LIKE BEFORE.
HERE YOU GO.
THANKS.
IT WON'T BE EASY MAKING UP THOUGH.
'CAUSE I KNOW HE WON'T LISTEN TO ME.
WE'LL PROBABLY TALK WITH OUR BODIES... YOU KNOW WHAT I MEAN, DON'T YOU?
YEAH, I DO.
WHEN RENE FIRST CAME TO SCHOOL, HE COULDN'T UNDERSTAND ENGLISH, SO WE WERE ALL TALKING WITH GESTURES.
THAT'S NOT QUITE IT, BUT IT'S SOMETHING LIKE THAT.
YOUR GRANDPA'LL BE HAPPY TO SEE YOU.
HE PROBABLY WON'T SHOW IT AT FIRST, BUT YOU ARE HIS FIRST GRANDCHILD.

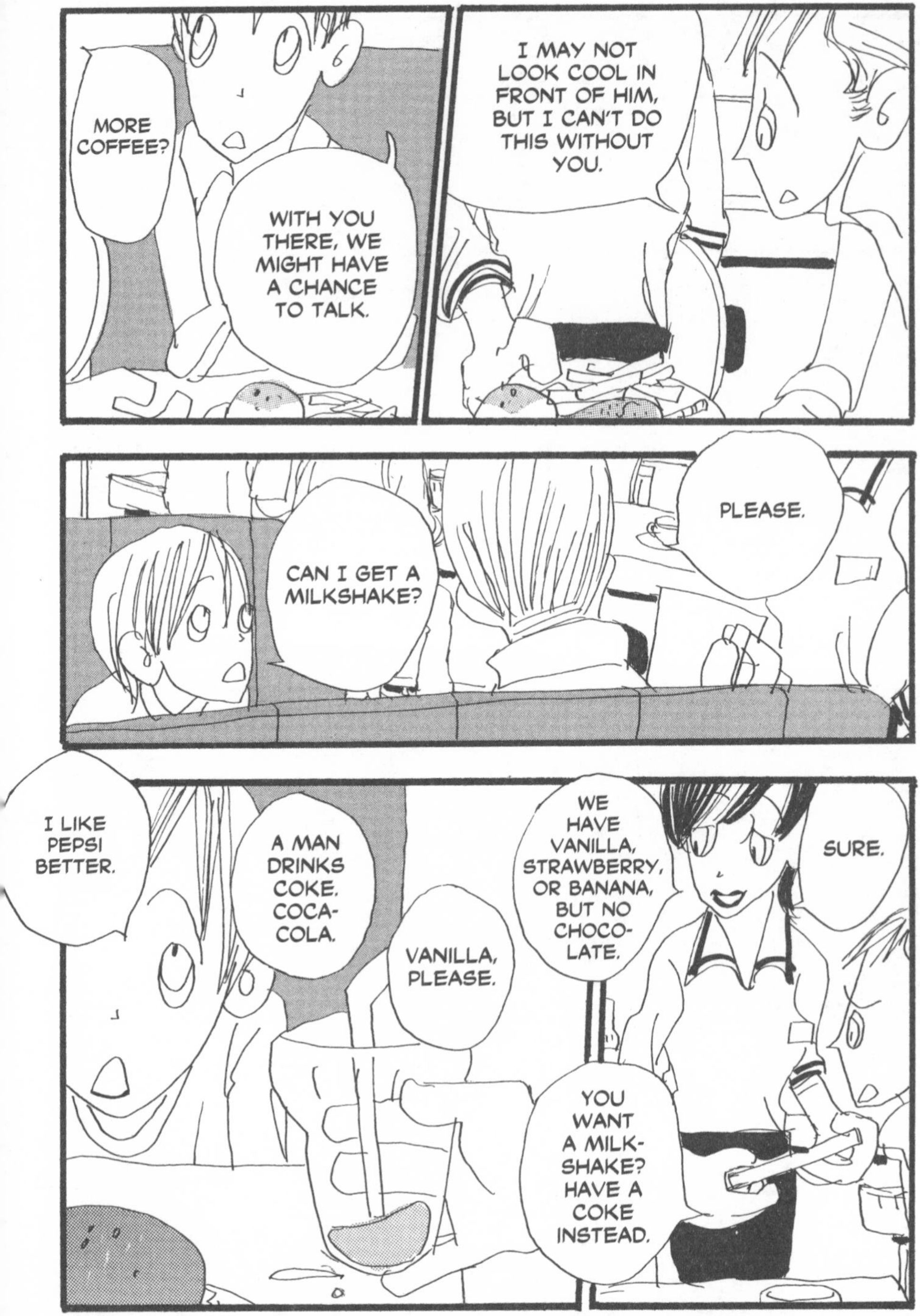

I MAY NOT LOOK COOL IN FRONT OF HIM, BUT I CAN'T DO THIS WITHOUT YOU.
WITH YOU THERE, WE MIGHT HAVE A CHANCE TO TALK.
MORE COFFEE?
PLEASE.
CAN I GET A MILKSHAKE?
SURE.
WE HAVE VANILLA, STRAWBERRY, OR BANANA, BUT NO CHOCO-LATE.
VANILLA, PLEASE.
YOU WANT A MILK-SHAKE? HAVE A COKE INSTEAD.
A MAN DRINKS COKE. COCA-COLA.
I LIKE PEPSI BETTER.

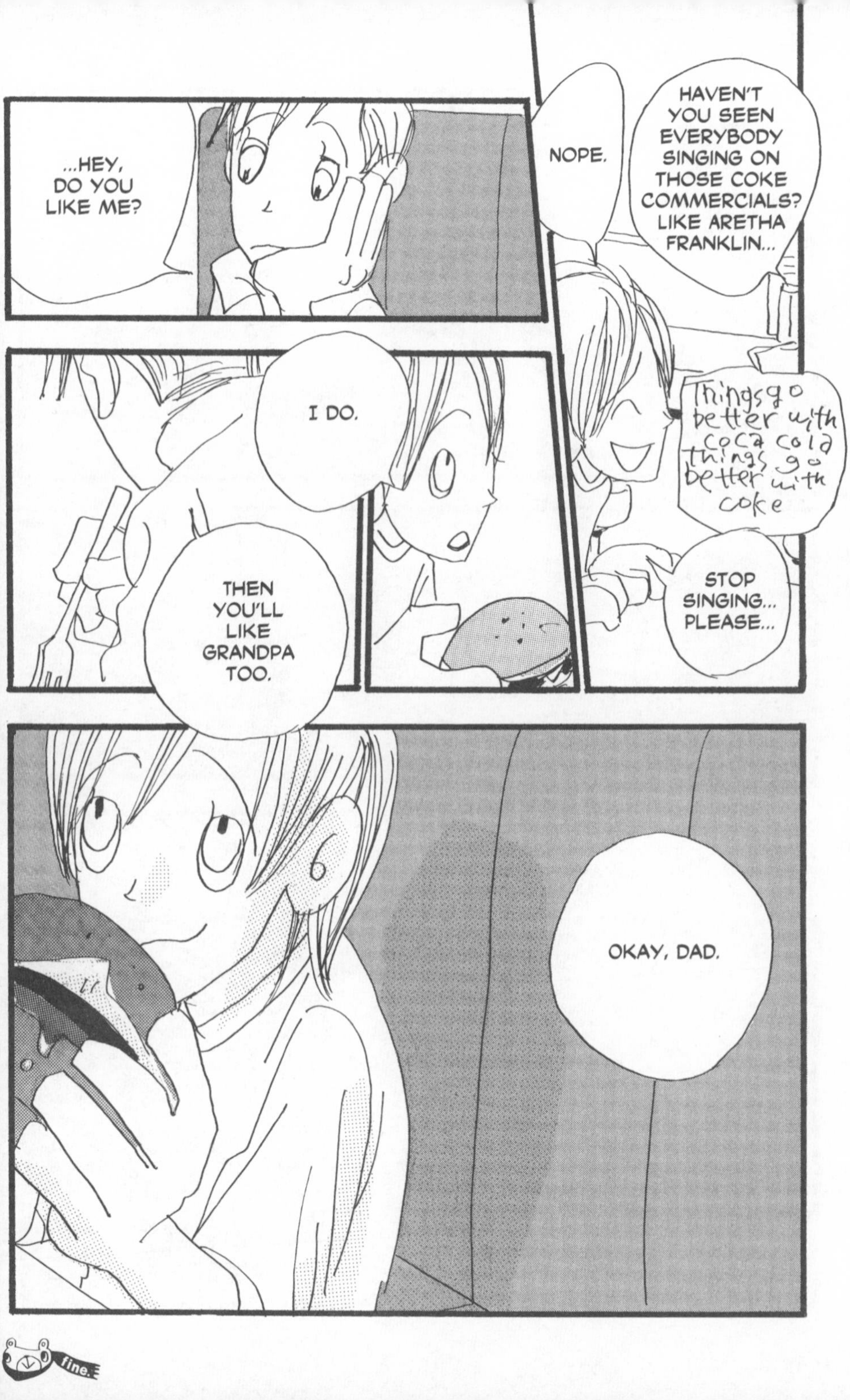
HAVEN'T YOU SEEN EVERYBODY SINGING ON THOSE COKE COMMERCIALS? LIKE ARETHA FRANKLIN...
NOPE.
Things go better with coca cola things go better with coke
STOP SINGING... PLEASE...
...HEY, DO YOU LIKE ME?
I DO.
THEN YOU'LL LIKE GRANDPA TOO.
OKAY, DAD.
fine.

***senza titolo* #3**
YOUR SMILE LIKE THE CARTOON (Dojinshi)
Published in April 1998

senza titolo #4

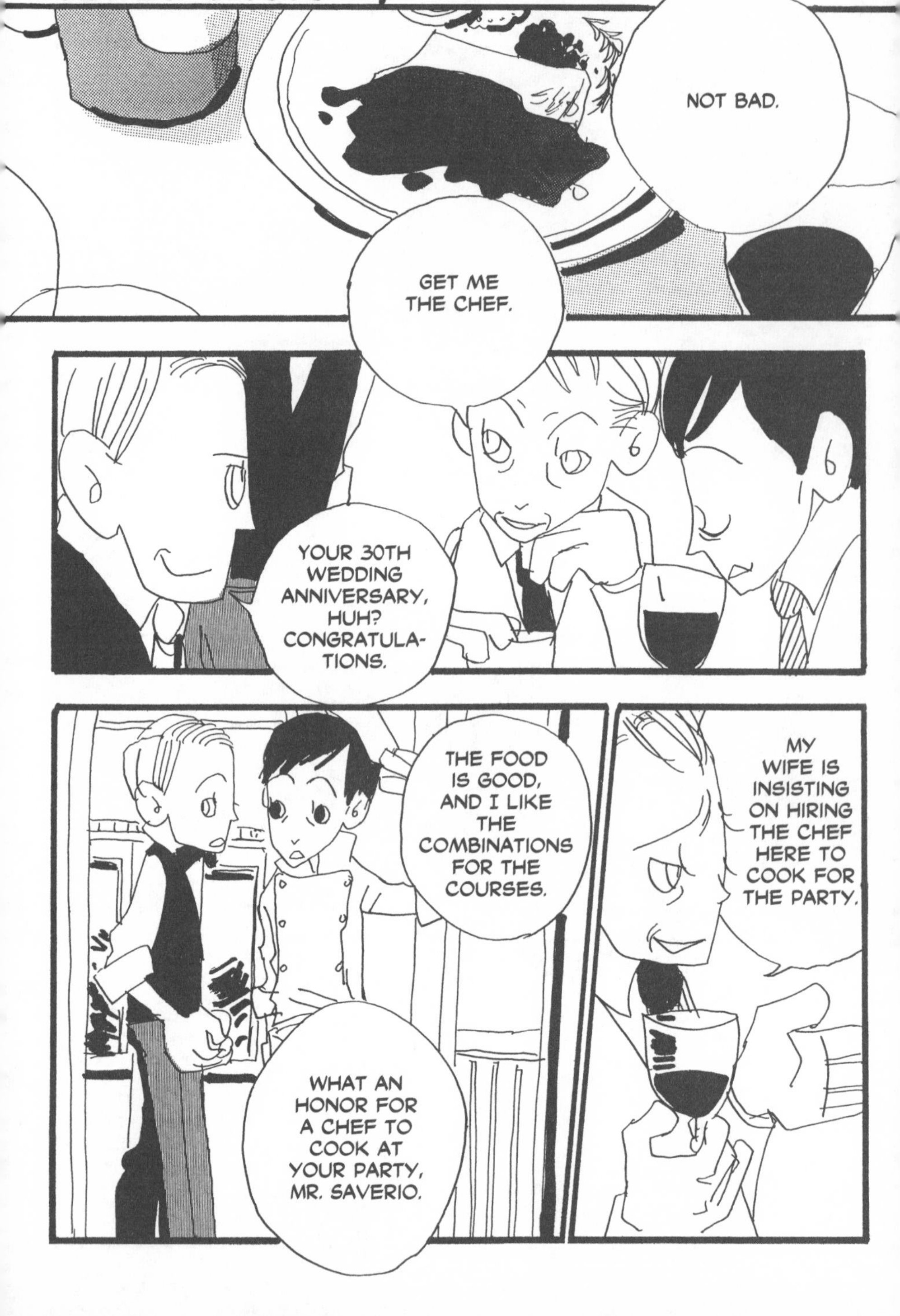
NOT BAD.
GET ME THE CHEF.
YOUR 30TH WEDDING ANNIVERSARY, HUH? CONGRATULA-TIONS.
MY WIFE IS INSISTING ON HIRING THE CHEF HERE TO COOK FOR THE PARTY.
THE FOOD IS GOOD, AND I LIKE THE COMBINATIONS FOR THE COURSES.
WHAT AN HONOR FOR A CHEF TO COOK AT YOUR PARTY, MR. SAVERIO.

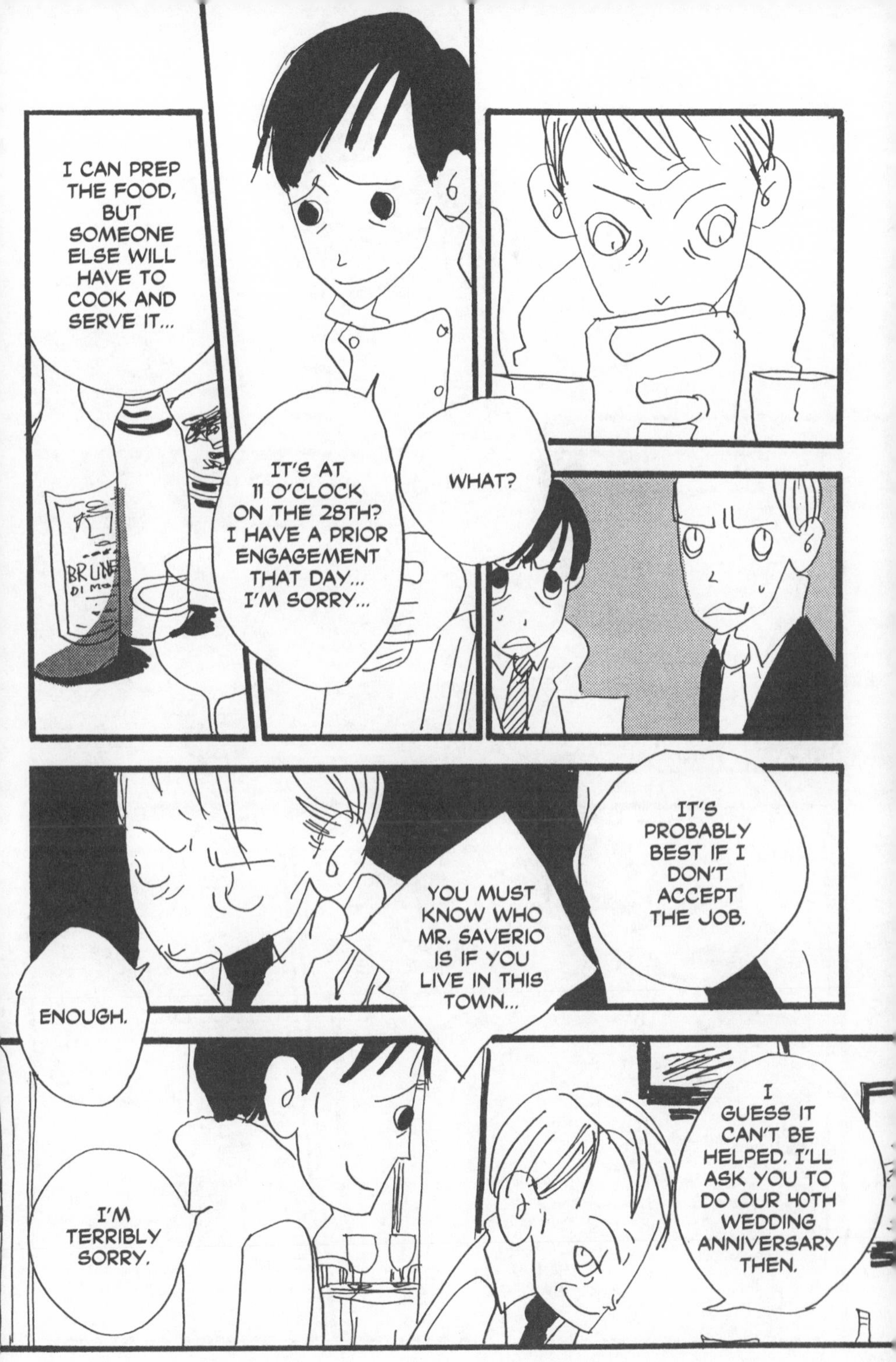
IT'S AT 11 O'CLOCK ON THE 28TH? I HAVE A PRIOR ENGAGEMENT THAT DAY... I'M SORRY...
WHAT?
I CAN PREP THE FOOD, BUT SOMEONE ELSE WILL HAVE TO COOK AND SERVE IT...
IT'S PROBABLY BEST IF I DON'T ACCEPT THE JOB.
YOU MUST KNOW WHO MR. SAVERIO IS IF YOU LIVE IN THIS TOWN...
ENOUGH.
I GUESS IT CAN'T BE HELPED. I'LL ASK YOU TO DO OUR 40TH WEDDING ANNIVERSARY THEN.
I'M TERRIBLY SORRY.

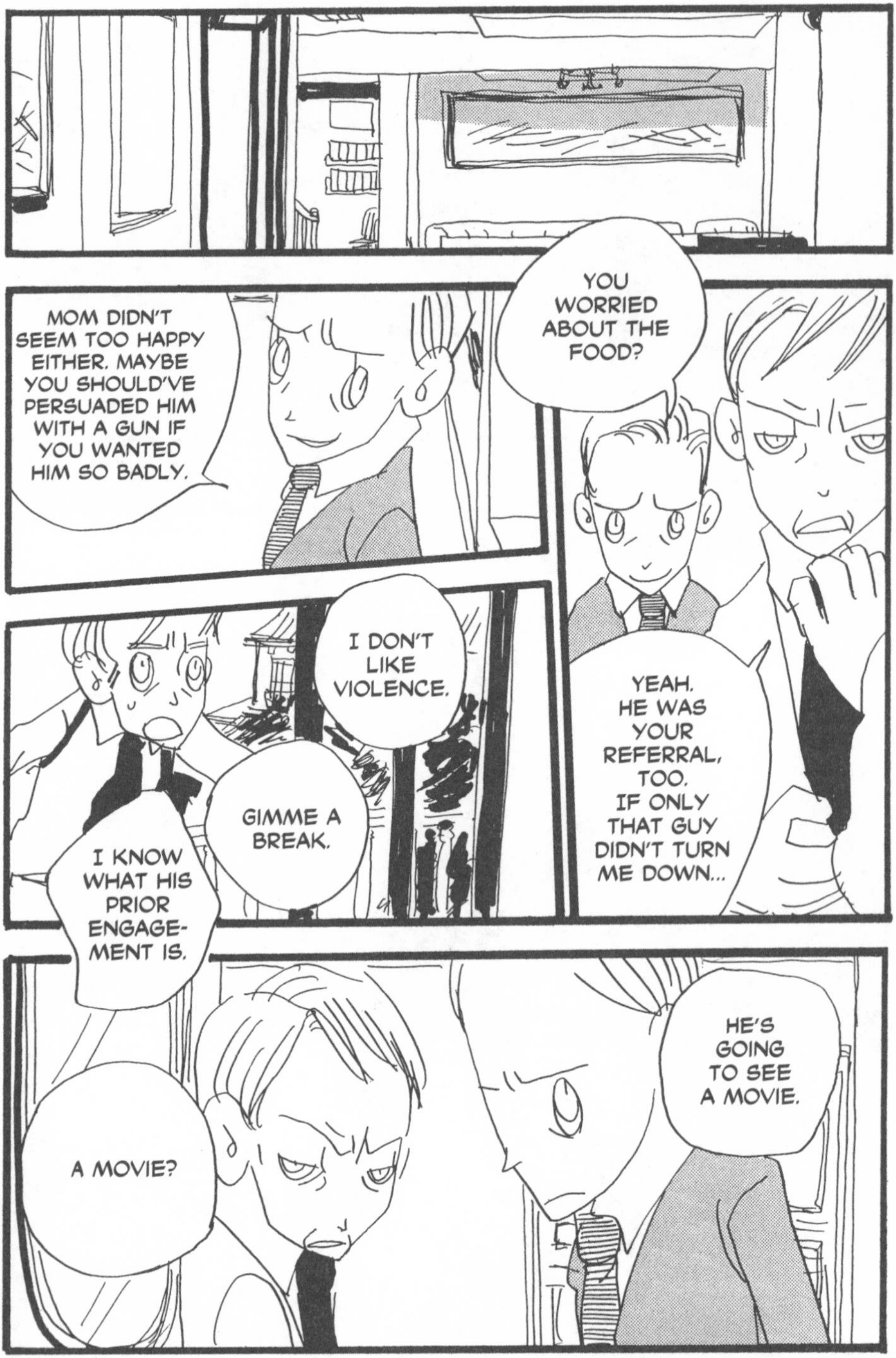
YOU WORRIED ABOUT THE FOOD?
YEAH. HE WAS YOUR REFERRAL, TOO. IF ONLY THAT GUY DIDN'T TURN ME DOWN...
MOM DIDN'T SEEM TOO HAPPY EITHER. MAYBE YOU SHOULD'VE PERSUADED HIM WITH A GUN IF YOU WANTED HIM SO BADLY.
I DON'T LIKE VIOLENCE.
GIMME A BREAK.
I KNOW WHAT HIS PRIOR ENGAGEMENT IS.
HE'S GOING TO SEE A MOVIE.
A MOVIE?

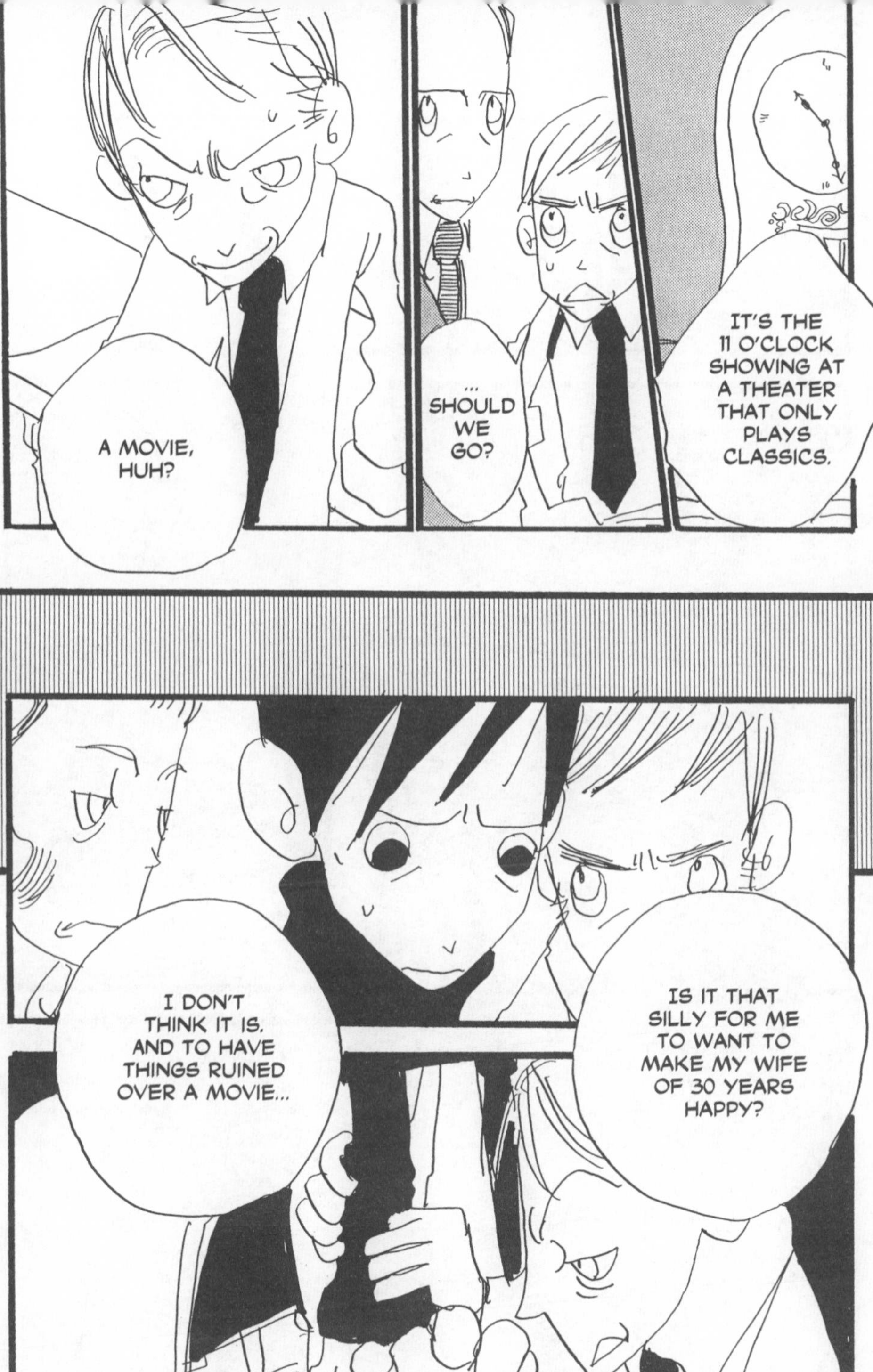
IT'S THE 11 O'CLOCK SHOWING AT A THEATER THAT ONLY PLAYS CLASSICS.
... SHOULD WE GO?
A MOVIE, HUH?
IS IT THAT SILLY FOR ME TO WANT TO MAKE MY WIFE OF 30 YEARS HAPPY?
I DON'T THINK IT IS. AND TO HAVE THINGS RUINED OVER A MOVIE...

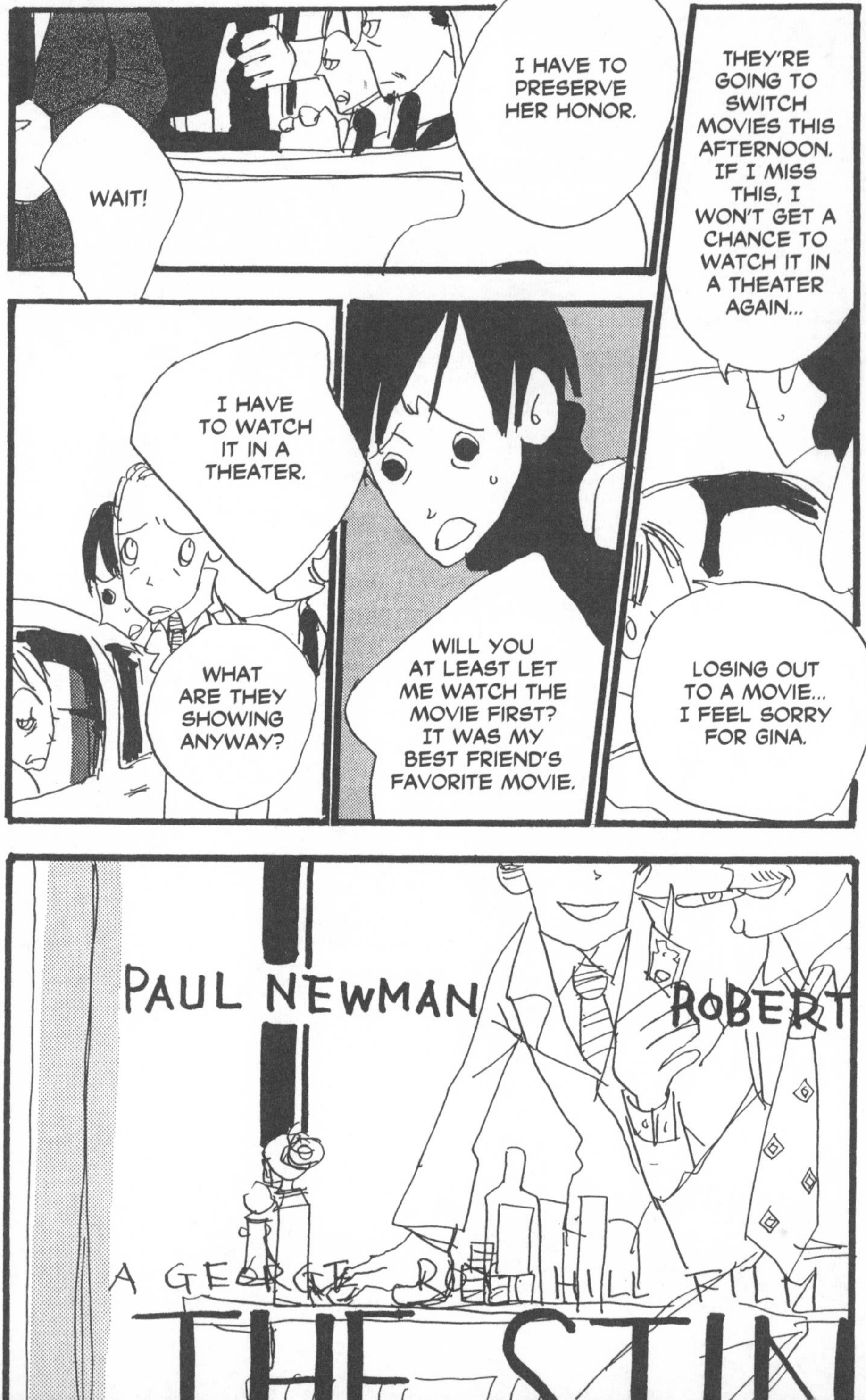
THEY'RE GOING TO SWITCH MOVIES THIS AFTERNOON. IF I MISS THIS, I WON'T GET A CHANCE TO WATCH IT IN A THEATER AGAIN...
LOSING OUT TO A MOVIE... I FEEL SORRY FOR GINA.
I HAVE TO PRESERVE HER HONOR.
WAIT!
WILL YOU AT LEAST LET ME WATCH THE MOVIE FIRST? IT WAS MY BEST FRIEND'S FAVORITE MOVIE.
I HAVE TO WATCH IT IN A THEATER.
WHAT ARE THEY SHOWING ANYWAY?
PAUL NEWMAN
ROBERT

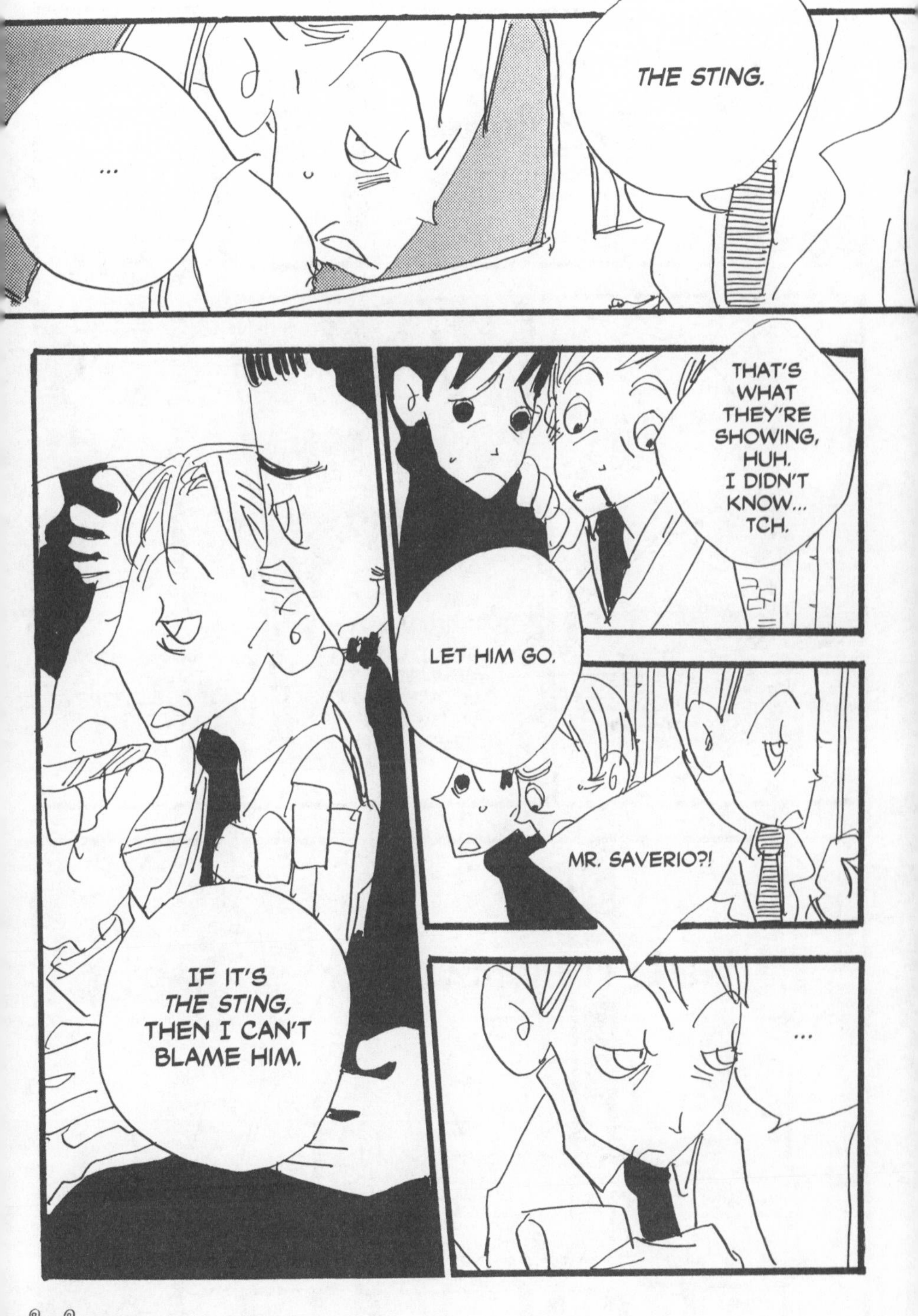
THE STING.
...
THAT'S WHAT THEY'RE SHOWING, HUH. I DIDN'T KNOW... TCH.
LET HIM GO.
MR. SAVERIO?!
IF IT'S *THE STING,* THEN I CAN'T BLAME HIM.
...

fine.

senza titolo #4
Gekkan Taruwaki No. 5 (Dojinshi)
Published in June 1998 (Taruwaki Shoten)

senza titolo #5

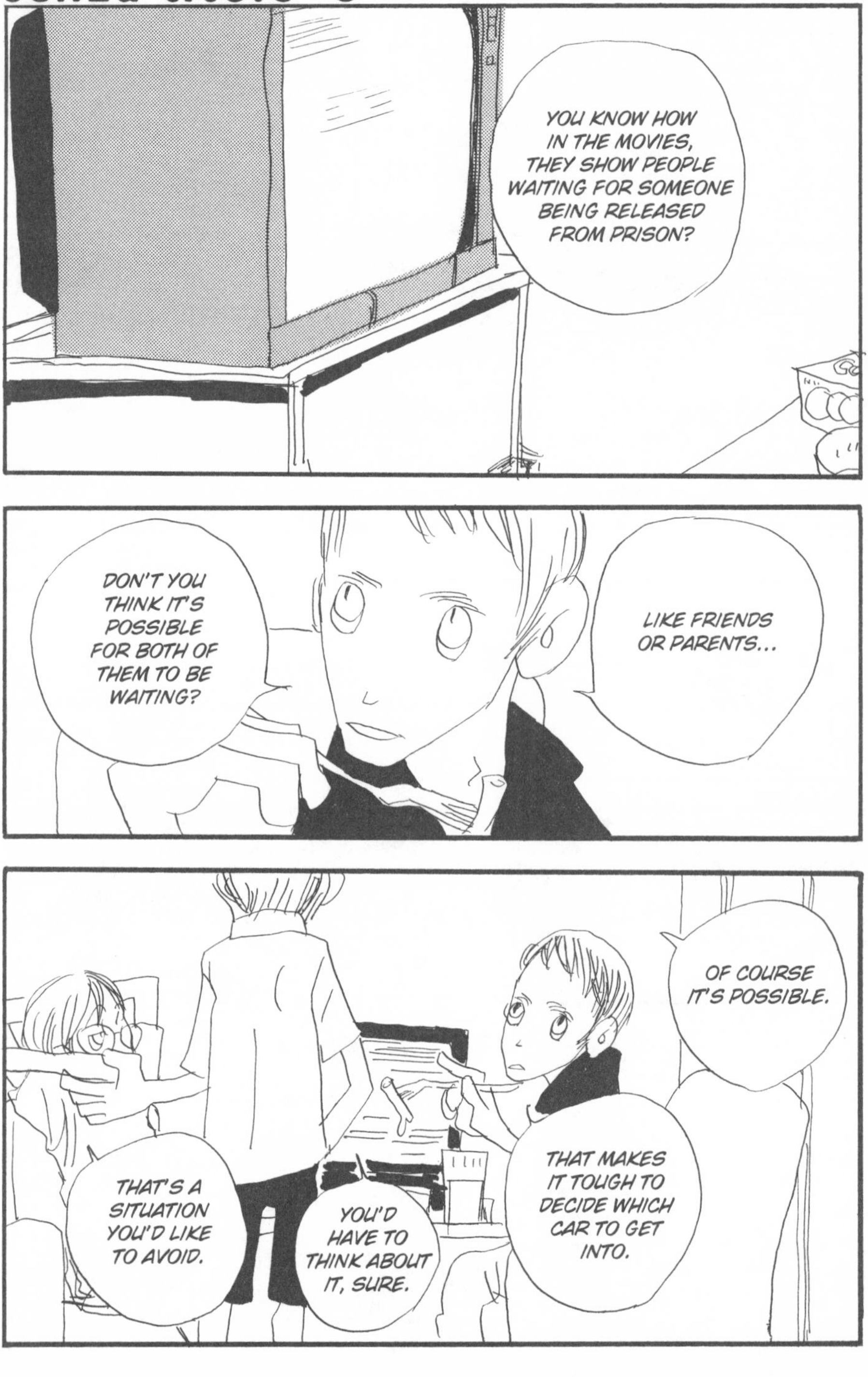
YOU KNOW HOW IN THE MOVIES, THEY SHOW PEOPLE WAITING FOR SOMEONE BEING RELEASED FROM PRISON?
LIKE FRIENDS OR PARENTS...
DON'T YOU THINK IT'S POSSIBLE FOR BOTH OF THEM TO BE WAITING?
OF COURSE IT'S POSSIBLE.
THAT MAKES IT TOUGH TO DECIDE WHICH CAR TO GET INTO.
YOU'D HAVE TO THINK ABOUT IT, SURE.
THAT'S A SITUATION YOU'D LIKE TO AVOID.

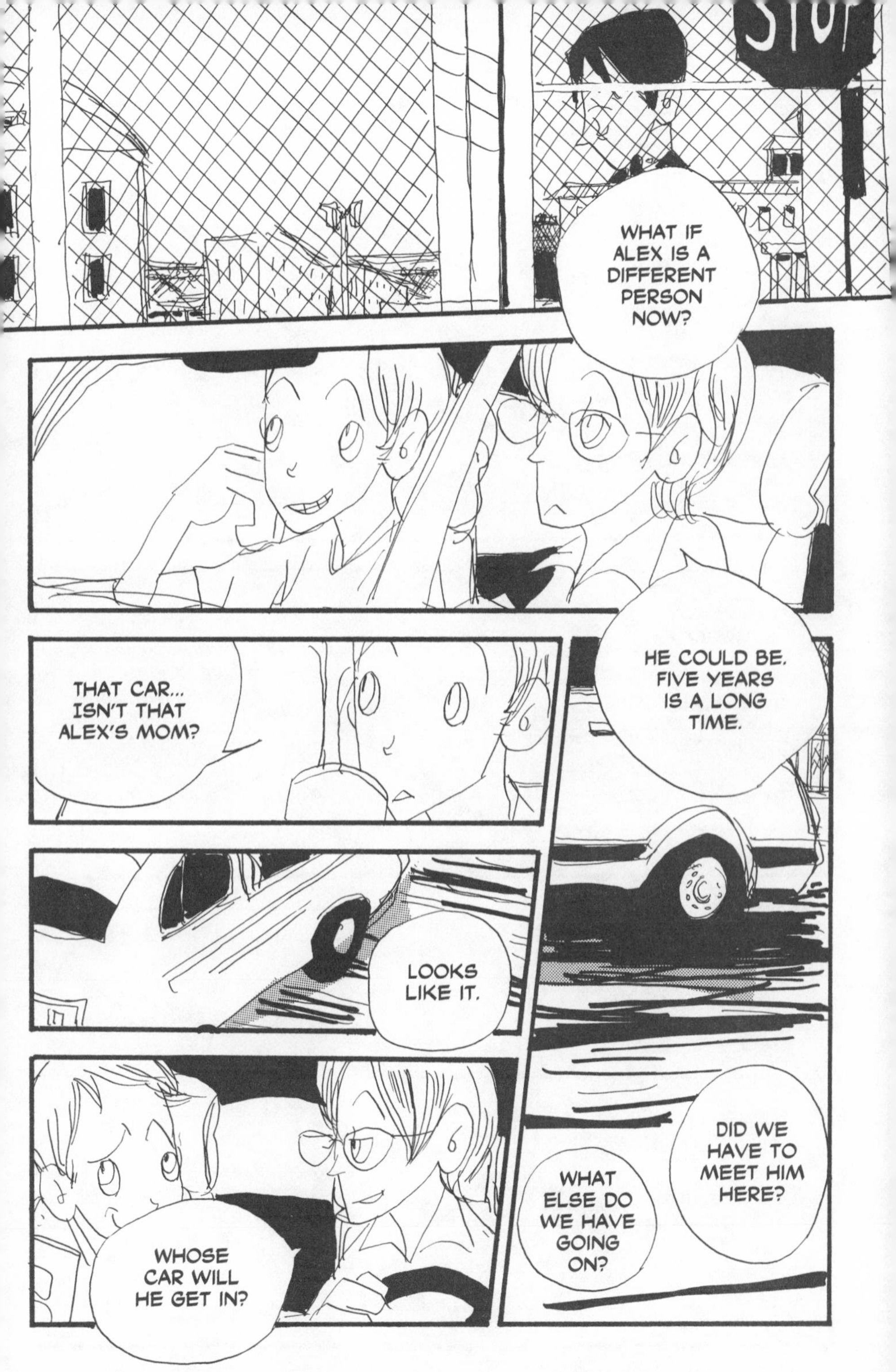
WHAT IF ALEX IS A DIFFERENT PERSON NOW?
HE COULD BE. FIVE YEARS IS A LONG TIME.
THAT CAR... ISN'T THAT ALEX'S MOM?
LOOKS LIKE IT.
DID WE HAVE TO MEET HIM HERE?
WHAT ELSE DO WE HAVE GOING ON?
WHOSE CAR WILL HE GET IN?

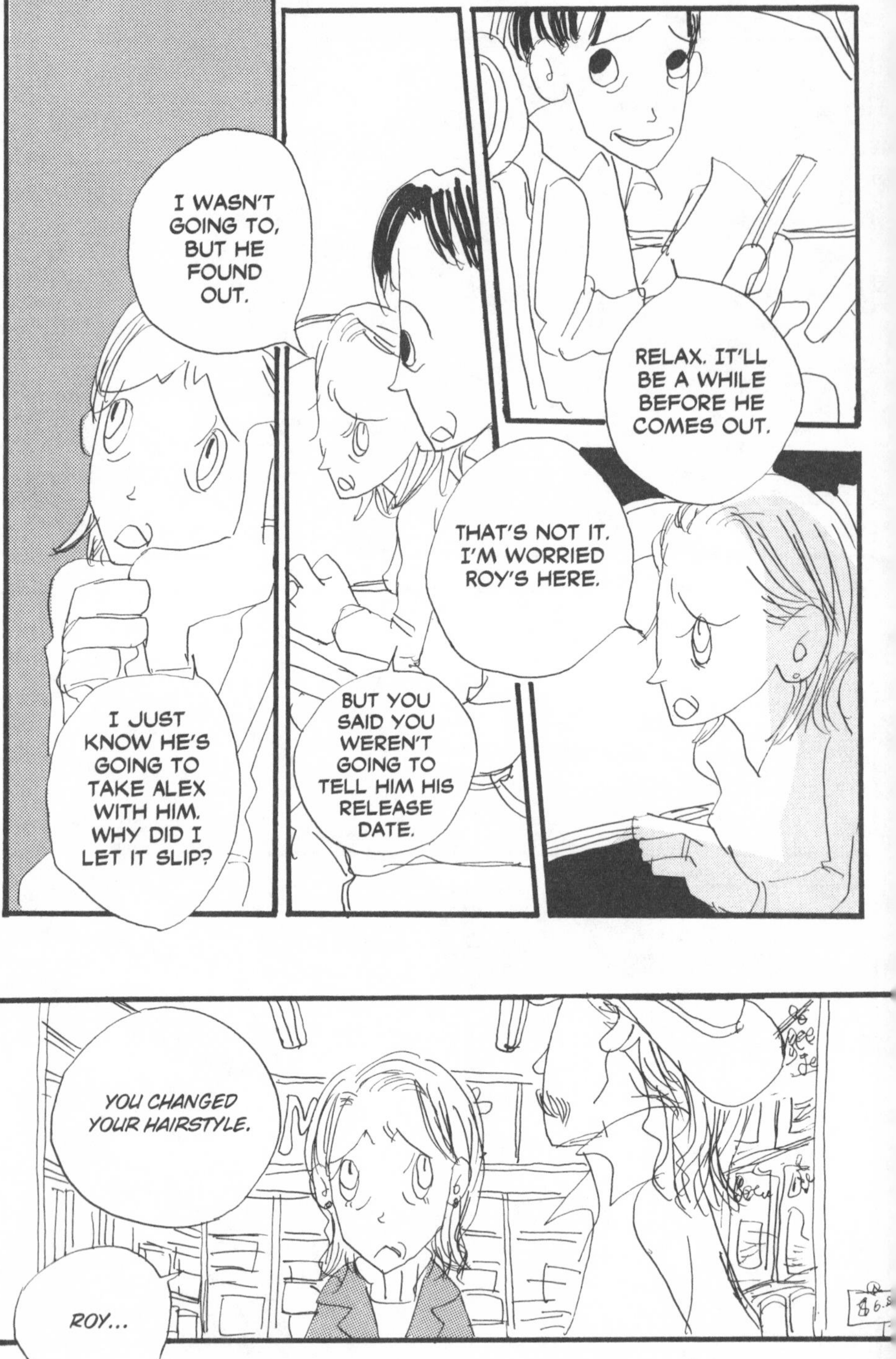
RELAX. IT'LL BE A WHILE BEFORE HE COMES OUT.
THAT'S NOT IT. I'M WORRIED ROY'S HERE.
BUT YOU SAID YOU WEREN'T GOING TO TELL HIM HIS RELEASE DATE.
I WASN'T GOING TO, BUT HE FOUND OUT.
I JUST KNOW HE'S GOING TO TAKE ALEX WITH HIM. WHY DID I LET IT SLIP?
YOU CHANGED YOUR HAIRSTYLE.
ROY...

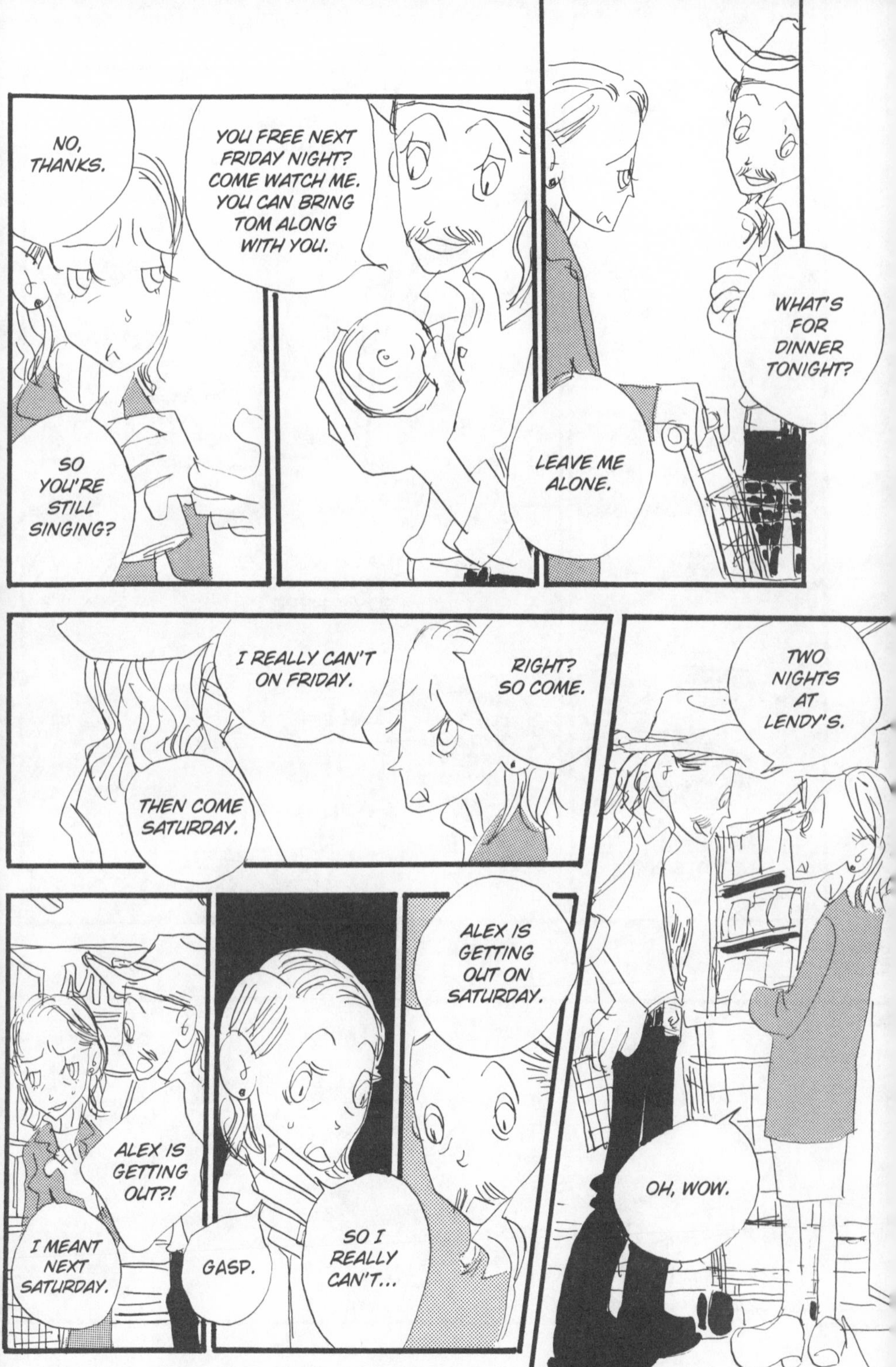
WHAT'S FOR DINNER TONIGHT?
LEAVE ME ALONE.
YOU FREE NEXT FRIDAY NIGHT? COME WATCH ME. YOU CAN BRING TOM ALONG WITH YOU.
NO, THANKS.
SO YOU'RE STILL SINGING?
TWO NIGHTS AT LENDY'S.
OH, WOW.
RIGHT? SO COME.
I REALLY CAN'T ON FRIDAY.
THEN COME SATURDAY.
ALEX IS GETTING OUT ON SATURDAY.
SO I REALLY CAN'T...
GASP.
ALEX IS GETTING OUT?!
I MEANT NEXT SATURDAY.

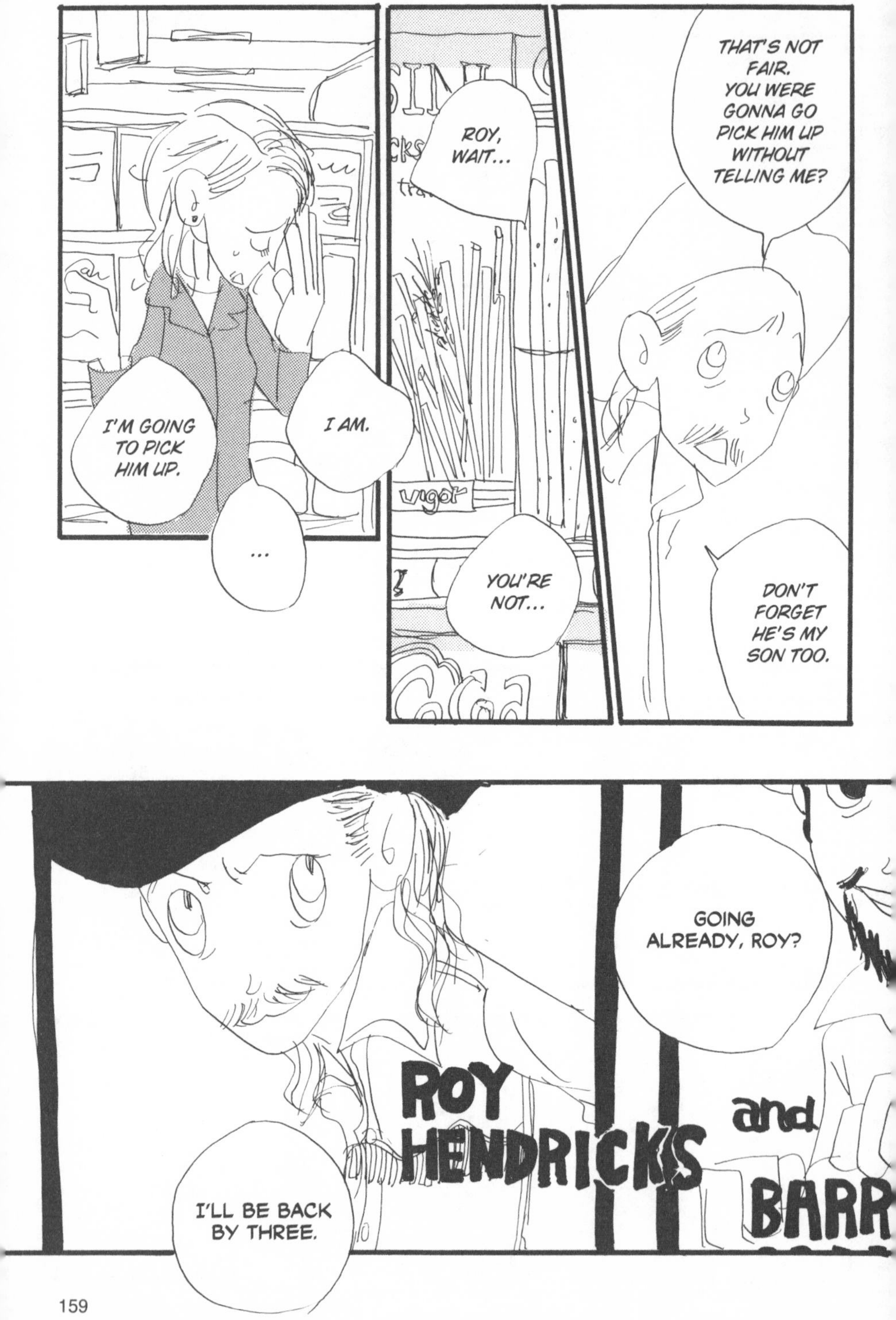
THAT'S NOT FAIR. YOU WERE GONNA GO PICK HIM UP WITHOUT TELLING ME?
DON'T FORGET HE'S MY SON TOO.
ROY, WAIT...
YOU'RE NOT...
I AM.
I'M GOING TO PICK HIM UP.
...
GOING ALREADY, ROY?
I'LL BE BACK BY THREE.
ROY HENDRICKS and BARR

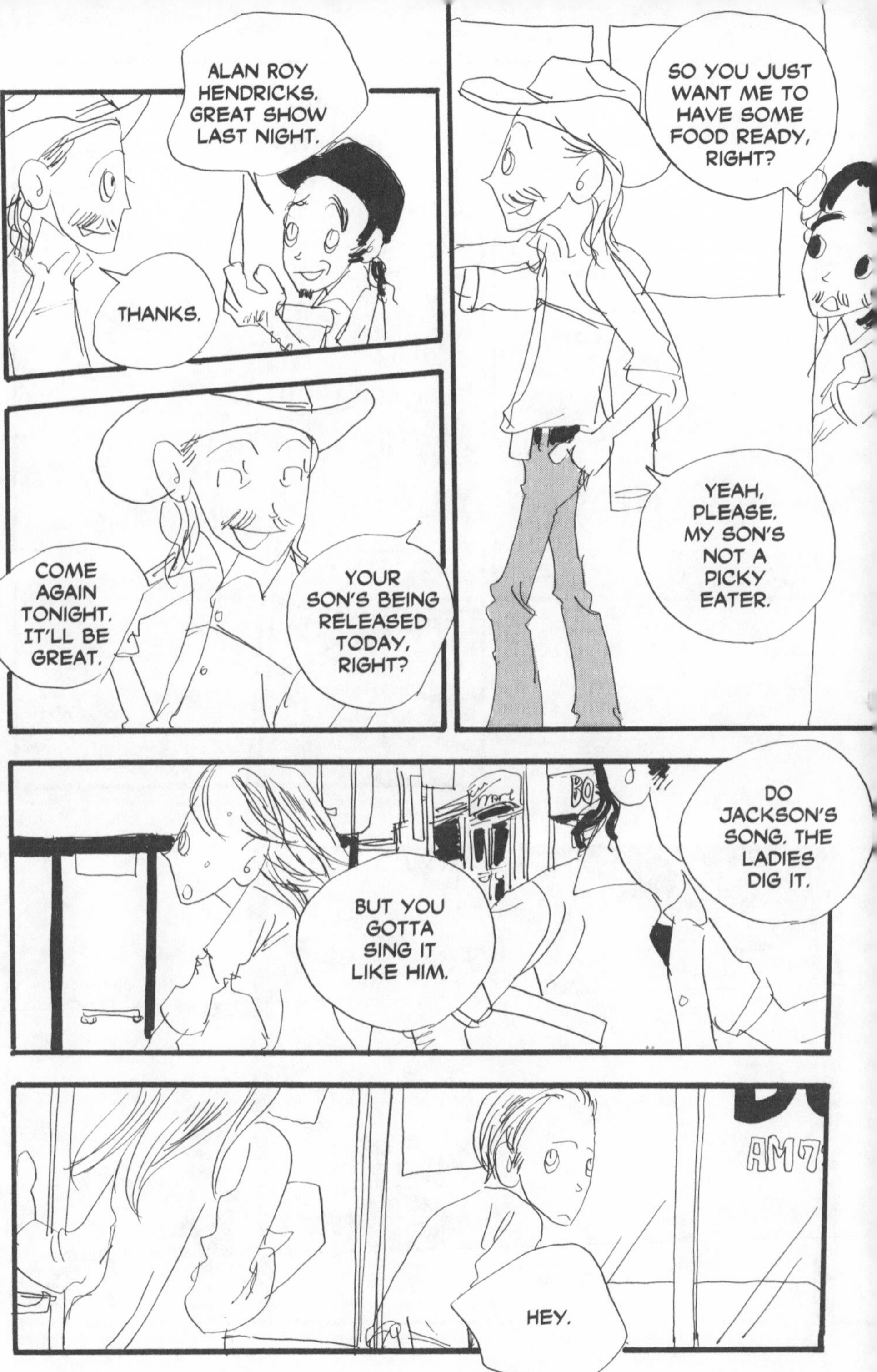
ALAN ROY HENDRICKS. GREAT SHOW LAST NIGHT.
THANKS.
COME AGAIN TONIGHT. IT'LL BE GREAT.
YOUR SON'S BEING RELEASED TODAY, RIGHT?
SO YOU JUST WANT ME TO HAVE SOME FOOD READY, RIGHT?
YEAH, PLEASE. MY SON'S NOT A PICKY EATER.
DO JACKSON'S SONG. THE LADIES DIG IT.
BUT YOU GOTTA SING IT LIKE HIM.
HEY.

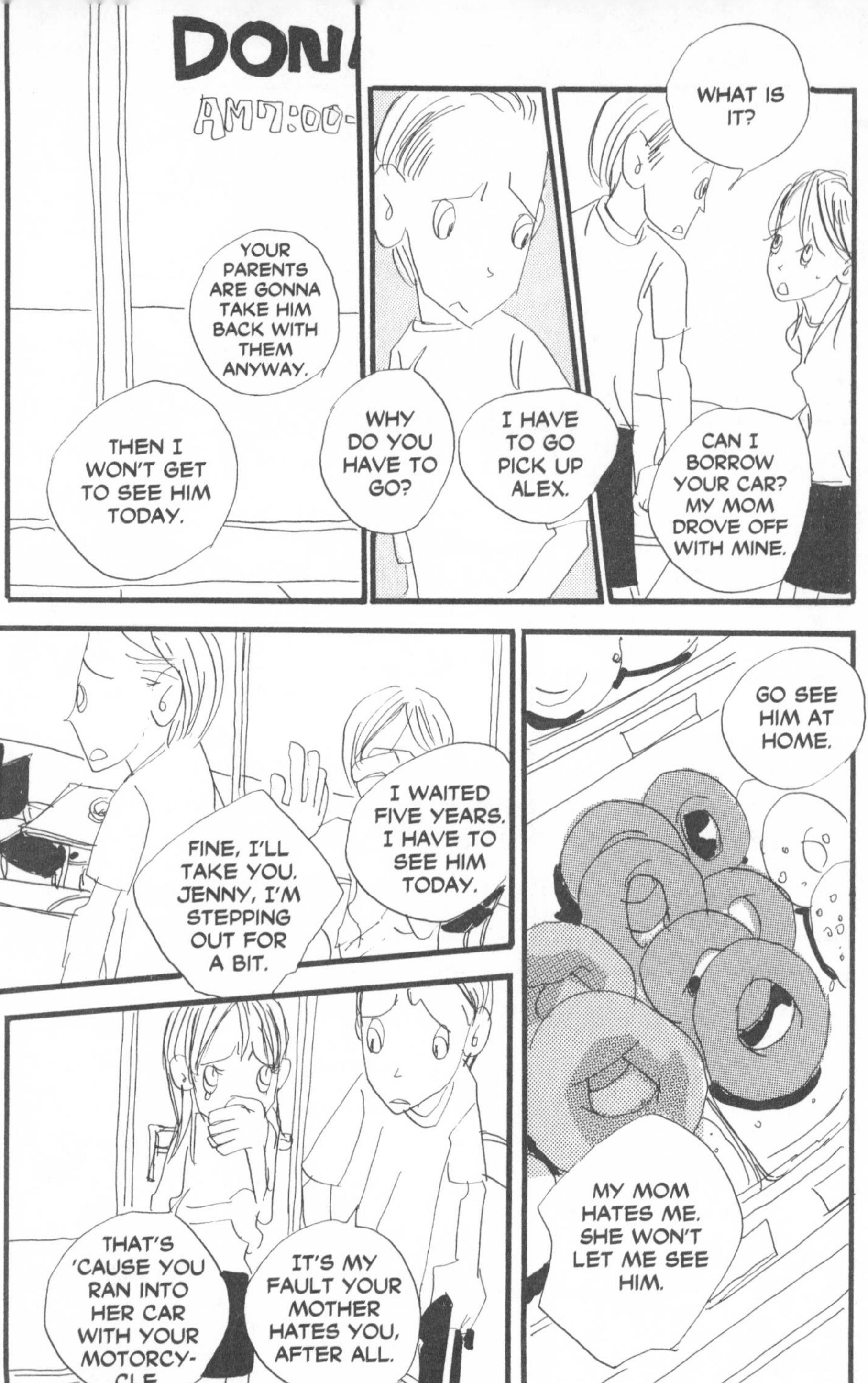
WHAT IS IT?
CAN I BORROW YOUR CAR? MY MOM DROVE OFF WITH MINE.
I HAVE TO GO PICK UP ALEX.
WHY DO YOU HAVE TO GO?
DON
AM7:00-
YOUR PARENTS ARE GONNA TAKE HIM BACK WITH THEM ANYWAY.
THEN I WON'T GET TO SEE HIM TODAY.
GO SEE HIM AT HOME.
MY MOM HATES ME. SHE WON'T LET ME SEE HIM.
I WAITED FIVE YEARS. I HAVE TO SEE HIM TODAY.
FINE, I'LL TAKE YOU. JENNY, I'M STEPPING OUT FOR A BIT.
IT'S MY FAULT YOUR MOTHER HATES YOU, AFTER ALL.
THAT'S 'CAUSE YOU RAN INTO HER CAR WITH YOUR MOTORCY-CLE.

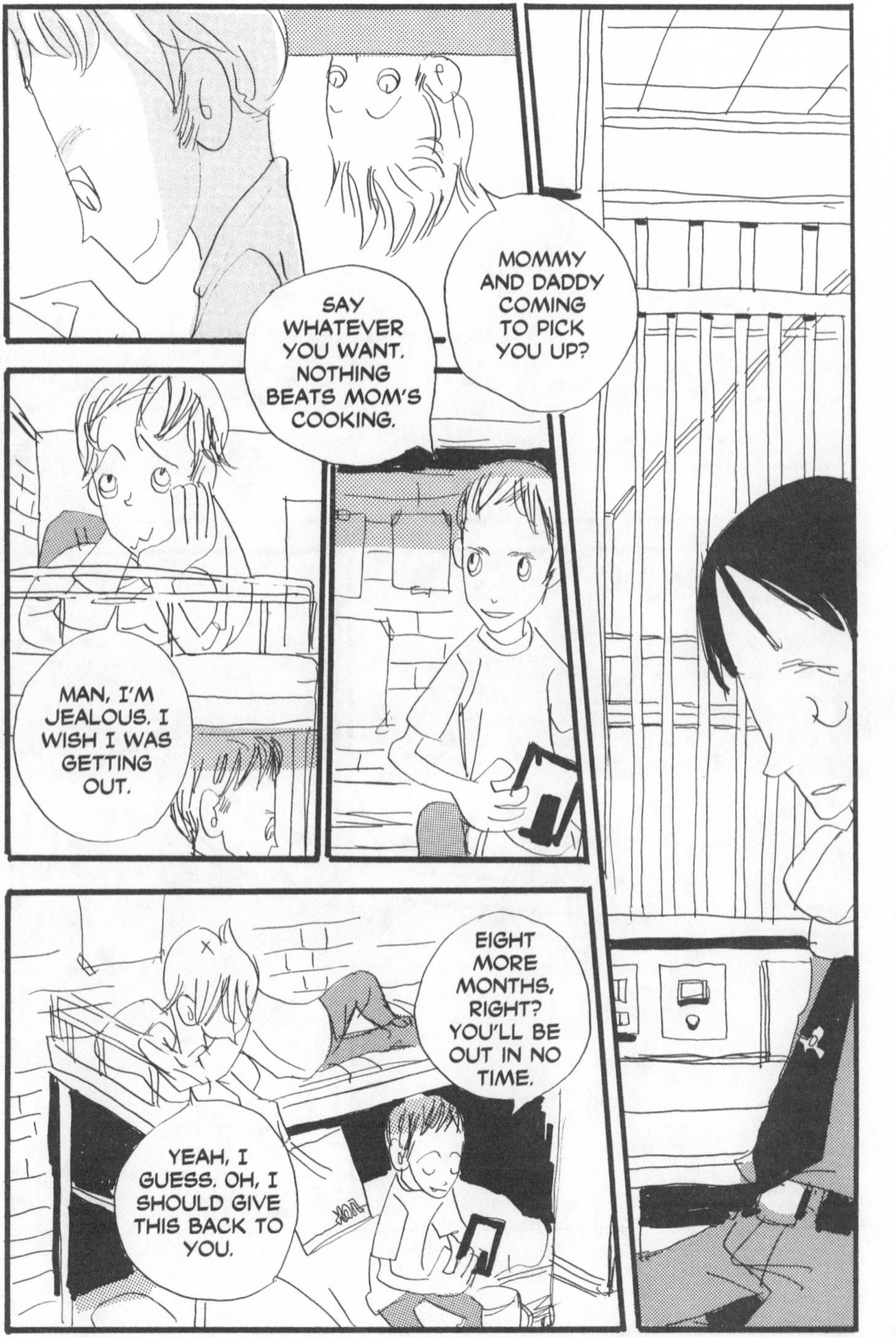

MOMMY AND DADDY COMING TO PICK YOU UP?
SAY WHATEVER YOU WANT. NOTHING BEATS MOM'S COOKING.
MAN, I'M JEALOUS. I WISH I WAS GETTING OUT.
EIGHT MORE MONTHS, RIGHT? YOU'LL BE OUT IN NO TIME.
YEAH, I GUESS. OH, I SHOULD GIVE THIS BACK TO YOU.

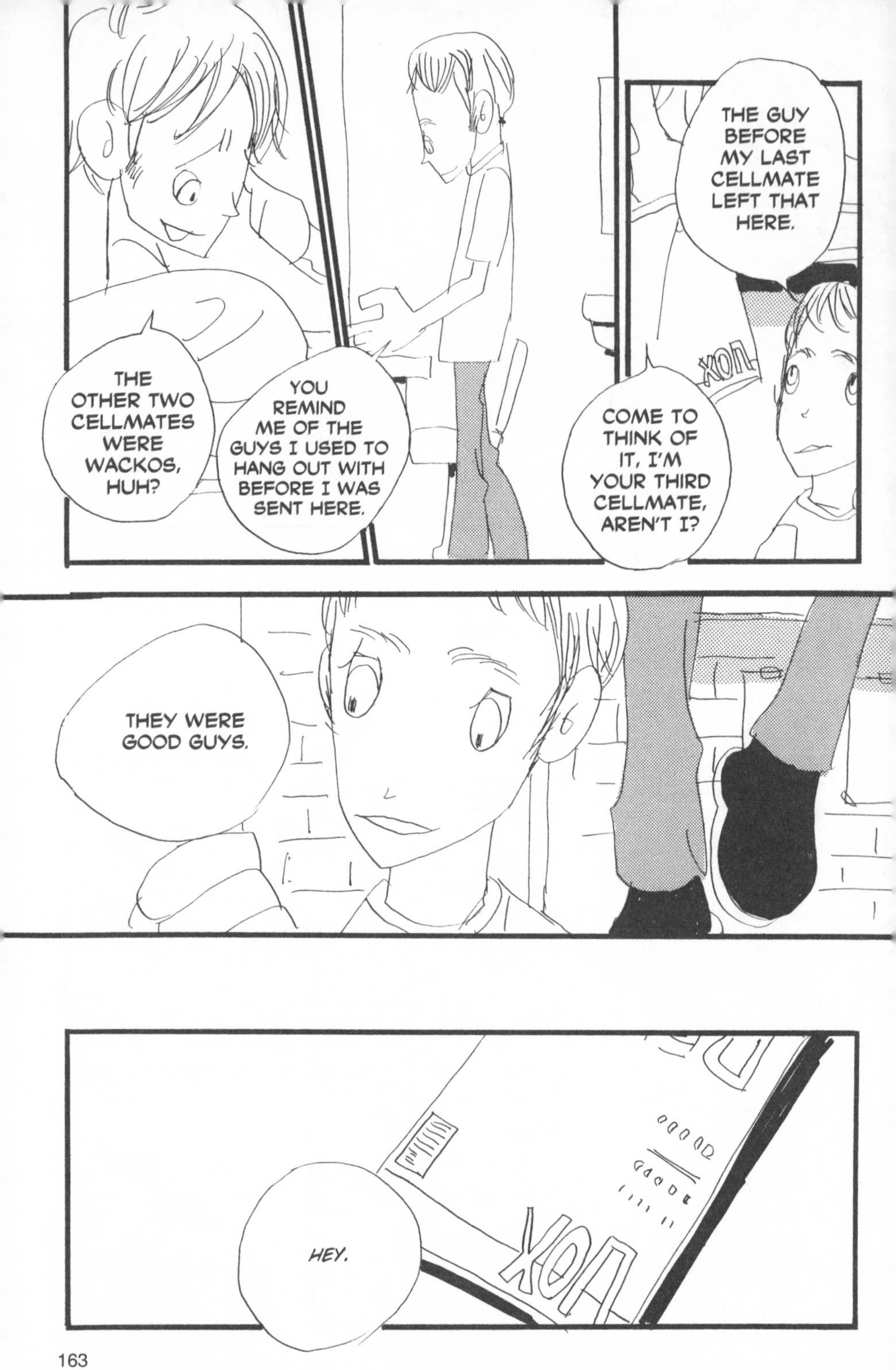
THE GUY BEFORE MY LAST CELLMATE LEFT THAT HERE.
COME TO THINK OF IT, I'M YOUR THIRD CELLMATE, AREN'T I?
YOU REMIND ME OF THE GUYS I USED TO HANG OUT WITH BEFORE I WAS SENT HERE.
THE OTHER TWO CELLMATES WERE WACKOS, HUH?
THEY WERE GOOD GUYS.
HEY.

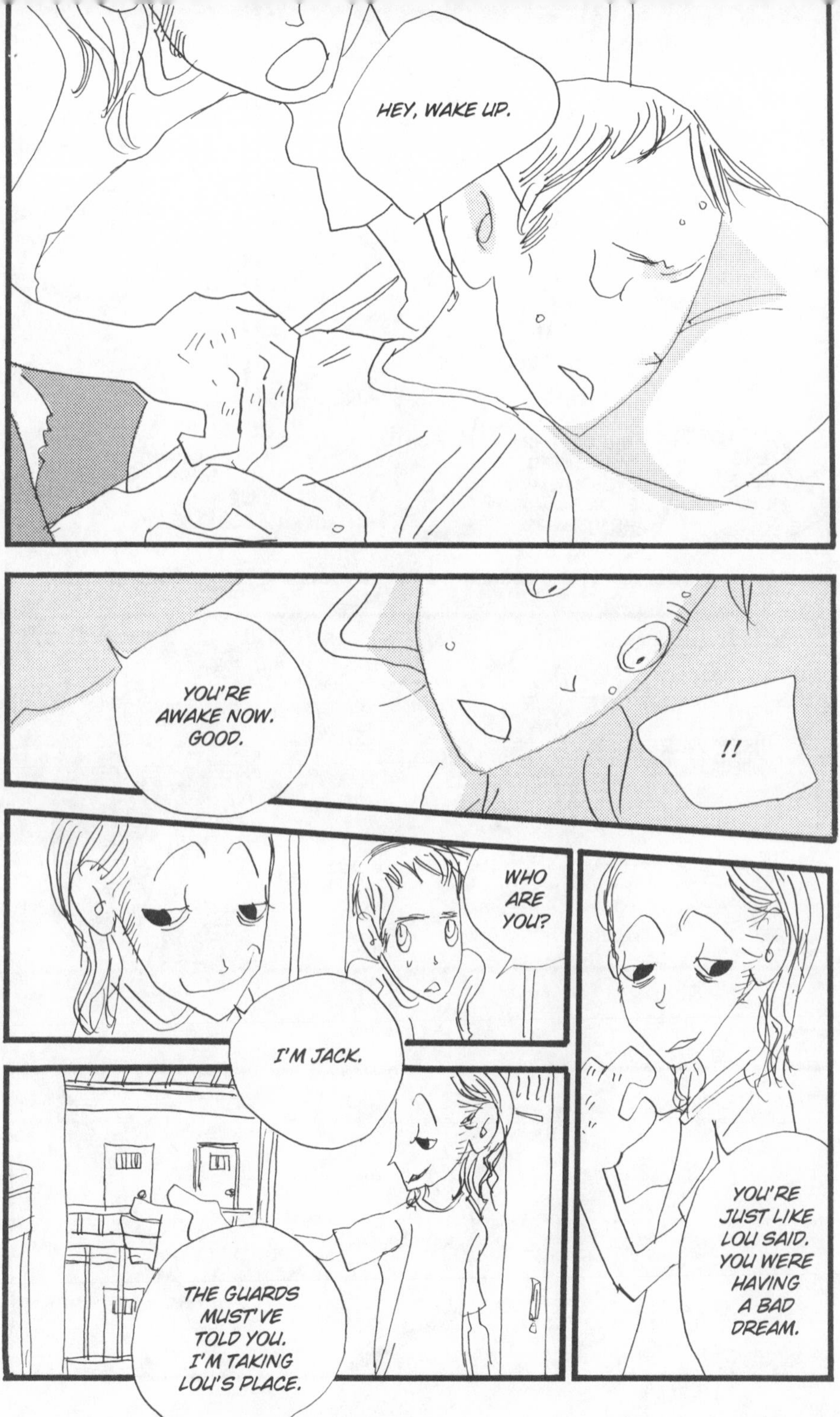
HEY, WAKE UP.
!!
YOU'RE AWAKE NOW. GOOD.
YOU'RE JUST LIKE LOU SAID. YOU WERE HAVING A BAD DREAM.
WHO ARE YOU?
I'M JACK.
THE GUARDS MUST'VE TOLD YOU. I'M TAKING LOU'S PLACE.

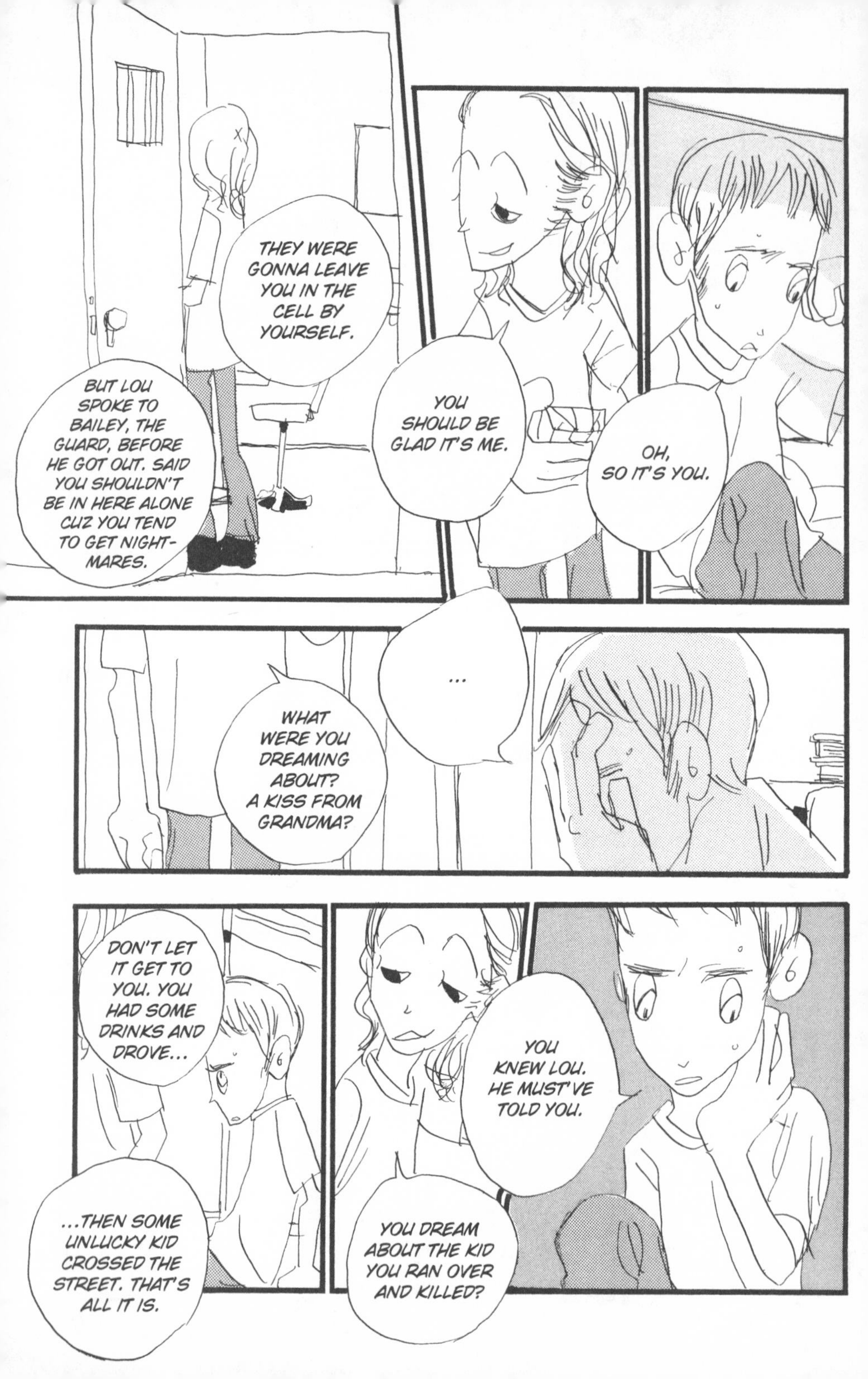
OH, SO IT'S YOU.
YOU SHOULD BE GLAD IT'S ME.
THEY WERE GONNA LEAVE YOU IN THE CELL BY YOURSELF.
BUT LOU SPOKE TO BAILEY, THE GUARD, BEFORE HE GOT OUT. SAID YOU SHOULDN'T BE IN HERE ALONE CUZ YOU TEND TO GET NIGHT-MARES.
...
WHAT WERE YOU DREAMING ABOUT? A KISS FROM GRANDMA?
YOU KNEW LOU. HE MUST'VE TOLD YOU.
YOU DREAM ABOUT THE KID YOU RAN OVER AND KILLED?
DON'T LET IT GET TO YOU. YOU HAD SOME DRINKS AND DROVE...
...THEN SOME UNLUCKY KID CROSSED THE STREET. THAT'S ALL IT IS.

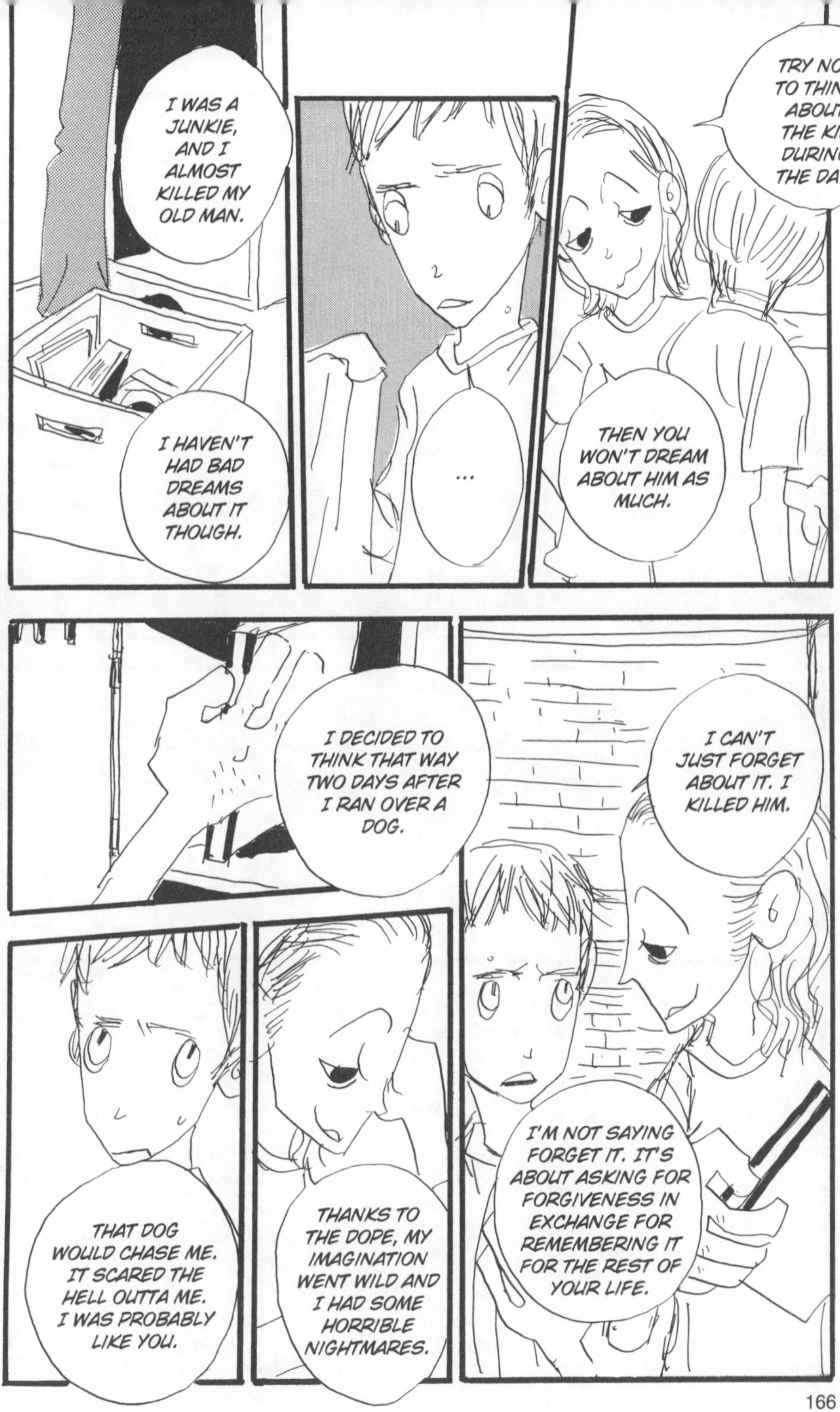
TRY NOT TO THINK ABOUT THE KID DURING THE DAY.
THEN YOU WON'T DREAM ABOUT HIM AS MUCH.
...
I WAS A JUNKIE, AND I ALMOST KILLED MY OLD MAN.
I HAVEN'T HAD BAD DREAMS ABOUT IT THOUGH.
I CAN'T JUST FORGET ABOUT IT. I KILLED HIM.
I'M NOT SAYING FORGET IT. IT'S ABOUT ASKING FOR FORGIVENESS IN EXCHANGE FOR REMEMBERING IT FOR THE REST OF YOUR LIFE.
I DECIDED TO THINK THAT WAY TWO DAYS AFTER I RAN OVER A DOG.
THANKS TO THE DOPE, MY IMAGINATION WENT WILD AND I HAD SOME HORRIBLE NIGHTMARES.
THAT DOG WOULD CHASE ME. IT SCARED THE HELL OUTTA ME. I WAS PROBABLY LIKE YOU.

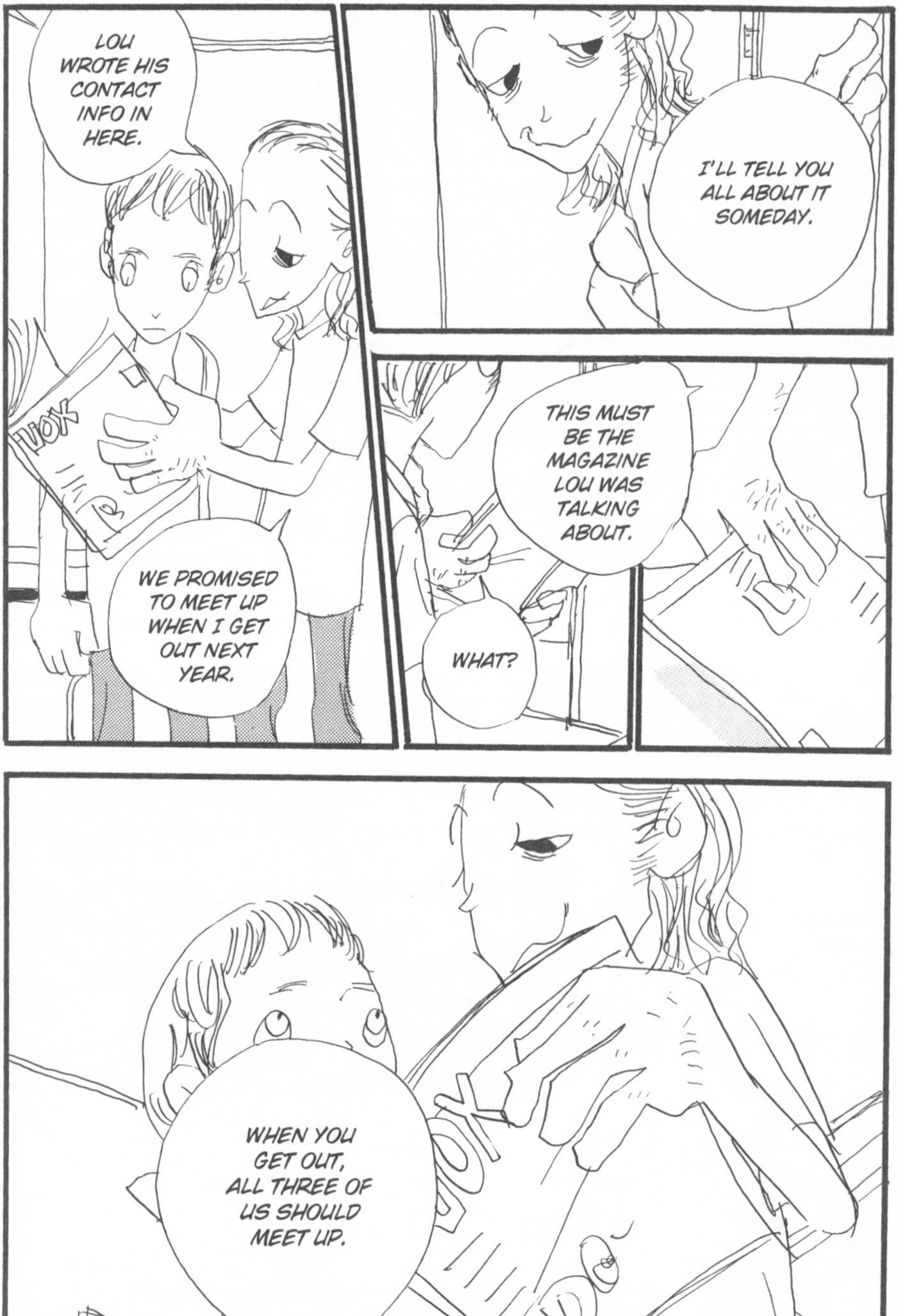
LOU WROTE HIS CONTACT INFO IN HERE.
WE PROMISED TO MEET UP WHEN I GET OUT NEXT YEAR.
I'LL TELL YOU ALL ABOUT IT SOMEDAY.
THIS MUST BE THE MAGAZINE LOU WAS TALKING ABOUT.
WHAT?
VOX
WHEN YOU GET OUT, ALL THREE OF US SHOULD MEET UP.

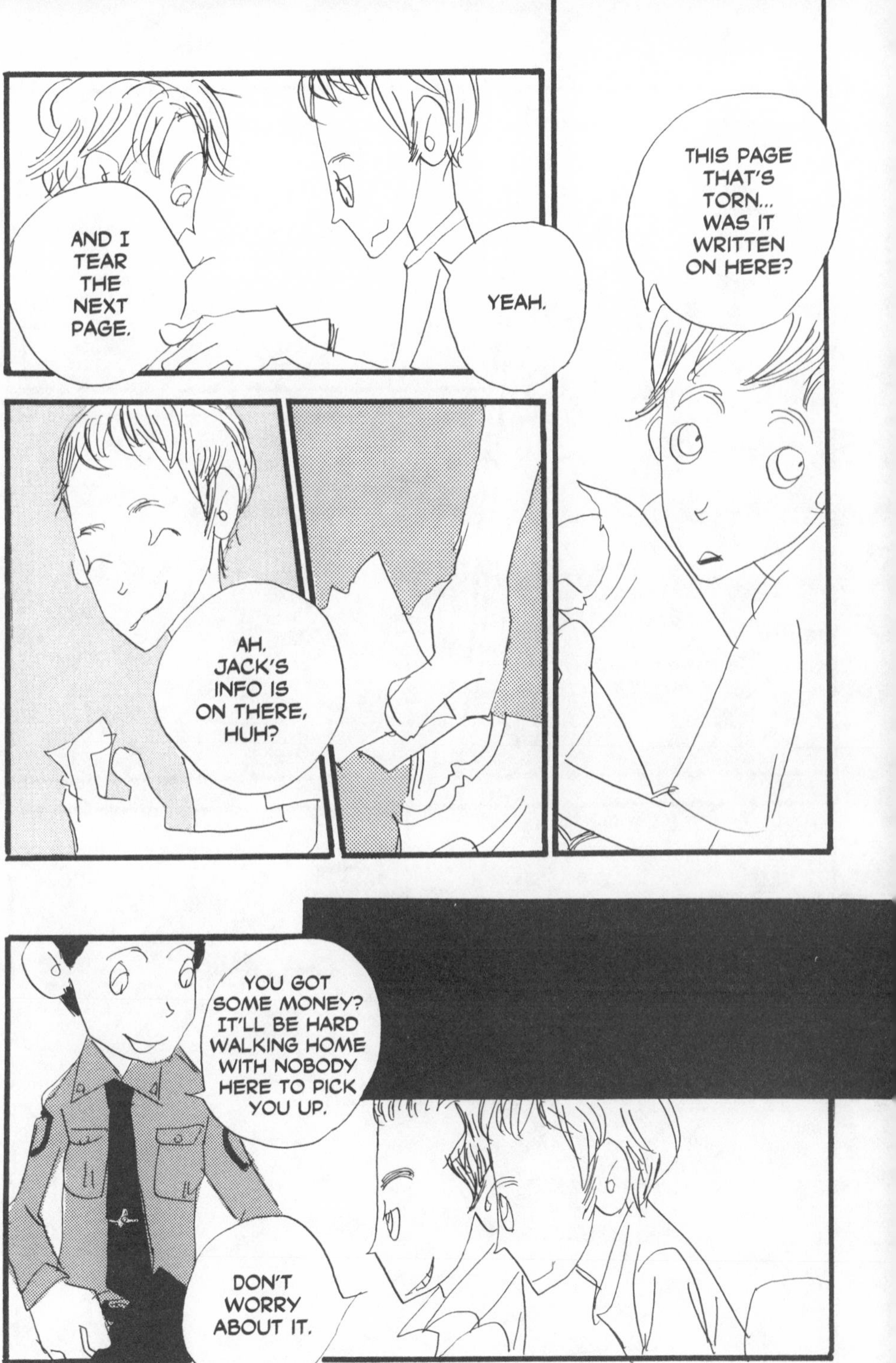

AND I TEAR THE NEXT PAGE.
YEAH.
THIS PAGE THAT'S TORN... WAS IT WRITTEN ON HERE?
AH. JACK'S INFO IS ON THERE, HUH?
YOU GOT SOME MONEY? IT'LL BE HARD WALKING HOME WITH NOBODY HERE TO PICK YOU UP.
DON'T WORRY ABOUT IT.

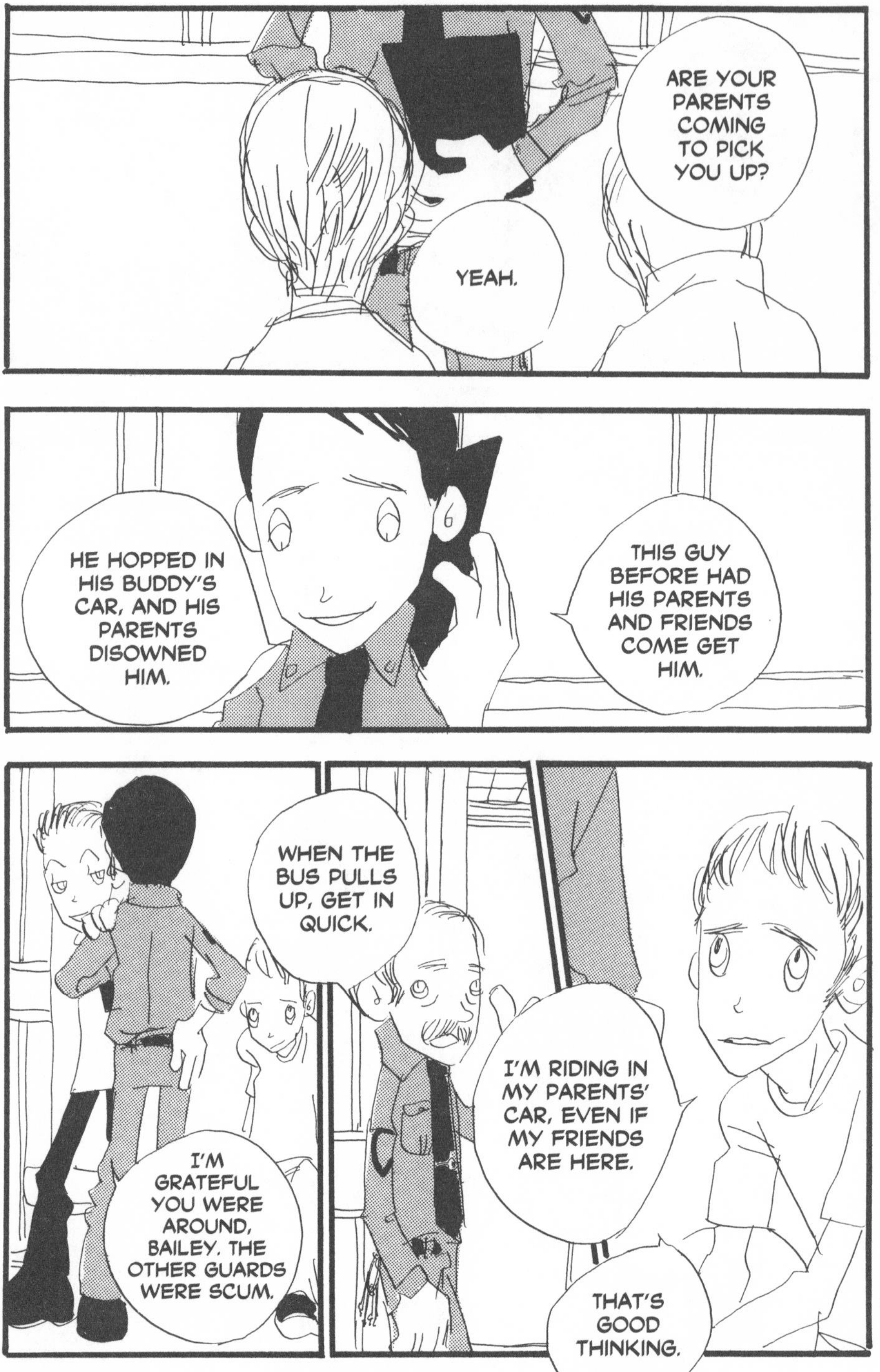
ARE YOUR PARENTS COMING TO PICK YOU UP?
YEAH.
THIS GUY BEFORE HAD HIS PARENTS AND FRIENDS COME GET HIM.
HE HOPPED IN HIS BUDDY'S CAR, AND HIS PARENTS DISOWNED HIM.
I'M RIDING IN MY PARENTS' CAR, EVEN IF MY FRIENDS ARE HERE.
THAT'S GOOD THINKING.
WHEN THE BUS PULLS UP, GET IN QUICK.
I'M GRATEFUL YOU WERE AROUND, BAILEY. THE OTHER GUARDS WERE SCUM.

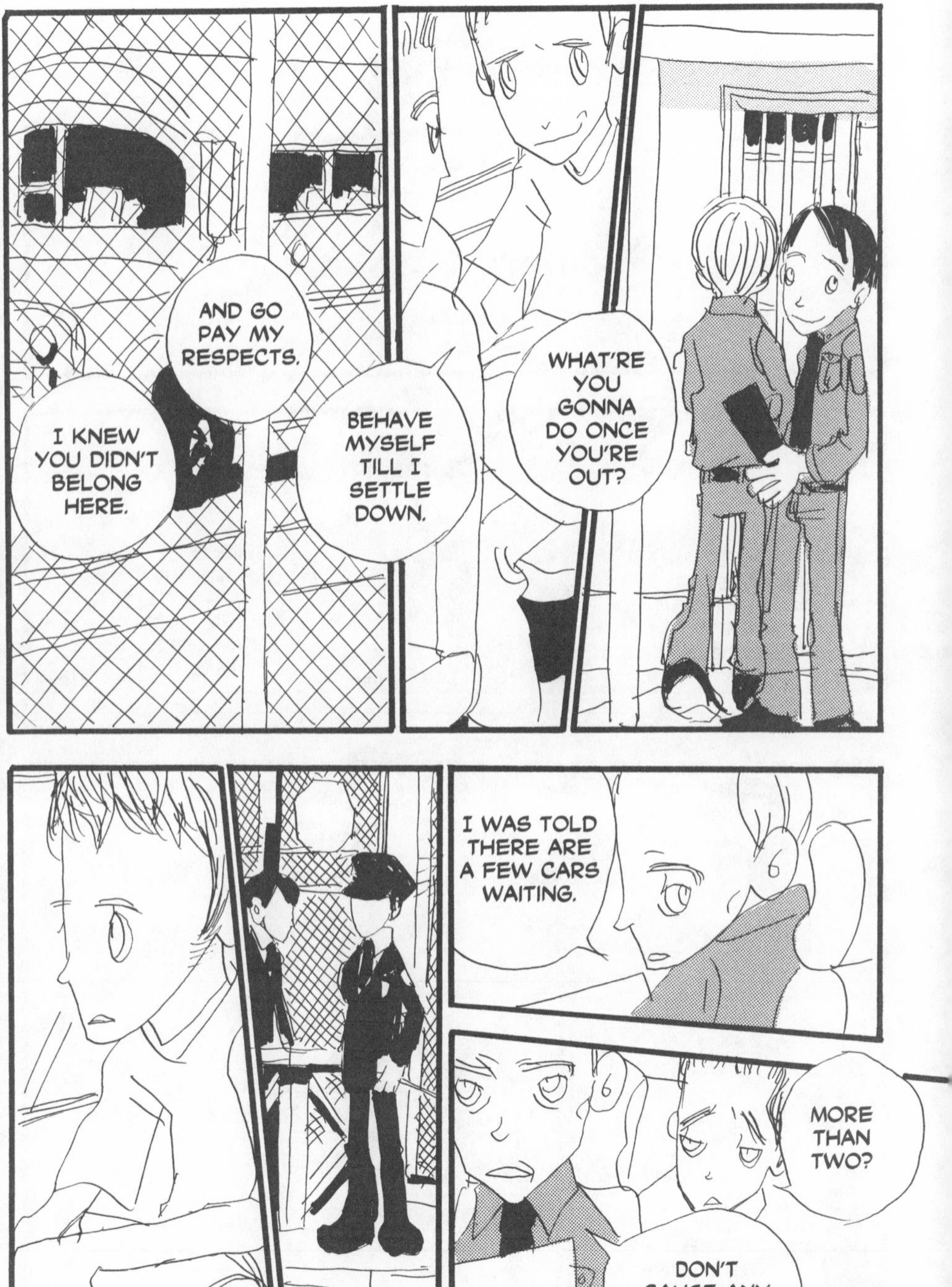
WHAT'RE YOU GONNA DO ONCE YOU'RE OUT?
BEHAVE MYSELF TILL I SETTLE DOWN.
AND GO PAY MY RESPECTS.
I KNEW YOU DIDN'T BELONG HERE.
I WAS TOLD THERE ARE A FEW CARS WAITING.
MORE THAN TWO?
DON'T CAUSE ANY PROBLEMS. JUST GO.

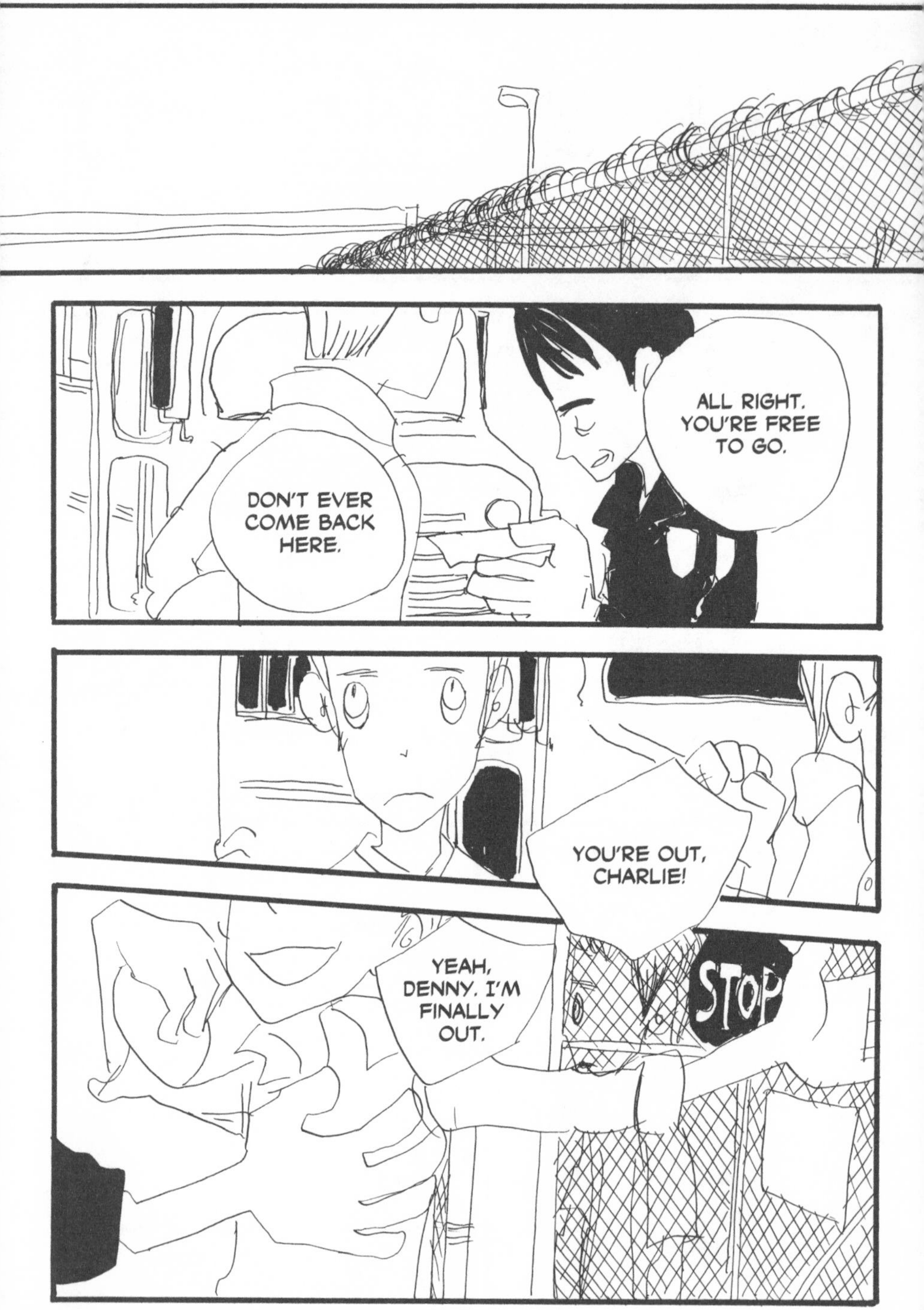
ALL RIGHT. YOU'RE FREE TO GO.
DON'T EVER COME BACK HERE.
YOU'RE OUT, CHARLIE!
YEAH, DENNY. I'M FINALLY OUT.
STOP

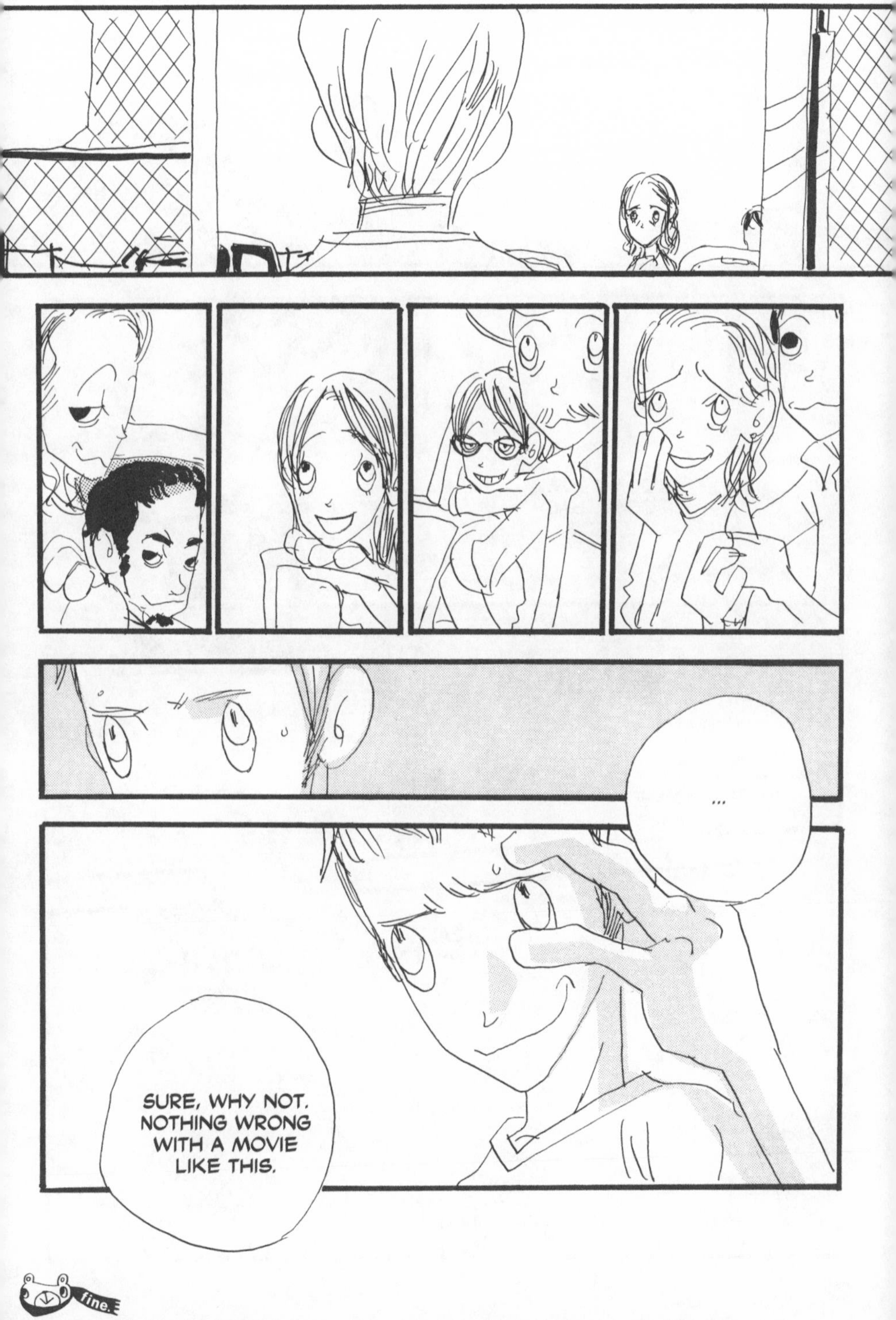
...
SURE, WHY NOT. NOTHING WRONG WITH A MOVIE LIKE THIS.
fine.

senza titolo #5
parking! Issue 3 (Dojinshi)
Published in August 1998

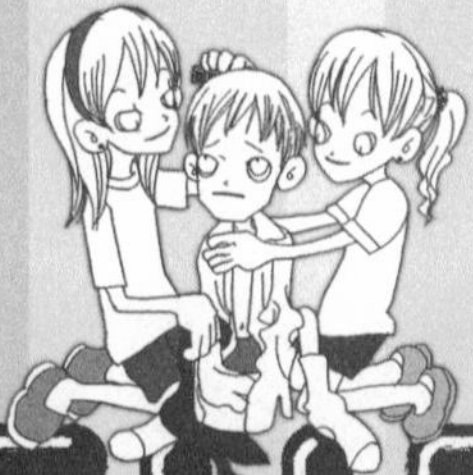

THE FROOMS

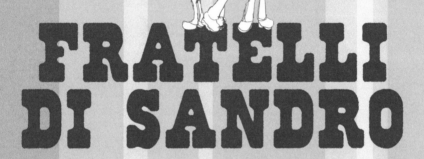

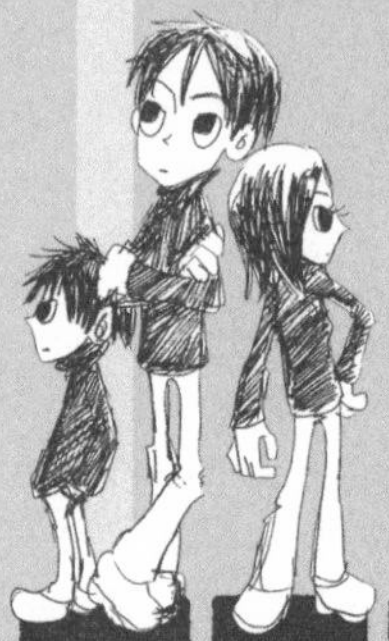

FRATELLI DI SANDRO

Stanley,
who lives in New York,
has two older sisters.

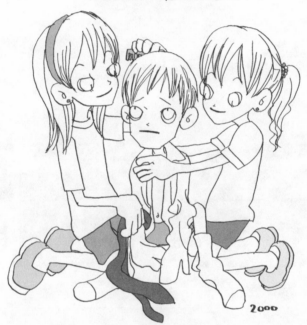

THE
FROOMS

Froom Family

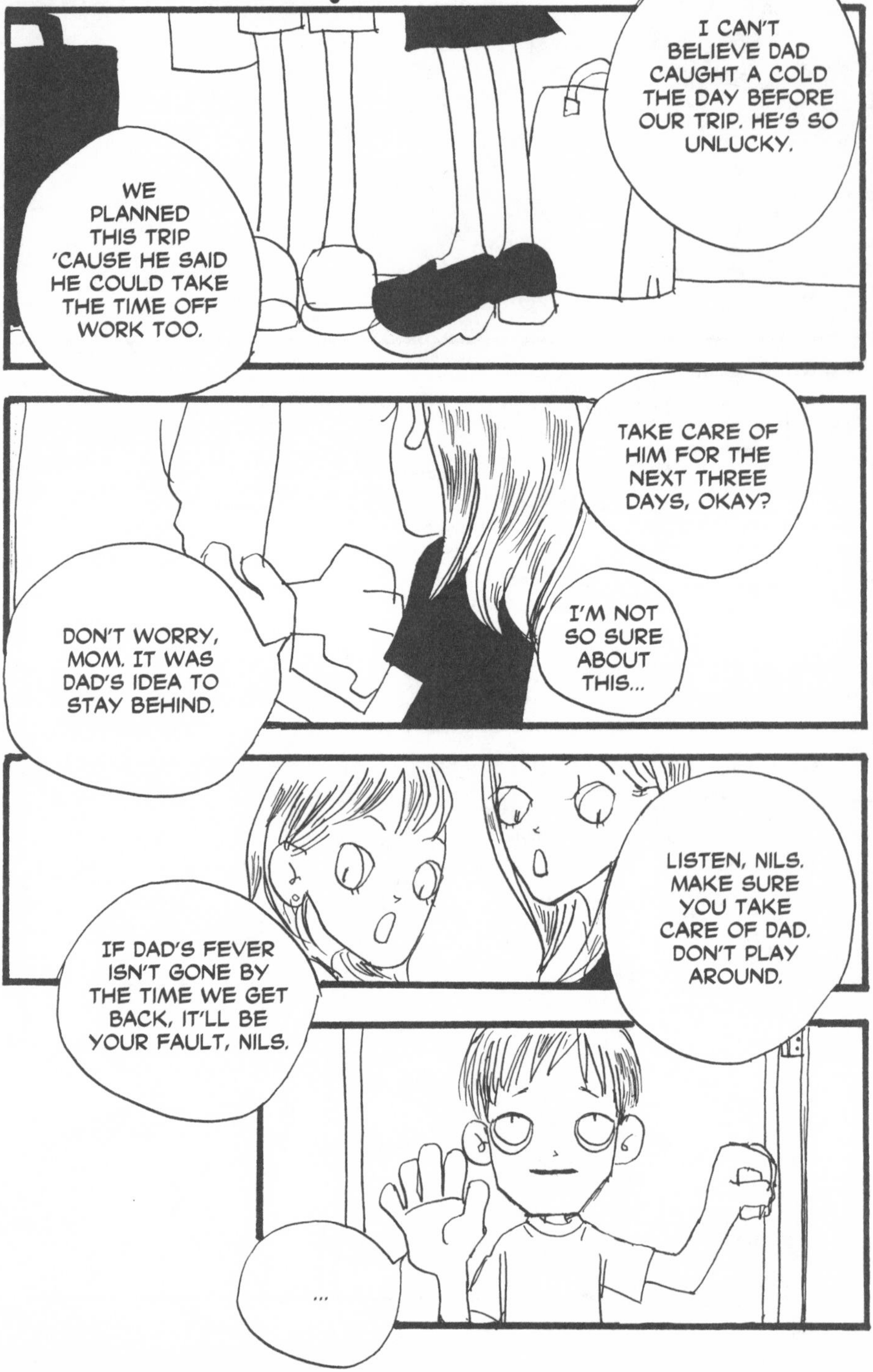
I CAN'T BELIEVE DAD CAUGHT A COLD THE DAY BEFORE OUR TRIP. HE'S SO UNLUCKY.
WE PLANNED THIS TRIP 'CAUSE HE SAID HE COULD TAKE THE TIME OFF WORK TOO.
TAKE CARE OF HIM FOR THE NEXT THREE DAYS, OKAY?
I'M NOT SO SURE ABOUT THIS...
DON'T WORRY, MOM. IT WAS DAD'S IDEA TO STAY BEHIND.
LISTEN, NILS. MAKE SURE YOU TAKE CARE OF DAD. DON'T PLAY AROUND.
IF DAD'S FEVER ISN'T GONE BY THE TIME WE GET BACK, IT'LL BE YOUR FAULT, NILS.
...

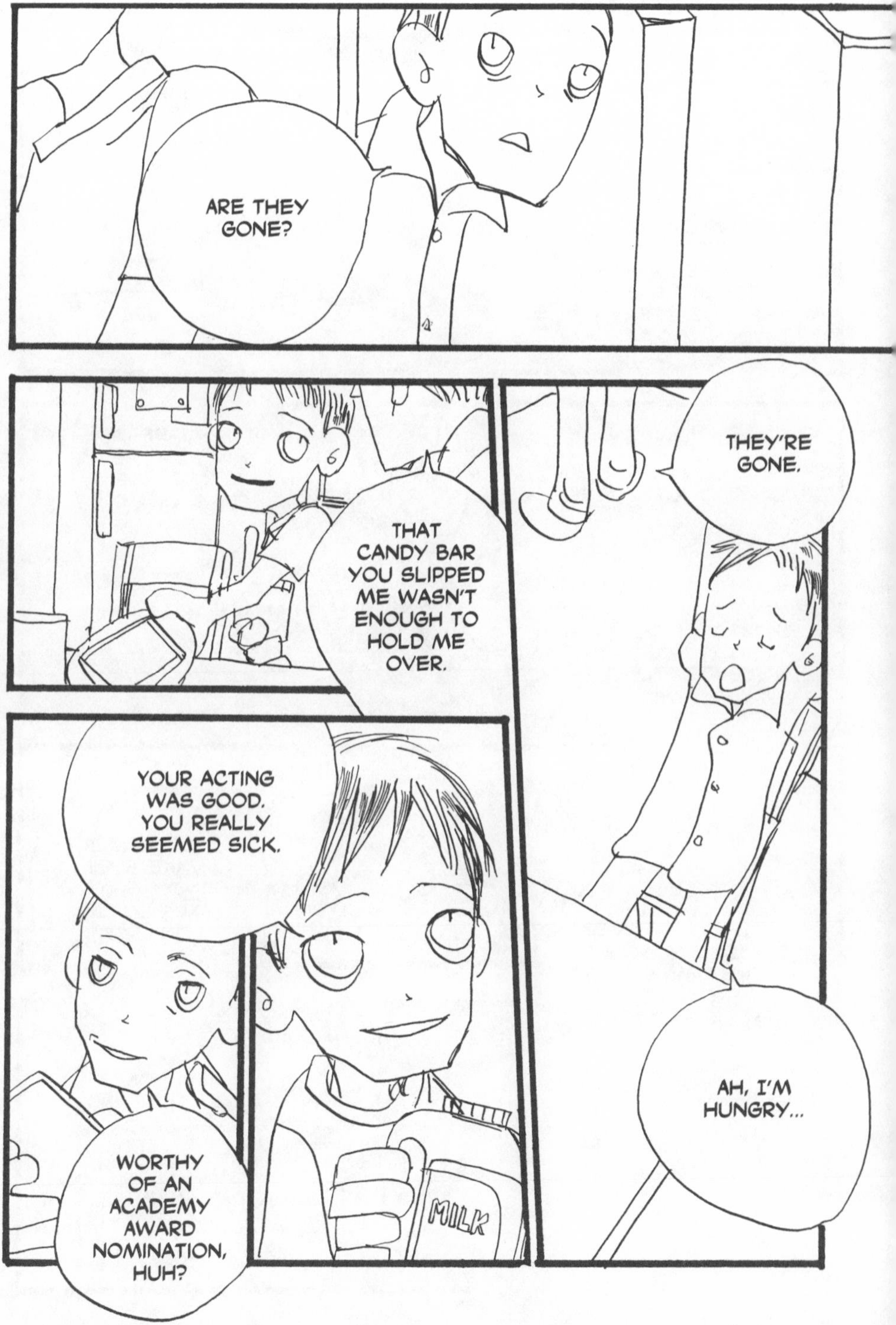
ARE THEY GONE?
THEY'RE GONE.
AH, I'M HUNGRY...
THAT CANDY BAR YOU SLIPPED ME WASN'T ENOUGH TO HOLD ME OVER.
YOUR ACTING WAS GOOD. YOU REALLY SEEMED SICK.
WORTHY OF AN ACADEMY AWARD NOMINATION, HUH?
MILK

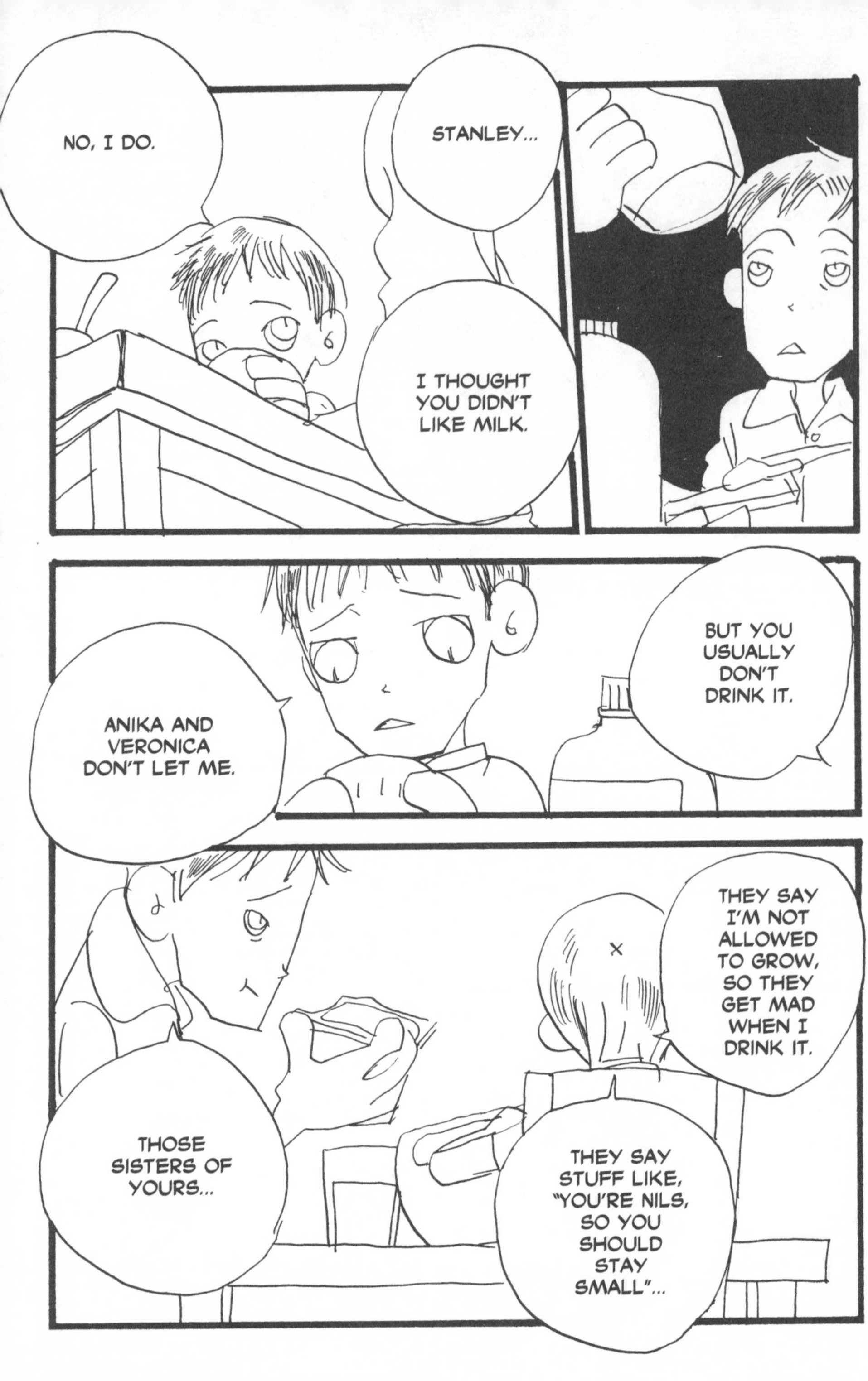
STANLEY...
I THOUGHT YOU DIDN'T LIKE MILK.
NO, I DO.
BUT YOU USUALLY DON'T DRINK IT.
ANIKA AND VERONICA DON'T LET ME.
THEY SAY I'M NOT ALLOWED TO GROW, SO THEY GET MAD WHEN I DRINK IT.
THEY SAY STUFF LIKE, "YOU'RE NILS, SO YOU SHOULD STAY SMALL"...
THOSE SISTERS OF YOURS...

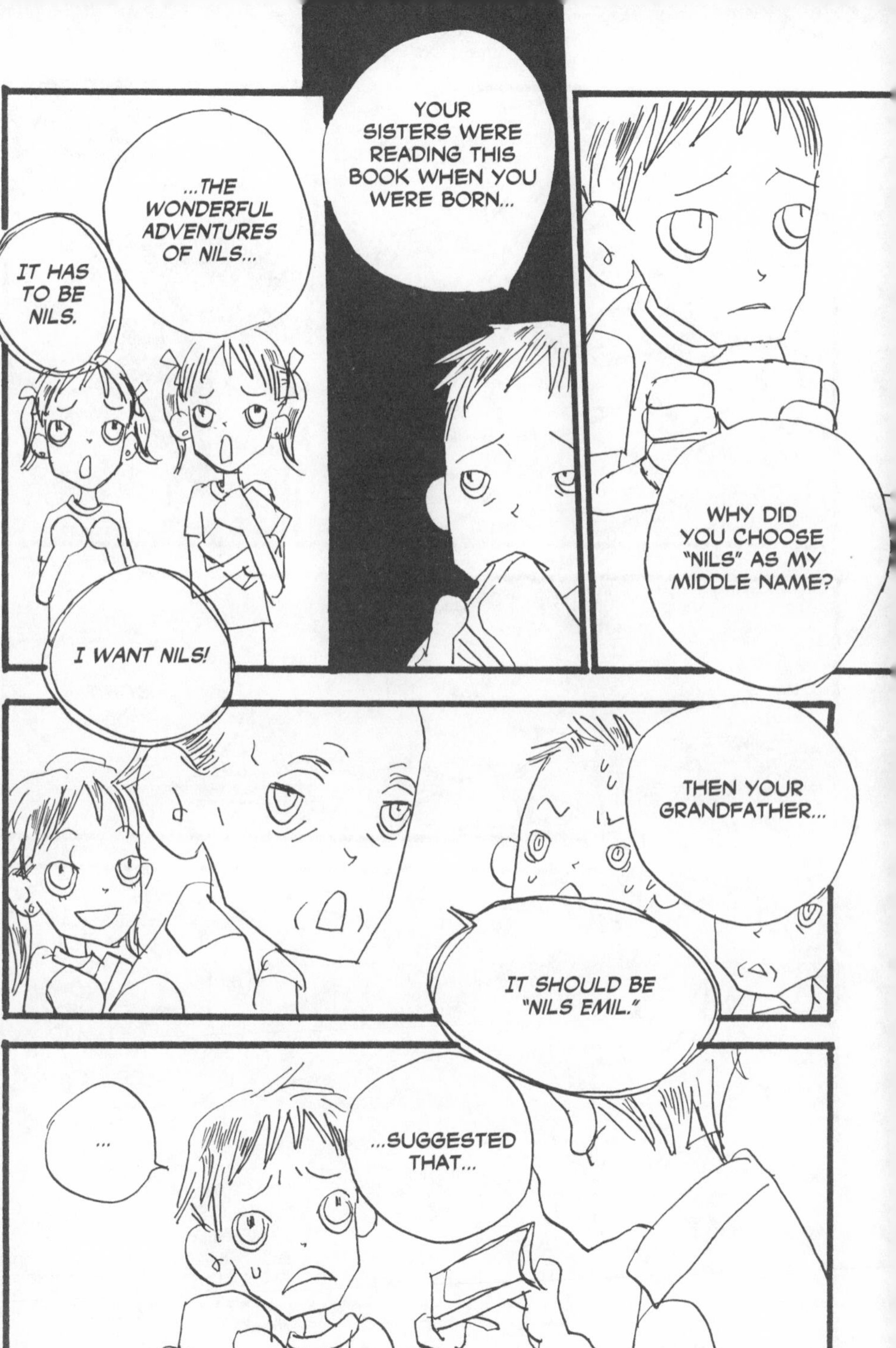
WHY DID YOU CHOOSE "NILS" AS MY MIDDLE NAME?
YOUR SISTERS WERE READING THIS BOOK WHEN YOU WERE BORN...
...THE WONDERFUL ADVENTURES OF NILS...
IT HAS TO BE NILS.
I WANT NILS!
THEN YOUR GRANDFATHER...
IT SHOULD BE "NILS EMIL."
...SUGGESTED THAT...
...

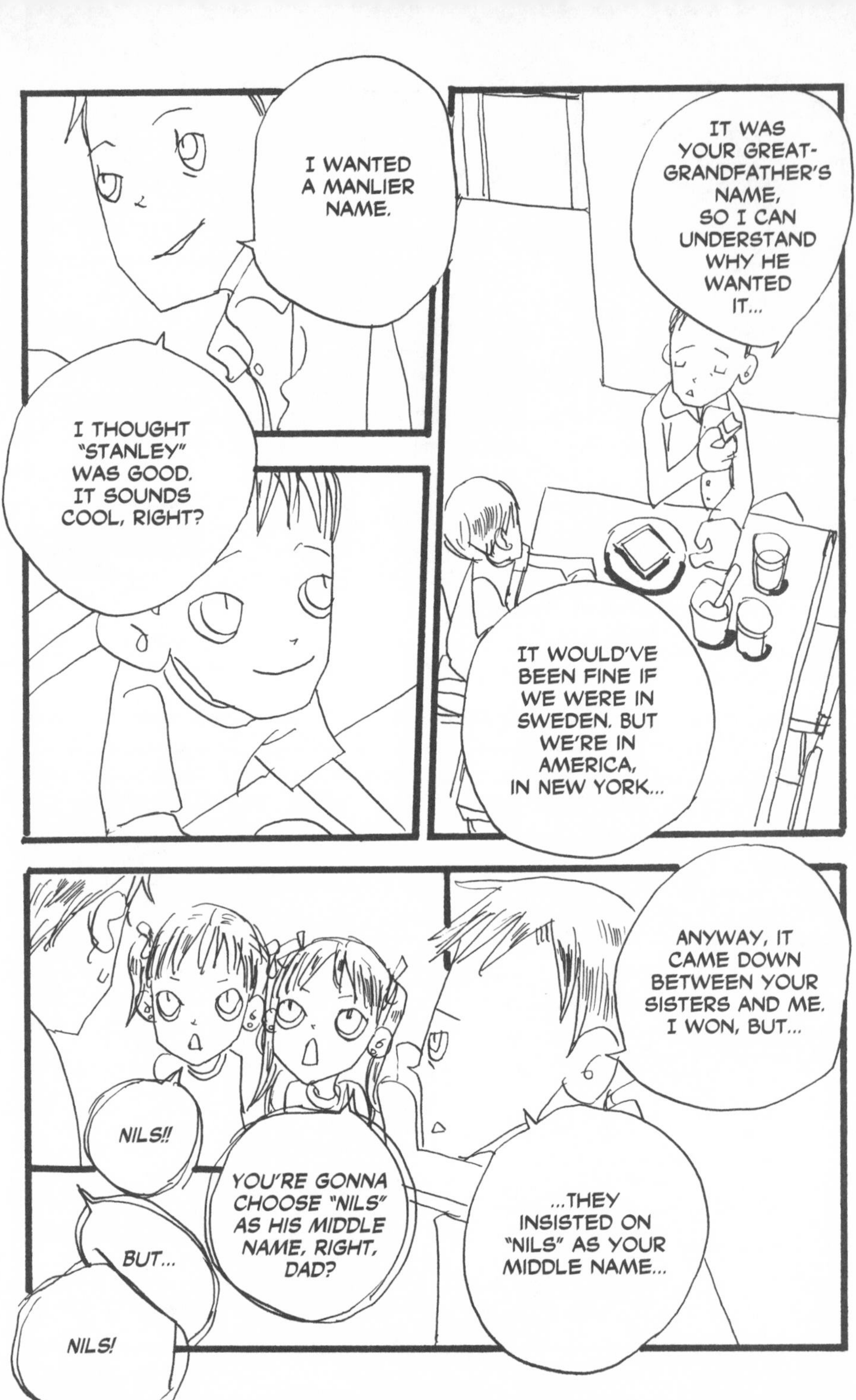
IT WAS YOUR GREAT-GRANDFATHER'S NAME, SO I CAN UNDERSTAND WHY HE WANTED IT...
IT WOULD'VE BEEN FINE IF WE WERE IN SWEDEN. BUT WE'RE IN AMERICA, IN NEW YORK...
I WANTED A MANLIER NAME.
I THOUGHT "STANLEY" WAS GOOD. IT SOUNDS COOL, RIGHT?
ANYWAY, IT CAME DOWN BETWEEN YOUR SISTERS AND ME. I WON, BUT...
...THEY INSISTED ON "NILS" AS YOUR MIDDLE NAME...
YOU'RE GONNA CHOOSE "NILS" AS HIS MIDDLE NAME, RIGHT, DAD?
NILS!!
BUT...
NILS!

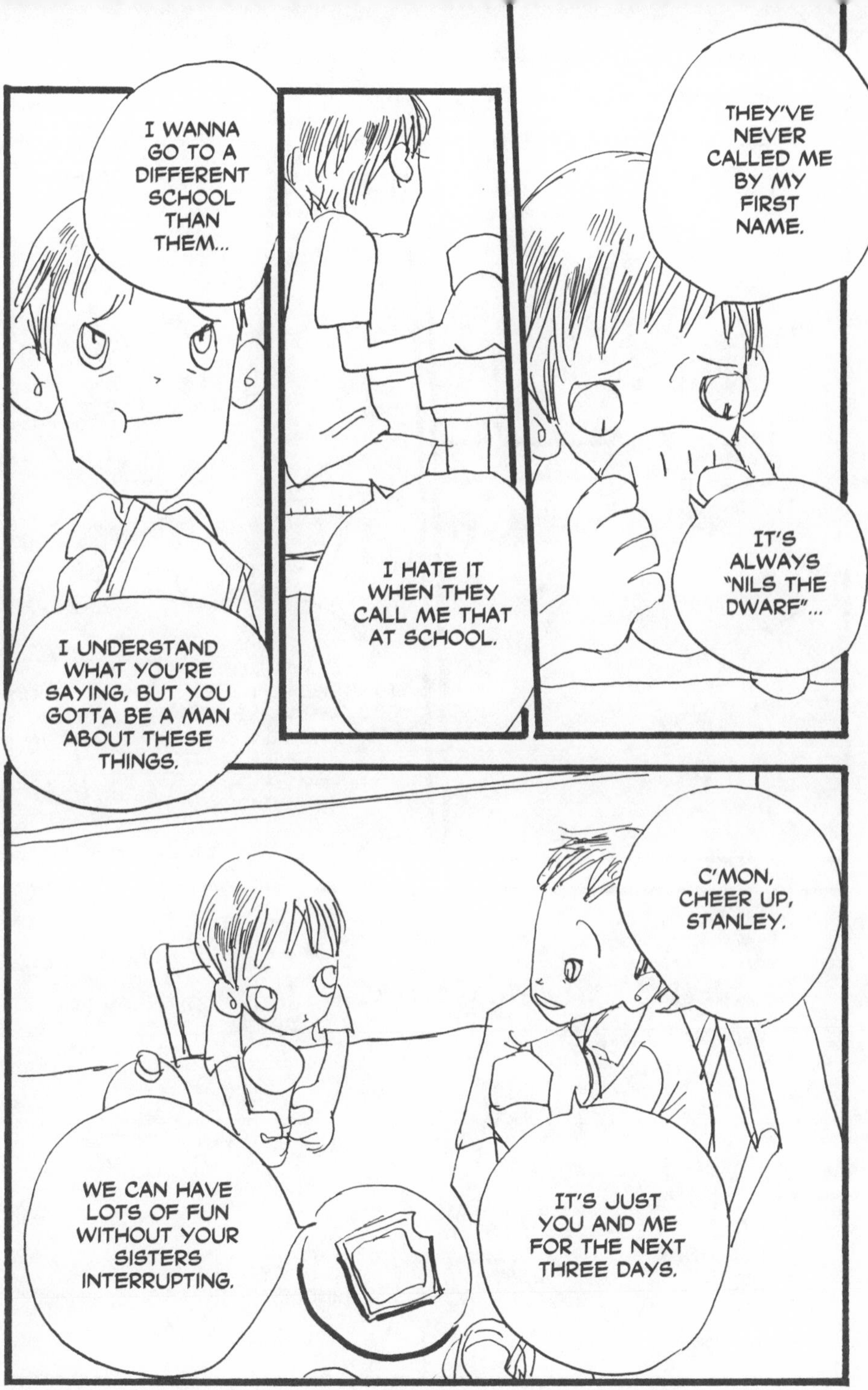
THEY'VE NEVER CALLED ME BY MY FIRST NAME.
IT'S ALWAYS "NILS THE DWARF"...
I HATE IT WHEN THEY CALL ME THAT AT SCHOOL.
I WANNA GO TO A DIFFERENT SCHOOL THAN THEM...
I UNDERSTAND WHAT YOU'RE SAYING, BUT YOU GOTTA BE A MAN ABOUT THESE THINGS.
C'MON, CHEER UP, STANLEY.
IT'S JUST YOU AND ME FOR THE NEXT THREE DAYS.
WE CAN HAVE LOTS OF FUN WITHOUT YOUR SISTERS INTERRUPTING.

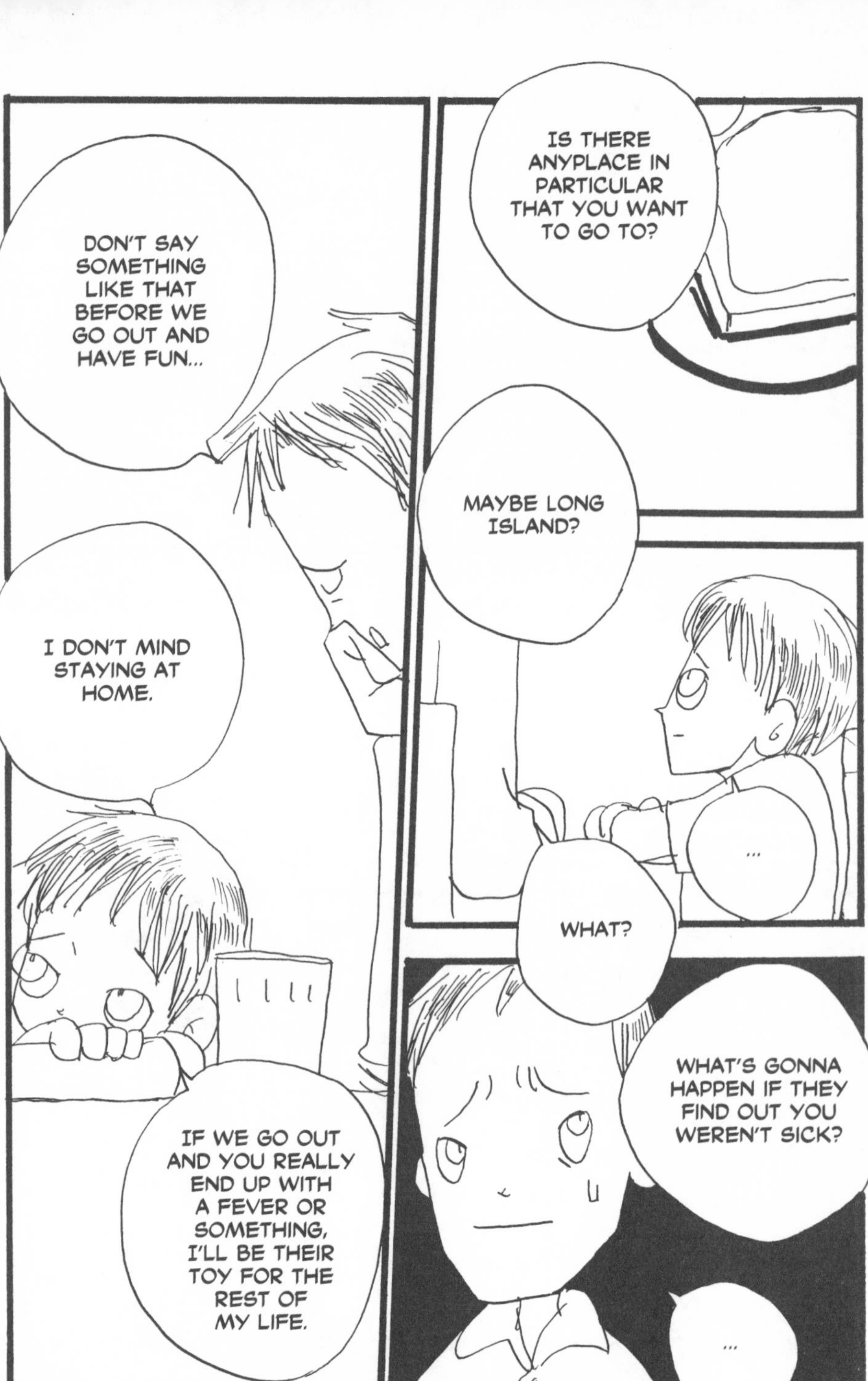
IS THERE ANYPLACE IN PARTICULAR THAT YOU WANT TO GO TO?
MAYBE LONG ISLAND?
...
WHAT?
WHAT'S GONNA HAPPEN IF THEY FIND OUT YOU WEREN'T SICK?
...
DON'T SAY SOMETHING LIKE THAT BEFORE WE GO OUT AND HAVE FUN...
I DON'T MIND STAYING AT HOME.
IF WE GO OUT AND YOU REALLY END UP WITH A FEVER OR SOMETHING, I'LL BE THEIR TOY FOR THE REST OF MY LIFE.

fine.

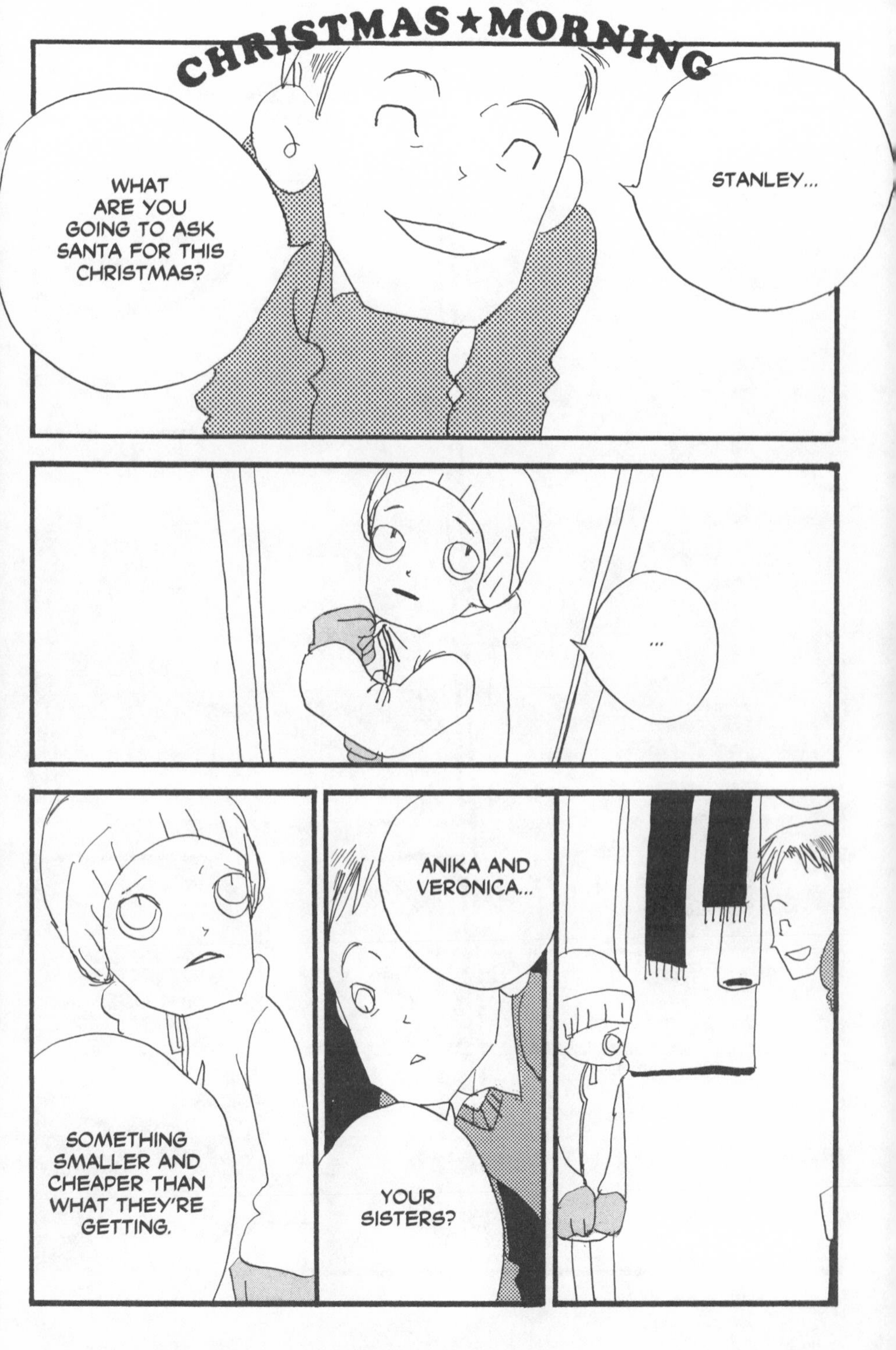
CHRISTMAS★MORNING
STANLEY...
WHAT ARE YOU GOING TO ASK SANTA FOR THIS CHRISTMAS?
...
ANIKA AND VERONICA...
YOUR SISTERS?
SOMETHING SMALLER AND CHEAPER THAN WHAT THEY'RE GETTING.

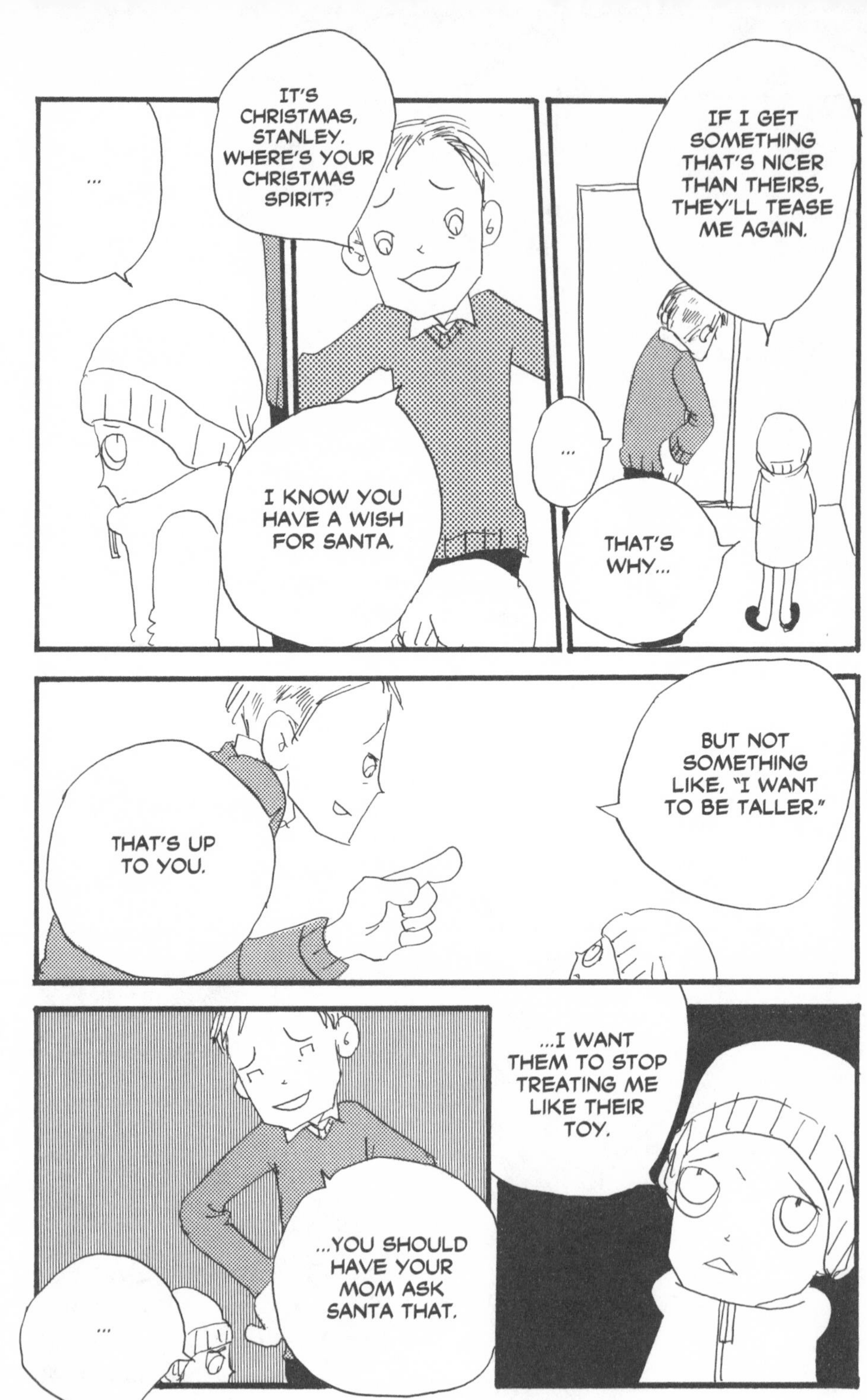
IF I GET SOMETHING THAT'S NICER THAN THEIRS, THEY'LL TEASE ME AGAIN.
...
THAT'S WHY...
IT'S CHRISTMAS, STANLEY. WHERE'S YOUR CHRISTMAS SPIRIT?
I KNOW YOU HAVE A WISH FOR SANTA.
...
BUT NOT SOMETHING LIKE, "I WANT TO BE TALLER."
THAT'S UP TO YOU.
...I WANT THEM TO STOP TREATING ME LIKE THEIR TOY.
...YOU SHOULD HAVE YOUR MOM ASK SANTA THAT.
...

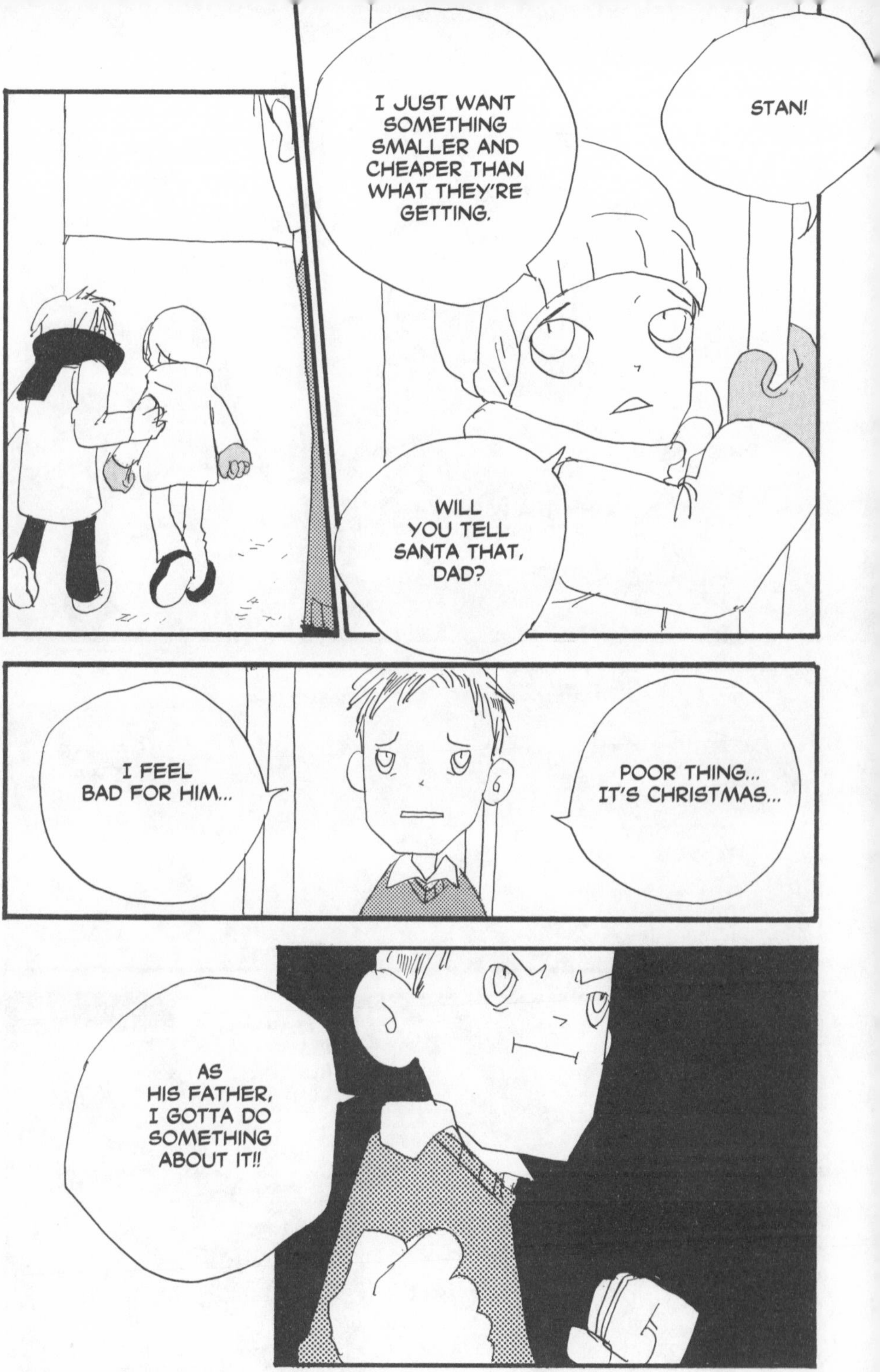
STAN!
I JUST WANT SOMETHING SMALLER AND CHEAPER THAN WHAT THEY'RE GETTING.
WILL YOU TELL SANTA THAT, DAD?
POOR THING... IT'S CHRISTMAS...
I FEEL BAD FOR HIM...
AS HIS FATHER, I GOTTA DO SOMETHING ABOUT IT!!

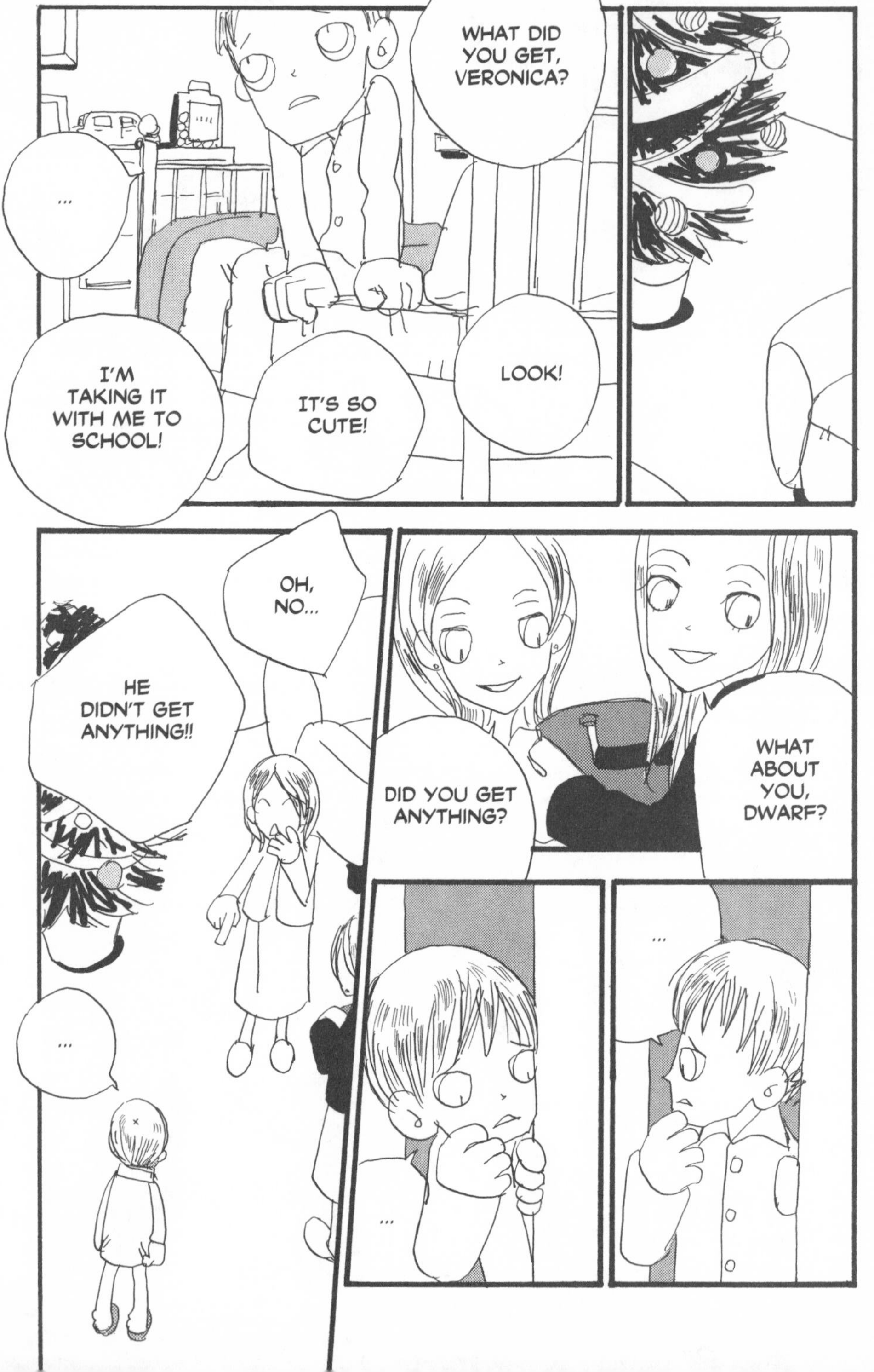
WHAT DID YOU GET, VERONICA?
...
LOOK!
IT'S SO CUTE!
I'M TAKING IT WITH ME TO SCHOOL!
WHAT ABOUT YOU, DWARF?
DID YOU GET ANYTHING?
...
...
OH, NO...
HE DIDN'T GET ANYTHING!!
...

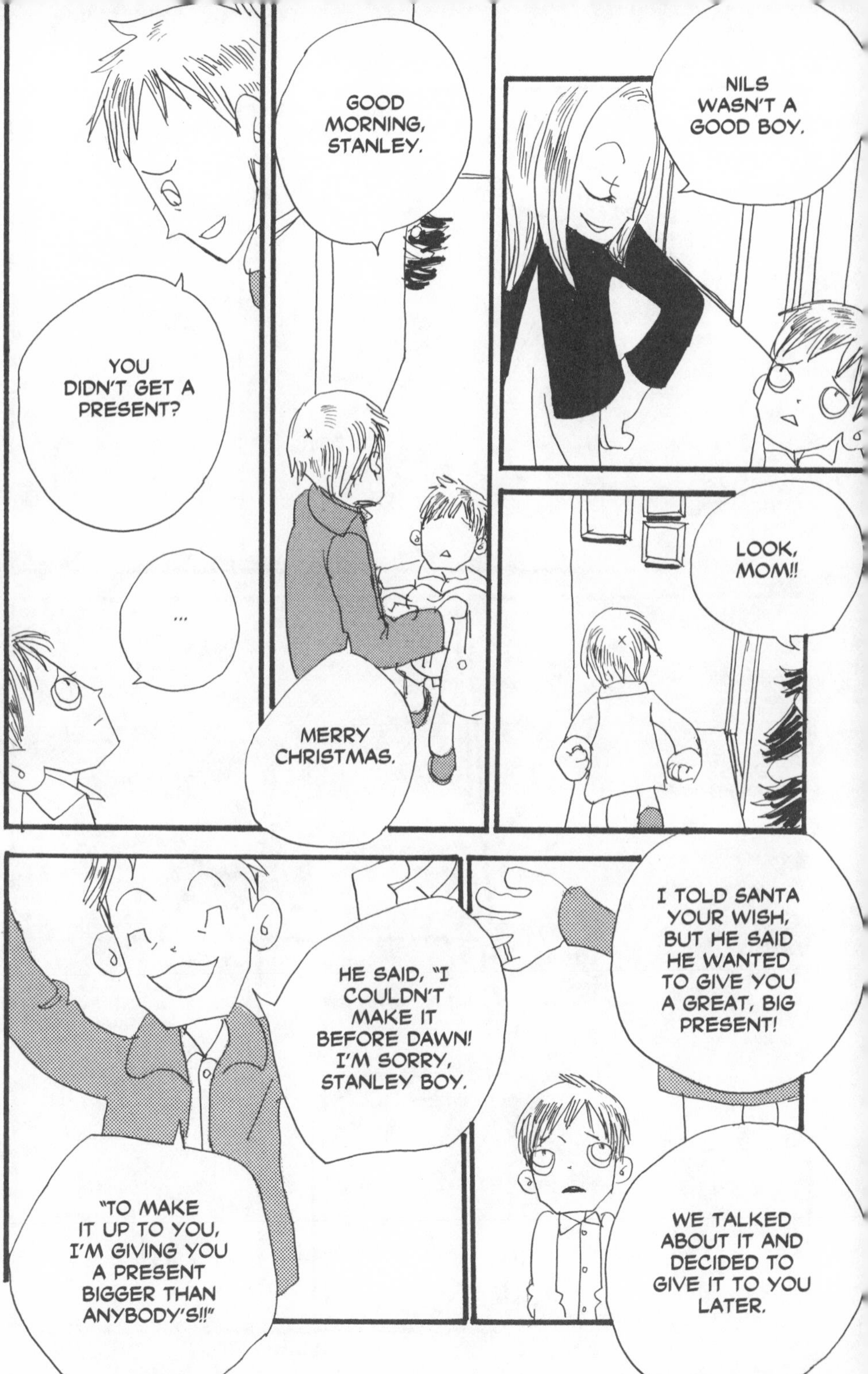
NILS WASN'T A GOOD BOY.
LOOK, MOM!!
GOOD MORNING, STANLEY.
MERRY CHRISTMAS.
YOU DIDN'T GET A PRESENT?
...
I TOLD SANTA YOUR WISH, BUT HE SAID HE WANTED TO GIVE YOU A GREAT, BIG PRESENT!
WE TALKED ABOUT IT AND DECIDED TO GIVE IT TO YOU LATER.
HE SAID, "I COULDN'T MAKE IT BEFORE DAWN! I'M SORRY, STANLEY BOY.
"TO MAKE IT UP TO YOU, I'M GIVING YOU A PRESENT BIGGER THAN ANYBODY'S!!"

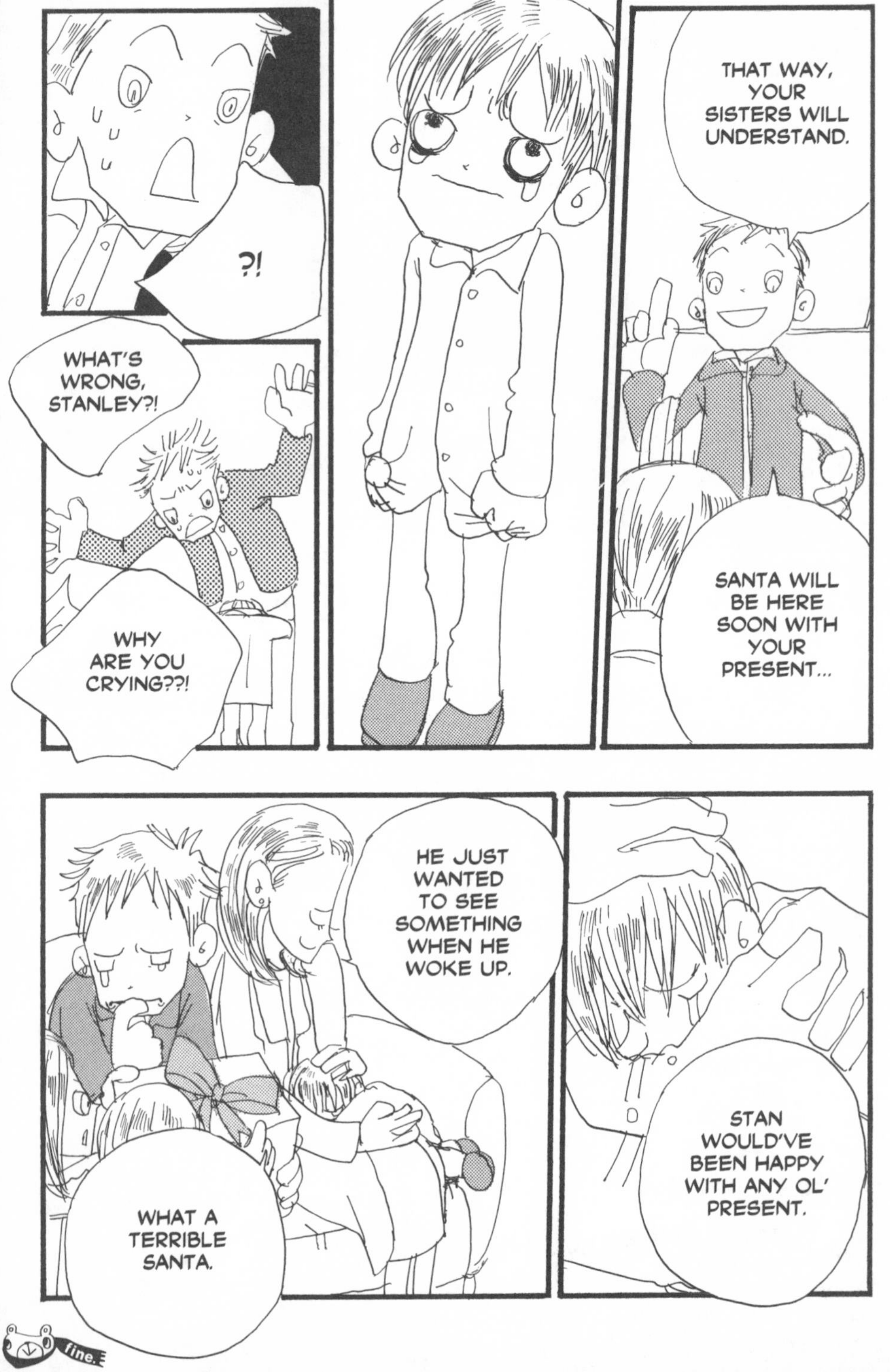
THAT WAY, YOUR SISTERS WILL UNDERSTAND.
SANTA WILL BE HERE SOON WITH YOUR PRESENT...
?!
WHAT'S WRONG, STANLEY?!
WHY ARE YOU CRYING??!
STAN WOULD'VE BEEN HAPPY WITH ANY OL' PRESENT.
HE JUST WANTED TO SEE SOMETHING WHEN HE WOKE UP.
WHAT A TERRIBLE SANTA.
fine.

Froom Family

CHRISTMAS★MORNING

PADRE (Dojinshi)
Published in May 2001

BROTHERS AND SISTER OF
A SWEETS STORE.
MONICA LEFT HOME TO
WORK IN MILAN.

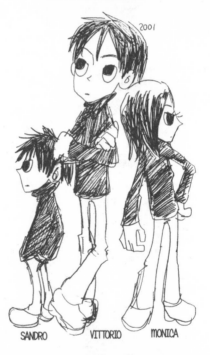

SANDRO   VITTORIO   MONICA

FRATELLI DI SANDRO

-Siblings of Sandro-

senza titolo #6

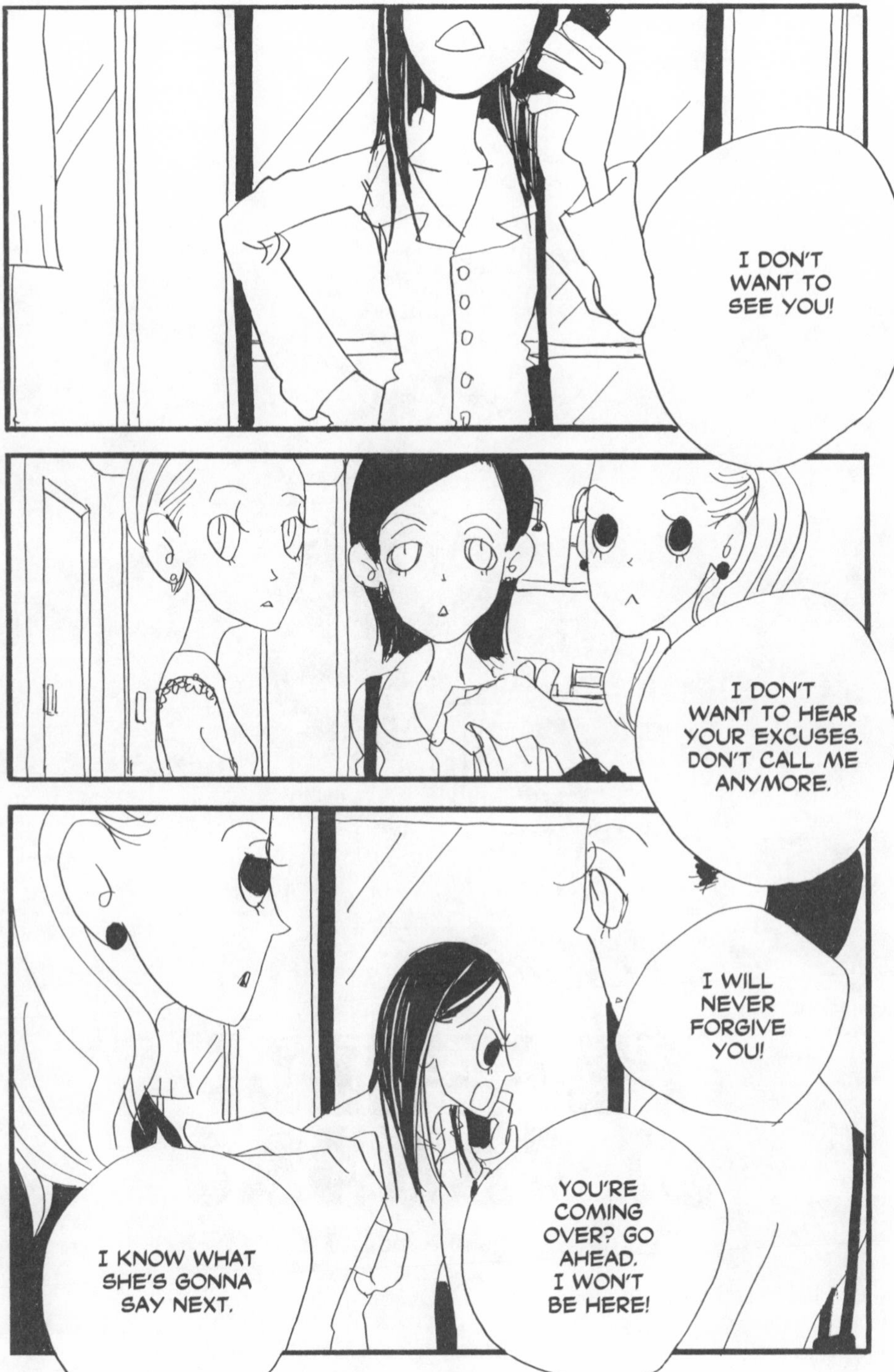
I DON'T WANT TO SEE YOU!
I DON'T WANT TO HEAR YOUR EXCUSES. DON'T CALL ME ANYMORE.
I WILL NEVER FORGIVE YOU!
YOU'RE COMING OVER? GO AHEAD. I WON'T BE HERE!
I KNOW WHAT SHE'S GONNA SAY NEXT.

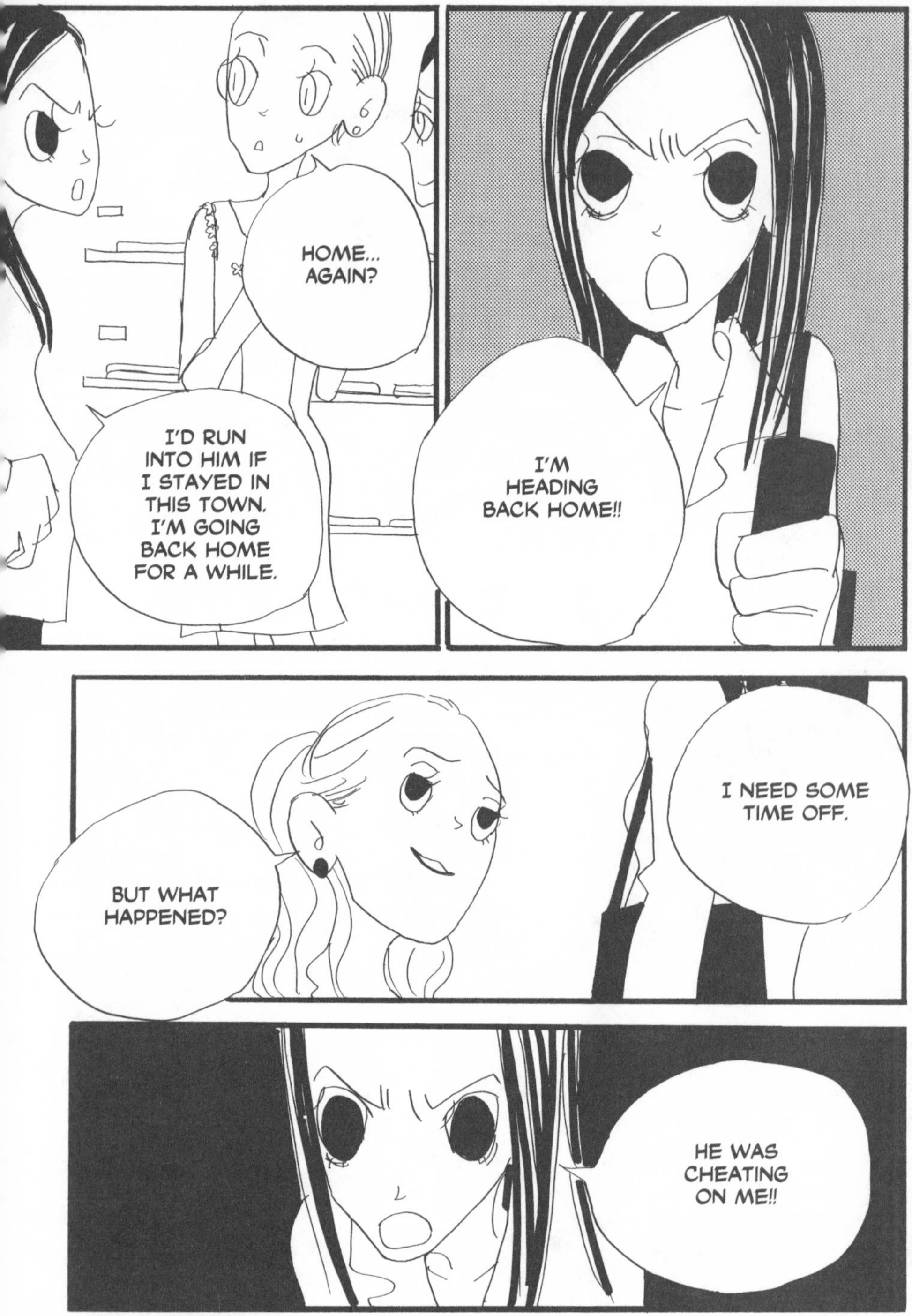
I'M HEADING BACK HOME!!
HOME... AGAIN?
I'D RUN INTO HIM IF I STAYED IN THIS TOWN. I'M GOING BACK HOME FOR A WHILE.
I NEED SOME TIME OFF.
BUT WHAT HAPPENED?
HE WAS CHEATING ON ME!!

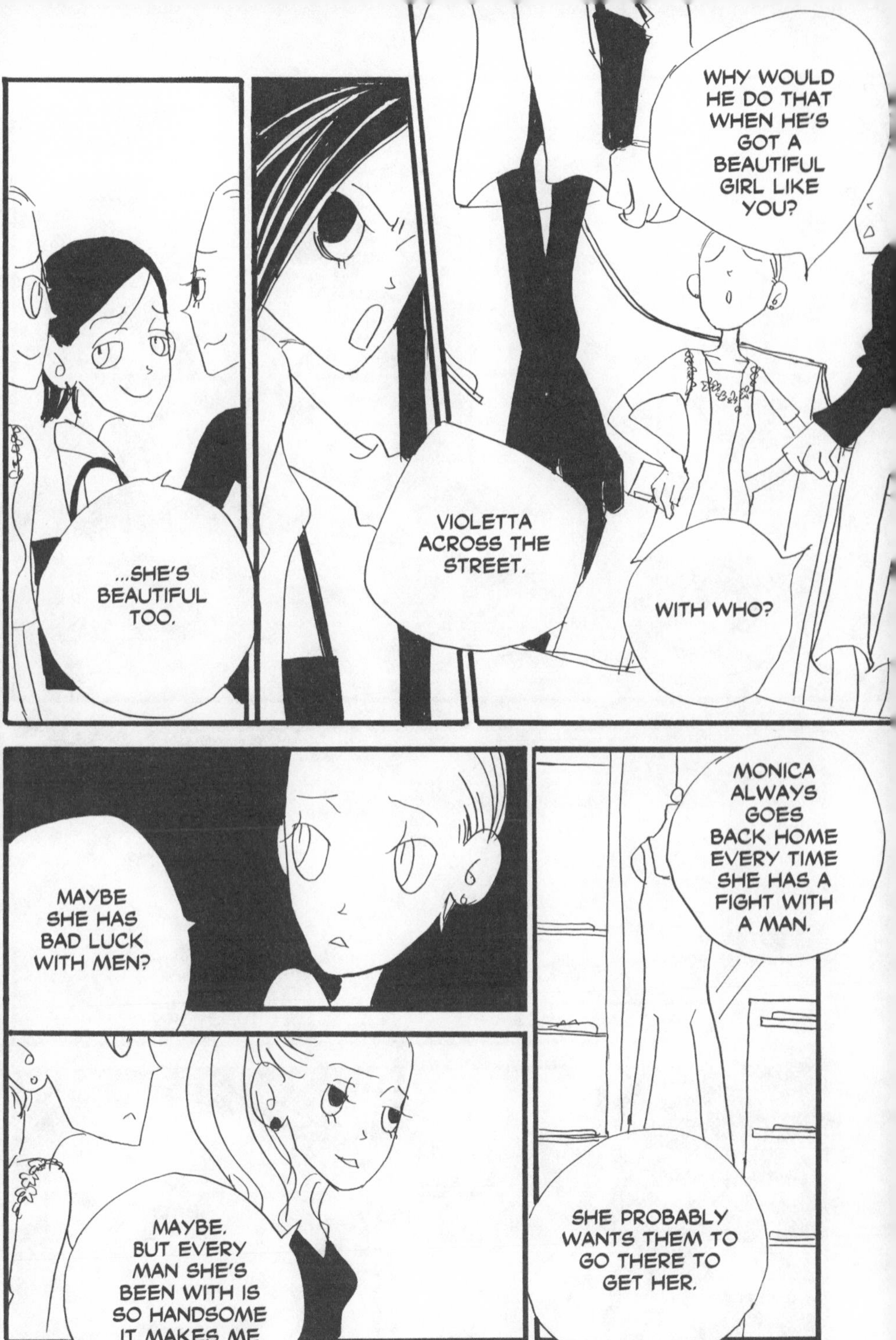
WHY WOULD HE DO THAT WHEN HE'S GOT A BEAUTIFUL GIRL LIKE YOU?
WITH WHO?
VIOLETTA ACROSS THE STREET.
...SHE'S BEAUTIFUL TOO.
MONICA ALWAYS GOES BACK HOME EVERY TIME SHE HAS A FIGHT WITH A MAN.
SHE PROBABLY WANTS THEM TO GO THERE TO GET HER.
MAYBE SHE HAS BAD LUCK WITH MEN?
MAYBE. BUT EVERY MAN SHE'S BEEN WITH IS SO HANDSOME IT MAKES ME JEALOUS.

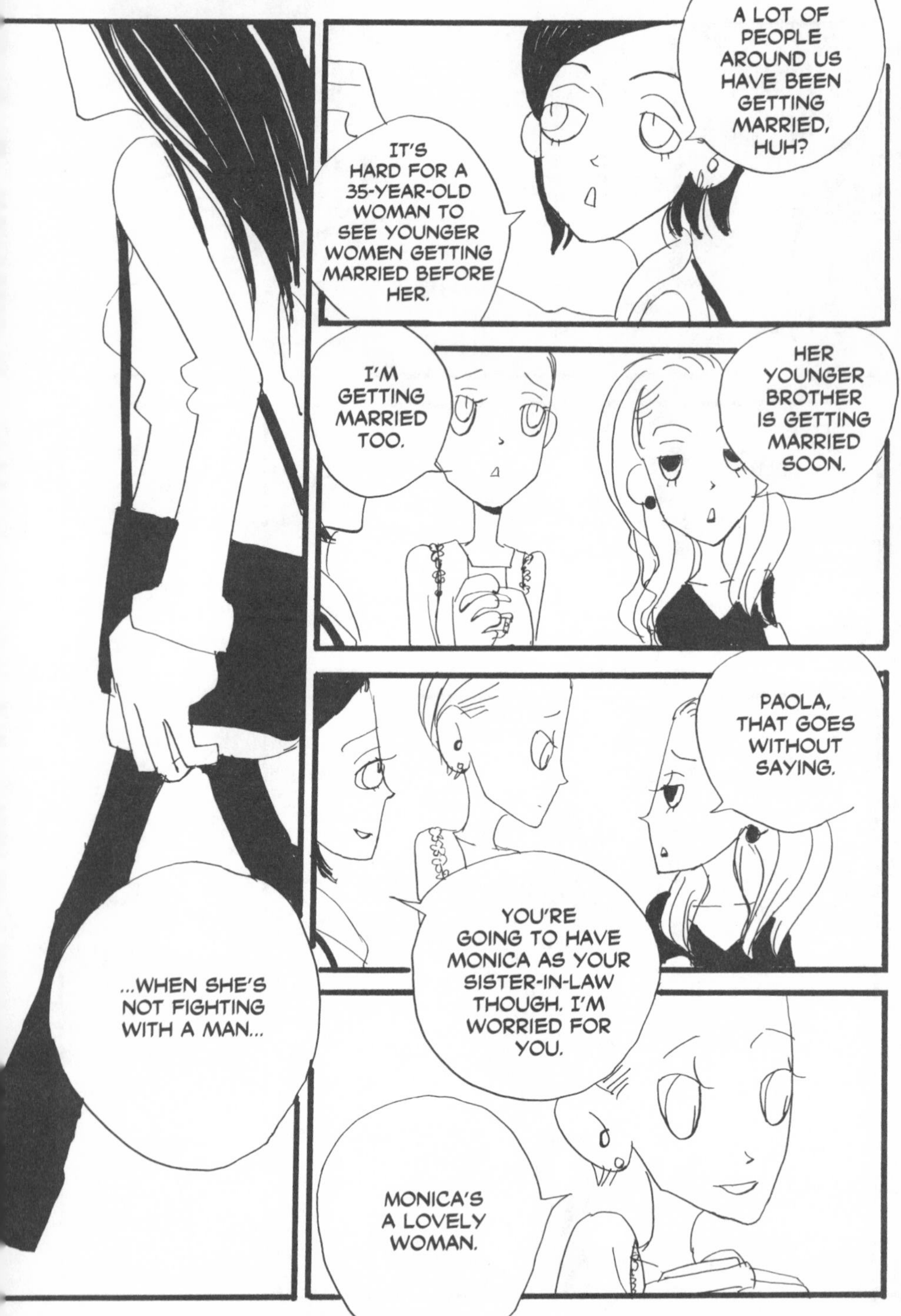
A LOT OF PEOPLE AROUND US HAVE BEEN GETTING MARRIED, HUH?
IT'S HARD FOR A 35-YEAR-OLD WOMAN TO SEE YOUNGER WOMEN GETTING MARRIED BEFORE HER.
HER YOUNGER BROTHER IS GETTING MARRIED SOON.
I'M GETTING MARRIED TOO.
PAOLA, THAT GOES WITHOUT SAYING.
YOU'RE GOING TO HAVE MONICA AS YOUR SISTER-IN-LAW THOUGH. I'M WORRIED FOR YOU.
MONICA'S A LOVELY WOMAN.
...WHEN SHE'S NOT FIGHTING WITH A MAN...

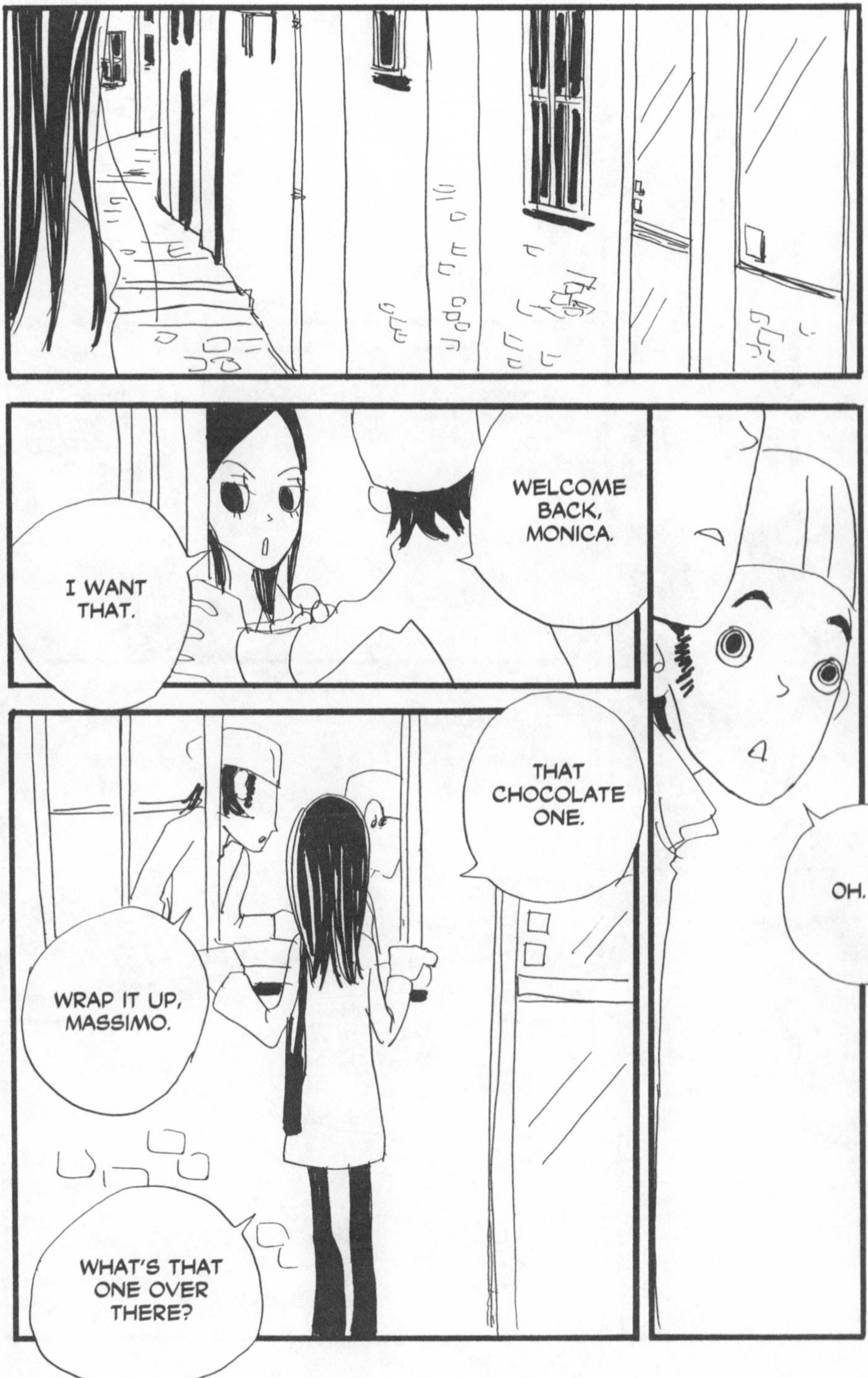
WELCOME BACK, MONICA.
I WANT THAT.
THAT CHOCOLATE ONE.
OH.
WRAP IT UP, MASSIMO.
WHAT'S THAT ONE OVER THERE?

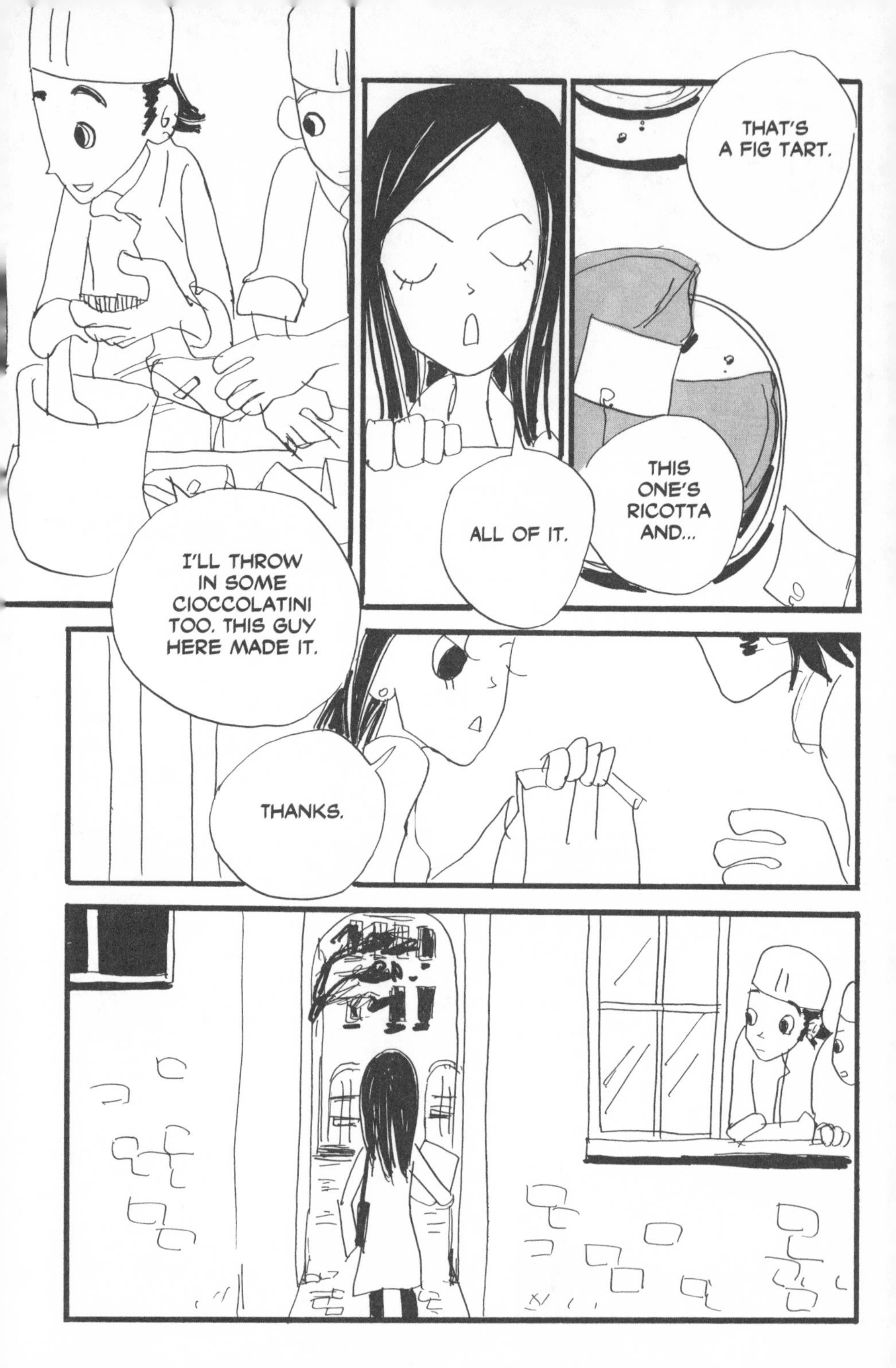
THAT'S A FIG TART.
THIS ONE'S RICOTTA AND...
ALL OF IT.
I'LL THROW IN SOME CIOCCOLATINI TOO. THIS GUY HERE MADE IT.
THANKS.

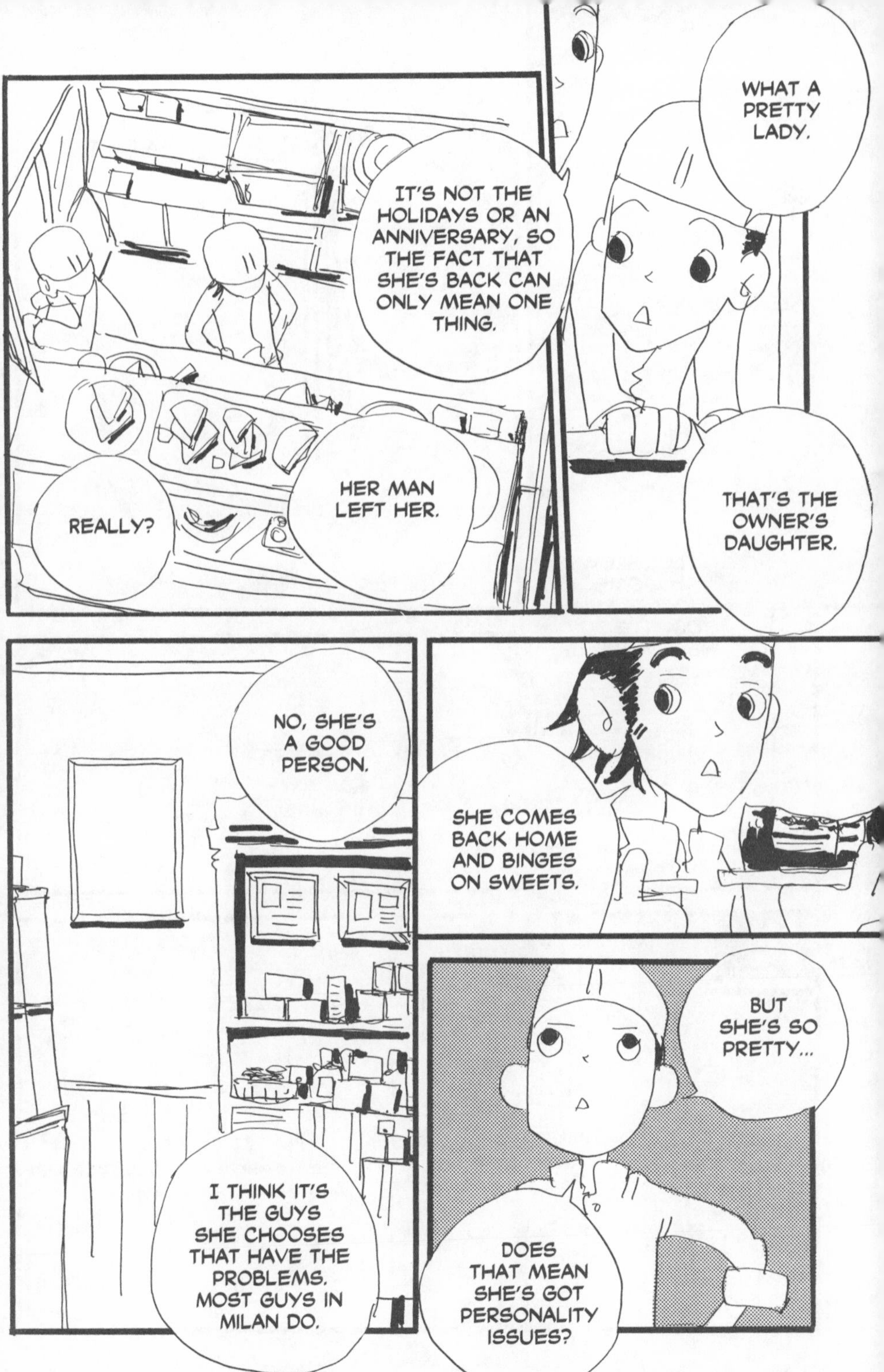
WHAT A PRETTY LADY.
THAT'S THE OWNER'S DAUGHTER.
IT'S NOT THE HOLIDAYS OR AN ANNIVERSARY, SO THE FACT THAT SHE'S BACK CAN ONLY MEAN ONE THING.
HER MAN LEFT HER.
REALLY?
SHE COMES BACK HOME AND BINGES ON SWEETS.
BUT SHE'S SO PRETTY...
DOES THAT MEAN SHE'S GOT PERSONALITY ISSUES?
NO, SHE'S A GOOD PERSON.
I THINK IT'S THE GUYS SHE CHOOSES THAT HAVE THE PROBLEMS. MOST GUYS IN MILAN DO.

GUYS IN THE COUNTRYSIDE HAVE BIG HEARTS...
THEY'RE KIND...
BUT SHE DIDN'T EVEN LOOK AT US.
TRUE.

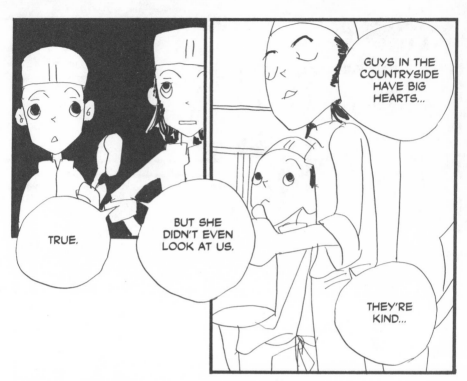

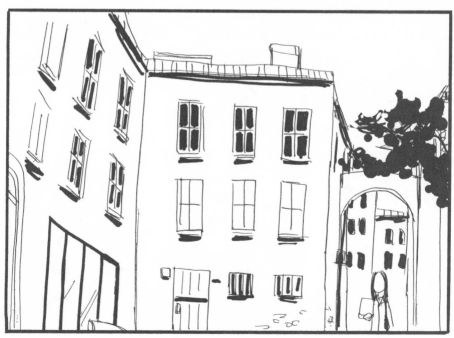

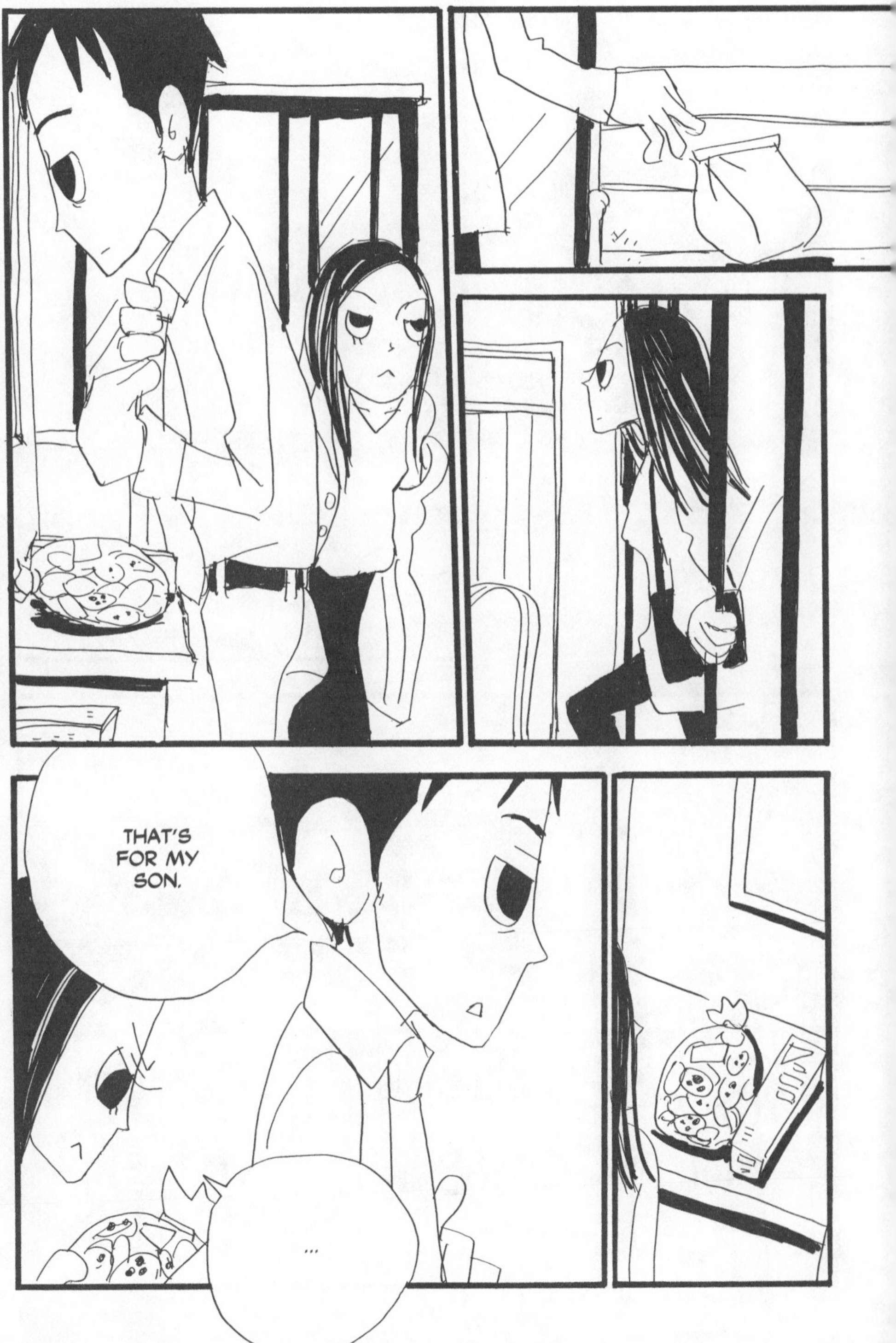
THAT'S FOR MY SON.
...

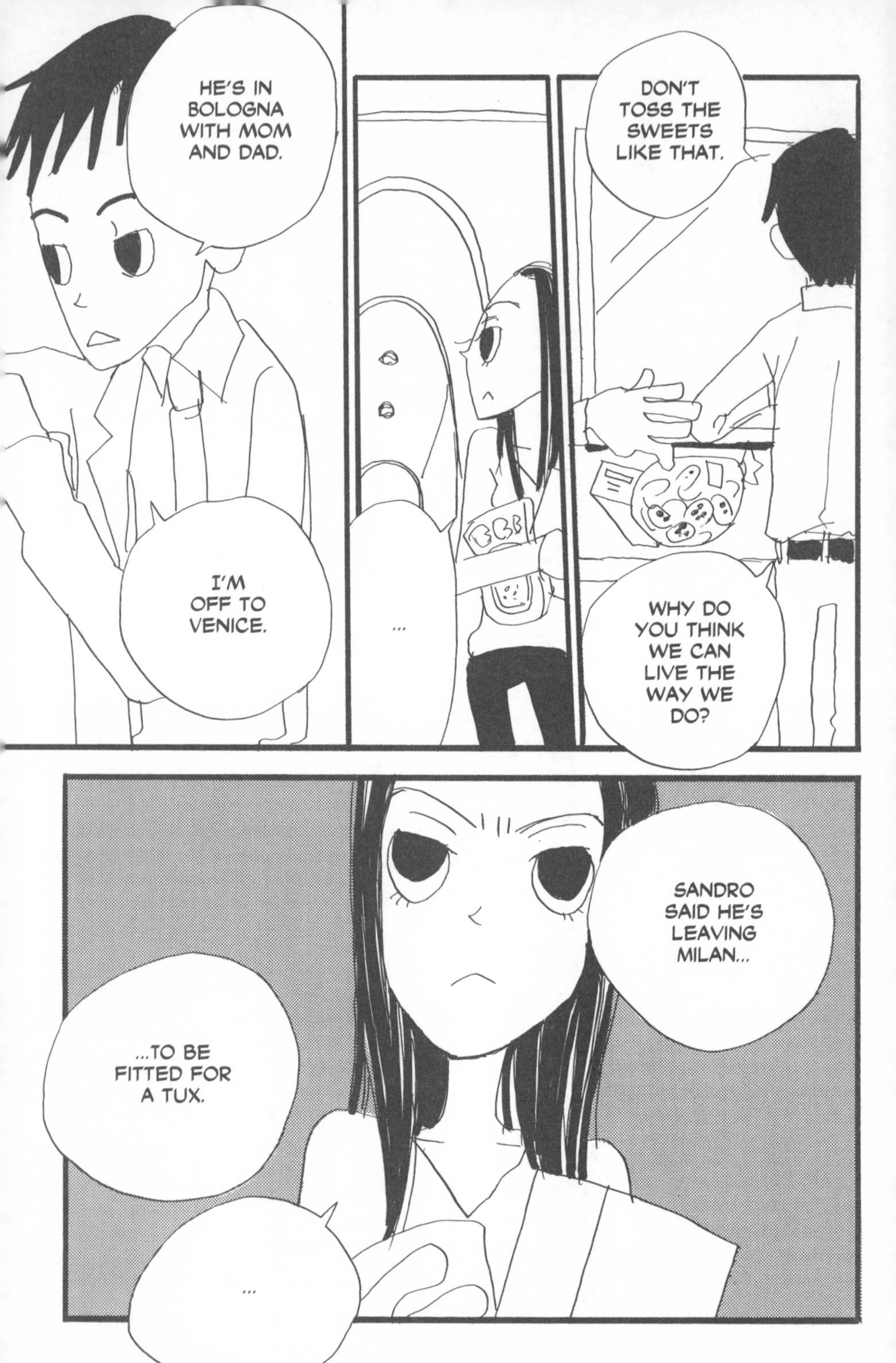
DON'T TOSS THE SWEETS LIKE THAT.
WHY DO YOU THINK WE CAN LIVE THE WAY WE DO?
...
HE'S IN BOLOGNA WITH MOM AND DAD.
I'M OFF TO VENICE.
SANDRO SAID HE'S LEAVING MILAN...
...TO BE FITTED FOR A TUX.
...

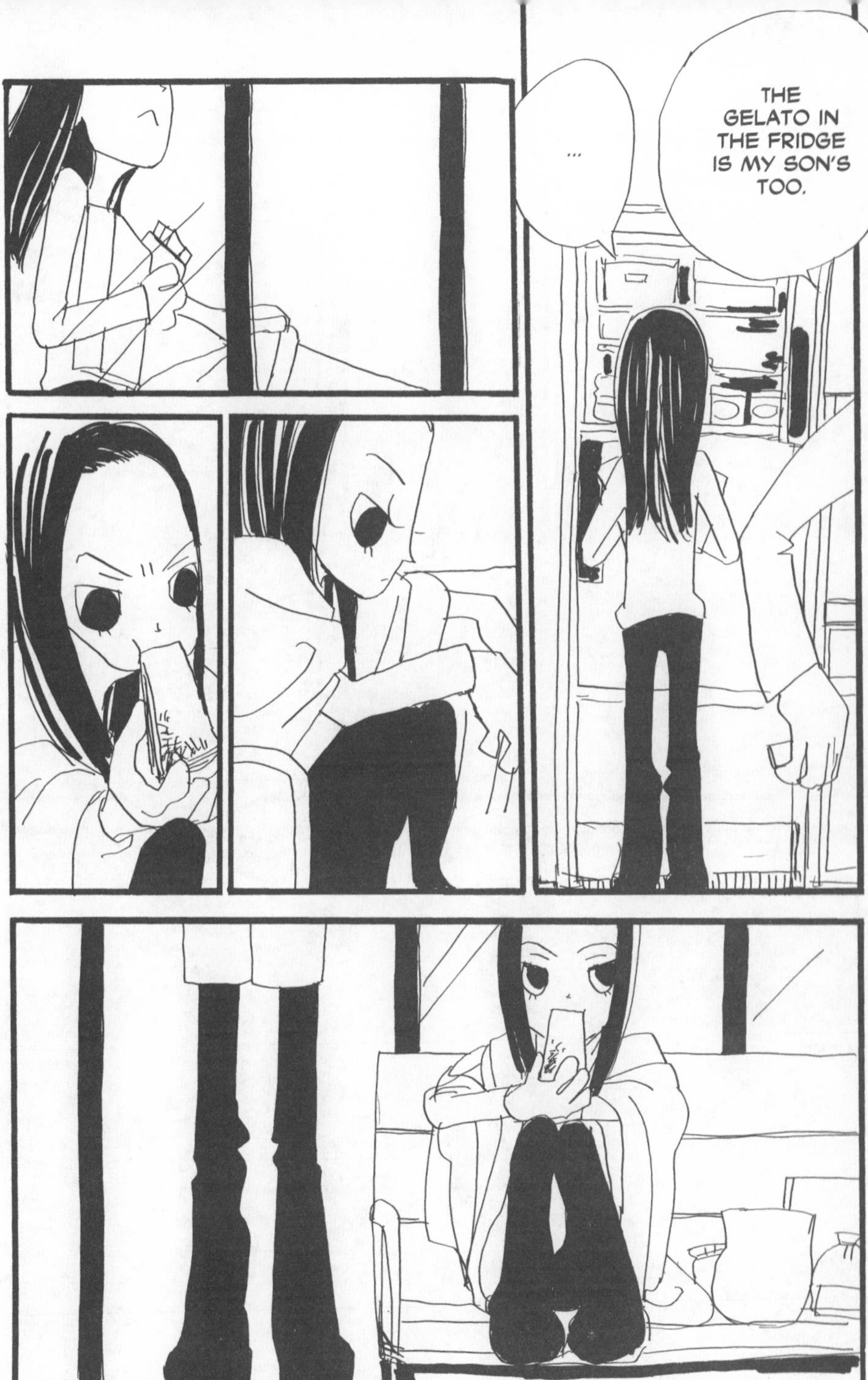
THE GELATO IN THE FRIDGE IS MY SON'S TOO.
...

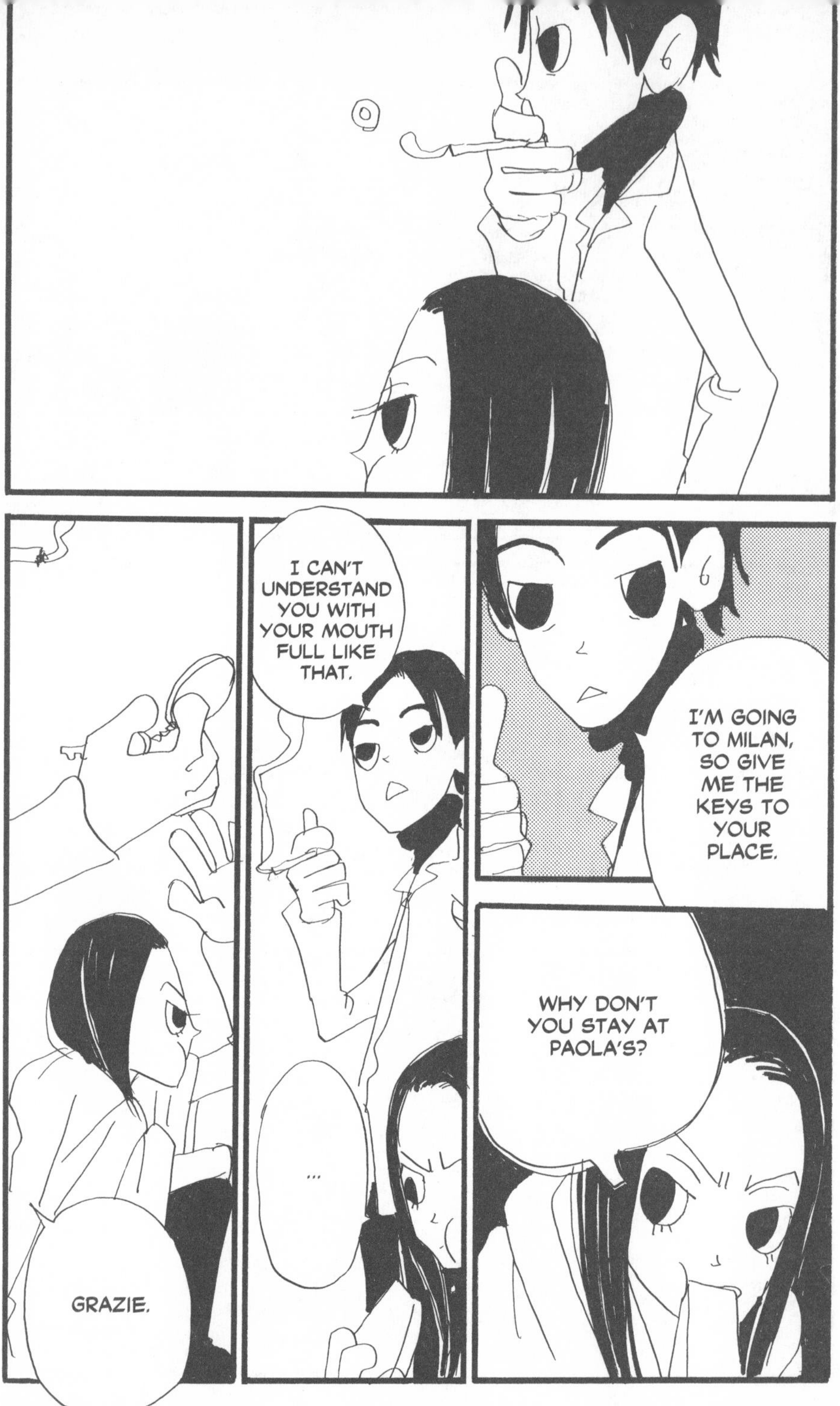
I'M GOING TO MILAN, SO GIVE ME THE KEYS TO YOUR PLACE.
WHY DON'T YOU STAY AT PAOLA'S?
I CAN'T UNDERSTAND YOU WITH YOUR MOUTH FULL LIKE THAT.
...
GRAZIE.

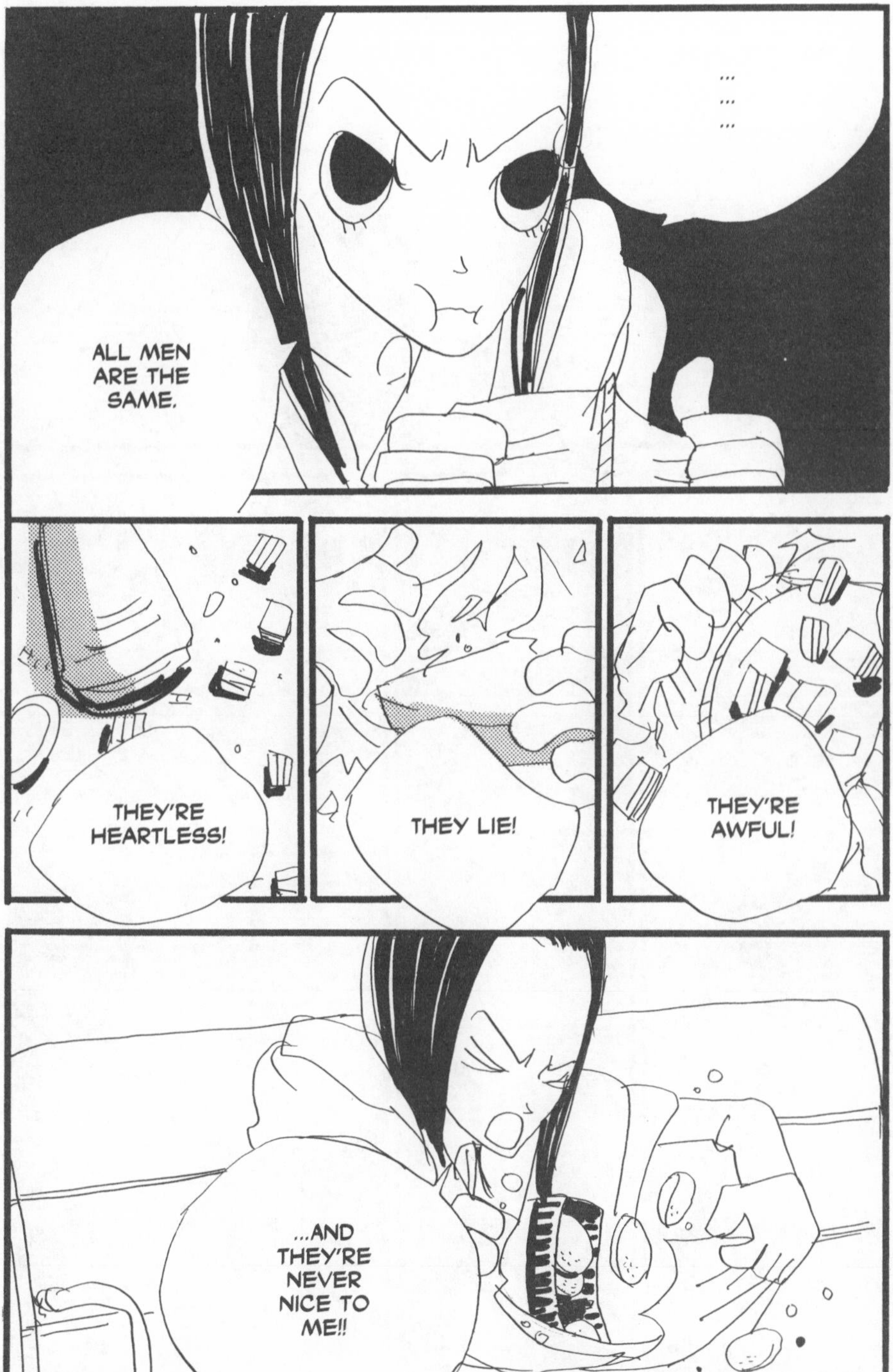

...
...
...
ALL MEN ARE THE SAME.
THEY'RE AWFUL!
THEY LIE!
THEY'RE HEARTLESS!
...AND THEY'RE NEVER NICE TO ME!!

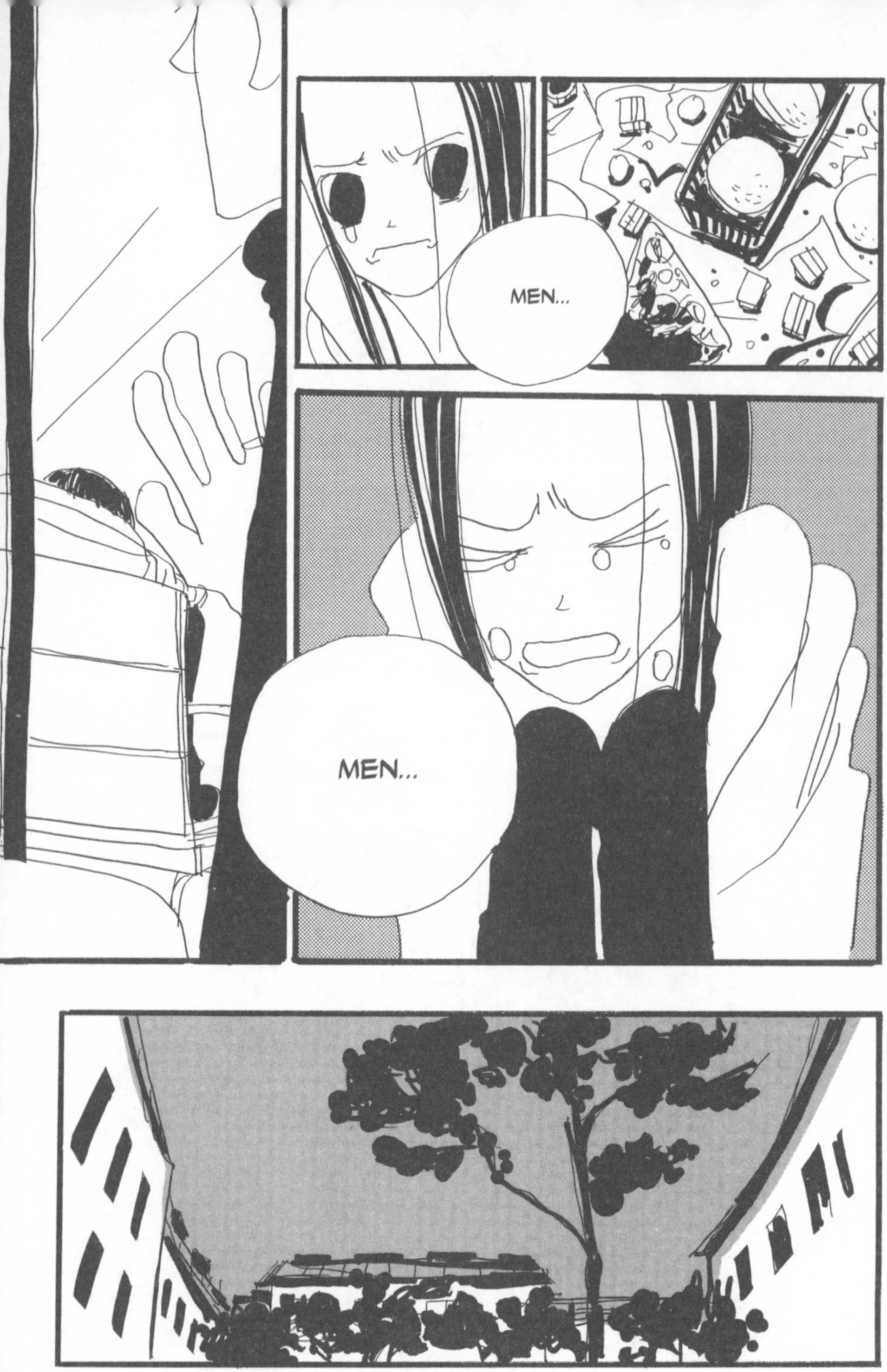
MEN...
MEN...

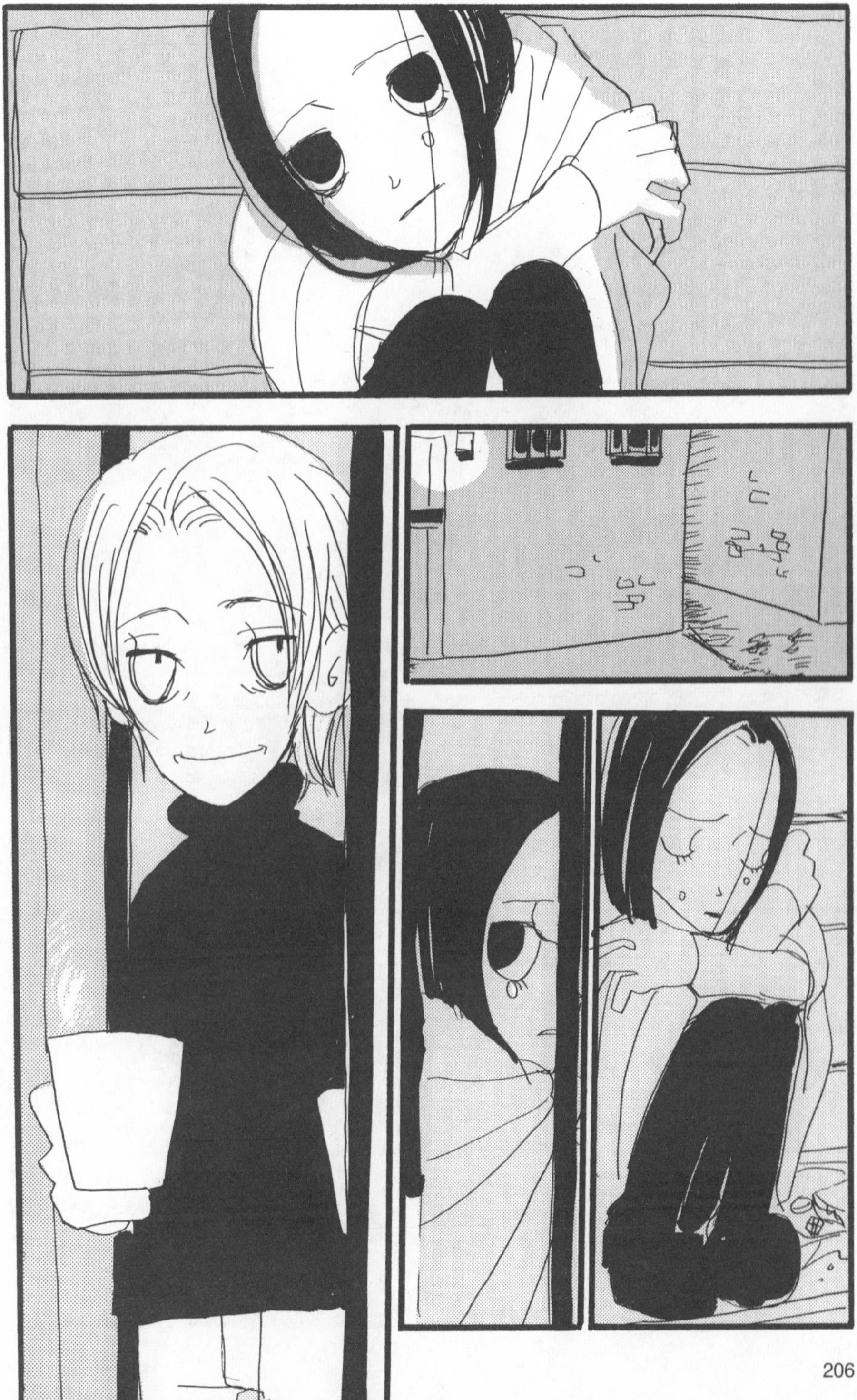

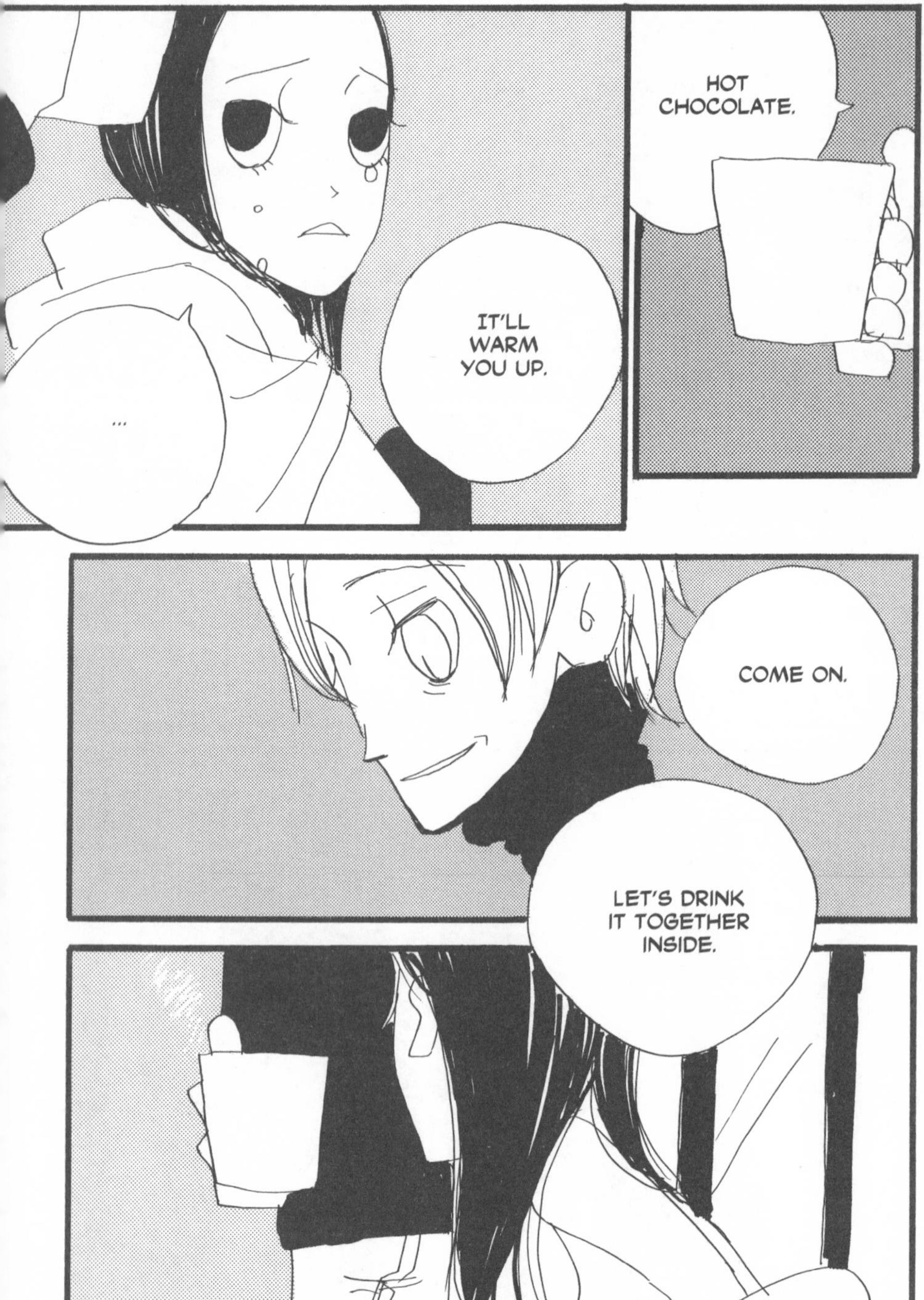
HOT CHOCOLATE.
IT'LL WARM YOU UP.
...
COME ON.
LET'S DRINK IT TOGETHER INSIDE.

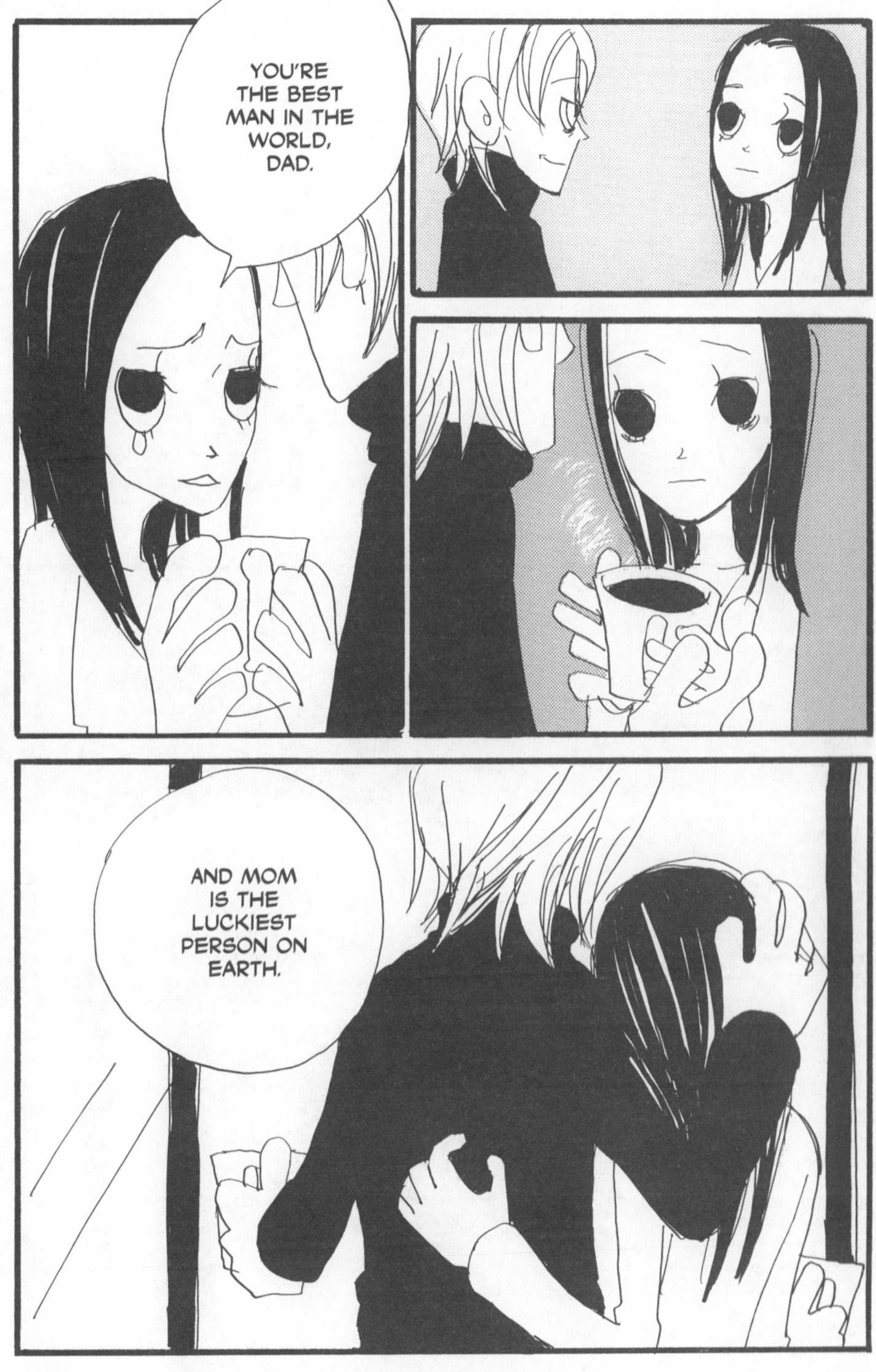
YOU'RE THE BEST MAN IN THE WORLD, DAD.
AND MOM IS THE LUCKIEST PERSON ON EARTH.
fine.

PADRE

-Father-

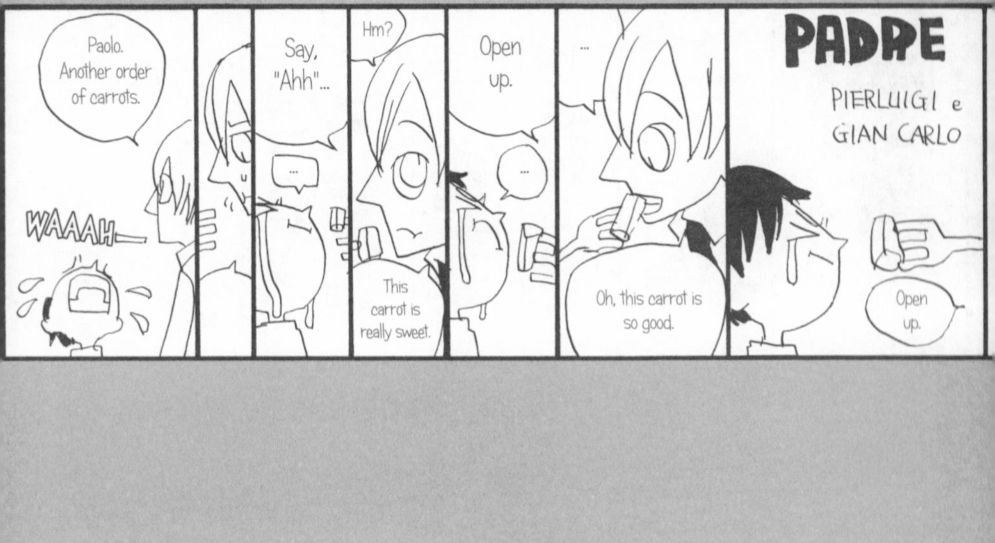
PADRE
PIERLUIGI e GIAN CARLO
Open up.
...
Oh, this carrot is so good.
Open up.
...
Hm?
This carrot is really sweet.
Say, "Ahh"...
...
Paolo. Another order of carrots.
WAAAH—

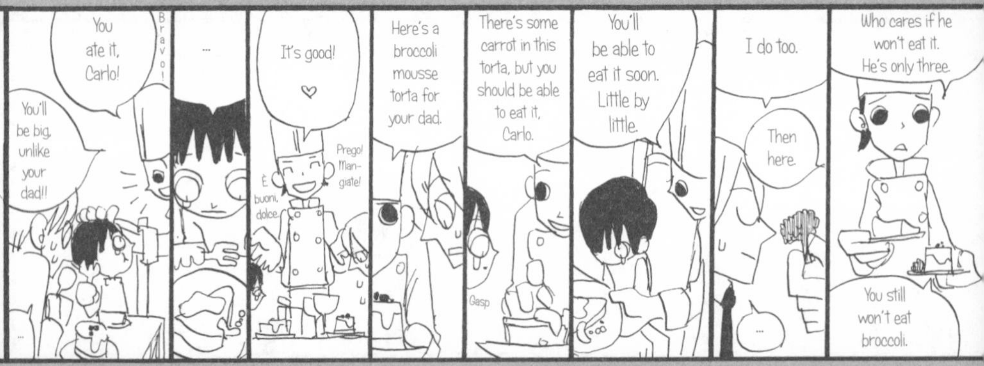
Who cares if he won't eat it. He's only three.
You still won't eat broccoli.
I do too.
Then here.
...
You'll be able to eat it soon. Little by little.
There's some carrot in this torta, but you should be able to eat it, Carlo.
Gasp
Here's a broccoli mousse torta for your dad.
It's good!
Prego! Mangiate!
È buoni, dolce.
...
Bravo!
You ate it, Carlo!
You'll be big, unlike your dad!!
...

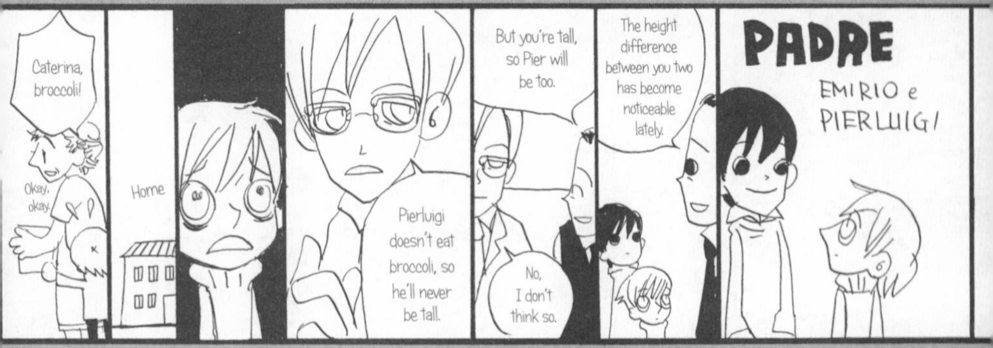
PADRE
EMIRIO e PIERLUIGI
The height difference between you two has become noticeable lately.
But you're tall, so Pier will be too.
No, I don't think so.
Pierluigi doesn't eat broccoli, so he'll never be tall.
Home
Caterina, broccoli!
Okay, okay.

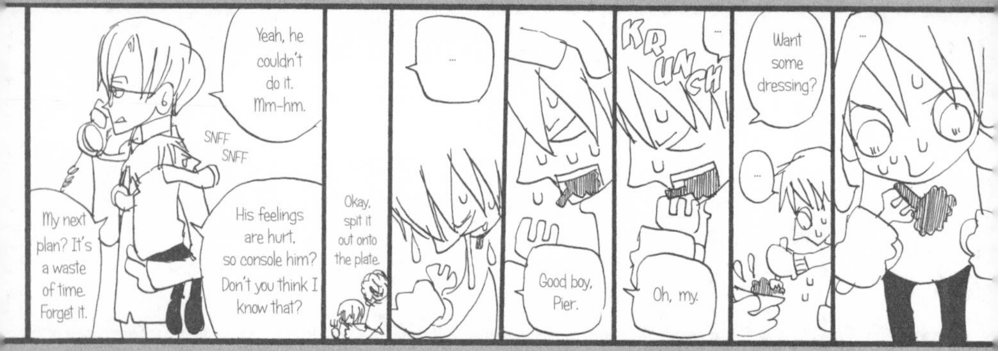
...
Want some dressing?
...
KRUNCH
...
Oh, my.
Good boy, Pier.
...
Okay, spit it out onto the plate.
Yeah, he couldn't do it. Mm-hm.
SNFF SNFF
His feelings are hurt, so console him? Don't you think I know that?
My next plan? It's a waste of time. Forget it.

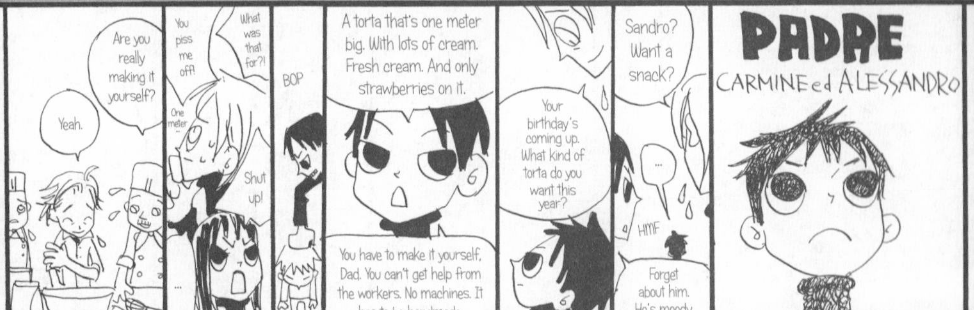
PADRE
CARMINE ed ALESSANDRO
Sandro? Want a snack?
...
HMF
Forget about him. He's moody.
Your birthday's coming up. What kind of torta do you want this year?
A torta that's one meter big. With lots of cream. Fresh cream. And only strawberries on it.
You have to make it yourself, Dad. You can't get help from the workers. No machines. It has to be handmade.
BOP
What was that for?!
You piss me off!
One meter...
Shut up!
...
Are you really making it yourself?
Yeah.

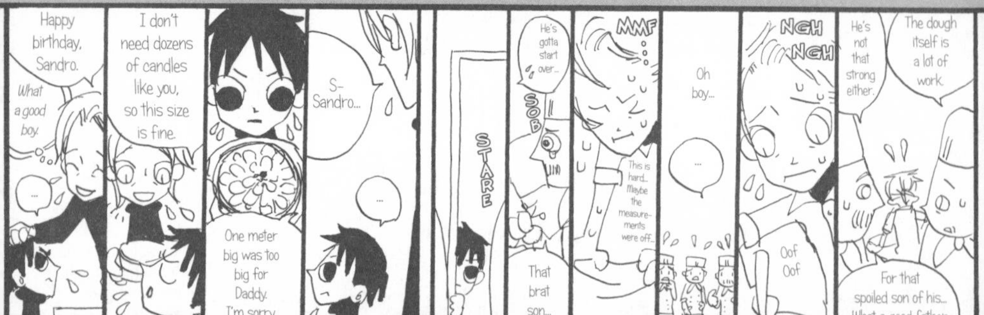
The dough itself is a lot of work.
He's not that strong either.
For that spoiled son of his... What a good father.
NGH NGH
Oof Oof
Oh boy...
...
MMF
This is hard... Maybe the measurements were off...
He's gotta start over...
SOB
That brat son...
STARE
S-Sandro...
...
One meter big was too big for Daddy. I'm sorry.
I don't need dozens of candles like you, so this size is fine.
Happy birthday, Sandro.
What a good boy.
...

fine.

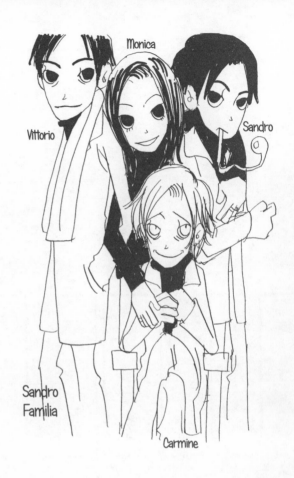

Vittorio

Monica

Sandro

Sandro
Familia

Carmine

senza titolo #6
PADRE (Dojinshi)
Published in May 2001

PADRE
Flyer, 2001

Natsume Ono
Tesoro⁵

galleria di illustrazione

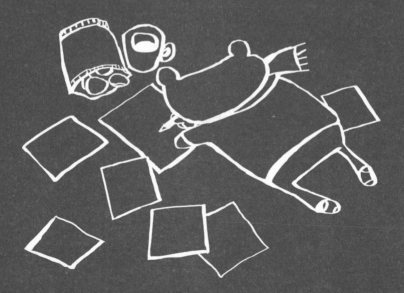

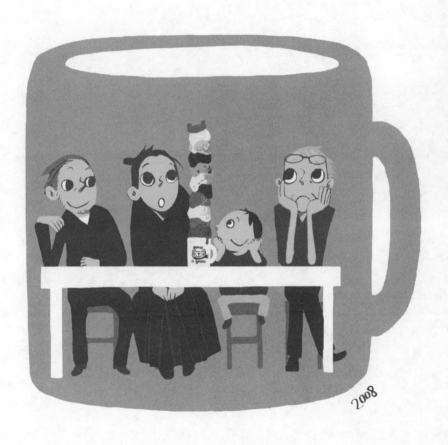

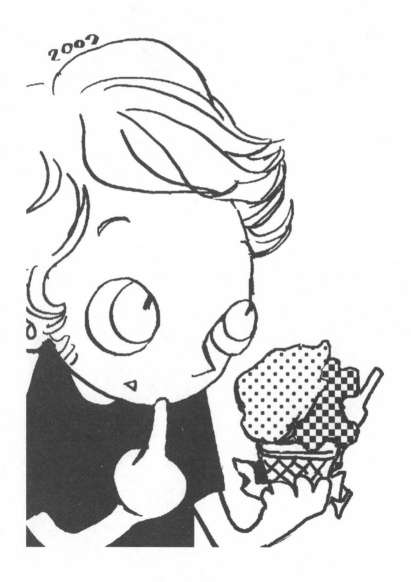

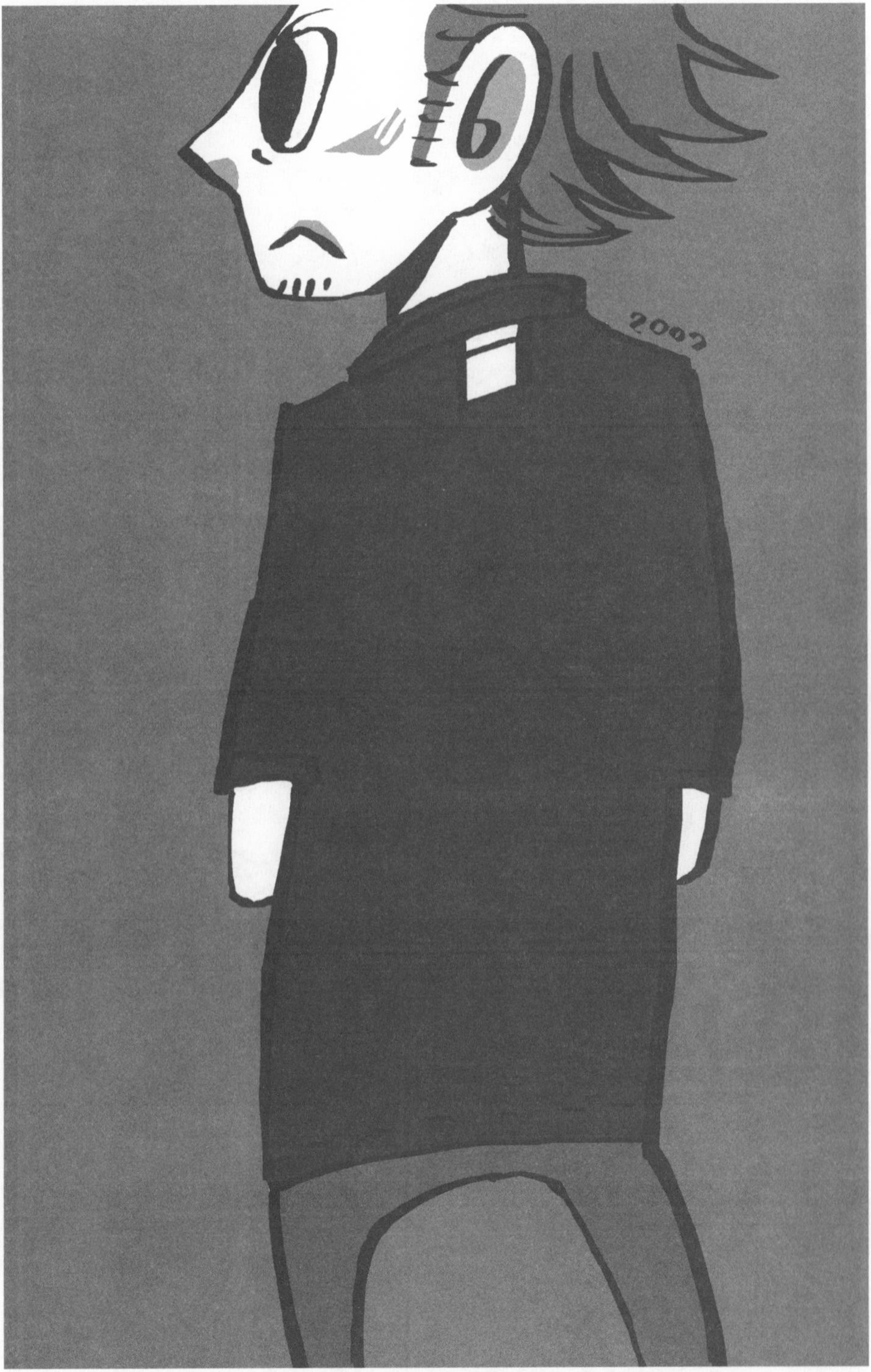

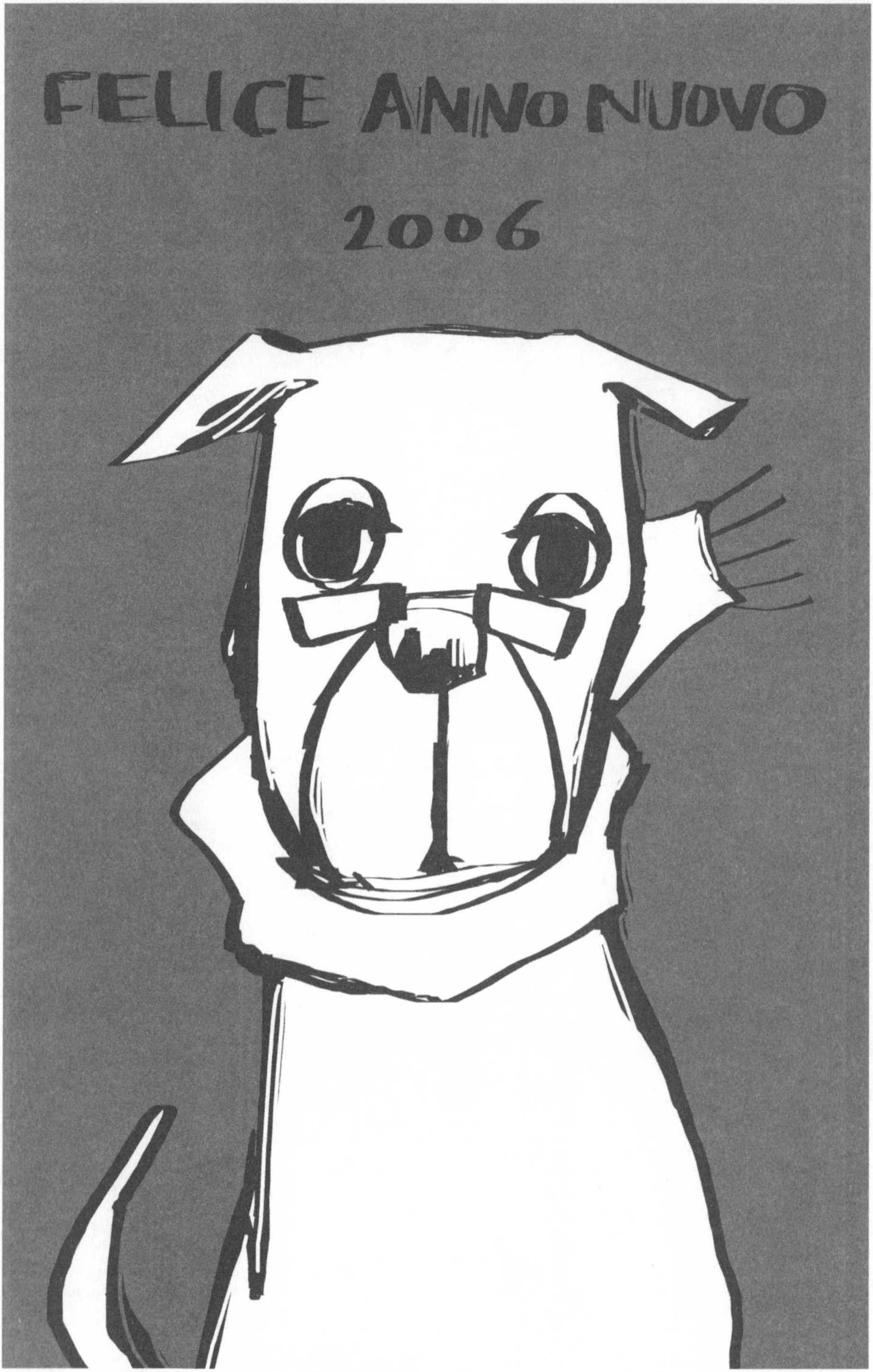
FELICE ANNO NUOVO
2006

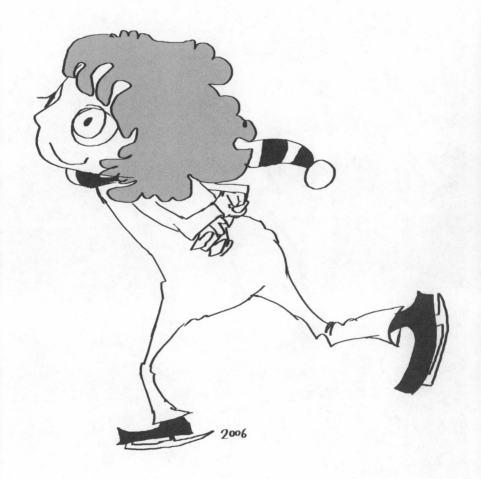

2006

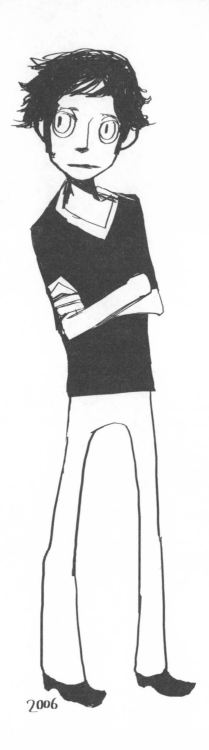

2006

Morning

Summer
Vacation

The radio
exercise card
my brother made
for me

2006

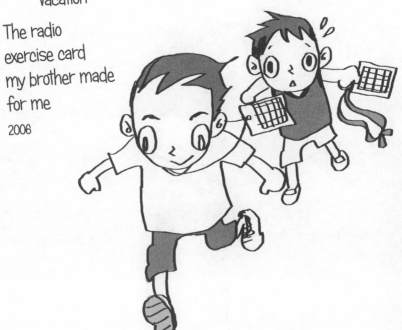

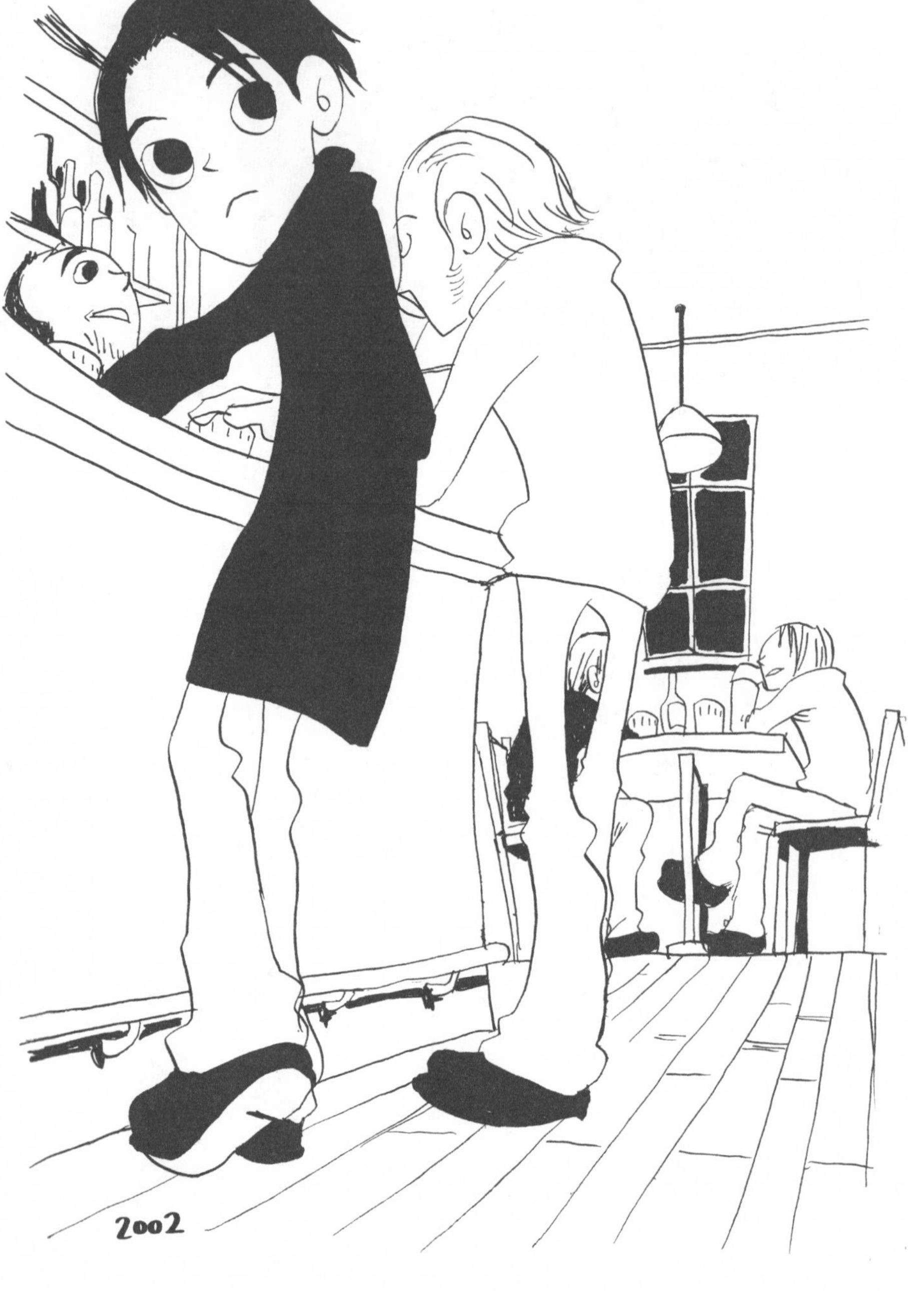
2002

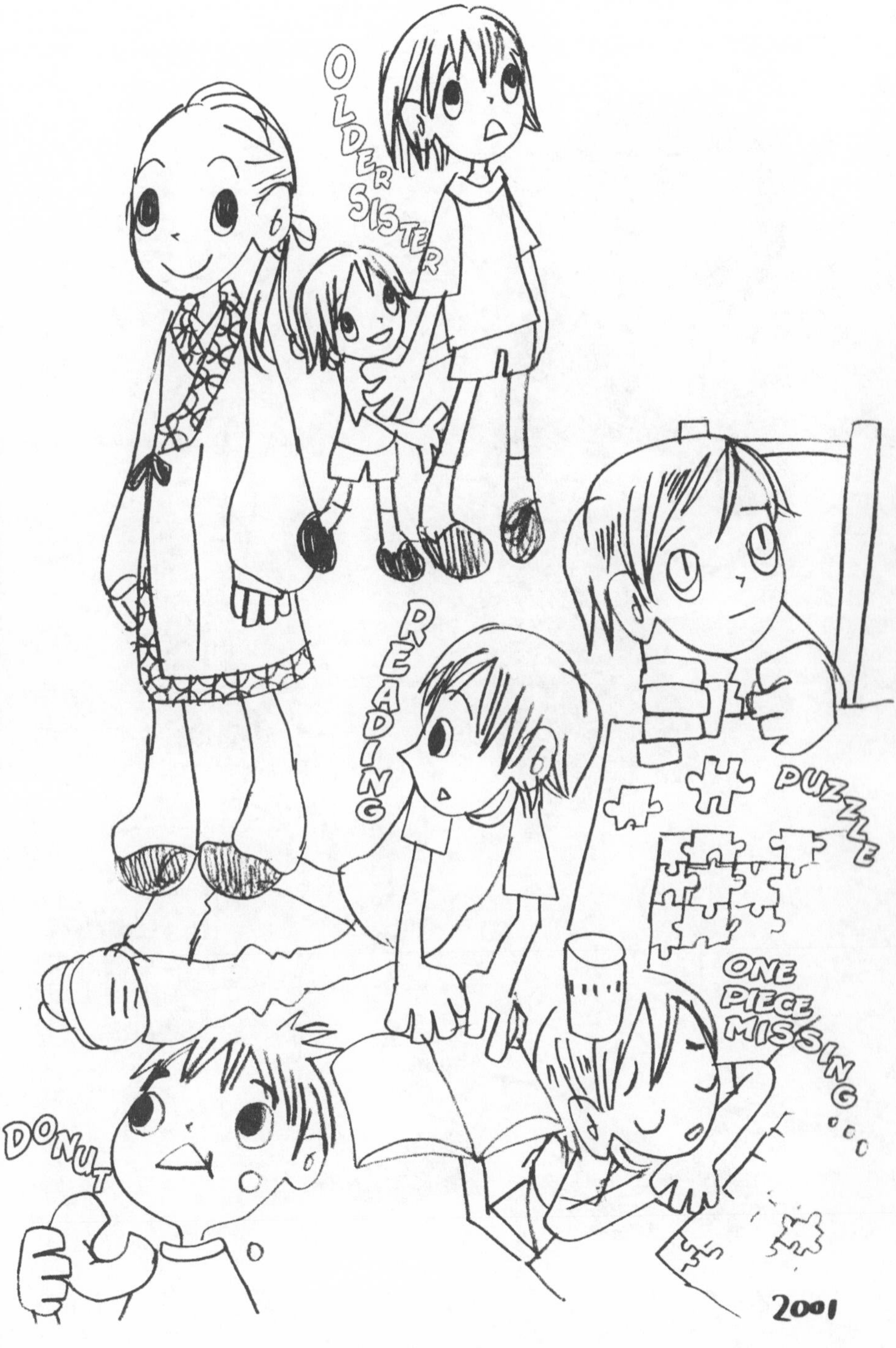
OLDER SISTER
READING
PUZZLE
ONE PIECE MISSING...
DONUT
2001

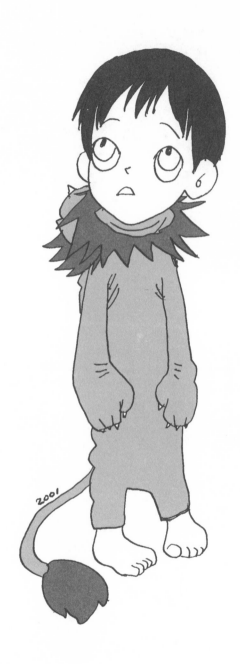

2001

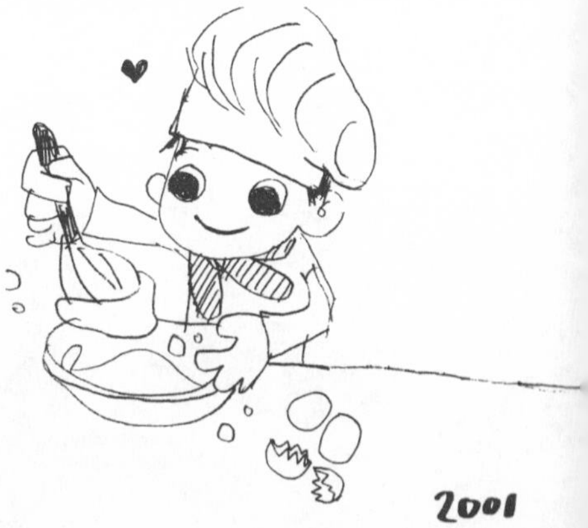
2001

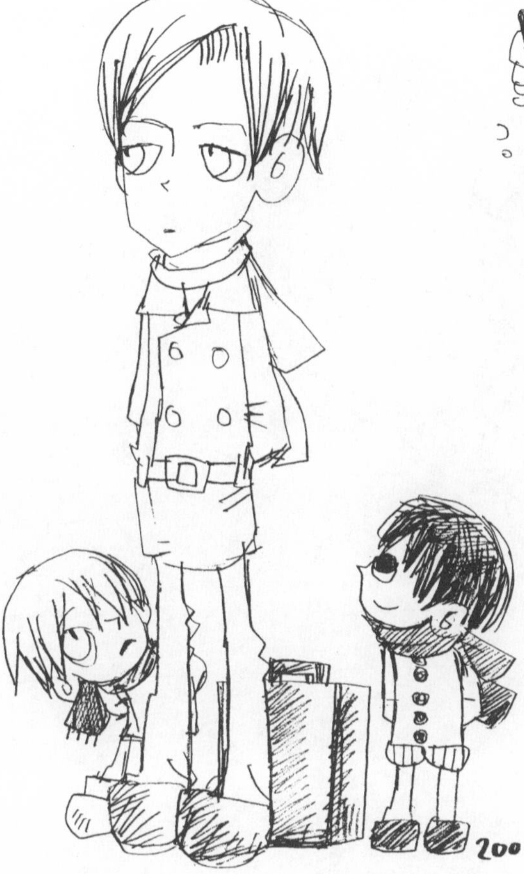
200

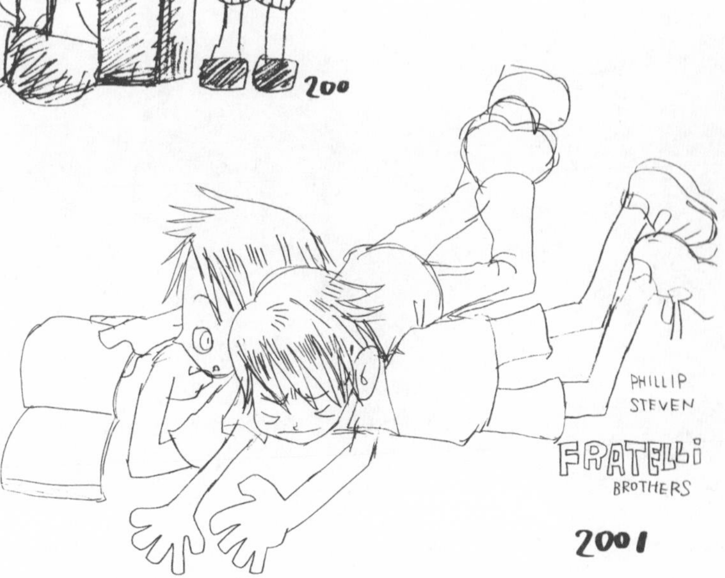
PHILLIP
STEVEN
FRATELLI
BROTHERS
2001

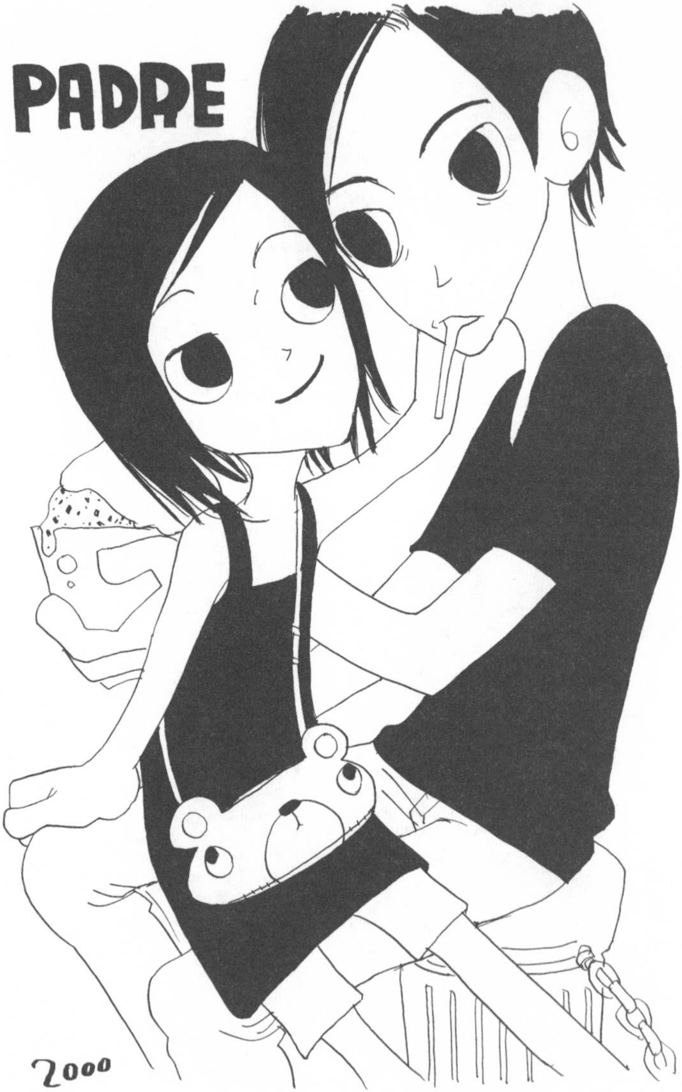
PADRE
2000

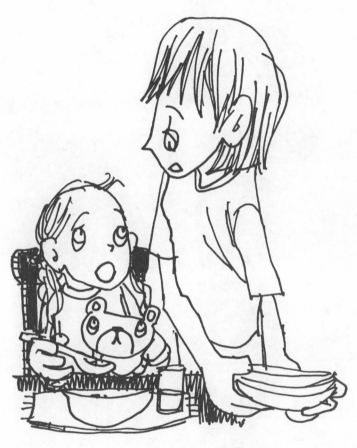

2000

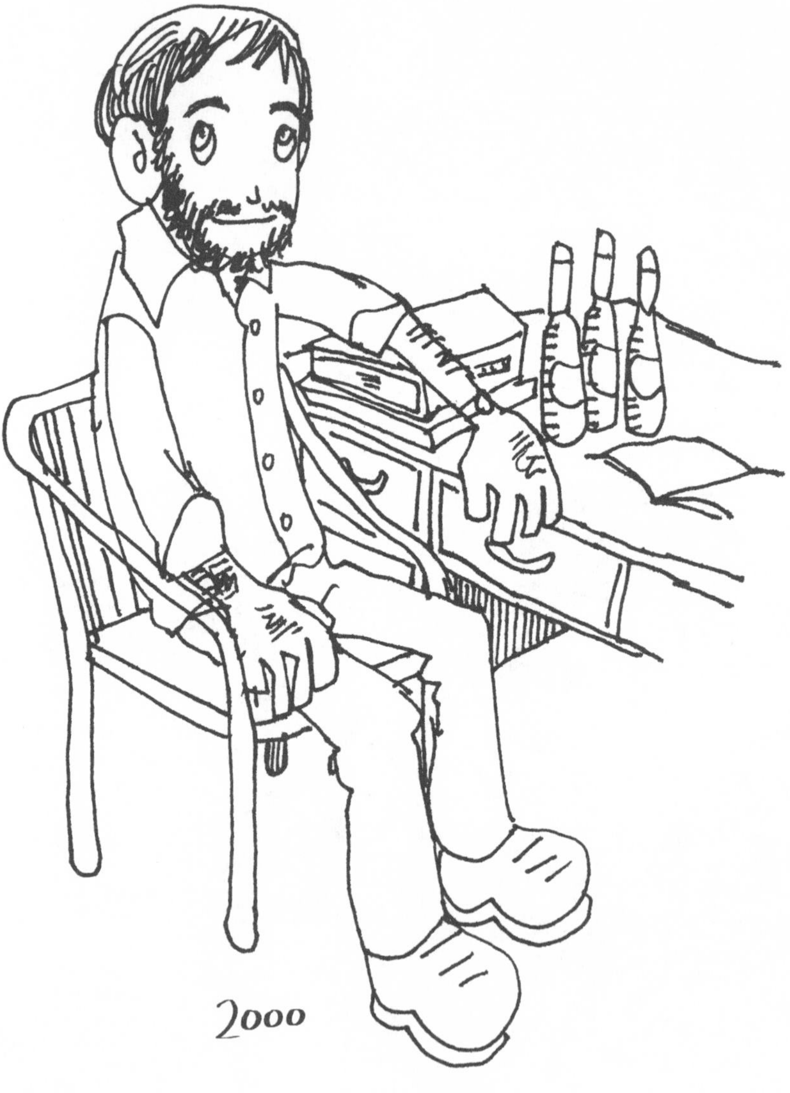
2000

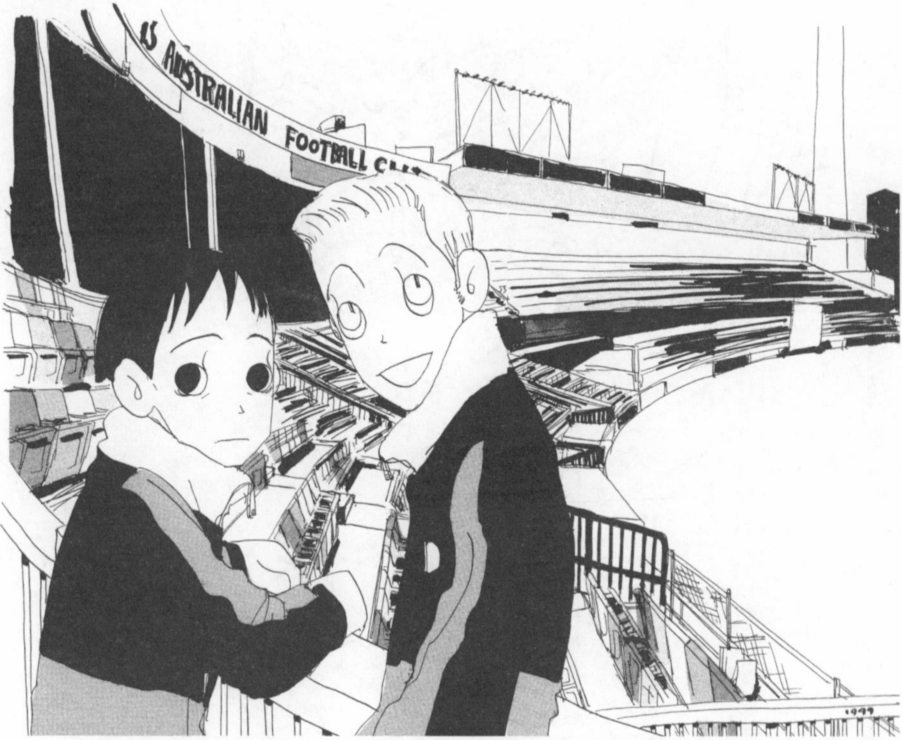
AUSTRALIAN FOOTBALL

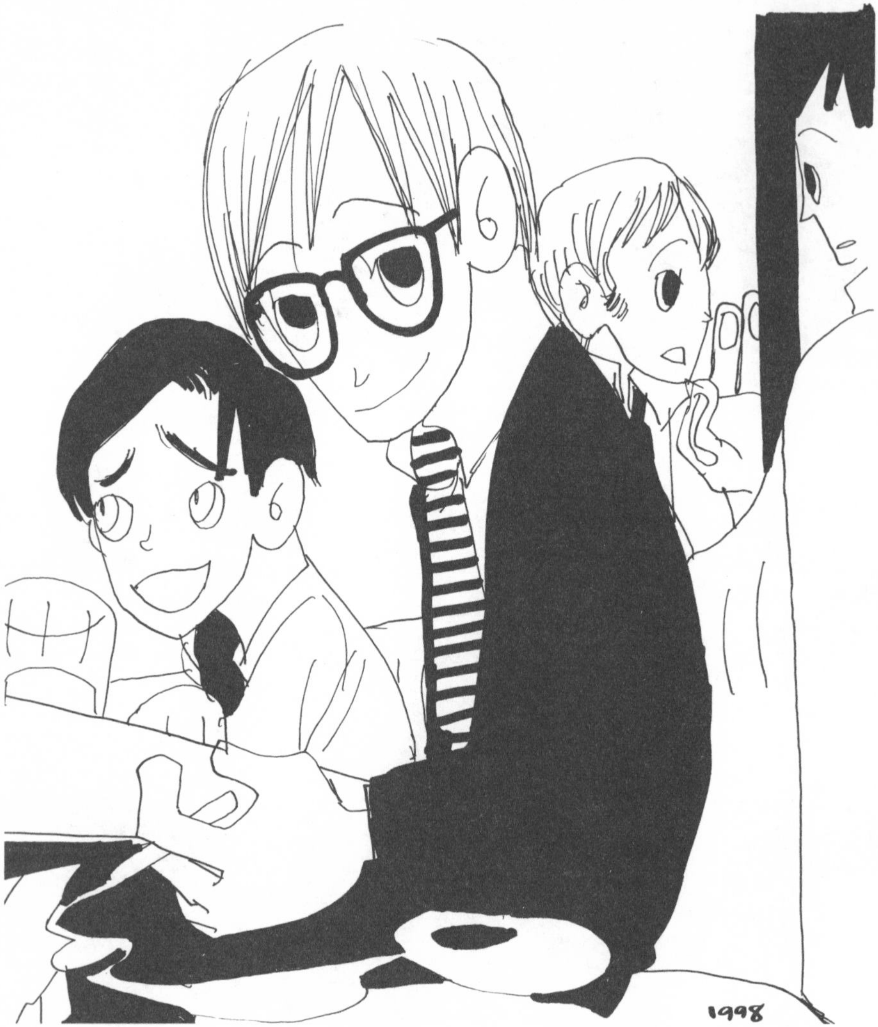
1998

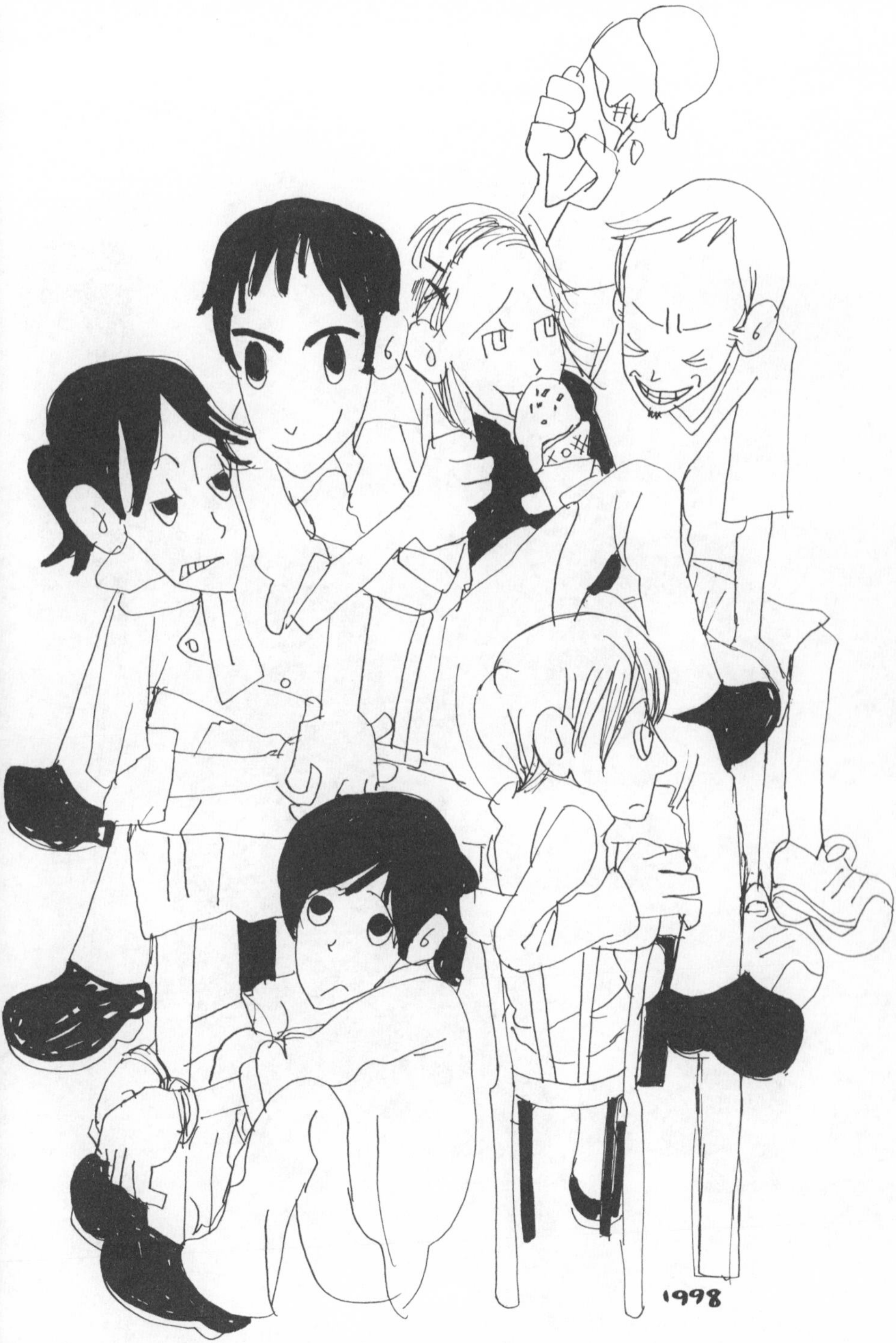
1998

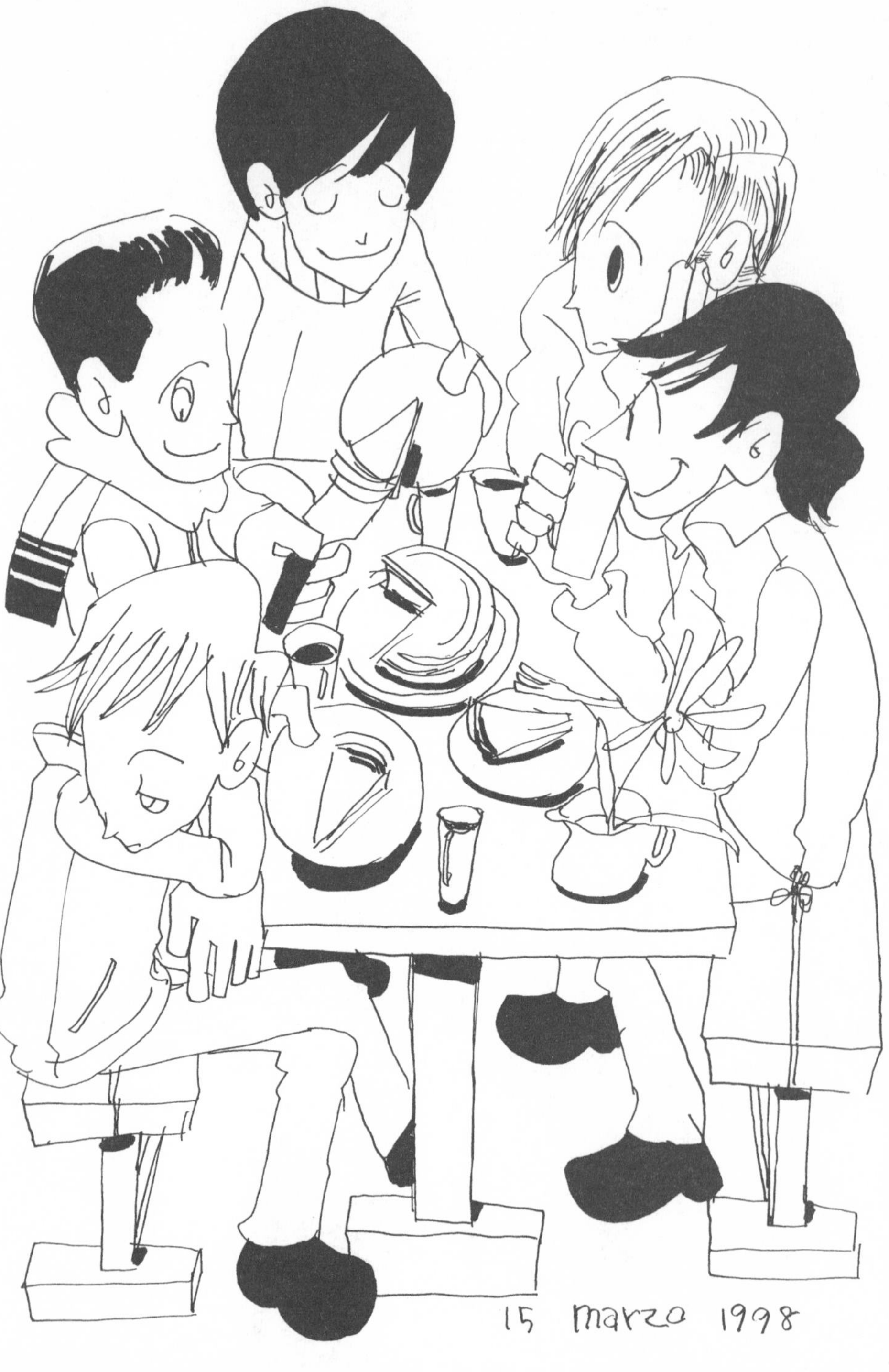
15 marzo 1998

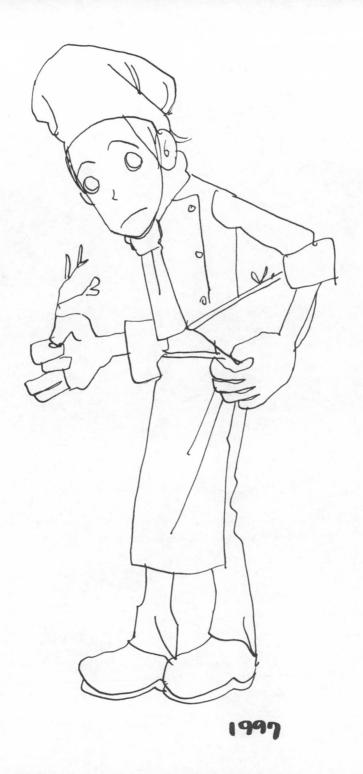

1997

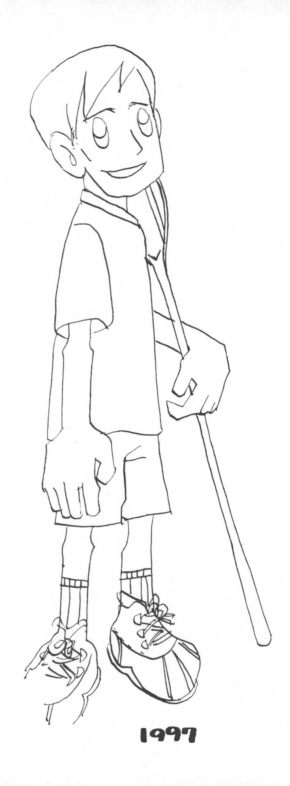

1997

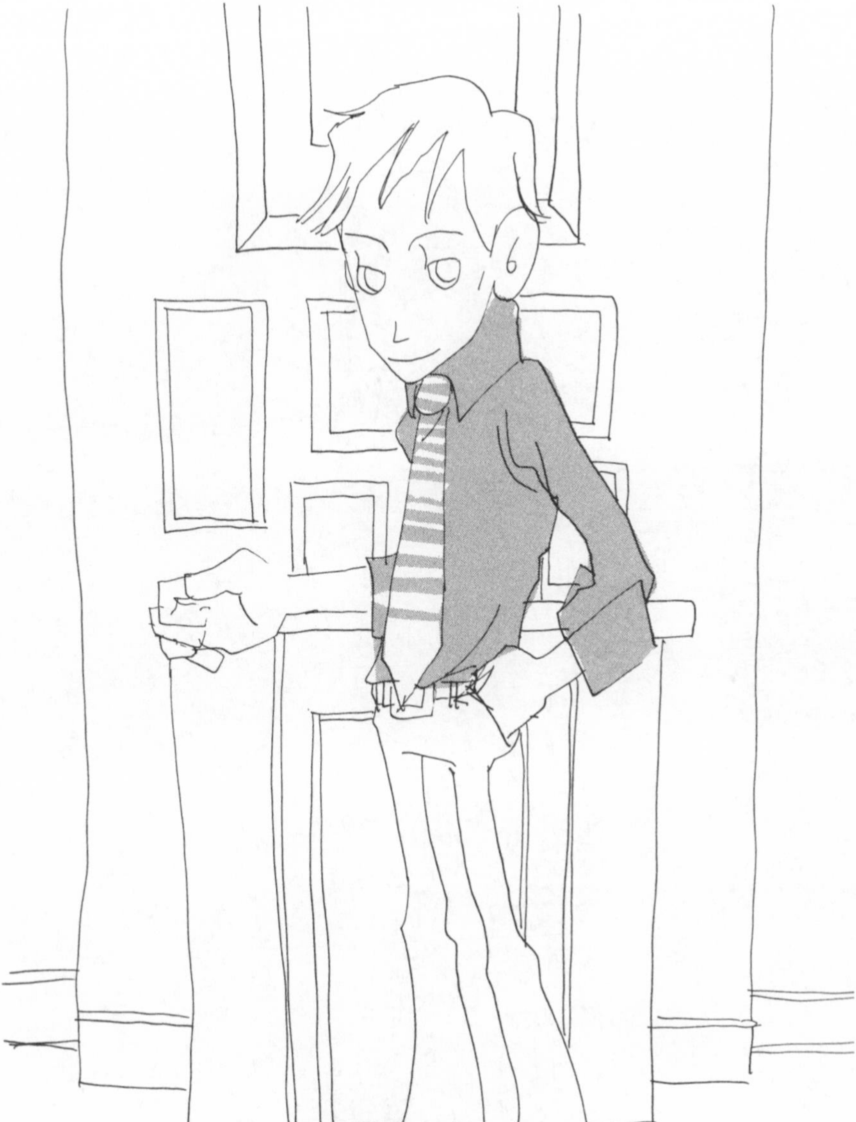
1997

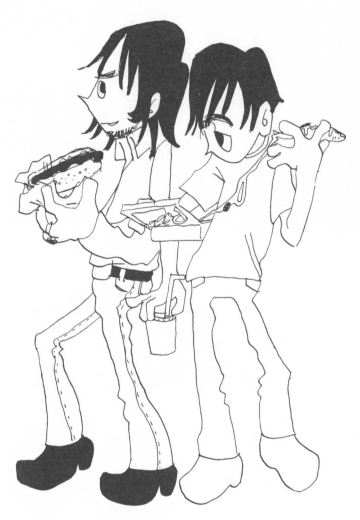

1996

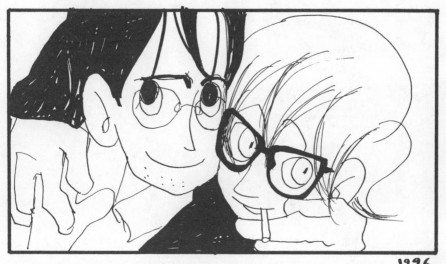

1996

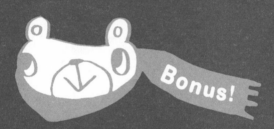

Bonus!

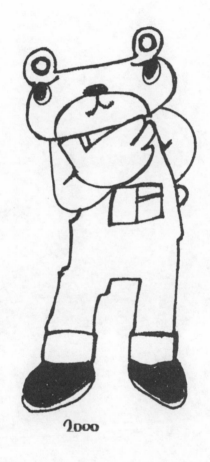

2000

A bear I drew in '99 or 2000.
I liked it, so I used it as the
opening image on my website.

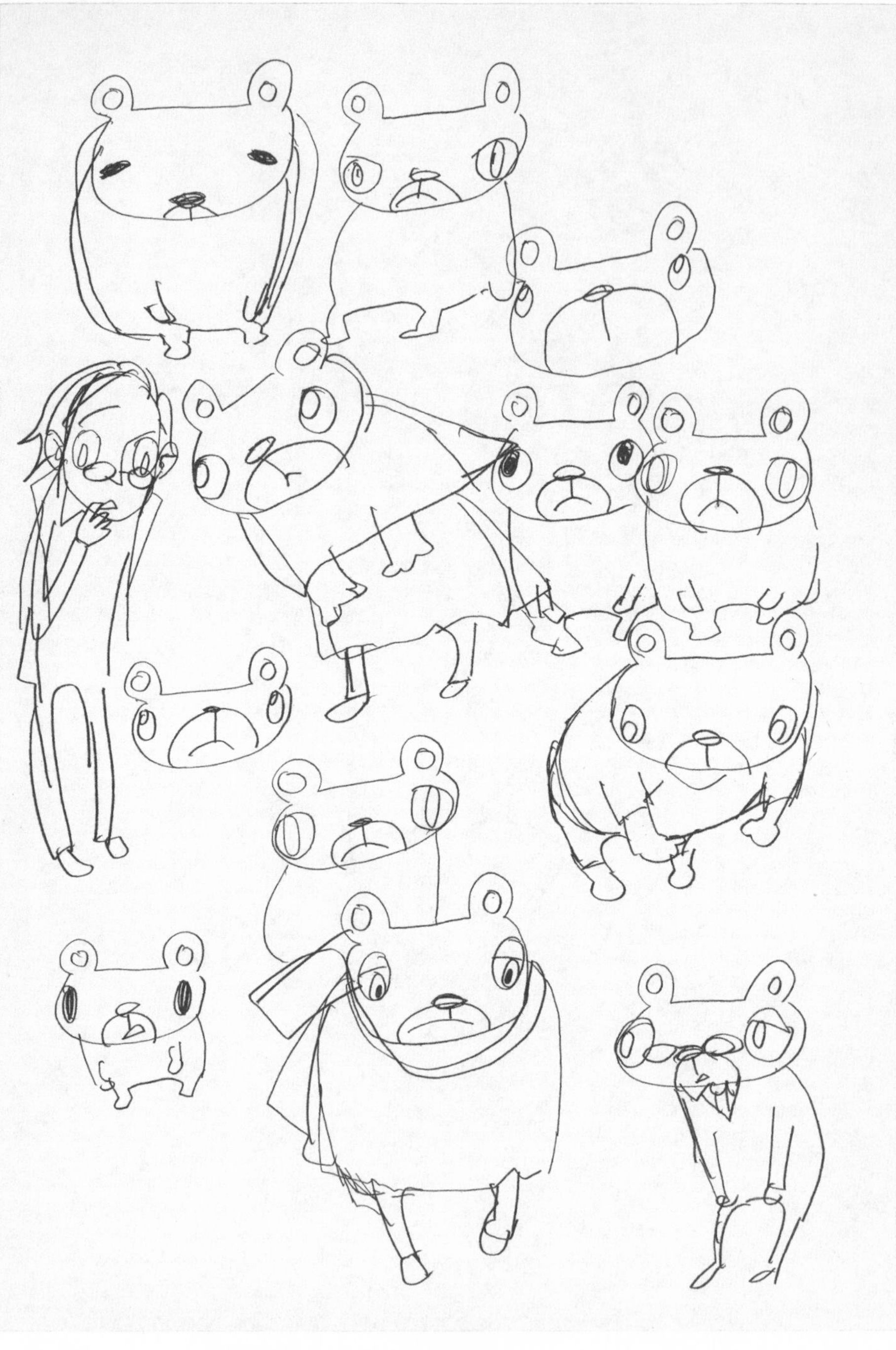

Doodle from 2007 or 2006.
Most of them are hunched over.

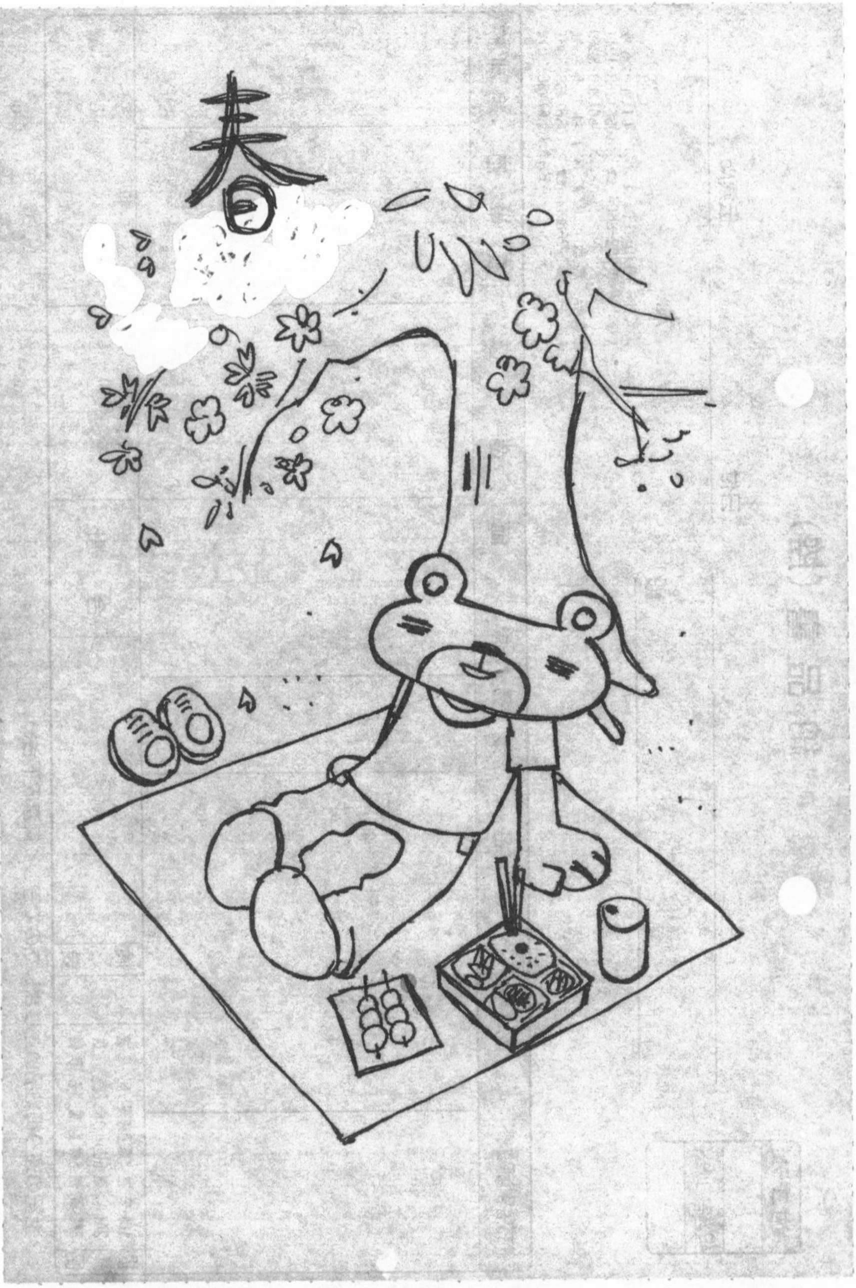
春

Probably the opening image for my website during Spring 2001. I change it every now and then. When I had an office job, there were extra delivery slips that were used as memo paper, and I drew this doodle on one of them.

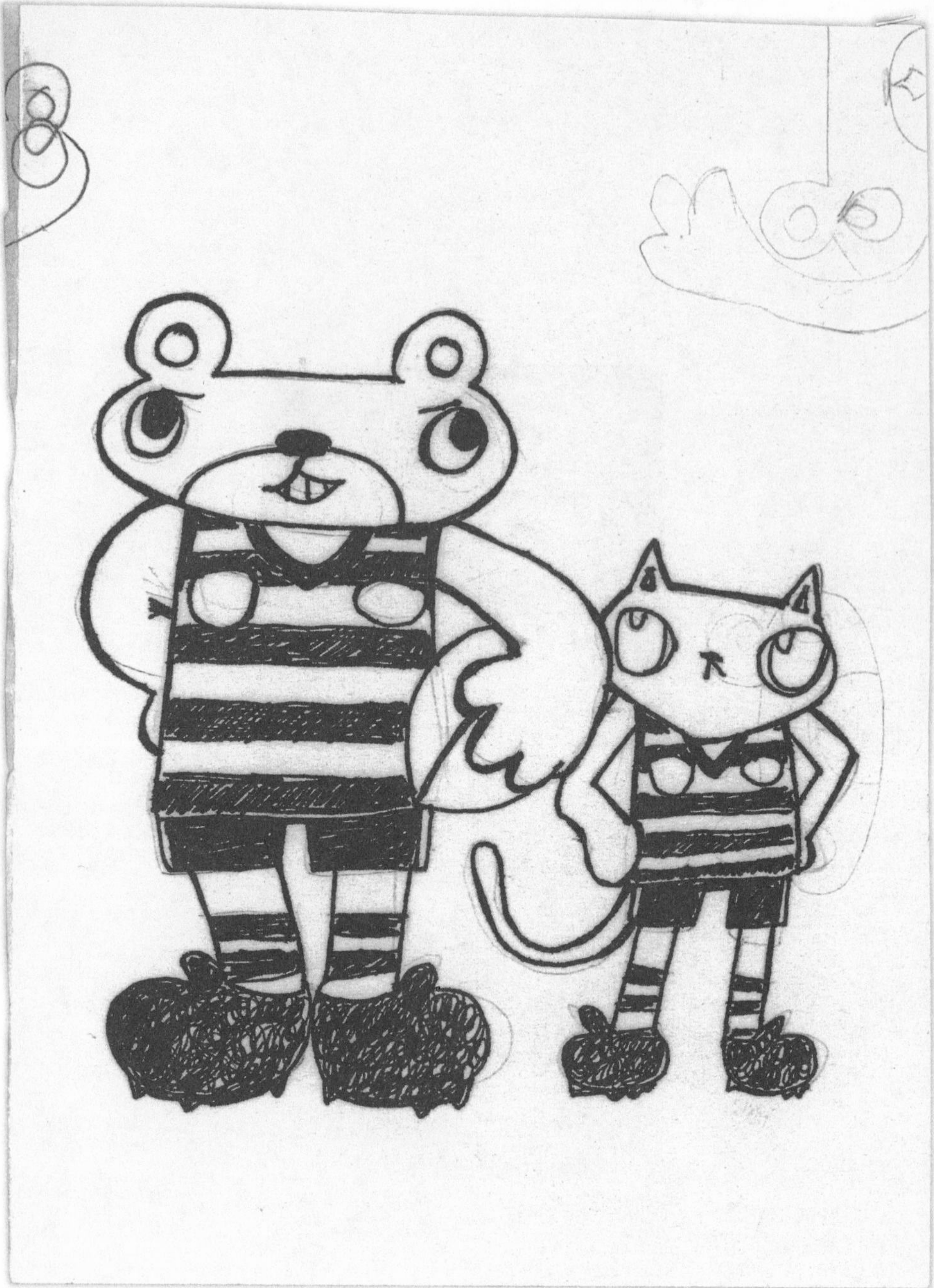

Probably from 2001. The opening image for my site during Australian football season.

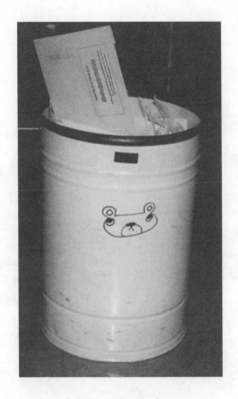

Trashcan I used when I
had an office job

I used to think I was no good at short stories. Now I think I've learned to like them.

The manga I drew as a hobby were mostly serial stories. The occasional short stories I'd create would be spinoffs of those series.

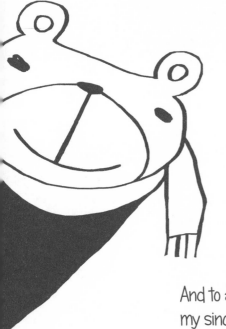

This book also contains a story that may require a bit of an explanation. These may be clumsy stories, but they've become memorable and important to me.

I'm grateful to have them all contained in one book. It's like a treasure to me.

I'd like to take this opportunity to express my deepest thanks to my editor Yuki Yasujima and designer Chutte.

And to all of you who picked this up, my sincerest gratitude.

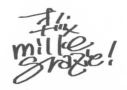

Tesoro

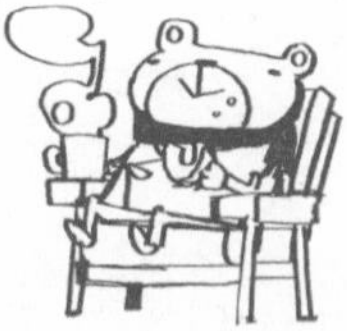

TESORO
VIZ Signature Edition

Story and Art by NATSUME ONO

© 2008 Natsume ONO/Shogakukan
All rights reserved.
Original Japanese edition
"TESORO - ONO NATSUME SHOKI TANPENSHU"
published by SHOGAKUKAN Inc.

Original Japanese cover design by **chutte**

Translation | Joe Yamazaki
Touch-up Art & Lettering | Elena Diaz
Design | Fawn Lau
Editor | Amy Yu

The stories, characters and incidents mentioned in this
publication are entirely fictional.

Printed in Canada

Published by VIZ Media, LLC
P.O. Box 77010
San Francisco, CA 94107

10 9 8 7 6 5 4 3 2 1
First printing, November 2011

www.viz.com

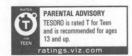
PARENTAL ADVISORY
TESORO is rated T for Teen
and is recommended for ages
13 and up.
ratings.viz.com

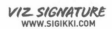
VIZ SIGNATURE
WWW.SIGIKKI.COM